THE HARDEST, LONGEST RACE

Ocean-to-Ocean Race for the Guggenheim Cup

Along a forty-one-hundred-mile route from New York City to Seattle, racers were required to stop at thirty checkpoints to demonstrate that they were genuinely driving and not shipping their cars by rail, and also to prove that the same crew members were present from coast to coast. At six points in the more densely populated East (Poughkeepsie, Syracuse, Buffalo, Toledo, Chicago, and St. Louis) they were required to rest for twelve hours as a safety measure, before a true free-for-all in the West.

Key

- • Official checkpoints
- □ *Climactic locations*

Official Checkpoints

1. Poughkeepsie, NY
2. Albany, NY
3. Fonda, NY
4. Syracuse, NY
5. Rochester, NY
6. Buffalo, NY
7. Erie, PA
8. Cleveland, OH
9. Toledo, OH
10. South Bend, IN
11. Chicago, IL
12. Bloomington, IL
13. St. Louis, MO
14. Centralia, MO
15. Kansas City, MO
16. Manhattan, KS
17. Ellsworth, KS
18. Oakley, KS
19. Limon, CO
20. Denver, CO
21. Cheyenne, WY
22. Rawlins, WY
23. Granger, WY
24. Montpelier, ID
25. Pocatello, ID
26. Twin Falls, ID
27. Boise, ID
28. Baker City, OR
29. Walla Walla, WA
30. North Yakima, WA

The HARDEST, LONGEST RACE

HENRY FORD AND THE CROSS-COUNTRY CONTEST THAT CHANGED AMERICA

Eric Moskowitz

ST. MARTIN'S PRESS
NEW YORK

First published in the United States by St. Martin's Press,
an imprint of St. Martin's Publishing Group

EU Representative: Macmillan Publishers Ireland Ltd, 1st Floor, The Liffey Trust Centre, 117–126 Sheriff Street Upper, Dublin 1, D01 YC43

www.stmartins.com

Map by Patrick Garvin

Designed by Omar Chapa

The Library of Congress Cataloging-in-Publication Data is available upon request.

ISBN 978-1-250-28267-5 (hardcover)
ISBN 978-1-250-28268-2 (ebook)

First Edition: 2026

10 9 8 7 6 5 4 3 2

For Hannah, Arlo, and Izzy

I like motoring because I have suffered for its sake.

—RUDYARD KIPLING, 1904

CONTENTS

THE HARDEST, LONGEST RACE

1
The Starting Gun

New York City, June 1, 1909

Lined up before New York's City Hall, the automobiles in the Ocean-to-Ocean Race trembled and snorted, vibrating in neutral, belching exhaust. Parted by police, thousands of people craned for a better view from both sides of the plaza, and hundreds more looked down from the skyscrapers lining Park Row. Mayor George B. McClellan Jr., the dashing son of the Civil War general, fingered a gleaming revolver plated with Yukon gold, raising it overhead. The hands on the cupola clock above City Hall nudged past 3 PM on Tuesday, June 1, 1909.

The automobiles strained; the crews in their dusters and driving caps shifted in their seats. They were racehorses at the gate, ready to bolt toward Broadway and charge across the continent. The loudest two were the smallest, a pair of new, moderately priced Model Ts from an automaker called Ford, stock models that had been stripped to the chassis, like prizefighters shedding final pounds before weigh-in. Even their exhaust systems and mufflers had been removed, so that four snub-nosed pipes jutted straight from each Ford's hood, unleashing a plume of smoke and a *rat-a-tat* growl. With the Fords idling at a few hundred rpms, their concussive bursts sounded like a pneumatic drill, or a couple of other recent inventions reshaping the world—the "endless chain saw" and the Maxim machine gun.

Any moment and the signal would come from Washington, where President William Howard Taft was poised to press the button on a ceremonial telegraph key encrusted with nuggets of Klondike gold. That would send a dual flash to special Western Union receivers in Seattle and here on the steps of Manhattan's City Hall, signaling the time to open the Alaska-Yukon-Pacific Exposition and start this Ocean-to-Ocean Race, which would run from New York to that World's Fair in Seattle.

Officially they dubbed this The International Automobile Endurance Contest for the M. Robert Guggenheim Trophy and A Motor Contest from Ocean to Ocean, rebranding it after the word *race* had caused convulsions in the auto world, though many still called it the Ocean-to-Ocean Race anyway. Opponents warned that a free-for-all dash across the continent could spill into a "saturnalia of reckless speeding" and carnage—setting back the progress of the motor car just as lawmakers were considering matters like speed limits, road improvements, and registration fees.

At least, that's what the 250 or so American automakers shunning the race claimed. Behind the scenes, they feared high-profile failure, with bad publicity in a crowded market worse than no publicity at all. No car had ever driven successfully between New York and Seattle, not even the pathfinder that had set out in March to chart the course for this race. That automobile, a famously rugged 60-horsepower Thomas Flyer that had circled the globe the year before, wound up needing two months to slog from Manhattan to Puget Sound—twelve times as long as it took by rail. Along the way, the car got mired in quicksand, pierced by a farmer's bullet (*just aiming for a coyote*, he said), and swarmed by a trio of roughs after the crew tried to bed down on a frigid night in a Wyoming locomotive roundhouse favored by tramps. After all that, the muscular Thomas couldn't even make it all the way on its own, crossing the Cascades by freight train, with deep snow choking the trail known as Snoqualmie Pass even in May.

So a rumored field of seventy-five cars in January shrank to a reported forty in March, then to an unlucky thirteen by the time entries closed in mid-May, despite efforts to rebrand the race as a safer contest. Tom Moore, a hustling promoter-manager hired by the young millionaire

Robert Guggenheim to finesse the details, deemed it an "ocular demonstration" of the most innocent variety, bringing the automobile to parts of the country where it remained rare. A glad-hander with a walrus mustache, Moore was a self-starter in the nascent field of public relations; he tried to convince the press that the contest was a wholesome affair celebrating the motor car's progress and affirming the Good Roads cause.

But neither Moore's lip service nor a set of safety-minded rule changes could mask the basic reality: This was a thrilling sporting event, meant to exhilarate auto-racing fans and gin up publicity for the Seattle World's Fair. Opponents trying to kill it begged Mayor McClellan and President Taft to consider that they had been duped by Moore and the speed-loving playboy signing his checks, twenty-four-year-old sportsman Robert Guggenheim. As chief example, they waved a brochure Moore had produced inviting wealthy New Yorkers to buy tickets for what he dubbed "The Wall Street Special"—a train to catch up with the race in St. Louis, Denver, and Seattle, bundled with a trip to Yellowstone National Park and a visit to the fair. "Twenty high-powered, space-annihilating automobiles will race across the continent to the great Alaska-Yukon-Pacific Exposition," promised Moore's brochure, contrasting the train's supple comforts with the pulse-pounding "excitements and perils of the race." Innocent contest, indeed.

McClellan and Taft dismissed the concerns. Opponents had far more luck applying pressure across the young auto industry itself, thanks to a feud between the venerable Automobile Club of America (ACA) and its more democratic rival, the American Automobile Association, or AAA. Every sporting event worth a place in the record book needed a sanctioning body, and Moore and Guggenheim had turned naturally to the ACA, which counted two Rockefellers, four Vanderbilts, and six Guggenheims among its members. The pioneering ACA had formed at the Waldorf-Astoria Hotel in 1899 to advocate for motorists in New York and promote the new sport of "automobiling." It matured quickly into an organization that lobbied lawmakers, produced maps and guides, posted directional signs, and published a newsstand journal, even as it remained an exclusive bastion for Manhattan millionaires.

Back in 1902, the ACA had helped create AAA as an umbrella alliance to unite motoring clubs around the country, but tension lingered over the ACA's first-among-equals standing and its reluctance to relinquish certain responsibilities to the wider AAA. That included racing, which the ACA initially controlled before handing over the sport after the fiasco of a Staten Island speed test that turned into a mass-casualty event. The ensuing arrangement worked smoothly enough when the ACA and AAA remained entwined, but a Hatfield-McCoy rift blew open for many reasons—riveting to the New York press; esoteric to most Americans—with personality conflicts and debates over the terms of racing among them. The two sides buried the hatchet in late 1908, with a precarious peace accord that gave AAA oversight for most domestic racing but preserved a special role for the ACA as America's authority for international contests and related rulemaking. But Guggenheim's race proved more than the treaty could handle.

Partly because of AAA's own grim record on sporting safety—with powerful cars leaping into the crowd on urban "hill climbs" or tearing through the fences of notoriously inadequate horse tracks at county fairgrounds, unpaved, unbanked, and a mere mile around—the American Automobile Association now came down hard against anything resembling racing on the open road, as opposed to a closed street course or proper auto track, the first of which were just being constructed. That made its opposition to Guggenheim's transcontinental race sound noble, but there was more to it. For the last five years, AAA had dominated summer motoring news with its marquee Glidden Tour, a long-distance "reliability run" born with a parade of motorists attempting to drive from New York to St. Louis for the 1904 World's Fair. Each year they picked a different region, with a loop this summer out West. Automakers loved the Glidden, with its ample publicity and its formula that crowned many of them as winners, speed only sort of a factor. Guggenheim's Ocean-to-Ocean thriller threatened to snatch that summertime attention away.

Soon a new alliance of automakers called the Manufacturers' Contest Association threw its hat in beside AAA, with threats swirling that anyone who entered the Ocean-to-Ocean affair could be banned from the AAA circuit, missing a number of major races coming up. That new association, which had formed to give manufacturers more say over the technical terms of racing, tried to pressure the ACA to drop its support, even hinting at an automaker boycott of U.S. Steel, which J. P. Morgan had founded with E. H. Gary, the ACA's current president. And if they couldn't kill the Ocean-to-Ocean Race outright, AAA leaders reportedly tried to extract money from Guggenheim in exchange for taking over the New York–Seattle contest themselves, running it with heavily modified rules.

Instead, Guggenheim, Moore, and the ACA's contest committee settled on amendments they hoped would placate everyone, asking racers to observe speed limits where they existed and to rest twelve hours a night while driving through the populous East, with those restrictions falling away in the wide-open country west of the Mississippi. It hardly mattered. By Memorial Day weekend, when the cars and crews needed to check in at the ACA's West Fifty-Fourth Street headquarters, the list of entries had shrunk to just ten. A few were so bold as to advertise their participation, but Moore worried others might get cold feet. Trying to lock them in, he released the list to the press.

Still, even ten powerful motor cars—plus swirling controversy—was enough to fill City Hall Park, with yet more people lining the sidewalks all the way to Upper Manhattan. Ten meant four more cars than had mustered on the same spot sixteen months back for the sensational New York–to–Paris Race of 1908. That one had left something to be desired as a sporting contest—it was disorganized, afflicted with disqualifications, and such a marathon that the crews stopped for leisurely banquets on their way across the United States before boarding steamers in San Francisco. But as a publicity stunt, that race was a sensation, captivating readers and making the winning Thomas Flyer the most famous car in America—a domestic hero defeating the supposedly superior autos of Europe.

The Seattle men planning the 1909 World's Fair got a load of that race and knew they wanted one of their own, starting in New York and ending at the exposition. They were happy to have people think of this

Guggenheim contest as the first true coast-to-coast auto race in America, with the less anyone recalled the time two Oldsmobiles had faced off in 1905, the better.

So the crowd converged on the park well before the two o'clock hour when the racers were scheduled to arrive, with one reporter pegging it at eight thousand people and another estimating twenty thousand, the masses encircling the cascading fountain and pressing in from beside both wings of the marble City Hall. In between, a cordon of bluecoats on foot and horseback had cleared the plaza in front of the steps into a paddock for the coming racers, displacing the usual newsboys, bootblacks, and bedraggled Bowery types seeking two cents for a night's lodging. A roar along Broadway shattered the lull, announcing the approach of the racers. But when the pack materialized, you could count the cars on one hand: two Fords, an Acme, a Shawmut, and an Itala.

Of the missing five, one had a good excuse: That car, a 45-horsepower Stearns, had been entered privately by a Brooklyn wire-mesh dealer named Oscar Stolp. A part-time inventor, Stolp wanted to demonstrate his patented aftermarket suspension, which would absorb enough shock to allow the use of thin, airless rubber tires, potentially saving time in the race—and money for future consumers. Pneumatic tires often burst or wore out in as little as a thousand miles, especially under strenuous conditions, making them an expensive, time-consuming bane to early motorists. But with the F. B. Stearns Company mindful of the mounting industry boycott, Stearns personally urged Stolp to drop out, warning that he was in over his head and could never compete with a factory team willing to spend $20,000 to win. Even *The New York Times* entered the fray, editorializing on behalf of rule changes to level the playing field for amateurs like Stolp. The Brooklyn businessman persisted, but after he sent his car to a garage for a final tune-up, it lay in pieces when he tried to collect it for the race, hinting at possible sabotage.

Of the others, three had simply caved to the pressure campaign, while the fourth—a pricey Welch entered by New York dealer L. H. Perlman—revealed itself to be a fleeting ploy by Perlman, a former patent-medicine promoter who now called himself "Motor King" of New York. Perlman was one of the few who had advertised his participation, boasting that Buffalo Bill Cody had introduced him to two Sioux guides, "Blue Hawk Jim and Long Feather Pete." He claimed the men had taken quickly to the powerful, easy-to-handle Welch and would excel in the race with their knowledge of the West. There was never any evidence they were real, but the press lapped it up.

The remaining five who pulled in now did so in defiance of the boycott—or out of desperation. They wore their racing numbers on their hoods, painted in order of application received, and lined up accordingly: the No. 1 and No. 2 Fords, the No. 4 Acme, the No. 5 Shawmut, and the No. 6 Itala. The gap created by the absence of the No. 3 Stearns accentuated the difference between the little Fords on one side and the powerful luxury cars on the other.

The 20-horsepower Model Ts had a showroom price of $850 (roughly $30,000 in 2025 dollars). They had been stripped from 1,200 pounds to 950 atop a one-hundred-inch wheelbase. The other three cars were two to three times as powerful, but they were far longer from axle to axle, weighed three to five times as much, and cost considerably more—$4,500 for the 45- to 50-horsepower Acme and $4,750 for the 40-horsepower Shawmut.

As for the price of the 45-horsepower Itala, don't even ask. Like other high-end European models, it came to the United States as a bare chassis to be finished by an upscale coach-builder, an outcome of a 45 percent tariff that made it cheaper to bring in the unfinished running gear than the completed auto. Even then, the Itala chassis-plus-tariff cost about $7,000, while a handsomely finished version turned out by New York's A. T. Demarest could set you back as much as $10,000—double the Acme or Shawmut.

Spectators sizing up the pack dismissed the runty Fords while favoring the Acme and especially the Itala. At a glance, the import from Turin appeared to be the car to reckon with, an elongated thoroughbred painted a sleek gray. Certainly it boasted the loftiest racing pedigree; Itala's international triumphs included smashing the record from Monte Carlo to London and winning the inaugural Targa Florio race through the mountains of Sicily in 1906, as well as the Peking-to-Paris Race of 1907, the wild contest that had inspired the 1908 New York–to–Paris affair, which in turn begat this race to Seattle.

The No. 6 Itala here also had a notable lead driver on its four-man crew in Gus Lechleitner, a hulking twenty-seven-year-old who wore a broad-brimmed Boss of the Plains hat and claimed to have experience as a "Western cowboy," giving him an edge in the far-off stages of the race. That was bluster; Lechleitner had grown up in Manhattan's heavily German Yorkville neighborhood, and there was little evidence he'd ventured west of the Hudson River. But he boasted nearly a decade of experience as a mechanic and road-tester for the famed racer and inventor J. Walter Christie and then for Demarest, and he could drive like mad. In the fall of 1908 he had finished third in the big sweepstakes race that christened Willie K. Vanderbilt's Long Island Motor Parkway, the first automobile-only road in the country.

At the No. 4 post, the Acme dazzled in yellow, a capacious six-cylinder "tourabout" with baby tonneau (the sofa-style rear seating on an open-air touring car, far roomier than the limited or nonexistent rear seats in the back of many roadsters), 118 inches from axle to axle, boasting a top speed of seventy miles an hour and ample room for a four-man crew of its own. For a company that emphasized racing, the Acme's decision to enter in spite of the pressure campaign on American automakers represented a gamble; if they won, it would be worth it, and if not, they could try to beg forgiveness later.

Based in Reading, Pennsylvania, the Acme boasted a solid reputation for craftsmanship and performance, but it had treaded water for an unusually long time. Amid America's teeming landscape of automakers, about ten were already building a thousand or more cars a year, including a couple flirting with ten thousand, Ford near the top. A few dozen automakers produced at least a hundred cars a year, the Acme among them. But the vast majority of car manufacturers were simply trying to get out of the gate, more starting up every month, hundreds of others already forgotten in the ash heap behind them.

Founded informally in 1900, Acme got serious in 1903, when the firm incorporated and brought over a Daimler-trained designer from Germany. Many of the factory hands went back to that founding, an eternity in a young industry with high turnover. That included foreman Jerry Price, chief mechanic and captain of the No. 4's crew. He had a gnarled left pinkie that had survived a run-in with the feed gear of a lathe, and a six-year-old daughter at home named Florence, growing up in a country that afforded women the vote in just four Western states—no way to imagine that she would one day become a nine-term member of Congress, a progressive Republican champion of civil rights and women's rights.

Financial miscues and a flurry of ownership changes had hamstrung the Acme company, but the heir to a nuts-and-bolts fortune had purchased it from receivership in 1907 with visions of racing glory and sales growth. The two often went hand in hand, and Acme got a jolt in 1908 with a third-place finish at a marquee race in Savannah, Georgia. Here in Manhattan, the company had found a new dealer with a gift for publicity, a slick former life-insurance and mining-stock salesman named Auckland B. Cordner. A few months earlier, Cordner had placed an Acme limousine into service on regular New York–Philadelphia runs between the Waldorf-Astoria and Bellevue-Stratford hotels. That was a wild idea; with the rise of the railroad, coach service between major cities had fallen from fashion two generations ago. The press loved it, dubbing it the "millionaires' inter-city express," while the breakdown-free performance so far attested to the Acme's reliability. Cordner pressed for the company to enter the Ocean-to-Ocean Race, at which point the Acme scored a huge coup by landing steely George Salzman as lead driver, with Salzman's name in the press typically followed by the tag *famous racer.* Star of the big E. R. Thomas factory racing team and head of that company's service department, Salzman had reportedly left Thomas recently, and now here he was driving for Acme. He certainly looked the part, one hand slung over the wheel, a cigar jammed in the corner of his mouth just like the famed Barney Oldfield, the first household name in American racing. Only later would it become clear that this Salzman character was an impostor, if a daring driver still. Already he'd run up a big Philadelphia hotel bill in the real George Salzman's name; addicted to the limelight, he would later claim to be a decorated war hero and an aviator contemplating the first transatlantic flight, amid stints in prison and time running a sophisticated stolen-car ring.

In between the Acme and Itala, the whitewashed No. 5 Shawmut was a bit of a mystery. It appeared to be smartly crafted, with a 40-horsepower four-cylinder engine and a top speed of sixty-five miles an hour, as well as a tighter wheelbase than the Itala or Acme, offset by bigger wheels—a canny combination for surmounting rough terrain. Still, few beyond Boston had heard of the Shawmut. The car was one of the only survivors of a factory fire that had wiped out the company just as it was about to begin real production. The Shawmut Motor Company had a purchase option on another building, but little else to its name besides some promising press clippings and a pile of debt. This entry was a long shot, a desperate bid to win publicity and generate enough investment to restart the business. In theory, the rules of the race had been democratized to put amateur entries and smaller firms like Shawmut on more even footing with giants by prohibiting the changing of major parts. The frame, axles, engine block, cylinders, transmission case, and steering gear on each car in the race were marked by the ACA with a specially coded pattern, using a stamping hammer, and would be inspected at the finish. If any of those parts broke, you had to stop and repair them, not swap them out for replacements stashed at dealerships along the way. Still, you could freely change any of the many other parts that were subject to wear and tear, making it hard to imagine that a team with limited factory support and few spare parts could reach Seattle at all.

Still, the Shawmut was undeniably handsome, and it fit in aesthetically between the Itala and Acme on the east side of the plaza. These were the motor cars people turned out to admire, lust objects of raw horsepower, with bold paint jobs—fifteen to twenty layers on a typical luxury car, applied over months—and burnished brass and nickel, priced far beyond the reach of most. Car ownership had exploded in less than a decade, from one in ten thousand Americans at the dawn of the century to around one in five hundred now, transforming the automobile from devilish plaything of the gilded class to functional luxury coveted by the masses. And for every car owner out there already, another fifty or sixty people loved to read about automobiles—or so *The Travel Magazine* had figured—if not necessarily hear endlessly about their neighbor's new wheels. They ogled magazine ads, strolled car shows pocketing three-color brochures, nodded along to talk of carburetors and crankshafts, and daydreamed about cradling the wheel of their own motor car. That day's *New York World* ran a front-page eye-catcher about a poor dressmaker in Pennsylvania coal country who had just inherited a surprise fortune from her uncle, and knew just how she'd spend it: FIRST SHE WANTS AN AUTO, the headline declared.

Even the dressmakers of the world were not generally dreaming about runabouts priced below $900. Affordable cars were notoriously poky and unreliable. As the joke went, the runabout got its name because it could run about a mile before failing. Olds had broken through in 1902 with the first mass-produced, moderately priced runabout, the curved-dash Oldsmobile, selling 2,500 that year at $650 apiece and even more the next. But the one-cylinder, 4½-horsepower Olds could barely pull three adults up a steep hill, and the bloom of that little car faded. Some still bought inexpensive high-wheelers that looked like buggies, and others skittered around in $375 Orient Buckboards (as comfortable as they sounded), but you generally got what you paid for. A cheap car was a starter car, or a car for puttering around town; it could no more win a cross-country race than it could soar to the moon.

To be fair, Buick had pulled a neat trick in 1908 with its $900 Model 10, a sporty two-seater—plus a rumble seat in back—on a compact, eighty-eight-inch wheelbase. It was so snazzy that they got away with calling it a *gentleman's light four-cylinder roadster* rather than a mere *runabout*, and it became the bestselling car of the year. But the homelier Fords lined up on the Broadway side of the plaza were no gentleman's roadsters, with a top speed of forty-five miles per hour going downhill.

All of the cars here had been stripped of their windshields and fenders, but these Fords had also been left unpainted—just plain metal, save for their numbers. In the light of the showroom, the Model T did have a certain utilitarian charm, its spindly frame topped with an assortment of interchangeable bodies, from three-seat runabout to seven-passenger town car. But these denuded Ts featured little more than a pair of bucket seats plunked onto a bare chassis, a canvas-covered platform in back where a rumble seat or tonneau might go, the fabric painted to read FORD in the rear and NEW YORK TO SEATTLE on the sides. (Each car had also been stenciled with a subtle *1212*, the Michigan registry number for all autos owned by the Ford Motor Company before standard license plates.) Lest *bucket seats* give the wrong idea, these were more like stiff chairs lifted from a farmhouse kitchen, not the tufted leather sofas of the big cars in the race. One reporter deemed the result a *buzz-cart*; another called these Model Ts *pygmies*, dwarfed by the muscular frames of the Itala, Acme, and Shawmut.

That was just fine with Henry Ford, the forty-five-year-old automaker taking in the scene from under a shade tree in back of the makeshift paddock, wearing a chesterfield and a derby. He was trim, and roughly five foot nine, but stood erect in a way that made him seem taller. The more people underestimated the Model T now, the sweeter victory would be in Seattle. Ford knew in his core that this car was fundamentally different. Thanks to an unusually light but strong alloy called vanadium steel, coupled with two years of obsessive designing and testing, he had solved the vexing problem of how to make a lightweight car that was also durable and reliable, instead of flimsy. By dispensing with frills and building them at scale, he had whittled the price below $900. And a flexible three-point suspension gave the high-riding car the ability to practically twist and step over country-road obstacles, not just grind through them. Most of all, Ford understood that for all the talk here about pure horsepower, what mattered more was the ratio of horsepower to weight. He was so fixated on leanness that his men had even swapped out the headlamps on these Model Ts from standard brass to humbler aluminum to shave another eleven pounds.

A limousine arrived, depositing Robert Guggenheim, his wife, Grace, and parents, Daniel and Florence, the women wearing Merry Widow hats as broad as the artillery wheels on the autos. An Edwardian dandy of gleaming stickpins and crisp club collars, Guggenheim sported a dusting of beard, a straw boater, and a lapel carnation as big as a saucer. An unapologetic rake, he was already the person he would always be (his motto: "Every wealthy family supports at least one gentleman in leisure. I have elected to assume that position in mine") but had not yet fully squandered his father's goodwill. With a cane in one hand, he popped around the paddock, chatting with the press and automotive elites. Putting the best possible sheen on the number of entries, he praised Ford, Shawmut, Acme, and Itala for their fortitude and faith in their machines, though he seethed privately over the small field. He did not mention that he had secretly bankrolled the Itala as a face-saving entry to assure his "International" race to the World's Fair had at least a dash of foreign flavor.

Some reporters less familiar with the barons of the age assumed the elder Guggenheim must be the race's sponsor, mistaking the tenacious Daniel for his fizzy son Robert. Among the many Guggenheim brothers engaged in the family business, Daniel had assumed control of the ever-expanding mining, smelting, real estate, and railroad empire after the death of patriarch Meyer Guggenheim in 1905. Though Daniel had bestowed on Robert his father's name—the *M* in *M. Robert Guggenheim* stood for *Meyer*—the mantle rested uneasily on the firstborn male of the third generation, an impish prankster, effortlessly charismatic but indifferent to work.

On his way to a lifetime of bobbing from one misadventure to the next, Robert had left Columbia University to tour Europe with a tutor, then proved such a loafer at American Smelting and Refining that Daniel had dispatched the lad to Seattle, ostensibly to keep an eye on the firm's

West Coast and Alaska interests but also to stay out of the way in New York. There the pleasure-seeking scion of America's most famously industrious Jewish family landed in print for flirting with Episcopalianism—as if it were just another club to join—and penning paeans to luxury products on company letterhead, repurposed in ads. Robert gushed about the Allen-Kingston Motor Car and Makaroff Russian Cigarets, the latter handmade and "blended scientifically" from "pure, clean, sweet tobacco," finished with your own gold monogram and sold in cedar boxes at $6 per hundred, not like the workingman's nickel-a-pack Piedmonts.

Needless to say, Robert had not exactly plunged into work at the family's Tacoma smelter upon arriving in Seattle the previous November. With his Cheshire cat smile and fashionable heels that made him a credible five foot eight, he secured multiple profiles in the city's dailies ("Robert the Young: Seattle Member of the House of Guggenheim," the Seattle *Sunday Times* declared, calling him an amiable millionaire who is "prouder of the dogs in his kennels than he is of his money in the bank"), frequented the exclusive Rainier Club, and fell in with the civic leaders planning the Alaska-Yukon-Pacific Exposition, a World's Fair to showcase Seattle's dominant role in the lucrative Alaska trade and the emergence of the Pacific Rim. It seemed a natural fit for Young Robert, given the Guggenheim interests in Alaska. Plus, he had expanded his champion kennels from English bulldogs to Alaskan sled dogs, too, though automobiles commanded much of his attention. William Sheffield, the ex-newspaperman who got the ball rolling on the exposition itself, merely had to whisper the idea of the race before Guggenheim took off with it, eager to become a sporting impresario. Until then, the only events he had planned were a tennis tournament at his parents' summer estate and, with other seaside millionaires, a hospital-fundraiser automobile race around a horse track in Long Branch, New Jersey. In the Northwest, he would pony up for aerial contests, motorboat races, dog cups, an all-day auto carnival, and a marathon footrace—the latest craze, which spoke to the public's fascination with distance and its hunger for witnessing humans push themselves to their limits in the age of machines. But the Ocean-to-Ocean Race became

Guggenheim's darling, promoting the prowess of the modern motor car and the possibility of an uninterrupted road one day linking dear New York to his new hometown.

He floated over to Ford. The two couldn't have been more different, the auto man a teetotaler who offered guests "nourishing and digestive" Malto-Grape—grape juice fortified with malted barley—and eschewed pretentious gatherings. But they had sure needed each other in April. At a time when the race organizers were starting to sweat about whether there would be any entries at all come June 1, Henry Ford had emerged to announce his participation and commit the entry fees for two cars, not just one. "This will be the first real auto contest ever promoted," Ford said, one that would demonstrate to consumers and manufacturers the soundness or shortcomings of any car that entered. "It seems to me that every manufacturer having faith in his product should welcome the chance to prove it." He called for others to buck the pressure campaign, offering to wager any amount they wished on the outcome. No one took the bet.

For Ford, whose disdain for the press was exceeded by his knack for working it, entering the race fit neatly with the iconoclastic image he cultivated for his firm. Founded in 1903, Ford Motor Company had sold nearly twenty thousand of its first eight car models combined before launching the Model T in October 1908. That made Ford one of the biggest players in the business. Certainly the firm was the largest of the "independents" refusing to pay tribute to the so-called Selden trust, which employed a questionable and initially obscure 1895 patent to crush or collect royalties from nearly anyone attempting to build a self-propelled "road-engine" powered by "liquid-hydrocarbon" fuel—at least anyone attempting to do so in serious numbers. The patent itself was widely mocked, having been drafted and slow-walked over sixteen years by a canny lawyer and aspiring inventor who never built a functioning automobile. But the trust that ultimately wielded that patent flexed enormous financial clout and threatened endless litigation. Ford's refusal to cave and insistence on being the first to fight a lawsuit from the trust all the way through trial, despite years of costly depositions and a mountain of filings, provided grist for a David-versus-Goliath campaign that presented Ford Motor as beholden to the consumer, not to the industry. It also made Henry Ford one of the most dynamic but polarizing figures in the auto world—though that world, to Ford's consternation, remained confined mostly to the sports pages, even the coverage of business dealings.

But the Selden lawsuit was draining, and his future was hardly certain. He was Henry Ford but not yet *Henry Ford*, the press sometimes mangling his name, a visitor who could pass anonymously through the streets of New York. He was successful, but not extravagantly so. After moving a dozen times in two decades of marriage, he could now afford to build a fine home on a corner lot along Detroit's Edison Avenue, with a sunken garden for wife Clara, and enroll their son Edsel in the prestigious Detroit University School at $100 a semester. His company turned a tidy profit, but for all the cars they'd sold, he'd invested heavily in the construction of a massive factory at Highland Park—on an old horse-racing grounds on the outskirts of Detroit—to build even more, and its opening was behind schedule. Henry Ford loathed debt, but he'd had to borrow personally to buy up the stock needed to gain majority control of his own company, amid a 1906–1907 coup to oust rivals on the board.

For all of Ford's outward defiance of the Selden trust and faith in the coming Model T, he had privately considered selling out to Buick's William Durant in 1908, as Durant began compiling the various companies that would become General Motors. Ford flirted with walking away for a tidy $1.8 million—reflecting his 58.5 percent ownership in Ford Motor Company, for which Durant had offered $3 million—to become a gentleman farmer in Dearborn, his bucolic hometown outside Detroit. But the deal crumbled over Ford's desire to be paid chiefly in cash, not stock in the future GM.

So he redoubled his commitment to riding out the Selden lawsuit and shepherding the Model T, which he believed would not only eclipse the Buick Model 10 as the bestselling car under $1,000 but also compete with automobiles twice its price. He had staked his company from the start on reliable cars at moderate prices, and this one blew all previous Fords out of the water. The Model T's fall debut had grabbed the attention of the trade, and most agreed it would be the star of the season. But what would that mean, and how long would it last?

Skeptical Eastern bankers had seen plenty of fads sweep the nation and vanish—roller skates in the 1880s, bicycles in the 1890s. The automobile seemed now to have staying power, but bankers suspected its wild growth would soon taper into a modest annual uptick. Last year, when American automakers were producing a record sixty thousand cars, Durant got laughed out of the room when he told financiers in New York that production might mushroom fivefold or tenfold in just a few more years. Even if you were audacious enough to believe it, it was hard to know what those fantastical sales might look like. The scene had evolved so quickly—steam and electric cars eclipsed by gas; one-cylinder engines giving way to two, four, even six; shaft drive competing with chains; luxury cars surrendering market share to mid-priced models after the Panic of 1907, but for who knows how long?—that Durant had embraced a Noah's Ark approach to gathering brands for GM, rounding up a bit of everything.

As for Ford, singularly focused on one style, he had shipped about two thousand Model Ts by the time he entered Guggenheim's race—a nice figure, but still just one for every forty-five thousand Americans. Demand was brisk enough that he would soon pause orders to catch up with production, not uncommon for popular new releases. But Ford had a bolder vision: that this car would bring middle-class families off the sidelines. With that big factory at Highland Park finally on the verge of opening, he imagined producing and selling twenty-five thousand Model Ts a year, double what any automaker had ever attempted. Many consumers who could afford a $1,500 touring car had held off because of exorbitant maintenance bills, especially regular rounds of new tires, easily $60 a set. Light cars ran easier on their shoes, but they had so many other ills.

He knew the Model T was the solution. Touting it in an ad was one thing, a drop in the ocean of superlative claims in automotive advertising. Demonstrating it in a cross-country race by defeating bigger, more powerful, more expensive competitors would cut through the clutter, prove it to the public. He needed the race every bit as much as Guggenheim needed him.

Because there was still that matter of the Selden lawsuit—all those legal bills and royalties on the line. Ford projected confidence, but if they lost, the hit could run toward a staggering million dollars. As it happened, the trial had finally opened on the previous Friday, May 28, 1909, after nearly six years of filings and depositions. And the case was being heard in a federal courtroom overlooking this very plaza, in the combination courthouse and post office that blotted out the southern end of City Hall Park like an overwrought layer cake—"Mullett's Monstrosity," people called it, for the architect who had concocted it in the 1860s.

As 3 PM neared, Mayor McClellan emerged, an avid motorist himself, strikingly hatless in the afternoon sun. The Guggenheims and assorted officials took their places around him, the smallest of them the one who would play the most decisive role on the far side of the finish if needed, superseding referee Guggenheim to sort out any lingering appeals: a "gentleman lawyer" named Robert Lee Morrell, a champion former coxswain of the Exeter and Columbia crews, and the esteemed chairman of the ACA's contest committee.

Arrayed on the steps, the dignitaries waited—and waited—for the signal from Washington. As the clock ticked, President Taft sidled up to a bistro table in the East Room of the White House, flanked by most of his family, his cabinet, and the congressional delegations from the Western states. The telegraph key sat before him, Klondike nuggets glued around its marble base solely for symbolic ornamentation, like an extravagant crafts project.

As the first automobile enthusiast in the Oval Office, Taft had secured $12,000 from Congress in February to purchase the first presidential limousines. In March, he had converted the White House stables into a garage, bringing over his personal chauffeur from the War Department, swapping feed bins for a gas tank, and hanging inner tubes and tire casings from pegs where harnesses had dangled.

And in April, when Robert Guggenheim sat down with the new president to pitch him on the race, he found a receptive audience. Joined by Colorado Senator Simon Guggenheim (Robert's forty-one-year-old uncle), the three shared a hope that one day a continuous motorway would connect the coasts, benefiting both commerce and the military. Though few in Congress yet believed the federal government should pay for road improvements, the anti-auto caucus was rapidly shrinking. Arguing against that $12,000 for Taft, Tennessee Representative Thetus Sims had blasted automobiles as "a dangerous means of travel" and "a genuine all-around nuisance," contending that even "Tennessee mules" would be better for the president. But the appropriation passed easily, 185 to 27.

At the White House, Taft reached now for the telegraph button. In New York, the hands of the City Hall clock showed 3:03, maybe 3:04. McClellan had let the revolver drop to his hip, resting his right arm. The telegraph machine snapped to life, picking up Taft's signal. "Go, with best success," the mayor declared, pulling the trigger. There was a flash, a puff of smoke, a sharp report. The crowd roared.

Spewing exhaust, kicking up dust, the racers turned and drove between the glass-and-copper entrances of the city's new subway system, threading through a set of bollards and out to Broadway, 4,106 miles and an untamed continent to go.

2

Up Automobile Row

New York, June 1, 1909

Near the back of the column turning onto Broadway, Shawmut mechanic Earle Chapin was raring to go, after four days idling in New York and half a year of uncertainty since the fire. He was a lanky six-footer with a mischievous gleam and a penchant for machine-shop patter peppered with occasional profanity. He loved to drive, never mind that he didn't have a license—a matter of coughing up a fee, not taking a test—and knew every inch of the Shawmut as a factory machinist and road technician. Chapin was twenty-six years old, with blue eyes and brown hair, a nimble third baseman on the company baseball team, dizzy in love with his wife Caroline and torn up over missing their upcoming first wedding anniversary for the race. But he also had a taste for adventure, and couldn't pass up this opportunity, not with the future of Shawmut hanging in the balance. He promised to write "Anita"—his playful nickname for Caroline, maybe because he *needed* her beside him—every chance he got.

She was twenty-four, a stenographer and a shopgirl, not yet a mother, with luminous eyes, delicate features, and a wry smile. They shared a cozy rental in a two-family home in Stoneham (a shoemaking town just north of Boston), decorated with fishnet and bits of whimsy—a set of antlers here, a small anchor there—and accented with family portraits and snapshots from their honeymoon. After supper they liked to recline together in a comfortable Morris chair, talking and listening to wax-cylinder records through a phonograph horn painted with morning glories. Their home was a third of a mile from the Shawmut factory—or rather it had been until that November morning when the clanging alarm bell atop the schoolhouse woke the town to the blaze at the auto plant.

You could trace the origins of the American automobile business, and an outsized share of American industry, to Chapin's hometown of Springfield, Massachusetts, ninety miles west of Boston, a picturesque city of fifty thousand and climbing in Chapin's youth that boasted the commercial clout of a metropolis. The horseless carriage had many would-be inventors, tinkering simultaneously with batteries, steam, and internal combustion, but it was Springfield where J. Frank Duryea managed to pull off the first recorded run of a gasoline-powered car in America in September 1893. In an age of one-off dabblers, Duryea also became the first to organize a company for manufacturing automobiles to sell to others, forming the Duryea Motor Wagon Company in 1895 with his brother Charles. That same year the duo made international news in a Thanksgiving Day "motocycle" contest sponsored by the *Times-Herald* of Chicago, running to Evanston and back. Amid drifting snow and frigid weather, an advertised field of nearly eighty conveyances of varying types shrank to just six starters, only two of which managed to complete the fifty-four-mile course. By crossing the finish line at Jackson Park in seven hours and fifty-three minutes, the Duryea machine won America's first recognized auto race by a margin of two hours.

That was just one achievement among many for Springfield, which had given rise to the adjustable monkey wrench, the game of basketball, and the American dictionary, and was best known as the heart of the industrial-innovation corridor that flourished along the Connecticut River, from Vermont to Long Island Sound. The sprawling Springfield Armory, the military's foremost arms supplier, had pioneered a system of interchangeable parts and division of labor among factory workers that spread first to private gunmakers and then to a panoply of industries, mass-producing affordable consumer goods for a modernizing nation—sewing machines, typewriters, steam radiators, pocket watches, bicycles, and now automobiles. By 1901, Springfield had even produced the first commercial motorcycle, Hendeen Manufacturing's "Indian."

That made it heaven to a scrappy kid with a technical mind like Earle Chapin, who at age twelve built a twenty-inch paddle-wheel schooner out of stray boards and the parts from an old clock. He was the third of five children; his father was a metal polisher who moved among private industry and employment at the armory. That young Earle could be counted on in a tight situation was clear by 1898, when the fifteen-year-old rushed to the rescue of a brick mason who had triggered the blasting cap on a makeshift cannon that literally fell from the sky into their neighborhood, the result of a preposterously ill-conceived real estate promotion involving an unmanned hot-air balloon. As flames spread over the frantic mason's clothing, Chapin helped tackle him, roll him in the dirt, and rip off his clothes to save him from serious injuries, burning one of his own shirtsleeves and singeing his arm in the process.

As a teenager, Chapin pursued a timeworn professional path as preordained as it was practical, apprenticing as a machinist. Soon he was precision-cutting game pieces at the Milton Bradley factory, when he wasn't raising trouble racing bicycles downtown. By twenty-one he was working for John W. Russell & Sons, a clattering all-purpose machine shop that developed the first aerial torpedoes for the Navy. This was the very place where Frank Duryea had built his first automobile a few years earlier, using the same steam-powered machine tools that commanded the floor. At night, Chapin earned a certificate in mechanical drawing at a trade school.

At twenty-three he moved across the state to Stoneham, where an enticing outfit named the Shawmut Motor Company was hiring skilled machinists. Shawmut was small, but it was backed by some of the wealthiest men in Boston, motor-car aficionados determined to build an automobile even better than any of them had owned so far, then develop a business around it. While many auto companies grew up around a visionary inventor, Shawmut was formed instead from the sudden departure of one, emerging from the remains of the Phelps Motor Vehicle Company, a quirky but semi-successful outfit organized by a restless polymath named Lucius J. Phelps. By the time Phelps turned up in Boston in 1899 he was nearly fifty years old, with a shock of bushy hair and a résumé of compelling contributions to the fields of railroad telegraphy, gas lighting, and pneumatic tires; he'd even built a better mousetrap, the bait-less Little Throttler. Still, he had little to show for it besides a zigzagging record of geographic moves and entrepreneurial false starts, his trail littered with guilelessness, impulsivity, and poor timing, laced with the agony of losing a young son to a skating accident.

While running a garage in Boston's wealthy Back Bay and trying to build his own steam car, Phelps befriended Elliot Cabot Lee, a Harvard-educated scion of multiple New England mercantile and banking dynasties who was so taken by the horseless age that he had just retired at forty-five to devote himself to automobiles—collecting, enjoying, and promoting them. Jowly and genteel, Lee wore a Garibaldi beard and a tweed motoring cap and lived with his aging mother and a few relatives on a Brookline estate with nine servants. The grounds boasted a chauffeur's cottage and one of the first true residential garages in the nation, no mere repurposed carriage house.

With money from Lee, Phelps finished the steamer and then designed a gasoline car, showing such promise that they incorporated and rented space in an old factory in Stoneham, hiring a few machinists. The Phelps car made a splash in 1903 with the first recorded ascent of Mount Washington, and by late 1904 they were employing seventy men, with plans to soon produce a hundred cars a year.

The three-cylinder Phelps was unusual, with the engine and transmission supported directly on the axles, and a body that lifted up from the front like the hinged jaw of a snake, exposing the mechanism for easy repairs. By 1905, they were determined to develop a four-cylinder car too. But Phelps's health was failing, and he suddenly abandoned the business for California, seeking refuge on an orchard near the Sierra Nevada mountains.

Lee had his hands full as president of the nascent, floundering American Automobile Association, stepping in as a respected authority to stabilize AAA and see it through incorporation and the publication of its first road maps. He had limited appetite to continue without Phelps, but he engaged a group of younger capitalists with a keen interest in automobiles to reorganize and keep the factory going, encouraging them and staying on as president. They briefly dubbed it Courier Motor Company before amending it to Shawmut, a popular moniker for businesses and place names derived from the misheard Indigenous word for Boston's central peninsula.

Initially, they plowed money and time into continuing what might have been the four-cylinder Phelps, selling a few at $3,500 before scrapping and starting over. They were not in a rush. They invested heavily in research and development, picking apart the finest European and American cars to study their construction, and sourcing materials from both sides of the Atlantic. By 1907, Shawmut had a showroom on Boston's Boylston Street and a dazzling line of models built around the same engine, winning plaudits at the city's annual auto show, and dispensing brochures suffused with the faith that "a motor car that is right is an exquisitely refined and sensitive mechanism capable in emergency of withstanding the most brutal treatment."

Even then they put more resources into perfection than production, going so far as to buy back some of the few cars they had sold, while focusing on still more improvements for 1908. By then Shawmut's vice president, guiding light, and chief financier was Quincy Adams Shaw Jr., heir to one of the nation's largest mining fortunes, and an amateur polo, golf, squash, tennis, and racquets player of the highest order. Described by one broadsheet as "one of the best known clubmen in New England," the thirty-eight-year-old Shaw could have breezed through life, but he dug in at multiple ventures, including Shawmut, where he helped design the car's curvilinear four-cylinder engine and water-jacket cooling system.

Shawmut earned respect from auto insiders at that April's Briarcliff Trophy Race, a grueling lap race around a twisting thirty-two-mile course in New York, submitted as a last-minute entry in a field of famous cars

(Renault, Benz, Fiat, Thomas, and others), helmed by drivers that included the speed king Barney Oldfield and the mustachioed Emanuel Cedrino, chauffeur to the Queen of Italy before achieving fame as a racer. Dismissed as an also-ran, the Shawmut achieved a surprising middle-of-the-pack performance before a hundred thousand spectators, but many people missed the achievement. The Boston car had been entered under the name of the New York luxury dealer Hol-Tan, scrambling for a substitute after an arrangement with another automaker had fallen through. Still, Hol-Tan was so pleased that it booked an order to sell Shawmut cars in Manhattan, provided the obsessive outfit could transition into real production.

Increasingly confident with their refinements, Shawmut entered another contest at the end of the summer, the 1908 Bay State Automobile Association (BSAA) Endurance Run. It was supposed to follow a 359-mile loop from Boston to the New Hampshire seacoast to the White Mountains and back, covering every type of road imaginable. Like other endurance runs, this one employed a formula that deducted points for breakdowns, mishaps, accidents, tune-ups, and other delays. The winner would be the car closest to perfect.

To everyone's surprise, nine of twenty-one remained flawless after twenty-four hours. So they kept going, and going, and going, determined to winnow the field like some sadistic game of musical chairs, in what the *Boston Evening Transcript* called "the hardest test ever given motor vehicles in this country and perhaps in the world." By the end of six brutal runs over eight days and sixteen-hundred-plus miles, the organizers gave up and crowned three winners, recognizing a Studebaker, a Franklin, and the Shawmut. That was an astonishing achievement for a firm that had built roughly a dozen cars, against Studebaker, a time-tested giant that had supplied wagons to the Union Army in the Civil War, and Franklin, a widely recognized technological leader with a massive engineering budget.

To Shawmut's backers, the result validated three years of intensive research and development. "We knew that we had the goods," said Horace Waite, the firm's general manager, telling *The Boston Herald* that "compared with the bulk of the cars marketed in America, the Shawmut can be best described as a custom-made car. Since the company has been in existence there is no record of a broken spring leaf or gear. The material used, while it may be bent as the result of an accident, has never been broken."

Earle Chapin had taken the wheel for some of those runs in the endless endurance contest, as had T. Arthur Pettengill, one of the most experienced machinists and testers at Shawmut, a steady, soft-spoken New Hampshire native who had worked in the factory since the first days of Phelps. Though Shawmut had used Hol-Tan's hired driver at Briarcliff, Pettengill had gone down there as a crew chief.

In October, Shawmut hustled out a new brochure ("A Car for the Man That Wants Only the BEST"), featuring a photo of the roadster with Chapin and Pettengill aboard, and capitalizing on the Briarcliff and BSAA performances: "After several years of study and experiment, we have a car that is certainly worthy of your inspection. The records . . . set at rest every question as to the Shawmut's reliability, speed and power. And also in beauty of lines and finish, in quietness and comfort, in smoothness and durability, in economy and ease in operation, the Shawmut product will compare favorably with any cars built in the world."

The factory crackled with an electrifying sense of purpose. The phones in Stoneham and at Shawmut's Boylston Street showroom in Boston jangled with people eager to tour the plant or take a test-drive. The company started to staff up, preparing to expand production dramatically for 1909. Then the fire alarm pierced the air at 1:30 AM on November 13—Friday the 13th—jolting Stoneham awake in the still of the early morning. A night watchman had been making the rounds at the Shawmut factory, casting the light of his oil lamp into the darkened corners as a strong wind knifed through the old timbers and rattled the windows. The man said he'd opened a door to the experimental room and discovered fire, though some suspected he'd struck a match to relight his lantern, unwittingly igniting a flash of unseen gasoline vapor. He tried to smother the flames before staggering out into the night, badly burned, the blaze growing behind him. The firehouse sat directly across the street, and there was an alarm box on the corner. But Stoneham still had a volunteer department—

a source of spirited debate around town in recent years—and by the time the firefighters came running from their homes, it was too late to save Shawmut, a lightly insured renter. The company lost all of its machine tools, a wealth of raw materials, ten finished cars awaiting shipment, and a handful of others in varying stages of completion. After three years and more than $300,000 invested (over $10 million in 2025), they had nothing left but charred rubble and a few test models parked elsewhere.

Some of Shawmut's directors had an interest in a small factory in Watertown, eleven miles away, that made industrial controllers and machine tools. Shawmut's Horace Waite, a son of privilege from Chicago whose family trust did not quite provide the means he desired, had already been running the business side of both ventures as general manager. And Frederick A. Meier Jr., a German-American engineer of precise standards and technical brilliance, had overseen the operations of both factories as superintendent, demanding from machinists what they called "micrometer fits."

On paper at least, they relocated Shawmut to Watertown—in reality, there wasn't much to move—and kept a skeleton crew employed. Actual automobile production froze, while they reorganized, scouted locations, and solicited new investment. It was harder than before, so they took a chance in the spring on the $350 entry fee for the Ocean-to-Ocean Race, even if the tab for sustaining a crew on the road for a month would be substantial, coupled with the cost of bringing the men and the car back afterward by train. If they won, the publicity payoff would be enormous.

As word spread around Boston, volunteers came forward, experienced track racers and wild-eyed venturers. But management turned to Earle Chapin and Arthur Pettengill, two reliable men who knew the car and had proven themselves at the factory and in competition. They were complementary characters, Pettengill five years older and five inches shorter, as taciturn as Chapin was peppy. Blue-eyed and balding, already a father of two, True Arthur Pettengill—who mostly went by Arthur or "Pet," though Chapin sometimes called him "True Pet"—had been raised on a dairy farm in central New Hampshire, where he studied in a one-room schoolhouse. As a young man he'd worked at a sawmill and a box factory before going off to Manchester, the Granite State's answer to Springfield, to apprentice in a machine shop. In late 1900, he married his childhood sweetheart, a schoolteacher named Edith Stevens, and two years later they relocated to Stoneham so Pettengill could join the new Phelps Motor Vehicle Company.

Though "Hod" Waite had gone to Yale, the Shawmut directors were mainly Harvard men. In the run-up to the race, they subjected Chapin and Pettengill to intensive calisthenics, as if they were training for "The Game" or "The Race," the annual Harvard-Yale battles on the gridiron and the water that gripped the sporting interest of the nation. They pushed the duo through a regimen of sleep deprivation in order to build stamina for grueling overnight runs ahead. At the same time, with no factory for building new Shawmuts, they used the skeleton crew in Watertown to customize a surviving Shawmut roadster for the race, beyond loading it full of tires, tubes, and implements of extrication, like shovels, crowbars, ropes, and an axe. Studying the struggles of the Thomas pathfinder, they designed attachments for securing and threading tackle lines around the exterior of the rear wheels, so that the car's own power could be used to propel it out of deep mud and quicksand, instead of the usual wait for a team of horses.

Even before these adjustments, the Shawmut was unusually durable and well designed, with major components machined from Krupp nickel steel imported from Germany—four times as expensive as standard American steel but superior in strength and lightness. An abundance of top-of-the-line ball bearings from German precision arms-maker Deutsche Waffen- und Munitionsfabriken—exacting producer of the new Luger pistol—reduced friction on moving parts. The magneto was protected by a special cover, the engine was as oiltight as possible, and the clever design of the fifty-one-disc clutch allowed it to be removed by loosening just eleven nuts, without disturbing the flywheel or transmission. Already the car boasted a high clearance compared to its center of gravity, but the Boston branch manager of tire supplier Diamond Rubber suggested raising the hubs higher still, to clear more humps and boulders and churn through deeper mud, by enlarging the wheels to forty inches in diameter from their original thirty-six in front and thirty-four in the rear.

In addition to a storage trunk behind the rear axle, the workers in Watertown added another along the passenger-side running board, for stowing foul-weather gear and a larder of canned foods. They painted that trunk with BOSTON and NEW YORK–SEATTLE while adding similar lettering, plus SHAWMUT, to the cover of the tire supply mounted on the back, with more tires stashed on the driver's side. Where the roadster had originally carried three bucket seats—two in front and a third behind—they ripped those out for roomier and more comfortable seating, installing a pair of high-backed, tufted-leather benches. That matched the look and tonneau seating of Shawmut's longer $5,000 touring car, but paired it with this roadster's tighter 108-inch wheelbase. The wider rear bench now had room for three seated passengers, if the crew took on guides or observers, or enough space for one man to stretch out sideways and try to snooze while the other drove, with special cushions affixed to each side as headrests. They also cut a section of white canvas oilcloth that could be unfurled as a sun or storm shield, without the weight and bulk of carrying a hardtop roof.

Pettengill would be captain and lead driver and Chapin mechanic, but they would share time at the wheel. The duo "know the Shawmut car down to the last bolt, and are full of honest fight and the 'get there' spirit," reported the *Boston Post* with boosterish pride. "They have before them a tremendous strain, but old-fashioned Yankee courage, judgment, coolness and grit can carry the Shawmut car first into Seattle, and the Shawmut crew has 'got the goods.'"

As the race approached, the Shawmut backers decided it would be wise to add a third crew member. They selected Robert Messer, a ruddy, ruggedly built twenty-four-year-old who was destined to succeed his father as a third-generation Stoneham undertaker. Messer already had his funeral director's license, but he loved automobiles, knew engines, and was known as one of the fastest drivers in town.

Following a big send-off for the Shawmut in downtown Boston six days before the race, they traveled west via Springfield, a brief homecoming for

Chapin in drizzly weather, before pointing south to New York City. After tuning up the car and checking in with the contest committee of the Automobile Club of America, the crew exhaled, and found themselves idle. The other automobiles were being displayed at their Manhattan showrooms, drawing crowds, but Shawmut alone didn't have one. So the trio explored the city as wide-eyed tourists, walking down from the Hotel Cumberland at Columbus Circle to the Theater District, where they took in *The Fair Co-Ed* starring the ingenue Elsie Janis, known for her French curls, comic mimicry, and keenly penetrating eyes. ("She is good and has got eyes something like yours, not so nice," Chapin wrote to Anita.)

On Sunday, Shawmut executive Horace Waite arrived bearing an envelope stuffed with those new American Express "travelers cheques" that let you pay without cash or letters of credit, and then Waite and a friend took the crew to Coney Island, where they couldn't believe the sight of so many young women drinking beer and dancing. On Memorial Day, Chapin and Messer wanted to join Waite at the Polo Grounds to see the great Christy Mathewson pitch, then catch another Broadway show, but Pettengill, sensible and serious at thirty-one, insisted they rest up for the big race.

Now it was Tuesday afternoon. The adrenaline rush that followed the starting gun had given way to a surreal parade up Broadway, moving so slowly that a dog could have run circles around them. A group of bicycle policemen set the pace up front, enforcing Manhattan's eight-mile-per-hour speed limit, followed by a lieutenant and an inspector from the traffic squad riding in an open-air taxi—a new one from W. C. P. Taxicab, the first in the city to paint its fleet yellow.

Other officials followed in taxis, too, but Guggenheim rode in an Allen-Kingston driven by Walter Allen himself, a former Mercedes importer who'd become one of the first to manufacture an American car modeled specifically on the techniques and materials of Europe, minus that stiff 45 percent tariff. Guggenheim had purchased a custom-built A-K racer on the spot in 1908, after it won a race in which his beloved Renault was totaled on a rain-slicked track.

Even then there was still one more automobile ahead of the competitors, which would remain in place through the East: a pacemaker carrying the veteran automotive journalist John Gerrie, acting as a rolling representative of the ACA, to monitor speeding and enforce those twelve-hour overnight controls until they reached the free-for-all beyond the Mississippi.

Those rules had been added, along with the prohibition on changing major parts, in that failed bid to placate the powers leading the pressure campaign against the race. That was all fine with Shawmut, but Henry Ford didn't like it, insisting that a race with fewer rules would be a simpler race, eminently fair. He thought the amendments complicated matters and amounted to caving under pressure—anathema to Ford, in his fight against the Selden patent—leaving unsaid that they could also cut into the considerable advantage conferred by his national sales-and-service network. Ford had eleven big-city corporate branch stores, with eight of them along the route of the race, plus nearly a thousand contractual dealers lined up to sell Fords in and around their hometowns. Although these agents held exclusive rights from Ford to sell on their turf, a lot of them were just part-timers—bicycle men, hardware merchants, even country doctors—moving a few Fords a year and taking a good horse for $100 trade-in credit. Many lacked proper showrooms, and fewer still had garages, but they were generally knowledgeable locals, respected in their communities. Most answered to the nearest branch manager, giving Ford a waiting network with a vested interest in assisting the No. 1 and 2 Ts all the way across the country. Only Buick had a network to rival Ford's, and Durant was too preoccupied to enter the race.

It was a good thing to advertise generally that with a Ford you were never far from a sales agent or someone who could help you secure factory parts quickly, if a dicey matter to broadcast in the context of the race. Better to maintain it as an unstated advantage and present objections to the new rules as a matter of sporting simplicity. There were rumors that Ford might drop out, but he stayed in, telling the press that even with these new rules he would still wager any sum against anyone, in or out of the race, who "does not believe in Ford cars, considers them too light, too cheap," and was willing to gamble on one of the others to win.

On top of that, Ford even furnished the very pacemaker automobile whose inclusion he opposed, the front-running car that would allow the ACA's Gerrie to keep a lid on speed and enforce the overnight controls. (Being first even in the East would still matter; if you broke down, got lost, or otherwise arrived late at these control points, your twelve-hour clock would not start until your arrival, meaning you would be held back when the leaders left the next morning.)

If there had to be a pacemaker, it might as well be a Ford—in this case a splashy Six-Forty, a sporty sibling to the roomy Model K, the company's rare foray into the upscale six-cylinder touring-car market, which dealers were now phasing out to make room for the Model T. This was one more stroke of promotional savvy, showcasing a car that needed to be sold while ensuring that the first automobile spotted by waiting crowds would be a Ford.

Rolling north out of Lower Manhattan, they glided past John Wanamaker's sprawling department-store complex and curled clockwise around Union Square, tracing Dead Man's Curve, the site of so many ghastly streetcar-pedestrian collisions. From there they approached the Fuller Company's "Flat-Iron Building," the wind-whipped triangular sensation where Broadway sliced across Fifth Avenue. They passed a short block and a world away from the United Charities Building, where the two-day National Negro Conference was at that very moment laying the foundation for the National Association for the Advancement of Colored People, or NAACP, propelled partly by a spate of lynchings in Springfield, Illinois, Abraham Lincoln's hometown.

Onward they chuffed past Gimbel Brothers, Saks & Co., and the massive R. H. Macy store, the police escort cutting with ease through the tangle of Herald Square, normally the most congested in the city, where Broadway and Sixth Avenue crossed amid a knot of streetcar tracks and a thicket of steel beams supporting the elevated train overhead. Now they approached Times Square, the rebranded Longacre Square, a fading carriage-manufacturing district undergoing a rebirth with an array of theaters and new hotels.

This marked the beginning of Automobile Row, the unrivaled sales capital of the auto industry, what *Motor Age* called "the liveliest 2 miles of business street in America," expanding outward and upward, low-slung wood-and-brick buildings giving way to more steel-frame warehouses and ten-story skyscrapers every year. Beckoning showrooms offered more than a hundred different makes of automobiles and a dizzying array of aftermarket accessories, from windshields and speedometers to exhaust-powered pedestrian-warning "surprise horns" and ornamental radiator caps, well into the West 70s.

Here the crowds and the cheers intensified, a homecoming for every car but Shawmut, the others enjoying a dealership in the district. First they passed Cordner Motor Company, the Acme agency run by the effervescent stock promoter who had persuaded the firm to enter the Ocean-to-Ocean Race, and whose sales-boosting ideas included the first prepaid maintenance plan in the industry.

Beyond West Fifty-Fourth Street they approached the expansive New York branch of Ford Motor Company, spanning 1721 and 1723 Broadway, fifty feet across, its polished plate-glass windows ready to track the progress of the race for passersby with posted bulletins and a painted map of the nation marked with the route, a rousing sight for the Ford convoy at the front of the procession. On the next block they passed Hol-Tan, a bittersweet reminder for the Shawmut men of what might have been; Hol-Tan was the agency that had booked Shawmut at the last minute for the Briarcliff race and then signed on afterward to sell Shawmuts in Manhattan, until the fire intervened. Now the Hol-Tan showroom offered a sporty little import called the Lancia instead.

On the far corner of the next block, Itala importer and coach-builder

A. T. Demarest & Co. was erecting one of the true stunners of Automobile Row, a nine-story Gothic Revival tower that would house their salesrooms, corporate offices, body-crafting shop, and automotive service center in one stack, with space to lease to other luxury dealers as well—a testament to the firm's long history in luxury coach-building and faith in its future. Beside the cowboy hat–wearing Lechleitner at the wheel of the Itala, the late A. T. Demarest's own twenty-year-old grandson occupied the front passenger seat as an adventure-seeking tourist and "mechanician." A recent graduate of Yale's Sheffield Scientific School, Francesco Bianchi Whittemore Jr. cut the most striking sartorial figure of anyone participating in the race, drawing notice along Broadway for eschewing standard motoring garb for a corduroy suit, knee-high lace-up boots, and a jaunty hat accented with a feather.

Behind them, backup driver Elbert Bellows rounded out the Itala's three-man crew in simple khaki work wear and a soft driving cap, Robert Guggenheim's own addition to the car he had enlisted and bankrolled for this race. A bootstrapping Spanish-American War veteran, Bert Bellows had been the mining and smelting heir's favorite chauffeur and chief mechanic for two years until Guggenheim got shipped off to Seattle, initially without his autos. He was five foot four but broad-shouldered, a thirty-four-year-old equally comfortable at the wheel or under the hood. He always called the young millionaire "Mr. Guggenheim" or "Mr. G," and had driven skillfully for him in Manhattan and at summer resorts north and south of the city, racing as well for Guggenheim in exhibitions. Despite his stalwart façade on the job, Bellows could be tender and funny; while courting his wife Margaret five years back, he'd once dropped her twenty postcards in forty-eight hours, giving each a wry or winking caption.

Raised by his grandparents in St. Lawrence County, Bellows, after school, had bicycled 340 miles from the North Country with two friends to seek adventure in the big city. The bike had no brakes, so he'd stop quickly by blocking the pedals hard with the back of his legs. By the time he reached Manhattan he had a case of necrosis. A doctor at Bellevue Hospital wanted to treat it by amputation, but Bellows gathered his clothing and walked out, saying he'd rather die in one piece; he found another doctor to scrape away the damaged area, and he healed without a limp. After finding work delivering milk by horse cart, Bellows got in on the ground floor as a driver when the first electric hansom cabs debuted in the 1890s, and soon found his way to gasoline autos.

For Manhattan's elite, good chauffeurs were hard to find. Grooms and coachmen who knew about horses weren't necessarily suited to newfangled contraptions. And many of the motoring men who proffered their services turned out to be grifters, faking credentials from evening chauffeur schools, taking automobiles for unauthorized "joy rides," and conjuring persuasive reasons to bring the car back to the shop for unnecessary service, while collecting kickbacks on the side.

Bert Bellows was never like that. Guggenheim wanted to persuade him to move to Seattle, but until then he had left him with a glowing letter of recommendation, calling him "entirely trustworthy and absolutely competent in every respect. He is honest, sober and obliging. He not only has driven Mrs. Guggenheim in the city, but has also driven my Renault Racer in numerous events; and I consider him thoroughly confident, as well as careful, when driving ladies in the city."

Of all the men in all the crews making their way up Broadway, only Bellows had an inkling of what they were in for. In April he had crisscrossed Idaho, and in May he had driven from Boise to Seattle, after Guggenheim had paid to ship his favorite chauffeur and his Allen-Kingston from New York to Boise by train. The millionaire had envisioned himself accompanying the Thomas pathfinder over the home stretch to great fanfare, but the Thomas Flyer was so plagued by hardship and delay that Guggenheim abandoned the idea and sent Bellows on his own. The drive had been nightmarish, but the journey was eye-opening. "I would never be content to be a chauffeur in New York again. I have seen too much independence out here," Bellows had written to his wife, awed by the comparative absence of class distinctions and the booming quality of the West. "Out here money don't count for much. All you have got to do is to make good in whatever you are into and you can get along all right."

He'd barely made it back East in time for the birth of his first child in late May, a girl they named Elisabeth, and he had little desire to turn around and leave again a week later for a second cross-country adventure. But Guggenheim wanted him to join the Itala. They needed the money, and it could open doors to more opportunity.

So there was Bellows, riding in the long, low-slung No. 6 Itala, carrying $500 from Guggenheim to cover the crew's expenses, and looking ahead at the No. 5 Shawmut, with its big letters stenciled on the spare-tire cover and a BOSTON MOTOR CLUB pennant flapping above. Earle Chapin sat beside Arthur Pettengill in the front of that Boston car, with Bob Messer behind them. Where Broadway widened beyond Columbus Circle they found a motoring haven, a smooth sheet of asphalt stretching all the way to the northern tip of the island, interrupted only by the double-tracked streetcar rails running down the middle. They followed Broadway to Columbia University, where they hung a left toward Riverside Drive and passed Grant's Tomb before rejoining Broadway through Harlem and up into Washington Heights and Inwood.

Brick apartment buildings were sprouting alongside the advancing subway line, intermingled with construction lots and the last vestiges of Upper Manhattan's country estates and untouched woods. As they neared the bridge over the Harlem River shipping canal, the leading convoy fell away, leaving only the pacemaker and the five numbered competitors. They could see Guggenheim and Morrell standing beside Broadway, waving them on toward the mainland, wishing them luck.

3

A "Frenzied, Foolhardy Speed Terror"

New York to Toledo, June 1 to 4, 1909

They could all see there was something different about the little Model Ts before they were out of the Hudson Valley. Up in the pacemaker, John Gerrie was accustomed to riding in substantial cars like this Six-Forty. He'd been writing about horseless carriages since the beginning, when they were all small and flimsy. As inaugural automobile editor of *The New York Herald*, he'd helped organize the nation's first auto show in 1900 at Madison Square Garden. As part of that show they set up a modest ramp on the roof of the Garden, and even that incline proved a challenge for those early autos. The next year, Gerrie was nearly killed with a group of fellow motoring enthusiasts, when the 10-horsepower car they were riding in on Long Island got struck by a locomotive at an unguarded railway crossing. They flew into the air, the car "landing in a shattered heap of debris," the men scattered. Gerrie was lucky to be hospitalized with just a broken shoulder. That seemed like ancient history now, the way cars had grown in size and power. The size gave you confidence, and the power helped you accelerate away from trouble when you needed it.

Gerrie had started as a bicycle reporter in Toronto and relished the role he'd grown into in New York, where there was no separation between the press and the auto realm they covered. He played toastmaster at automotive banquets and served as a judge at major races, rubbing elbows with rich men and riding in the mightiest and most refined motor cars. Amid the parade through Manhattan, he had given short shrift to the two entries he considered "midget competitors" behind him. He assumed those Model Ts would fall away when they picked up the pace in the countryside or encountered some hills. Now he saw that they couldn't be shaken. Their top speed might be modest, but they had pep, and they seemed to take "the grades as easily as the levels."

Bert Bellows could see it too. These Model Ts were nothing like the cars he had driven for Guggenheim—the roomy Rainier ("The Pullman of Motor Cars"), the racy Renault, the roaring Allen-Kingston, or now this elongated Itala. The Model T was more like a water bug or a spider, with that twisting frame and light construction. It wasn't much to look at, stripped down like this, but it seemed surprisingly fast and sturdy. Those "two Fords are special built cars, and they can go," he would soon write home to Margaret.

To Henry Ford, it was obvious. The virtues he prized in a car were the same he favored in people. Strength coupled with lightness; leanness, efficiency, coiled power, fighting trim. The very qualities he prized in himself. The lithe farm boy who had walked nearly two miles to school each morning with a lunch prepared by a mother who considered sweets a moral weakness had grown into the wiry executive who shed his suit jacket to wrestle workmen on the factory floor and shoved his desk aside to tangle playfully with visiting salesmen, eager to prove that size and strength were not the same. And vanadium steel was the magic ingredient for achieving what he wanted in an auto, obliterating the competition when it came to strength against weight.

It even sounded mystical, named for a Scandinavian goddess of beauty and youth. It was the open secret Ford was shouting from the rooftops, touting it in ads adorned with "micro-photographs" of steel alloys that supposedly made vanadium's structural superiority obvious to the naked eye, even if they just looked like blotches to most people. He evangelized it in interviews and letters to motoring magazines and even wrote about it for a special *Harper's Weekly* automobile issue—well, the piece carried Ford's byline; he wasn't even much of a reader, never mind a writer—all about a natural element that, "when judiciously used, imparts to steel qualities that are little less than magical, and which are well calculated to meet the most severe requirements of the automobile engineer."

For all the eons that vanadium had waited in the earth's crust, only in the last few years had British metallurgists started experimenting and testing it as an ingredient in heat-treated steel alloys, with initial applications in custom European racers. Ford was one of the first to incorporate it in America, using vanadium in some custom racers and adding it as an ingredient in existing consumer models. But designing a car stem to stern with vanadium was another matter. In the winter of 1906–1907, Ford cordoned off a special lair on the third floor of his Piquette Avenue factory in Detroit, where he would hold court from his late mother's rocking chair while prodding and coaxing a handpicked collection of designers, draftsmen, and machinists through nearly two years of drawings, models, and prototypes, of probing and refining and testing, before the car he yearned for was ready: the Model T.

For the first time in a Ford, all four cylinders were cast in a single block, covered by a detachable head. The engine, transmission, and flywheel—with built-in magneto—were enclosed in one case. It promised efficiency (better than twenty miles to the gallon) and economical operation. And the steering column had been sensibly relocated to the left. Americans had always driven on the right, but carmakers put the steering wheel on that side, too, because it matched the seating arrangement in carriages and buggies, with the dominant whip hand out on the right, to avoid striking a passenger. Plus, when automobiles were designed with chauffeurs in mind, it made sense to have the driver on the right, to more easily step out and open doors at the curb. But the left side made more sense for gauging oncoming traffic. Besides, Ford was designing a car for people to drive themselves, and carry passengers who weren't waiting for a servant to open the door.

Though serious production would not begin until winter, the car officially launched October 1, the annual start of the new model year. A few days before that, Henry Ford took the first official Model T out for a long-haul test run to the hunting grounds of northern Wisconsin, eager to demonstrate what the car could do. To drive, he tapped factory men Bernard W. "Bert" Scott and C. J. "Jimmie" Smith. Scott was a skilled road-tester and occasional company racer. Smith was a machinist who had earned special notice from Ford for his zealous efficiency, after jury-rigging his station to bore eight engine camshafts at once instead of one. That helped Smith get picked for the secret team that developed the Model T. They drove by way of Chicago and Milwaukee, with Ford leaving the boys at Iron Mountain, Wisconsin, and Scott and Smith returning on their own, 1,357 miles round trip. They reached Detroit thoroughly covered in mud, having consumed sixty-eight gallons of gasoline and more than eleven gallons of oil. But other than a punctured tire, they hadn't needed to make a single adjustment—early proof to them of what the Model T could do on a long run in demanding conditions.

Now Scott and Smith were paired again for the Ocean-to-Ocean Race, roaring north along the east side of the Hudson River in the No. 2 Ford. Scott was five foot nine, with brown eyes and dark hair, the twenty-six-year-old son of a popular police sergeant on Detroit's health squad. A former competitive cyclist, he had started as a teenage apprentice electrician at Detroit's Edison Illuminating Company, just missing the opportunity to overlap with Henry Ford himself, an Edison supervisor who left the lighting plant in 1899 to plunge into automobiles full-time. They met a few years later when Scott was bicycling near the docks—a chance encounter that would change the young man's line of work and the trajectory of his life.

Jimmie Smith, the enterprising cam miller, was five foot six and lean as a jockey, with gray-blue eyes and sandy hair. Just twenty-four, he had worked at Ford for three years already. A native of the Canadian side of the Detroit River, Smith had initially followed his father into Detroit's robust shipbuilding industry, a manufacturing base that made the city a natural home for the emerging auto industry—particularly as that industry's center of gravity shifted from the myriad smaller firms of the East to Michigan companies like Cadillac, Olds, and Ford producing cars at scale.

If Scott and Smith were natural picks for one of the racers, the crew in the No. 1 Model T made it clear which one Ford imagined breaking the tape at the finish. At the wheel, Frank Kulick was the company's unquestioned driving star, his acclaim in the sporting world at odds with his quiet nature and modest personal life, living at home at twenty-six with his parents and siblings. Another former competitive cyclist from a working-class Detroit family, Kulick was an exceptionally gifted mechanic who had come of age with the infant auto industry. By twenty-one, he had already built engines for Olds and tested motors for Northern. As one of Ford Motor's first employees in 1903, he rose quickly to head road-tester and handpicked racer. Readers of sports pages and auto weeklies knew his name through achievements in stock cars as well as specially designed racers—until a pair of spectacular crashes in the fall of 1907, with a freak Ford concoction too powerful for its slender wheels, nearly killed Kulick twice in a matter of weeks. The second crash threw him so far and so hard that Kulick fractured his kneecap and broke his right femur in two places; he would forever walk with a limp, quietly enduring lifelong discomfort. With no ambulance nearby, Henry Ford hacked off the seats of a touring car with a saw and crowbar to fit a makeshift stretcher, rushing Kulick to the hospital on a cot borrowed from a groundskeeper. While the steely driver yearned to compete again as soon as he was off crutches, Ford was so shaken that he outwardly denounced racing. As with other Ford proclamations to the press, this one came with caveats far below the headline; his racing denunciation applied chiefly to powerhouse machines on overmatched horse tracks. The Ocean-to-Ocean Race was just fine, an endurance showcase for consumers.

The man Ford teamed with Kulick as "mechanic" in the No. 1 knew relatively little about auto repair and maintenance: Henry B. Harper, known as H.B. and Harry, the polished, studiedly self-deprecating Ford Motor advertising manager who doubled as editor of the *Ford Times*, a bimonthly newspaper for factory employees, dealers, and Ford owners. Harper looked snappy in his goggles and motoring cap above a tidy mustache, but whether the twenty-eight-year-old office dweller could drive or wield a wrench was beside the point. Kulick would handle all that.

Harper was there for one reason only—to generate copy. He would pump out dispatches for the house organ, compose paeans for advertisements, and lionize the story of the victory that the boss expected and craved, these affordable cars tackling the continent and taming bigger, pricier, heavier rivals. He would also send frequent telegrams, so that Ford Motor could relay them to branch managers and dealers as well as Firestone tire outlets, to post in showroom windows and reprint in local papers, as if good old Harry Harper was taking time from the race to personally wire them all.

Ford knew what he was doing by entering two cars and by submitting the application first, with hood numbers assigned in order of entry. That meant they would invariably be referred to by the press as "the No. 1 Ford" and "the No. 2 Ford"—which had an undeniable ring to it, equating them with the vanguard irrespective of their actual position on any given day. The two cars were instructed to drive cross-country together, as long as they could manage. That way they could help one another as needed, each vehicle an insurance policy for the other, while one car could power ahead if something truly went wrong.

That was hardly Ford's only built-in advantage. The company's dealer network stood out for both its size and its structure, organized under that hierarchy of eleven branch managers in the biggest American cities, company executives running direct-to-consumer showrooms. Some thought you couldn't get a salaried man to work as hard selling cars, unlike commissioned salesmen or self-employed agents. But the branch managers were trusted field lieutenants, bolstered by profit sharing, with faith in the company and what they saw as its bright future. They competed against one another in sales contests published in the *Ford Times* while angling for potential stock bonuses and future promotions. They also lined up most of the company's thousand dealers, a term used interchangeably with *agents* meaning the independent operators contracted to sell Fords in their communities, each with an exclusively designated area. With a few exceptions, those dealers—who bought at a slight discount and made a modest profit with each sale—booked their orders through the nearest branch manager instead of Detroit.

In late spring, those branch men traveled up and down the line in their territories, recruiting the most trusted dealers as guides and seeding supplies as needed. In a nation with few marked roads, where countryside directions were given largely around landscape features or notable buildings, good guides would be essential. The Thomas pathfinder crew had prepared a booklet with town-by-town directions, but one glance and you could tell it was a recipe for getting lost. The race rules prohibited anyone who was not a coast-to-coast crew member from taking the wheel, but local "pilots" could ride along or drive ahead to show you the way.

For the other entries, that was an ad hoc matter, recruiting guides along the way or with help from their tire suppliers. Only Ford had an uninterrupted relay waiting to guide the Model T racers from New York to Seattle.

A deliberately lighter schedule over the first three days allowed the crews to get their sea legs but limited the opportunities for anyone to pull away, with the cars largely bunched through Yonkers and Poughkeepsie, Syracuse and Rochester, then on into Buffalo by the evening of June 3. That was the third of the six overnight control stations that had been added for safety in the East. Buffalo also doubled as the sixth of thirty nationwide checkpoints where the cars needed to stop, at least briefly, so the crew members could prove that they were traveling with their automobiles continually and also that they weren't shipping these cars point to point by rail, a problem in the New York–to–Paris Race. Around those thirty stops, the organizers had arranged with Standard Oil to provide lubricating oil for free and to offer gas at no more than fifteen cents a gallon, though gasoline of varying qualities could also be found at most hardware stores, a combustible cleaning product ladled from the barrel.

Each crew carried a passport with a page for every checking station, from the Nelson House in Poughkeepsie to the Yakima Hotel in central Washington, most of them naturally placed at hotels where you could find someone working at all hours. At each of the stops, the crew needed to present the booklet and obtain the signature of one of the various "named Gentlemen" listed on that respective page, typically hotel owners or clerks lined up by the pathfinder to confirm each car's appearance. In return, the checkpoint attendants would give each crew a card for everyone to sign and mail to Seattle, where Guggenheim's personal secretary would check the signatures against a master list as a way to verify they were really all there, not cheating by substituting fresh crew members.

With everyone gathered at Buffalo's Iroquois Hotel, they understood that June 4 would bring the most ambitious day yet, a three-hundred-plus mile run to Toledo, starting in the gray light of 5 AM. Speed limits were strict in densely settled districts, but on the wide-open roads between towns, New York State allowed a brisk twenty miles per hour, Pennsylvania permitted twenty-four, and Ohio again twenty. If they kept that pace, the run might last about fifteen hours. That was a big *if*, provided they didn't break down, get lost, or become mired in mud, with rain in the forecast. They would need to hit two checkpoints in between, in Erie and then Cleveland, before stopping for the night at Toledo's Secor Hotel. Even if the real free-for-all wouldn't begin until St. Louis, they all felt a sense of urgency already, knowing any delay that day would require them to be held back by the same amount when the pack left again the next morning.

There was an extra wrinkle now, with the big red Ford Six-Forty that pacemaker John Gerrie had been riding in turning back at Buffalo for Manhattan. From here to St. Louis, the rolling representative of the Automobile Club of America would shift among the bigger cars, his yellow-and-green ACA banner carried along with him. With their expert guides, that would make it even easier for the two Model Ts to shake off Gerrie—fall back, then pick up an alternate road—and drive as fast as they wanted.

Among that day's pilots, Ford's Toledo dealer, Stanley Roberts, waited at the far end of the line to lead the way over the final thirty-five miles, anticipating their arrival with the nerves and excitement accompanying the anchor leg in any big relay. Just twenty-five years old, Roberts had already glimpsed the future and grabbed hold. He was five foot seven, clean-shaven, at once affable and unshakably determined. For three years he'd worked at Ford headquarters, starting as a clerk and rising in the sales department under the masterful Norval Hawkins, traveling to recruit new dealers and serving as a contact for them in Detroit.

Then Roberts got a look at the coming Model T—and decided his days in middle management were over. Wanting a cut of the action, he became a Ford dealer himself, though not one of the thousand with a small patch of turf and limited independence, nested below the eleven branch managers. A small number of independent dealers with unusual seniority or other connections commanded much larger terrain and answered directly to corporate, functioning more like branch managers, often with big showrooms and their own local network of satellite dealers. That's what Roberts had carved out, commanding Ford sales across all of Northwest Ohio.

Certainly he had learned a thing or two in Detroit, studying the sales-and-marketing prowess of Hawkins and E. LeRoy Pelletier, two figures who were equally outsized and brilliant, and who between them had contributed significantly to Ford's market share. Pelletier was the first advertising manager, the role that the buttoned-up Harry Harper in the No. 1 racer was now trying to fill. A Barnumesque bantamweight with a rakish mustache, Pelletier had been a Klondike gold seeker turned newspaper correspondent who flirted with mounting a motorized North Pole expedition and served as an advance man for the circus before joining Ford. Everything he did commanded attention. He'd left in 1908 in order to get in on the ground floor of a bold new automotive venture, the E-M-F, cofounded by breakaway figures from Ford and Cadillac.

For his part, Ford sales manager Hawkins was charismatic, classically handsome, and so likable that when he served a prison stint for embezzlement as a Standard Oil cashier early in his career, a group of influential friends advocated for his early release, then helped set him up again—as an accountant, no less. Arriving at Ford initially as a consultant, Hawkins brought creativity, rigor, and polish to the nascent sales department, not just lining up dealers but imparting a vision. Hawkins believed firmly that Ford agents were selling ideas, not goods, and should appeal to emotions, not bombard potential customers with facts and figures. He created the *Ford Times*—overseeing editor Harper—and traveled the country to teach people how to generate leads and close deals, motivating them with carrot and stick. In time, he would become known in Detroit as the "daddy of super-salesmen" and write multiple business-tips bestsellers.

Steeped in this Hawkins-Pelletier school, Stanley Roberts didn't just scrutinize his thirty-five miles of the Ocean-to-Ocean route to determine the surest path or uncover any roadblocks. He wanted to wring as much publicity out of the passing race as possible. So he recruited two reporters to accompany him on a thrilling ride-along, the *Toledo Blade*'s Jerry Winters and the *News-Bee*'s Fred Mollenkopf, while booking ads to accompany their coverage in the papers. That morning in Toledo, he followed the race's westward progress by wire. He knew the cars remained clustered at Erie, Pennsylvania, where they'd rumbled in so fast that a police officer pinched one of the crew members for speeding—grabbing Fay Sheets, the Acme's backup driver, in a rush to set an example. ("Life has its pin-points as well as its velvet cushions," one paper would quip, poking at the officer's "lack of 'sporting' instinct.") The cop dragged Sheets to the station for booking, a common practice before written citations and standardized fines for driving infractions. Nabbed speeders were routinely arrested, then needed to post cash bail or wait behind bars until arraignment. Though judges were often forgiving when the drivers appeared before them, bail forfeited by the many motorists who simply skipped town served as both a de facto fine system and just one more cost of driving for the wealthy. In this case, with pacemaker John Gerrie present, and with everyone clustered, the competitors were obliged to wait for the Acme crew to post $25 bail and free Sheets from lockup—even as Cleveland Ford salesman Fred Van Patton, who'd been in Erie overnight awaiting his turn as guide, was eager to pick up and race off toward Ohio.

Van Patton helped the Model Ts gain a modest edge by Cleveland, and they really began to pull away on the west side of that city, as rain descended. Without expert guides of their own, the Acme, Shawmut, and Itala muddled through waterlogged mishaps and misdirection, Shawmut's Pettengill consulting a silver dollar-sized compass he kept in his pocket, while the Model Ts took a shortcut inland to Elyria, where the next Ford dealer in the relay waited to grab the baton and lead them fifty miles to Stanley Roberts, who was poised to escort them on that final leg from Fremont to Toledo. As those three big cars meandered alongside Lake Erie—at least that way they knew they were heading roughly in the right direction—the Acme ran off the road twice. First it skidded into a ditch near Lorain, but a passing trolley—one of Ohio's many electric "interurbans"—helped tug the car back onto the road. If the map of the Northeast was laced with the major arteries of the big steam-powered railroads, the interurbans looked more like a neural network, an intricate lattice of city-to-city streetcar connections running well beyond the trolley lines within cities. They made it possible to travel from Boston to New York City and from New York City all the way to Chicago entirely by streetcar, albeit in disjointed fashion, with innumerable transfers and frequent stops. Recognizing that he was falling behind, the ACA's Gerrie left the struggling Acme there to catch one of those trolleys—the Lake Shore Electric—all the way to Toledo, to reliably reach that night's control station in time. Back on the road without him, the Acme made it only a few more miles before slip-sliding off once more, this time careening over a steep embankment toward a swamp. Striking a tree saved the Acme from plunging in entirely, and the car and crew escaped with only damaged headlights and a dizzying shakeup, but this time it took four horses, a dozen people, and at least two hours to drag the car back to the road. The Shawmut and Itala both happened upon the scene, and their crews did the sporting thing and pulled over, helping the Acme men get going again.

That played out forty miles and a far cry from Fremont, where Roberts gave Toledo newsman Winters the impression that even in this semi-controlled stage east of St. Louis, nobody "is waiting for or helping anybody during this race. Every car is out for itself and there will be no quarter shown." He made sure they were in place in plenty of time—no room for error, and eager to attract notice—and by midafternoon people began gathering near State and Front Streets in downtown Fremont, a community of ten thousand typical of the small but thriving industrial cities that straddled the intersections of river and rail across the Northeast and Midwest. Fremont's factories produced a bounty of silverware and safety razors, steel shears and sauerkraut, sustaining a brick-and-limestone downtown studded with confectioners and jewelers, motion-picture houses and pool halls, and leading out to leafy boulevards lined with fine homes. Webb Hayes, a manufacturing executive and decorated combat hero, still lived here on the estate that his father, Rutherford B. Hayes, called home before and after the White House.

Finally, the Model T racers with their shotgun-blast motors roared onto the scene, rattling across the iron State Street bridge over the Sandusky River into downtown, near a handsome railway station and turret-topped hotel. Trolley tracks and steam-railroad lines radiated from the area, and a dock for passenger and cargo ships sat nearby. From sales manager Norval Hawkins, Roberts understood that he wasn't selling Fords so much as freedom: freedom from the timetables and fixed tracks of those streetcars and railroads, freedom from mucking out horse stalls. They pitched the automobile as a means of shortening distances and gaining time, liberating local doctors, real estate agents, and traveling salesmen to make house calls, take clients around, and ply their trade faster and better than before. They would free farmers and their families to traverse the countryside and visit the city on their terms, delivering them from isolation and greasing the wheels of commerce. It was an entirely benevolent vision that didn't foresee the role these motor cars would play in ending the passenger rail and steamer traffic that coursed through places like Fremont, let alone the construction of the bypass highways and later the interstates that would hollow out their downtowns.

With the reporters in his own Ford and the No. 1 and No. 2 right behind him, Roberts took off, churning up the West Main Street hill, where spectators lined the road in spite of the rain. They crossed a series of railroad tracks and followed the old Maumee and Western Reserve Turnpike out into the countryside, throwing open the throttle—a right-hand lever cradled beneath the steering wheel that served as the Model T's accelerator. With the Shawmut or Acme, you could adjust the speed with a similar hand throttle or give it a burst by flooring a gas pedal, but the Model T's three foot pedals had nothing to do with acceleration; the right one controlled the transmission brake, the middle pedal moved the car in reverse, and the left was the clutch.

The turnpike was one of the nation's oldest roads, cleared by the new state of Ohio in the early 1800s as a log-planked byway through the Great Black Swamp, on land ceded by Congress to encourage westward expansion. By mid-century, the swamp had been drained to create farmland, while the seasonally passable wooden planks of the notorious "Mud Pike"—laid crosswise as a "corduroy" road through the mire—had been replaced with macadam, meaning graded dirt topped with tightly rolled layers of crushed stone. Now even along the most rural stretches of the turnpike, trolley tracks ran down one side and utility poles shared space with old limestone mile markers, carrying the wires—telephone, telegraph, electricity—that crisscrossed the nation and made the Guggenheim copper smelters so lucrative. Less than 10 percent of the nation's roads had even been "improved" like this from simple dirt, but macadam was suddenly falling from fashion. The crushed-stone surface that had proven so durable for hooves and iron wheels was being chewed up rapidly by speeding automobiles, leading engineers to experiment with tar, petroleum, and other binders to hold those rolled-gravel layers together, or ponder new paving methods entirely.

On this soggy evening, the Maumee Pike macadam was a mess. The newspapermen clung to their seats "over roads flooded and over bumps that threatened a hundred times to hurl the drivers into the ditches," as Winters from the *Blade* put it. Six years earlier, he'd been reviewing paperwork at Sandusky City Hall as a cub reporter when a rifle shot pierced the window and whistled past his head, striking a wall, but this sprint was as harrowing as anything he'd experienced. Clearly Ford dealer Roberts—and Kulick and Scott, buzzing close behind in the official T racers—had no plans to follow the speed limit, tearing toward Toledo at forty miles an hour. Ignoring the usual slowing for bridges and bumps, they powered through giant puddles almost as if they were aiming for them, skittering down the road and kicking up fifty-foot sheets of water. However fast Roberts was going, Kulick seemed determined to go faster, his old track-racing juices flowing, smoking past the guide to take the lead. The mud was flying so wildly that the men riding shotgun had to keep bailing out their drivers' goggles until finally they stripped them off altogether. They hit the outskirts of Toledo in just fifty-five minutes, barely stopping even when Roberts smacked a buggy on East Broadway, causing damage but no injuries. Navigating to the intersection of Jefferson and Superior, the Ford caravan pulled up at the Secor Hotel checkpoint at 7:15 PM, forty-five minutes before anyone expected them, no telling just how far back the big cars were now.

Henry Ford was there at the checkpoint, waiting with friend and tire supplier Harvey Firestone. Stanley Roberts had done his job and then some. Ford greeted the mud-caked men as they entered the splendor of the Secor, with its glimmering green marble and opulent oriental rugs, a million-dollar monument to the flourishing metropolis of Toledo. Harper located a telegraph agent and sent a short message to be relayed from the home office, reprinted in newspapers, and posted on showroom windows: "Ford cars arrived first and second. Only cars to arrive in Toledo on time. Too muddy for heavy cars."

The Acme finally pulled in a little after eleven, followed closely by the Shawmut and the Itala, which had sideswiped a few kegs of cement at a bridge-construction site and limped in with minor damage. All three were at least four hours behind the Fords. The next day, both papers carried compelling accounts of the front-running ride with the Model Ts, the Toledo *Blade* bearing a particularly breathless story from Winters. OCEAN-TO-OCEAN CONTEST IS FRENZIED, FOOLHARDY SPEED TERROR read the headline, the story omitting the part about the accident with the buggy. Accompanying both articles, Stanley Roberts had placed a big ad:

FORD CARS WINNING

Our competitors have said that Fords were too light—wouldn't stand the gaff. From New York to Toledo in three days—from Buffalo to Toledo in one day—the last forty miles in an hour—isn't that enough to test the stamina of a car? Why were the Fords the only low priced cars entered? Why didn't those other fellows who prate about their heavier cars, enter their machines? Compare the Fords' work with the high priced cars in the race, and remember, you can get a duplicate for $825. Come in and see us.

ROBERTS-TOLEDO AUTO COMPANY

218 SUPERIOR STREET

At that showroom, one block north of the Secor Hotel on Superior Street, Stanley Roberts had adorned his display windows with a giant map of the race, just like some of the big corporate branches. For the first time, he moved the markers for the little Model Ts comfortably into first.

4

Muscling Through the Middle West

Toledo to St. Louis, June 5 to 7, 1909

As far as purgatory went, you could do worse than the Florentine palace of the Secor, but that was little consolation for the Shawmut crew, trapped in Toledo as the Fords tore away at eight on the morning of June 5. For three hours, they sat on their hands, thinking about all the extra miles the Model Ts were now piling up. It was one thing to trail because of engine failure or blown tires or because you'd been outclassed at the wheel. This was different. Sure, they'd been slowed some by the mud after the skies opened up around Cleveland. And they'd stopped to help the Acme. But much of the gap could be pinned on the navigational expertise of the Ford guides, not to mention how they must have shattered the speed limit.

At least the No. 5 car remained in "first class condition," as the Shawmut men wired to general manager Horace Waite back in Boston. And they felt rested after a night sleeping at the Secor. As they waited, Earle Chapin penned a note to Anita on a postal view of a local church: "Hard roads and rain to Toledo . . . mud 12 to 16 ins. deep. was tired last night. all OK now."

Eventually eleven o'clock arrived, and the detained cars were released in sequence. Today's schedule called for an all-day run to Chicago, second to last of the twelve-hour overnight controls. The organizers envisioned a thirteen-hour trip running 244 miles, an undulating route linking Lake

Erie and Lake Michigan. Neither figure was realistic. The estimated time was another matter of state law and arithmetic, accounting for speed limits. In Ohio, that meant eight miles per hour in densely settled districts, fifteen in outlying areas, and twenty in the country, with an added requirement to slow near any horse and to stop fully if the person with the horse signaled you to do so. Indiana's laws were similar, though you could legally pass any horse there at six mph without stopping. But that 244-miles-in-thirteen-hours calculation didn't account for varying road or weather conditions. Plus, some of the intrepid local motorists who'd actually attempted the drive said the distance the pathfinder claimed was just plain wrong, pegging it more like 260 to 300 miles, typically spread over several days.

If nothing else, the crews could at least figure on encountering gravel macadam on the main byways between towns, the last place this would be true. The three thousand miles west of Chicago would be mostly dirt roads and wagon trails, save for improvements around scattered cities. That didn't make it any easier to navigate. From Toledo to South Bend, there are "very many points where one way looks as good as another and road signs are lacking," one recent motorist who'd covered those 170 miles put it.

Not that the Shawmut crew even knew it was 170 miles to South Bend. Because here the directions pamphlet hastily prepared by the pathfinder didn't even list the town-to-town mileage. As they consulted the pages in question, the limitations of that slim guide revealed themselves in full. The New York section had at least presented each town in sequence as a list of boldface names paired with two mileage figures—the incremental distance from the previous town and the cumulative odometer total—and an accompanying sentence or two describing the route in between. Those descriptions left something to be desired, and the lack of even a single map meant you were out of luck if you lost the route. But they were a gift from heaven compared to what followed.

Starting with Buffalo, the pamphlet abandoned the easy-to-read list for a narrative in paragraph form. The syntax was choppy, the punctuation unpredictable, but at least you could sort of follow along while finding mileage figures sprinkled in parentheses. Suddenly with Toledo those mileage numbers vanished, as did the paragraph breaks. The directions unfurled as an eye-glazing word salad across two pages. Glance down and your eyes might land on the following:

> Cross the tracks again, take the right fork and cross over the railroad tracks again twice. Then turn to your left, school house, cross the trolleys. Then turn to your left, school house, cross the trolleys, into Archibald; turn to your right at the hardware store, cross the trolley and then make your turn to the left. At the fork turn to the left, cross the trolley track and RR. At the end of the road turn to the left into Stryker. Cross over the bridge and the RR tracks and the trolley. Pass, take right fork, turn to your left, follow the telegraph wires . . .

And on and on it went, all the way to Chicago, where the dizzying directions abruptly ended at Michigan Avenue—leaving the bearer to guess the remaining route from there to the checkpoint at the Chicago Automobile Club, address unspecified. Good luck keeping your finger on the page and not losing your place or getting lightheaded while standing still, let alone jouncing along bumpy roads.

The title read *Route: New York to Seattle Automobile Contest*, but they called this twenty-four-page pamphlet the "Blue Book," because that was the cover's color, but also because that had become shorthand already for any directional guide, the way *yellow pages* would take hold for commercial telephone directories. Blue books of varying qualities dated nearly to the birth of the automobile, their name and color a nod to the existing social-register "blue books" that served as guides for the upper crust and those striving to reach it. Early automobile versions were more likely to list the names of car owners and chauffeurs than contain practical directions, until the *Official Automobile Blue Book*, which encouraged touring by offering detailed routes coupled with mileage figures and a list of "supply stations" along the way. That guide, first published in 1901 by a Hartford, Connecticut, automobile oil-and-grease manufacturer, quickly became the bible of recreational motoring. But it focused on the Northeast, where most automobile owners lived. When the grease manufacturer failed to pay his corporate taxes, an automotive trade publisher took over and stamped the new editions with AAA's logo, while splitting the Blue Book into three volumes, separating New England, New York, and the Mid-Atlantic at $2.50 each. The rest of the country remained a no-man's-land, but the Class Journal Company was diligently working on Volume 4 of its *Official A.A.A. Automobile Blue Book*, covering the "Middle West." That one would be released in midsummer—just a few weeks too late to help the Shawmut crew.

Around Chicago, a quirky set of books with turn-by-turn photo directions for select routes had circulated since 1905, pioneered by a local auto dealer, H. Sargent Michaels, and expanded by a doctor turned auto parts retailer named Gardner Chapin (no relation to Earle in the Shawmut). The books contained photos showing every turn and intersection along a particular route, augmented with mileage and directional arrows, like Google Street View a century before its time. Chapin dedicated one to the dream of "A National Highway . . . When a Road Map along this Route will no longer be necessary." But those books remained virtually unknown in the East, and would not get a signal boost until Chicago mapmaker Rand McNally & Company acquired the rights, with a multivolume series of "Photo-Auto Maps" spanning Chicago to New York City now due for release—also in summer 1909, just a few weeks too late for the Shawmut.

If only that crew had any of those volumes, to say nothing of actual experts waiting to show them the way in a convoy of matching cars. Because even the most detailed printed directions couldn't provide the updated insight of locals who knew, say, that the bridge in Stryker, Ohio, over the Kettle Run was out for repairs, so you'd need to take the southern route from Archbold, entering Stryker by way of the Universalist church. As it was, the pamphlet prepared by the pathfinder misspelled that town as "Archibald" and didn't name the creek. But the Shawmut trio would have to make do with what they had, their intermittently helpful Blue Book and Pettengill's pocket compass.

And yet they covered the first sixty-five or so miles to Bryan in three hours, keeping pace with the Fords far ahead of them—or so they gathered, gleaning bits of information at occasional stops—and drawing even with the Acme. As for the Itala, it faltered on the outskirts of Toledo and fell behind, a mere prelude to a cascade of calamities to come.

Around the same time, Oscar Stolp, after laboring with mechanics to get his No. 3 Stearns into shape, finally succeeded in reaching the starting line in Manhattan, four days late. A big crowd watched as an official from the Automobile Club of America stamped the many parts that could not be changed under the terms of the rules. Stolp felt good, after a fifty-mile-an-hour test run to prove the durability of his solid tires and the special "equalizing lever" he'd invented and patented. Joined by an experienced crew, Stolp vowed to run day and night to catch the race leaders—bolstered by an official decree allowing him to skip the twelve-hour rest stops in the East, to give him a sporting chance of closing the gap. (Though even then he would probably "need a pair of wings to make St. Louis before the leaders," the *Chicago Daily News* mused.)

Stolp and his crew cranked up and roared north on Broadway, disappearing out of sight. His transmission failed in Tarrytown, requiring a tow back to the city. That was the end of Stolp's voyage, thirty miles traveled in all.

Out in the "Middle West," the Shawmut crossed from Ohio into Indiana, jockeying with the Acme, sometimes pulling ahead, sometimes falling back, just out of sight. They'd been on the road five hours when they spotted the yellow No. 4 again in Kendallville, stopped as a freight train thundered before them on the Lake Shore and Michigan Southern railroad tracks, blocking the road. The Shawmut pulled beside the Acme just after 4:15 PM, and they waited together as one freight car after another rumbled past, every stalled second an advantage for the Model Ts ahead.

Already those Fords had met up with their latest secret weapon, Chicago branch manager Tom Hay. He'd come all the way to Goshen, Indiana, to oversee the final 130 miles himself. Even by the standards of Ford's eleven American branch managers, Thomas Jefferson Hay was intense and competitive, with a piercing stare and a penchant for burying opponents with verbiage at the first hint of debate. Debonair and fastidious, he loathed seeing unwashed Fords on the road, every car its own advertisement. At forty, he was sensitive about his vanishing hair, retaining a little forelock that other Ford managers ribbed at their own peril. But he could also be genial and generous, with a gift for closing a deal and a knack for fostering salesmen who would go on to lead other branches in the expanding organization.

In May, like his peers, Hay had set out in both directions to study the route and line up local guides. But where some might watch from afar when the time came, or ride along for perhaps fifty miles, Hay would cover every inch himself, leading a two-day convoy from one end of his terrain to the other, Goshen to Chicago, and Chicago to Springfield, Illinois.

He'd always been this way, from his days as a teenager in the 1880s racing perilous high-wheeled bicycles. That was nothing compared to what his father, a top Indianapolis lawyer, had endured as an infantryman in the Civil War, surviving three dozen battles—including Antietam and Gettysburg—and multiple stints in grim Confederate prisons. Frank Hay, who once escaped a prison transfer by hacking his way out of a boxcar, had transmitted his tenacity to his son.

When "safeties" replaced high-wheeled "ordinaries," fueling the national bicycle craze, Tom Hay became an organizing force in Indianapolis's renowned Zig-Zag Cycling Club, and a bike retailer. Hay was still in his early twenties himself when he took a liking to a talented adolescent named Marshall Taylor, hiring the youngster to perform riding tricks outside his shop in a military uniform. That getup earned the African American Taylor the nickname "Major," beginning a journey that would see the powerful sprinter become the world's first Black sports superstar, and a magnet for racial animus.

Hay rode the dizzying highs and lows of the boom-bust bicycling craze. Expanding into manufacturing, his Hay & Willits firm produced the popular Outing model from a factory with 275 hands. But the company succumbed to receivership, part of a national wave of bike makers who went under or consolidated amid cutthroat price competition and wild overproduction. By 1900, Hay was selling newspaper advertising, while also promoting bike races of waning interest at the Newby Oval, an Indianapolis velodrome built to seat twenty thousand by bicycle magnate Arthur Newby, Hay's mentor. When Newby branched from bikes to horseless carriages with the National Motor Vehicle Company, he brought Hay along in sales and advertising. Soon, Tom Hay was serving as the official starter of Indianapolis's first automobile race (1902), six years before Newby and three partners would begin building the Indianapolis Motor Speedway, now due to open in the summer of 1909.

Having seen both booms—first bicycles, now automobiles—Hay pounced into the fray whenever he heard someone suggest the automobile was a fad like the bike. In the 1890s, American bicycle production had exploded roughly thirtyfold in just a few years, everyone clamoring for one of these new machines, which put freedom and fresh air in reach of people living in crowding industrial cities, brought men together in social clubs, and afforded women some independence, along with less restrictive clothing. Then, sales plummeted.

It wasn't fair to attribute the collapse to the arrival of automobiles; cars were still scarce when the bike business went bust. Instead, sky's-the-limit manufacturers failed to recognize market saturation—most people who wanted a bike now had one—at the same time that popular interest waned. Fashions come and go. Urbanites who used bikes for transportation found they could get around more easily on proliferating streetcar lines, while turning to other forms of recreation. Almost overnight, the bike got relegated to child's toy and tool of necessity for the underclass. But the automobile, Hay insisted, was different. This was no flavor of the moment; it would be here forever—or at least until a flying car came around.

If Henry Ford supplied the singular vision for his company, James

Couzens—all-in-one bookkeeper, secretary, sales manager, and cashier out of the gate in 1903—imposed the corporate discipline and structure that helped make Ford Motor Company more successful than Henry Ford's first two ventures, the Detroit Automobile Company (1899) and the Henry Ford Company (1901), the latter of which became Cadillac after things went south between Ford and the board. Couzens created the branch-and-dealer system and lured true-believing Hay to Chicago in late 1905 to open one of the first six branches beyond Detroit, at $175 a month plus an enticing one-third share of the branch's net profits. It didn't take long before Hay noticed that not a single local sportswriter owned an automobile—not even Chris Sinsabaugh, the writer and editor who had first branded the local National League baseball club the "Cubs" in a headline, and who was making ends meet for his family by juggling three jobs at once, with *Motor Age*, the *Chicago Daily News*, and the *Chicago Tribune*. A decade before automobile payment plans would become popular, Hay struck a deal with Sinsabaugh to give him a new Model N in exchange for $200—the newsman's life savings—and a work-off agreement to write publicity for Hay's Ford branch.

When the race approached, Hay believed Ford's national network of salesmen-navigators wasn't some advantage to conceal—fair, unfair, or otherwise—but a selling point to emphasize, a way to remind potential customers that they'd never be far from someone offering Ford parts at factory prices. He also planned to showcase the expected success in the race not with the usual sidewalk window display but by plastering all the windows of his two-story branch with signage, easily visible to passing traffic along Michigan Avenue's "Motor Row" and pedestrians across the street. Noting his advance spadework, the *Chicago Daily News* called Hay the "man on the job" to make sure the Nos. 1 and 2 Fords made it from Indiana to Illinois to Missouri in the lead.

Whipping them from place to place, assisted by a couple of his salesmen and joined for intervals by local delegations of Ford owners, Hay guided the Model T racers to the South Bend checkpoint around 3:30 PM, to Michigan City at 5:30, and to Munster, Indiana, at 7:30, crossing into

Illinois ahead of schedule. The Ford convoy slowed a bit in the dark but still reached the Chicago Automobile Club a few minutes before 9 PM, beating the thirteen-hour prediction by a shade, a brilliant run.

Harper, the Ford adman riding with Kulick, sent his expected telegram to Detroit, to be relayed to dealers: "Both cars arrived in Chicago on time without trouble. Other cars not in but said to be seven hours behind."

That was a twist of the knife. Wire reports had put the Shawmut and Acme only half as far back—three and a half hours—at South Bend and again at Michigan City, roughly sixty miles away. Even if they got a little lost in the dark, the Shawmut and Acme would likely roll in five hours behind, the *Chicago Examiner*'s auto writer predicted in his big Sunday column, going to press when only the Fords had arrived.

That columnist, who went by "Magneto" and may have been *Examiner* auto editor Pete Estey, a former Studebaker copywriter, got right to the crux of the race, as a test of whether a lightweight, affordable car could compete with more substantial rivals: "Much interest pertaining to the contest is wrapped up in the work of the two little Ford cars, the smallest contestants in the race, and there will be considerable curiosity in the attempt of such small machines to negotiate the entire course from New York to Seattle."

Hay predicted the Fords would win, saying the race out West would be a test of stamina, not speed, where the gap would only widen. Chapin, Pettengill, and Messer weren't in yet to speak for themselves, but amid assorted references to the unfamiliar "Shaumut," "Shawnut" and "Shawmuz" in some other papers, Magneto showed his automotive knowledge by giving due credit to the Shawmut for its perfect score in that grueling Bay State Automobile Club endurance run last summer.

As the Shawmut ground along in the dark, the mood turned irritable at times, the teammates frustrated by the limitations of the guidebook and the indecipherable landscape, sparks flying about which way to go. Making matters worse, Pettengill, the steady captain, was doubled over with cramps, his stomach churning, forcing him from the wheel. Chapin took over the late-night driving. Finally, they hit Illinois, sticking close to the lake. Jackson Park eventually came into view, and they wound their way over to Michigan Avenue, where automobile dealerships lined both sides of Motor Row for more than a mile leading to the downtown district known as the Loop.

It was after 1 AM when they turned onto Plymouth Court, where the Chicago Automobile Club's six-story clubhouse-garage retained an Old World grandeur amid the skyscrapers nearby, with green-shuttered French windows, bountiful flower boxes, and delicate iron balconies. The press had disbursed, and only the hardiest club members remained amid the Spanish-leather upholstery of the lounge or oak fittings of the basement rathskeller, the messy workings of the multistory garage separated by a brick firewall and iron doors. The clubhouse included several studio apartments furnished in mahogany and brass, but those were for visiting clubmen of equal standing.

The Shawmut boys got their passbook signed, filled out the cards for Seattle, and left their car in the club garage before trudging over to the Great Northern Hotel—no slouch either, a sixteen-story Burnham and Root masterpiece with Turkish baths and rooftop Palm Garden, rooms running $2.50 to $4 a night. They collapsed into bed before even wiring Horace Waite in Boston, who was surely asleep anyway.

In the morning, they telegraphed home: "Roads very poor. Deep mud. No trouble. No tires. Fords two hours ahead"—maybe an earnest mistake, maybe they were hoping Waite hadn't yet seen reports showing they'd arrived four-plus hours behind—"Acme with us. Itala four hours behind." They closed optimistically: "Will catch Fords today."

Chapin was less sanguine in a three-page letter to Anita. On the cream-colored stationery of the Great Northern, he drew a fountain pen and cut to the chase: "My dearest Honey: Here in Chicago four hours behind time and what I have seen of the place is rotten and it stinks."

He skipped the surpassing beauty of Jackson Park, the imposing might of the grain elevators, the dazzling heights of Chicago's skyscrapers, several approaching or exceeding three hundred feet. He was human, grumpy about trailing in the race, stung in the eyes and scratched in the throat by the inescapable smog and industrial tang of arguably America's smokiest city.

Chapin told Anita about Pettengill's stomach and the squabbling in the car but asked her to keep it to herself so neighbors wouldn't gossip, the Shawmut entry the pride of Stoneham. He craved hearing from her. He knew she'd been back to Springfield visiting friends and family, had written to her so far in care of others, but he meant for this letter to be waiting when she returned to their cozy little home. For all the places he'd dropped her cards or written notes already, he wished he could have penned even more; he was unable to do so in the moving car. "I wish that I was there with you in the back yard it is better than all the Hotels ever," he wrote, while making clear he wasn't "homesick or yellow." He vowed to fight on and hoped things would get better in the open country west of the Mississippi: "The Ford agents guide them along from place to place and there are plenty of crooks to guide us different but it won't be that way after we leave St. Louis and if we win honey we will be all right won't we."

It was heartening to imagine how they might put the Shawmut's power to the test once the speed controls fell away. In the meantime, they enjoyed a dash of celebrity here, with Chicagoans recognizing the "sun-tanned drivers and mechanicians" by virtue of their "greasy canvas jackets and dust-grimed caps," in the words of the *Record-Herald*. A crowd gathered around the mud-spattered cars as the crews waited for permission to depart, first the Fords, later the Shawmut and Acme, the unfortunate Itala not even in yet. Right before they cranked up, Chapin jotted Anita a postcard—a view of the Chicago Academy of Sciences in Lincoln Park—that would reach her in western Massachusetts before she returned home and found the letter from the night before, when he'd been marinating in the struggles of the race.

Wrote you this morning. Have got a nice day to go to St. Louis. Kind of warm.

As ever
Earle

They were off, leaving at 1:04 PM, charging southwest across Illinois to St. Louis, 260 miles as the crow flies. The schedule called for a fifteen-hour, 283-mile run, but the mileage was a clerical error. Even the pathfinder in March had calculated the route at 317 miles. In the hasty preparations of the Blue Book pamphlet, the organizers must have conflated the more direct and well-established mileage of the two leading railroads connecting the two cities (284 and 293). But some Chicagoans who had driven all the way to St. Louis insisted it was even longer still, more like 350 to 370 miles, a two- or even three-day expedition given the notoriously atrocious roads in this railroad-dominated state. Anyone with sense knew you could glide to St. Louis on the Illinois Central or the Chicago & Alton in eight to ten hours for as little as $7.50, no charge for a recliner, a supply of fresh magazines at the ready. (You could upgrade to the parlor car for another dollar, guaranteeing more room and an assigned seat, or plunk down $2 extra for a Pullman sleeper on an overnight run.)

As for fifteen hours, that seemed even more ludicrous than the mileage error. If the organizers truly intended to respect speed limits, it was impossible to cover 317 to 370 miles that quickly under the laws of Illinois (six mph around corners, ten in business districts, fifteen in residential areas, and twenty in the country, with a full stop for any frightened horse). But those limits only mattered in the driest months anyway, in a state defined by soft clay and trampled sod. Beyond fifty or a hundred miles from Chicago, the map for motorists might as well have read, "Here be dragons." Even leaving on time and with ample help waiting, the Fords would be lucky to reach St. Louis by midnight, while the Shawmut and Acme—leaving four hours later—would surely be slogging well into morning. But all they could do was try.

The Shawmut reached Joliet, about forty miles out, that afternoon in roughly two hours, discovering they'd matched the Fords' morning pace but fallen behind the Acme, already through. The roads out of Joliet could be tricky, so a young lumber executive with a taste for automobiles offered to show the Boston crew the way. As they burst out of town, from the main boulevard onto what they called the Troy Road, they were trying so badly to make up time that they skidded and tore off two tires. The local man, C. H. Latimer, watched the Boston crew leap from the car to tackle the problem.

Changing a tire was no minor feat. The new *American Cyclopedia of the Automobile* devoted twenty-three pages to tire maintenance, repair, and replacement, from fitting the butterfly nuts on the bolts to ensure they're flush with the felloes, to taking care not to nip the inner tube between the head of the valve and inside of the beaded edge of the tire. The work required both strength and finesse, not to mention "forked manipulators" and "actuating levers." "Before fitting the new casing, rub the beads with French chalk to facilitate their slipping into position, and polish the inside of the rim thoroughly with blacklead, using a stiff brush for the purpose," the *Cyclopedia* advised. "The operation of getting on a new cover, as a rule, entails much kneading and thumping with the hands, which seem to have the effect of increasing its flexibility." If that sounded daunting or inscrutable, Henry Copley Greene had put the agony of a shorn tire more eloquently in a recent motoring essay in *The Atlantic Monthly*, provided you had the foresight to carry a spare: "If so, you unstrap it, lay it by your wheel; then prod, pry, and pull at the old tire-casing, pull, pry, and prod again at the new; insert its intestinal tubing; and pump, pump, pump in the hot sunlight till the firm, replete, and distended tire encircles your wheel like some Gargantuan sausage."

Even if you knew what you were doing, a single tire could take an hour. Dorothy Levitt's breezy *The Woman and the Car: A Chatty Little Handbook for All Women Who Motor or Who Want to Motor*, another new release, was full of genuine pointers for identifying faulty spark plugs and addressing engine knock. But when it came to tires (or "tyres" in England, where famed "bachelor girl" Levitt had earned the title "Champion Lady Motorist of the World"), she did not mince words: "There is only one trouble regarding which you are really justified in feeling angry—that is a punctured or burst tyre. It *is* possible for a woman to repair a tyre, but I am sure I am correct in saying that not one woman in a thousand would want to ruin her hands in this way. Nowadays there is a repairer in nearly every village, and the best plan is to drive very slowly on the rim to this nearest repair-shop."

Joliet had five garages—up from two the year before—but the Shawmut had no time to waste pulling into a shop. With Latimer tracking it on his pocket watch, the crew unbuckled two new tires, jacked up the car, and replaced both shoes in an uncanny twelve minutes. Then they took off, telling Latimer they were determined to catch the Fords and reach Seattle first.

One checkpoint lay between there and St. Louis, at Bloomington's Illinois Hotel, nearly 150 miles out. The Fords made it in under seven hours, speed limits be damned. Even as they told a reporter that the roads here were the worst they'd seen since New York, the Model T crews felt good. They sat for a proper dinner with Tom Hay at the hotel, remaining in Bloomington until after 5 PM.

The Shawmut arrived three hours later, having shed the Acme, which had wandered fifty miles off the route. Learning that they'd cut into the Ford lead, the Boston men didn't linger for dinner. They could pry open a can of something in the car, stay awake with coffee from a thermal bottle. They tarried only as long as necessary to vise their passbook at the desk of the Illinois Hotel and sign those cards for Seattle, leaving by 8:05.

Then they ran into some trouble. The Fords had covered the thirty-eight miles from there to Lincoln in two hours, reaching that small city—the only one named for Abraham Lincoln *before* he was president, as a prairie lawyer who platted the area for the railroad—before sunset. Alerted by Hay, local dealer W. L. Wasson had ginned up a big crowd, watching eagerly as the Model Ts "cavorted and bounced down the street," stopping briefly at Wasson's before leaving "a bunch of interested people and a faint trail of combusted gasoline" in their wake, per the *Lincoln Daily Courier.* The Shawmut labored in the dark, arriving four hours behind the Fords, with no fanfare.

At Springfield, the capital, Tom Hay signed off and handed over responsibility for the Model Ts to the convivial Warren "Fuzzy" Anderson, Ford's St. Louis branch manager. Anderson had brought along one of his top salesmen, with another deputy waiting down the line to join them for the home stretch. It was well after 10 PM, and they still had one-hundred-plus miles to go, meaning even disciplined, determined Tom Hay couldn't meet the fifteen-hour pace the organizers had imagined, not on roads this meandering and muddy. No matter; if the Model Ts were running behind, then the other cars must really be mired. They telegraphed the Hotel Jefferson, the St. Louis checkpoint, to tell a group of Ford executives who'd come from Detroit that they expected to arrive around 3 AM. As the team stopped for a late-night meal at Springfield's Leland Hotel, wide-eyed onlookers noted that the men were nearly as mud-caked as the Model Ts parked outside. But they were in fine spirits. "We have had a hard race so far, but have made excellent time considering the roads. The motors have stood the strain fine and the tires have held up well," No. 2 driver Bert Scott told a reporter. "We are well in the lead and unless we have awful hard luck, should be the first to arrive in Seattle."

From there it was a grind, taking them nearly six hours to go eighty miles. It was 5 AM when they finally reached Edwardsville, Illinois, a county seat of five thousand less than twenty-five miles from St. Louis, finding brick pavement downtown. Taking advantage of the solid terrain, the Fords flashed by the county courthouse "so rapidly that they were merely a blur," to the eyes of an early-rising reporter. They hit Collinsville and East St. Louis, crossed the Mississippi over the massive Eads Bridge, and reached the checkpoint at 6:55 AM. The Hotel Jefferson, St. Louis's answer to the Waldorf-Astoria, sat along busy Twelfth Street between St. Charles and Locust, an auspicious corner of the world for Ford. A few months earlier, the company had erected a massive billboard across the street festooned with multicolored lights, one of a few like it in big cities around the country. The blinking bulbs gave the illusion of movement, in this case a Model T driving by a river.

The Ford crews shuffled in, adjusting their eyes to the Jefferson's marble lobby. Once again, Henry Ford was here to greet them. The men had crossed Illinois in twenty-two hours, a truly remarkable showing, the irrational fifteen-hour schedule on the books notwithstanding. Tom Hay, the Chicago branch manager, called it a "cracking good drive," one they might have done in as little as seventeen hours on firmer soil. The Ford men told the press the roads they had encountered in the "Sucker State" were the worst they'd seen, hoping it might somehow get better from here. They stayed awake through breakfast and then headed upstairs to sleep, but not before spreading the word that they would take a full day of rest here. This was the last twelve-hour control point, so technically they could leave at 6:55 PM. But there was something to be said for twenty-four hours of recovery before the true ordeal began, a reset for man and machine alike. Fuzzy Anderson's team took the No. 1 and No. 2 cars out to the branch to give the Model Ts a full cleaning and tune-up.

To everyone's surprise, the Shawmut blew in at 9 AM—not the seven- or eight-hour gulf the Ford men had figured but just two hours behind. Somehow the Boston crew had gained ground overnight, despite their heavier weight, lack of a guide, and need at one point to rip the rails off a fence and lay the planks across the muck to gain traction. The Acme arrived just after ten, another surprise. Henry Ford must have been furious. Hay steamed, sure these cars must have left Chicago early, wondering if maybe their watches were still on Eastern time.

Earle Chapin napped, then drew a pen to write another letter to Anita, his second three-pager on fine hotel stationery in twenty-four hours. This one showed an engraving of the Jefferson ("European Plan, Absolutely Fire Proof").

"My sweetheart," he began. "Here at St. Louis all right . . . and but 2 hours behind the Ford cars so you see we pulled there lead of 5 hours down to 2 hours, and all we had was a Blue Book."

He told her they'd gone all night over shoddy roads, twice encountering mud twenty inches deep. "We are one hour ahead of the Acme #4 and I don't know how many ahead of the Itala #6."

Everything seemed better now in the midday light, flush with knowing they'd narrowed the gap. Messer had been dead tired when they'd rolled in, and captain Pettengill was still feeling some lingering effects from the bug that struck on the way to Chicago, but they'd be full of vigor by the time they left tomorrow, appreciating the report that the Fords were going to wait until morning. The idea that they might wipe the slate clean and all set off at the same time for the West was exhilarating. St. Louis might be a "smoky Burg" like Chicago, but Chapin liked it from this vantage, one last way station before the wide-open race.

"Well my little honey I am out for that $600 now," he wrote, feeling good about their chances of carving up the first-place prize, a $2,000 purse and a massive trophy to the winner. They even had a good guide lined up now, an expert on Missouri motoring, ready to show them the way clear across the state to Kansas City.

5

Guile at Glasgow

St. Louis to Kansas City, June 7 to 8, 1909

The idea that the Fords would rest for twenty-four hours in St. Louis before setting off for the West was certainly compelling. After all, when Henry Ford bemoaned the rule changes that cluttered the contest in the East, one of the wagers he dangled was for any automaker to meet him in St. Louis and start there on an even footing the rest of the way to Seattle. And since the Ford team was sure that the twenty-five hundred miles remaining would pose a test of endurance more than speed, what was the harm in relinquishing a two-hour lead over the Shawmut or three hours on the Acme? Let them all line up together once more, thoroughbreds waiting to burst forth for the full-fledged start of the race—never mind the straggling Itala, which was just now leaving Chicago. Except it was all a bluff. The Fords planned to leave as soon as they could, cutting out at 6:55 PM on June 7, exactly twelve hours after arrival.

That Monday unfurled languidly, no one else the wiser. The mercury broke eighty at 10 AM and neared ninety in the afternoon, humidity making it feel more like one hundred. Earle Chapin shrugged it off, everything feeling better on account of cutting down that Ford lead. "Seems about 80," he wrote to Anita late in the day, following his letter with a postcard showing the double-decker Eads Bridge they'd crossed to enter St. Louis, the familiar symbol of the city as gateway to the West. Completed in 1874 at nearly $10 million, the Eads had been built to bring eastern trains over the powerful Mississippi, ensuring St. Louis would retain prominence as commerce shifted from steamboats to steel rails. It accomplished it in high style, with three sweeping spans in the middle—the first steel-truss bridge in the nation—and rows of satisfying stone archways closer to shore. "It is indeed a structure of perfection and beauty unsurpassable, and I never tire of it," Walt Whitman had written. A second deck above the railway level carried foot traffic, cattle, horse-drawn vehicles, electric streetcars, and now automobiles, too, though locals bristled at the tolls, twenty cents for a runabout or one-horse buggy, thirty-five cents for a touring car or two-horse conveyance.

The Hotel Jefferson where they waited, built for the 1904 World's Fair, boasted an international flavor—Louis XVI rotunda, Louis XV ladies' parlor, French Renaissance gentlemen's café, Japanese tearoom, Elizabethan library—steeped in regional history, with a panoramic frieze depicting the 240 years since the arrival of the first French fur traders. Now it hummed as the momentary capital of the modern motoring world, flush with automotive reporters and industry types soaking up stories of the hardships the racers had endured so far. John Gerrie, the rolling pacemaker for the ACA, delighted in holding court, ever the toastmaster. Just as he did going into Toledo, he'd needed to reach St. Louis by rail, after abandoning the Acme in a mudhole near McLean, Illinois, and walking to catch a late-night train to St. Louis. Relieved to be done with his official duties, he called this the hardest endurance contest he'd ever seen and marveled at the surprising performance of the little Fords. As a New Yorker, Gerrie shuddered over the frightful state of the roads in Illinois, but he would soon put the "nerve-destroying rush" behind him and glide home on the train. The racers weren't as lucky, though they agreed they couldn't imagine conditions being any worse than Illinois, either—no idea yet just how bad things would get.

A stringer for the *New York American* noted that all the cars remained in excellent condition, despite the strain. The Acme crew sounded especially optimistic, looking forward to traveling a bit lighter, having carried Gerrie most of the way since Buffalo. They got a jolt from finding themselves once more in a city with an Acme dealer, who would pilot them across Missouri. Beyond that, they were busy spraying the West with telegrams, trying to line up guides to match the Fords.

The Shawmut men buzzed about, too, arranging with tire supplier Diamond to move a stash of shoes and some other supplies to points in Kansas, Colorado, and Wyoming. Thanks to a local tip routed through Horace Waite in Boston and back again, they had lined up an ideal guide in Nelson Gutelius, former editor of a Midwestern motoring mag, *The Auto Review*. In that post he'd compiled the *Missouri State Automobile Blue Book* in 1908. Though most of its 136 pages were devoted to the names of the state's 3,171 automobile owners and 827 registered chauffeurs, a list of Missouri motoring laws, and a gallery of "Good Roads" views, it also included seven maps, with known auto routes marked in black. Around Christmas, Gutelius had taken charge of automobile coverage for the big *St. Louis Post-Dispatch*. Though that gig had ended abruptly a few weeks back, you could hardly ask for a better guide. It was satisfying to think they might leave on even footing with the Model Ts for once.

Henry Ford had brought some of his most trusted deputies to the Jefferson from Detroit, a signal of how seriously he viewed the contest. The group's blend of youth and experience reflected both how new the industry remained and how quickly it had grown. The men included Charles Sorensen and Gus Degener, each in their mid-twenties. Degener had been with Henry Ford already for seven years, helping him as a machinist and draftsman on the "999" racer that Barney Oldfield drove to fame in 1902, an achievement that helped position Ford to start the Ford Motor Company. A cigar maker's son with little formal schooling, Degener had fashioned himself into an in-house expert on the heat treatment of steel, helping develop the vanadium components that were so crucial to the Model T. He would soon become superintendent of inspection.

No one commanded a room like the twenty-seven-year-old Sorensen, five foot eleven, powerfully built, impatient, explosive, with blue eyes and a chiseled jaw like Tom Mix, the skilled horseman who was about to become the first Wild West star of the moving pictures. Equally respected and feared, Sorensen had started at Ford four years back as a $3-a-day patternmaker, coming from the stove industry. A good patternmaker is as much an interpreter as artist and tradesman, able to translate drawings into the three-dimensional models needed to create molds for casting liquid metal into auto parts. In that capacity Sorensen had a special gift for channeling the visions and musings of Henry Ford, often carving rough mock-ups without even waiting for drawings. That ingratiated him with the self-taught Ford, who preferred tactile models to technical blueprints. The boss also liked Sorensen's fiery nature. He promoted him swiftly, first to lead the pattern department, and now to assistant superintendent of the entire factory. In a few more years, he would become a father of the moving automobile assembly line. Rising ever higher, the man known as "Cast-Iron Charlie"—fiercely loyal lieutenant, uncanny operator, unflinching hatchet man—would hold the company together during a Ford family succession vacuum in the 1940s, before his own unceremonious exit.

All of that lay ahead, including the day in 1927 when Sorensen and Degener would stand beside Frank Kulick and five others to ceremonially hand-stamp the eight-digit serial number on the fifteen millionth Model T, the honor bestowed upon those longest-serving veterans who had yet to fall from favor with Henry Ford or grow weary of his prejudices and peculiarities. No one had any inkling of this car's staggering reach and staying power that day at the Hotel Jefferson; even to sell 150,000 would have been incomprehensible, to say nothing of fifteen million. They were focused on selling this year, this season, this week, proving that a lightweight car could actually be durable. No way they were going to concede an inch in the coast-to-coast race, let alone give away two or three hours and leave beside the Shawmut and the Acme.

The Ford team waited until evening, when it was clear the other crews had retired for a full night's sleep. That way they might be halfway to Kansas City by the time anyone else woke up. But they hit a snag, discovering a fuel leak in Kulick's No. 1 racer just as they were about to spirit away from St. Louis. By the time they'd fixed it, they'd lost eighty minutes, rolling out at 8:15 PM.

Word spread back at the Jefferson, somehow. Roused awake, the Shawmut men rallied, threw together their things, and jumped in the car with guide Gutelius by 9:30 PM, tearing off after the Fords. The Acme had to wait a little longer, its twelve-hour clock not expiring until 10:05.

The dash out of St. Louis wasn't just the beginning of the wide-open race. It was a sprint to Glasgow, 160 or so miles away, where a creaky wooden craft served as the only means of crossing the Big Muddy, the Missouri River. The Shawmut crew might not have even known about the ferry at all. But everyone involved with the Ford side knew Glasgow was a pinch point, crucial to this stage of the race. The little wooden ferry could hold two cars at a time. There were, of course, two Fords. They would be first onto the ferry, come hell or high water.

That morning, a stringer for *The Sun*, the popular New York broadsheet, had spotted Henry Ford with his team at the Jefferson and assumed he was there to see his "two lilliputian competitors . . . start upon the actual race." He was, but not in St. Louis. Ford left soon after, to get out ahead of his own racers—and meet them in Glasgow, to wait for the real action.

He set off with Fuzzy Anderson, the St. Louis branch manager who had met the Ford convoy the day before at Springfield, where Tom Hay's Chicago territory ended and Anderson's St. Louis domain began. Anderson had lined up local dealer-pilots all the way from central Illinois to central Missouri, but unlike last night—when he'd ridden alongside those Ford racers and pilots—he was now sprinting far ahead of the pack with the boss.

The good-time Charlie of the Ford branch men, Anderson favored a lucky horseshoe stickpin and wrote an essay for the *Ford Times* called "Don't

Be a Knocker," encouraging salesmen to smile. He enjoyed cocktails and rich food, with an ample waistline at thirty-nine. He formed a Ford owners' club in St. Louis, organizing weekend motoring trips to foster camaraderie. That bonhomie belied keen instincts and an intensely competitive spirit. The club outings boosted visibility and increased word-of-mouth sales. And as a lean bicycle salesman-racer in Chicago in his youth, Anderson had taken a daring detour through a construction site in the annual Pullman Road Race in 1892, surging to a surprising second-place finish before thousands of spectators. After selling bicycles and automobiles around the Midwest, he joined Ford as a traveling recruiter of dealers, then won the job to run the new St. Louis branch in late 1907. Starting off with a bang, he wagered a $60 suit that his branch would outsell all others per capita—and quickly made good.

Now Anderson and Ford, two men of varying natures who would both do anything to win, hurtled west across Missouri in Anderson's car. They were more than seventy miles out by the time the No. 1 and No. 2 left St. Louis, passing through the city of Mexico around 11:30 that night. No time to rest, they were spotted next by a reporter in Armstrong at 4 AM, ten miles shy of Glasgow, stopping there to receive reports on the progress of the race. They hit their destination in plenty of time for breakfast.

To the east, the cars had been jockeying all night. Tearing out of St. Louis, the powerful Shawmut shaved half an hour off the Ford lead over the first twenty miles, getting to St. Charles around 10:30 PM. Amid local confusion about what time the cars might come through, a huge crowd had gathered earlier at the city's highway bridge, anticipating the most excitement in town since a pair of circus lions had escaped the previous week. (Showmen with pistols and lassos tracked and subdued the lions in a trolley yard before anyone could be hurt, though not before a fatal attack on one of the circus's trick ponies.) By the time the Shawmut passed by, just a handful of folks remained.

Two main roads split west from there, each originally pioneer trails, neither easy to follow at night. The Fords and the Shawmut took the northerly Salt River Road. The Acme, bringing up the rear, decided with their dealer to take the southerly Boone's Lick or Boonslick Road, originally used by Daniel Boone's sons to connect St. Louis to a salt-producing spring way out in the wilderness. If less popular for motorists, the Acme crew picked it partly because they'd arranged to meet a shopkeeper another ten miles out in Cottleville who promised to take them nearly to Glasgow for $10. The alternate route proved shrewd. With the Acme's six-cylinder power, coupled with the merchant's knowledge of the terrain, they caught the leaders by early morning.

By then the Shawmut had nabbed the Fords too. Around 2:30 AM, the pack passed through Jonesburg, where a local newspaperman tipped off by telephone got out of bed and clocked the cars at forty miles an hour. The darkened town of 450 had no automobiles and no street lamps, but the editor mused that if they could somehow "be rigged up to use some kind of horse or mule power, betcher-life we'd have street lights."

As word spread down the line, people got out in their nightclothes to see the racers roar through Montgomery City at 3:50 AM, roughly halfway to Glasgow. With the air crisp and the dirt roads firm, the cars seemed to be flying by at fifty miles an hour.

Dawn approached. With St. Louis now far behind them, the Shawmut men discovered that their expert guide, Nelson Gutelius, wasn't all he was cracked up to be. That he did not seem to be listed among the 3,998 Missouri automobile owners and chauffeurs in his own guidebook might have been a sign of his limited practical experience. That the same volume described the route between St. Louis and Kansas City in just a single paragraph, with one vague map, was another bad omen. Closing in on forty, Gutelius was less a Missouri motoring expert than a restless dreamer who'd bounced among gigs. The son of a small-town newspaper editor-publisher in Pennsylvania, Gutelius had left the predictable path of succession to a younger brother. Never satisfied, he cycled through newsrooms and print shops as far north as Niagara Falls and as far west as Idaho, setting type, writing stories, selling ads. Always he was hustling for a way to make more money on the side, selling household coal additives, novelties made of "Aluminum, the New Metal," illustrated history books, and special fountain pens that could supposedly write two pages instead of two lines before needing to be dipped again in ink. Naturally, he'd become smitten with autos. Though neither the *Auto Review* editorship nor the *Post-Dispatch* gig had lasted, he would resurface again soon as an automotive advertising man. In barely a decade more, Gutelius would drop dead in a rear church pew in Detroit, succumbing so quietly that the service would continue uninterrupted. Here, in the gray light of early morning, west of Mexico, Gutelius—no doubt meaning well, trying his best—lost the way, sending the Shawmut twenty miles south and twenty miles back again. They recognized the error only when they hit a clearly defined town that wasn't on the route.

The organizers placed one checkpoint between St. Louis and Kansas City, at the New Globe Hotel in Centralia, about forty miles before Glasgow. Surging ahead with vigor, the Acme burst into Centralia first by a matter of minutes. Despite state law restricting speeds to eight mph in heavily settled areas, and six mph coming around corners, the Acme hurtled around the bend from Singleton Street onto Allen in downtown Centralia as fast as "the flicker of a motion picture machine," in the words of a reporter waiting with the crowd outside the checkpoint. The Acme and then the Ford teams had their passports endorsed, signed the cards for Seattle, and sat down to a quick but hearty breakfast, famished from the all-night drive. They must have been gone forty minutes by the time the Shawmut finally pulled in. Lead driver Pettengill tried to sound optimistic; the car remained in top shape, and they believed they would make up the time to Kansas City if the roads remained firm.

They took off again quickly, the weather heating up by the hour on a day that would approach ninety. On they sped in the Shawmut toward Armstrong and Glasgow—except they lost the road again, going all the way to Moberly, adding twelve more miles.

In Glasgow, the crowd had filled in along the river all morning, a buzz spreading about the automobile folks who'd appeared in the city, first three

Ford men from Kansas City coming in from the west the night before, and now Henry Ford himself arriving from the other direction with his St. Louis branch manager. Ford wore a three-piece suit, open in the heat to reveal his pocket watch, and Anderson a flat-crowned, broad-brimmed hat, the brim snapped forward to shield his eyes from the sun. The roads in and out of Glasgow were empty, most seemingly gathered here, others hunkered down in fear of being run over by a racer. Thanks to the ferry, locals understood that even if Glasgow was not one of thirty official checkpoints in the race, the cars would have no choice but to stop here, too, giving everyone a good look down by the wharf.

Candidly, the city of sixteen hundred had seen better days. Up through the 1860s, Glasgow was a prosperous Missouri River trading post, the end of the line for packet ships that plied the Big Muddy between there and St. Louis. That made it a clearinghouse for the considerable tobacco and hemp grown in Missouri's Little Dixie, the plantation belt settled by Southern slaveholders after the Compromise of 1820 made Missouri a slave state. For a time Glasgow even rivaled Chicago and Kansas City in pork packing. Then the railroads asserted their might, and Glasgow's river trade withered. There was grandeur still in the Greek Revival and Italianate manses from that golden age, and a sturdiness to the downtown commercial blocks, but *The Kansas City Star* had run a cruel feature the week before detailing the tragic decline of "sleepy old Glasgow," its warehouses boarded and rotting, the whistle of the steamboats a faded memory.

The community sat on a bluff, downtown separated from the waterfront by railroad tracks and a scruffy hillside. Most days that forlorn riverbank could be ignored, but with notables here, the editor of the local paper saw with clear eyes the weeds and the "mass of refuse and filth," as well as the "simply wretched" condition of the dirt road leading to the wharf. Understanding that the race was cementing Glasgow's position on the cross-Missouri and cross-country motoring maps, he would pen an editorial calling on the Woman's Improvement Club to mount a beautification project.

The modest ferry at the wharf was less a boat than a raft, a wooden platform partly surrounded by split-rail fencing and powered by a small motor. That it was a tough way to make a living could be seen in how frequently the operators turned over. The latest ferryman, W. B. Stevens, was a river fisherman who also scratched out an income repairing gasoline engines. At forty, he had a history of back pain and kidney problems. He'd been the ferry operator since the previous winter, but he would give it up by fall, selling the craft for $500.

Already Stevens had made a run across the river to take Henry Ford and his men to the opposite bank, which was agricultural bottomland known as West Glasgow. The river marked the end of Fuzzy Anderson's territory and the beginning of Charles C. Meade's turf as Kansas City branch manager, a vast domain stretching through Texas. Meade, another former bicycle racer and salesman, was a handsome, crisply dressed man with a tight-set mouth and a punctilious reputation; he believed that "selling automobiles is a business, not a game." He'd brought a few Ford men from western Missouri, including an especially colorful dealer named Joe Lightner, who covered Lafayette County. At twenty-five, the five-foot-two Lightner tipped the scales at just a hundred pounds, but he had already opened his hometown's first motion-picture house and toured the vaudeville circuit as a magician, dubbed "Lightner the Wizard."

Maybe the magician cast a spell. Maybe money changed hands, with Ford, Anderson, or Meade opening a billfold. Maybe they simply discussed the weather. No one else would ever know for sure. But at 9:30 AM, the No. 1 and No. 2 Fords roared into Glasgow, piloted from Armstrong by Dr. Walter S. Thompson, a respected small-town physician who had bought a Ford to make his house calls, then liked it so much that he became a dealer on the side. The convoy scrambled down to the waterfront, where the No. 1 and No. 2 Fords rolled carefully onto the ferry. Excitement coursed through the crowd, people straining to get a look at the dusty little racers, and at the drivers with their bug-eyed goggles and long cotton-duck coats. A small boy, Henry Rose, stepped barefoot on the point of a nail while scrambling over a pile of timbers for a better view, howling in pain. (Though wounds like that could often be fatal, the five-year-old would make a full recovery and live into his eighties, raising a family and running an appliance store, active with the Rotary Club and as a volunteer firefighter.)

The ferry shoved off. It puttered across the broad river, a good thousand feet wide. Finally, it reached West Glasgow, tying up on the other side. Kulick nudged the No. 1 off first, followed by Scott at the wheel of the No. 2, a photographer capturing the scene around 10:15 AM. Then boatman Stevens declared the propeller was broken, and the ferry called it quits.

Some accounts would claim the Shawmut arrived on the eastern bank while that ferry was still midstream, tantalizingly out of reach. The reality was hardly less dramatic. The Shawmut muscled in at 11:30 AM, having passed the Acme—which got badly lost after Centralia, squandering its lead over the carefully guided Fords—to reach Glasgow third. Pettengill nosed the car down to the riverfront, expecting to cross immediately and chase the Model Ts. But for all the people gathered, there was no boat at the wharf. The little craft remained on the far side of the river.

Confusion, indecision, no good options. Every ticking second represented a growing lead for the Fords. Minds racing, the Shawmut men tried to size up the situation. *Was the ferryman taking a break? Was that boat really not returning, so close they could see it?* In one telling, the Boston crew hired a rowboat to go across and investigate. More likely they simply found out by word of mouth: The ferry was finished.

They learned the next nearest ferry was down in Boonville, eighteen miles as the crow flies, even farther by automobile. It could easily take an hour to drive there, and considerably longer to find your way back again on the other side. Time wasn't the only consideration. The Boonville ferry wasn't exactly auspicious. A few days back, a local Ford dealer scouting the area to evaluate alternate routes for Fuzzy Anderson had lost a new Model T in the river when the hillside sands above the Boonville dock shifted, and the car slid backward into the water, plunging into the murky Missouri. After an hour, divers had located just a single seat cushion.

Theoretically there was one other option, looming overhead: the massive Chicago & Alton Railroad steel-truss bridge spanning the river high above Glasgow, half a mile long, easily sixty feet up, maybe higher at the center of the river. From the bank they could see through the rails and ties to the sky, making it easy to imagine how terrifying it would be to bump along and look down through those rails to the water. For that matter, they didn't even have to imagine. Edward Payson Weston, the nation's most famous pedestrian, had written about the terrors of crossing this very bridge just a few weeks earlier in one of his daily dispatches to *The New York Times*. Going coast-to-coast at age seventy, Weston refused to take ferries, so he could walk every inch of the way from the Atlantic to the Pacific. Not easily cowed, the white-whiskered Weston had already been besieged by a blizzard, pelted by hail, knocked under a fence by hellacious winds, and arrested by a police officer who assumed he had escaped from an asylum, while persevering through road and weather conditions that frequently foiled his supporting auto. But none of this compared to the Glasgow bridge, which had no real guardrails.

"To my horror I discovered the trestle was nearly 150 feet above the river"—or so it seemed to Weston—"and nearly a mile in length. In case a train approached I had no way to escape except to jump into the river. I got very nervous and was getting dizzy," the seasoned pedestrian wrote in that dispatch for the *Times*, describing how the bridge haunted him that night in his dreams. "I walked that trestle again in my sleep, and when I arose at 6 o'clock I was so dizzy that after eating breakfast I had to lie down again."

What choice did the stalled Shawmut men have, especially when the Acme crew rolled in beside them? They resolved to cross the railroad bridge, and together drove up the hill to the Chicago & Alton depot, consulting the schedule. The eastbound No. 14 train, the Daily Missouri State Express, would thunder across any minute, at 11:55, and then the bridge should be clear. A local bank cashier, George Sellmeyer, offered to climb in with the Shawmut, to show them how to find their way to something resembling a road on the other side. Now they were five, counting Nelson Gutelius too. Maybe they said a prayer. Arthur Pettengill backed the car up

Jackson Street, nosing it onto the viaduct leading to the four spans of the bridge. A jerk of the wheel and they might all be dead, to say nothing of what would happen if there was an unscheduled train. The Shawmut went first. Pettengill drove straight and true, edging across, displaying "a bit of Yankee grit and courage," his hometown paper would later call it. Still jouncing along the far end of the bridge, they crossed over the bottomland on the west side, where Henry Ford had posed for a picture that morning with Anderson and the Kansas City men. The ties now had ballast, the bridge reconnecting with solid ground. Sellmeyer pointed the Shawmut toward the town of Gilliam, and they raced off.

The ferry fiasco should have cost the Shawmut half a day, if they'd gone down to Boonville. By dint of braving the bridge, it hardly slowed them at all. Racing on toward Kansas City, struggling to find and keep the route, the Boston crew scarcely had time to consider whether the boat's breakdown was coincidence or foul play; in time they would become sure it was the latter, based on conviction. *The Glasgow Missourian* would give the ferry operator the benefit of the doubt, but others in Central Missouri were dubious, questioning how the little boat had broken down by chance right after depositing the Fords on the far bank. When *The Daily Intelligencer* up the road in Mexico revisited the moment a few weeks later, it called the matter casual bribery, no questions asked: "In addition to the usual ferry charge the driver of the leading car paid to the ferryman an additional amount if he would conveniently permit his engines to break down, thereby as he believed, placing an insurmountable delay in the path of his following competitors."

Even while losing the way at multiple points, the Shawmut still made up time west of Glasgow. It wasn't because Missouri had great roads. Some farmers aided the cause by tugging "road drags" behind their teams when they went out to see a neighbor or set off for town, towing split logs or metal-edged boards that smoothed out some of the lumps and bumps behind them. In a few places they even formed brotherhoods or engaged in competitions to incentivize the work, especially on postal routes. But those were still just dirt trails they were dragging out, like an infield crew smoothing the base paths between innings of a ball game. Macadam was rare in Missouri, asphalt paving rarer still. Had the racers come through even twenty-four hours later, rain would have churned everything into gumbo, and "Missouri roads would have gotten a lot of bad advertising," the *Armstrong Herald* would note. But June 8 remained warm and dry, leaving the dirt firm for the time being. The Boston crew could let the big car have its head on the country roads between towns. The Shawmut boasted direct drive in third gear—meaning the engine transmitted power to the driveshaft directly without being reduced or multiplied by gearing, so they rotated together at the same speed, a 1:1 ratio—allowing for unusually efficient and quiet operation at up to forty-five miles an hour; they may even have pushed it into fourth, edging above fifty mph in places.

Finally, they reached Kansas City, hitting the Baltimore Hotel checkpoint around 6:45 PM, twenty-one-plus hard hours out from St. Louis. The Fords had beaten them by about an hour and forty minutes, the Acme by a few. All the men were so spent that they "swayed exhaustedly in their seats and waved occasionally and sleepily to motorists and passengers on street cars" as they edged toward the hotel, one paper noted.

Over supper, Harry Harper—the Ford adman in the No. 1—boasted to the press that the Fords would win. "We believe that the smaller cars in the long run will do the work and stand up better than a heavier machine. We have not had a single accident," he said. He claimed that it was "greatly through the influence of our company" that the rules had been changed to prohibit replacing major parts, a nifty bit of revisionism, given Ford's objections in April. "If we can keep up the gait we have been going, we will run into Seattle ahead of the rest."

The Baltimore, newly renovated, was Kansas City's crown jewel, lavish as any hotel in the nation. It sat on a prime stretch of Baltimore Avenue, around the corner from the palatial Convention Hall, where William Jennings Bryan had just addressed twenty-five hundred people. The "Peerless Leader" of prairie populism had railed against money as "the root of almost all" evil, never mind that he did so while wearing an alpaca coat and wielding a Japanese fan. Bryan denounced the "temptation to sell the soul" in everyday life and hammered against the influence of corporate interests on the press.

The crowd at Bryan's "Price of a Soul" speech, hosted by the Society of Christian Endeavor, would have deemed the nearby Baltimore Hotel a temple of Mammon, with its Falstaffian boasts ("there is not another hostelry in the United States possessing furnishings as sumptuous and massive") and its many themed halls for dining or drinking: Egyptian Room, Pompeiian Room, Heidelberg Room, Italian Room. Even an "Automobile Room," believed to be the first in the nation, furnished in Circassian walnut and lined with murals that depicted handsome touring cars in a variety of settings. Coupled with art-glass windows that suggested a forest, the murals—per the hotel's one-hundred-page brochure—fostered "the impression of outdoor life which is so dear to the hearts of all lovers of the automobile."

The Shawmut trio had no time here for a heavy repast or round of imbibing. The men stayed just long enough to register their appearance, refuel the car, rest their legs a bit, and confer with Albert Gustin, an astute farm boy who'd made a fortune already at thirty-three, as a retailer and now manufacturer of railway and industrial supplies. Dabbling in the automotive world, he'd also become a distributor for Diamond Tires, Shawmut's supplier. He helped the No. 5 crew secure an unusually good guide across eastern Kansas (the less said about the last one the better; "Grutelius [*sic*] no good," the team had telegraphed home) and gave the Shawmut as many tires as they needed, though they wanted just two casings and three tubes. Gustin was pleased to hear how their Diamonds were holding up, with two still full of New York air. The powerful automobile should thrive in Kansas, with its broad expanses. He wrote to Shawmut GM Horace Waite in Boston, impressed with the car and crew:

> *In making a comparison of the cars in this race, it does seem that you should win very easily, as your car is built on more substantial lines and you have a very conservative crew. We wish you success, and hope you may finish a long way ahead of the other contestants. Your boys were somewhat tired, but were feeling much better than the other crews, as*

they were very careful about the water they drank; they were not smoking and being very modest in their habits, should make the trip without any trouble whatever.

Gustin sent it the next day: Wednesday, June 9, 1909. By then the cars were deep into Kansas, the skies pummeling them with rain, those promising expanses churning into gumbo.

6

"Mud, Water, and Glue"

Mired in Kansas, June 8 to 11, 1909

No one was eager to pick up and leave Kansas City Tuesday night on the heels of that all-night-and-all-day race across Missouri, especially with rain looming and dusk descending. But the end of the enforced twelve-hour stops meant any recovery time now came at a cost. Speaking to reporters at the hotel, Harry Harper from the No. 1 Ford sounded resigned. "After twenty-one hours on the road I am about all in, and if I can't sleep pretty soon and have to go out again tonight, I guess I will have to sleep between bumps," he said that evening, June 8. Even car mate Frank Kulick, known for feats of endurance as well as speed, found the thrill of daylight racing faded at night. "It's hard work steering the car over a road that's very strange to you and make any time in the dark," he said. "And when you're not at the wheel it's almost impossible to sleep—the country roads are too rough."

Their boss, on the other hand, could relax in the comfort of a night at the resplendent Baltimore, though productivity-obsessed Henry Ford was more apt to appreciate the hotel's "scientific construction" and "army of efficient, trained employees" than the rococo splendor of its themed dining rooms. The next morning, the rested automaker struck reporters as a man of practicality and vigor, seeming more like a traveling salesman than the "popular idea of an inventor," that disheveled dreamer with "double lens glasses" and "far-away expression" imagining "the day when airships shall be sold for $8.50 each." Ford told the Kansas City press not to dismiss lightweight, affordable autos as consolation cars or starter vehicles, relegated to those who could not yet afford a bigger, better model. Instead, he predicted that the improved runabout—his runabout, to be sure—"is certain to be the popular car of the future . . . because it is the handiest car, is simple in construction and costs little to maintain."

As Ford dispensed wisdom in Kansas City that morning, the leaders were only about sixty miles west, amid an ominous introduction that signaled they were in for something different than the pathfinder had enjoyed back in April. For all the horrors of the Thomas Flyer's two-month nightmare from New York to Seattle, Kansas had been a placid interlude, five-hundred-plus miles of rolling hills and flat prairie from Kansas City clear across to Kanorado, with nary a mountain or metropolis to slow them in between. Across that flat landscape—the nation's straightaway—there were just two communities exceeding ten thousand people (Lawrence and Topeka), though even in the most remote stretches the Thomas had been cheered by farmers who shared word of its advance by barbed-wire telephone, a technological hack that turned steel fencing into an electrified party line without the need for expensive poles and extensive copper wiring. Like the Thomas before them, the Shawmut and Acme crews envisioned opening the throttle here to achieve the top speeds that had been held in check in the East. Mother Nature had other ideas.

The Shawmut men left Kansas City an hour behind the Fords, riding with William Henry "Gilly" Gillmore, the guide that tire dealer Albert Gustin had lined up. A car salesman and top local motorist, Gillmore had shouldered much of the driving in a 1907 sprint from Kansas City to Denver that set two records, as both the fastest drive between the two cities (twenty-nine hours, still standing in 1909) and the first completed without an overnight rest. Given the open-road speeds the Shawmut could hit, it was tempting to think they might reach the Colorado border—and maybe even Denver itself—in similar time, arriving by Thursday morning.

Of course, there was a catch to that 1907 record. Gillmore's boss had picked his spot, delaying the departure for dry weather. Even then, the twenty-nine-hour mark recorded by an accompanying sportswriter tallied only forward-progress "driving time." The journey had actually consumed forty-eight hours, counting numerous stops for blown tires and delays, everything from assisting an overturned buggy blocking the road to waiting on a team of horses to tow their own car out of a sinkhole. But surely the Shawmut would reach Denver, seven hundred miles off, by Thursday night or Friday morning.

The Ford side knew what Kansas roads were really like: a tale of two states, depending on the weather. In May, when Kansas City branch manager Charles Meade drove most of Kansas to scrutinize the route over his territory, a mere half-inch of precipitation transformed dirt roads into such stubborn mud that he managed just fifty-three miles one day. The next week, the sun shined generously on a group of young Kansas friends setting off on a motoring adventure for the ages, attempting to drive two thousand miles to Seattle for the World's Fair. Though they would eventually encounter such trouble in the Rockies that they would abandon their car and take the train, they sailed across Kansas during a warm, dry start to June. "We could not wish for better roads, better weather or better success," one of the guys wrote home from Denver.

Alternating weeks; alternating realities. Now rain threatened again, and much more than Meade had encountered. That posed separate problems for the crews and their vehicles. The men, with no roof, windshield, or windshield wipers, would get drenched. They could stay semi-dry from the neck down by donning rubberized cotton gowns or more durable and breathable (if slightly less waterproof) oilcloth slickers, like Boston-based A. J. Tower Co.'s popular "Fish Brand" line. The former smelled heavily of India rubber and industrial solvents, while the linseed oil that waterproofed the latter gave off a cod-liver aroma that either reminded you of the sea or jolted you back to choking down Scott's Emulsion. But the rain would pummel their bare faces, leaving a choice between blinking into the flying droplets or constantly wiping smeared goggles.

And now that they were on the far side of St. Louis, driving through the dark, they would need headlights, no mere matter of flipping a switch.

The lamps were all gas-powered, requiring the men to fuss with matches or primitive lighters even in the rain. Though magnetos and batteries had made portable electric lights possible, the incandescent bulbs of the age could not generally withstand the jarring of an automobile or produce enough candlepower to illuminate the road. Instead, car lights were typically fueled by acetylene, like miner's headlamps. In a tank resembling a fire extinguisher mounted by the running boards, carbide and water combined to form the acetylene gas, which flowed through flexible tubing to lamps containing a Y-shaped burner, copper reflector, and heavy glass lens. You opened the lens on each headlight, turned the valve at the tank to start the flow of the gas, waited for the acrid odor of the gas, then added flame—and voilà, you had enough light to see a few car lengths ahead. The Shawmut and Acme also had brighter dash-mounted searchlights that worked on the same principal. That helped on a clear night, but in heavy rain those beams illuminated the droplets like a swarm of fireflies.

Beyond discomfort and difficulty seeing, the real problem with the rain was what it would do to the clay soils of the Plains, which transformed from brick-solid when dry into "gumbo mud" with water. Easterners who thought all mud was the same were in for a surprise. Water plugged up the pores in this Midwestern soil, expanding it into gelatinous goop, slick and greasy on top, thick and tacky overall. One writer said gumbo mud clung "tighter than a long-lost brother." Alice Ramsey, a noted New Jersey motorist—"one of the most daring chauffeuses in America," as *The Los Angeles Times* put it—poised to embark on the first all-female cross-country drive, would soon encounter the same stuff in Iowa, likening it to "mucilage." It didn't just grab hold of metal or wood and wrestle cars into submission; it adhered to itself, so that soon you were straining to lug hundreds of extra pounds of earthen baggage, making every mile harder. And the farther west you went, the worse the gumbo. At that very moment, a Salina milliner named Lillian Hoyt was returning from Denver after tracing five hundred miles of the Ocean-to-Ocean Race route in a Maxwell runabout. (Though Hoyt left the driving to her chauffeur, the fact that a woman owned the car and oversaw the long-distance journey was notable enough to make headlines.) The trip west had been a pleasure cruise, but the return became such a slog that Hoyt and her driver abandoned the car at Hays City and took the train home. Attempting to drive through gumbo was a revelation to the Salina hat seller, even after living most of her life in Nebraska and Kansas. "It wasn't mud," Hoyt said. "It was a combination of mud, water and glue."

This was exactly what lay before them. No wonder the Acme, last to leave, made it only a few miles into Kansas before stopping at a farmhouse around midnight, overcome and praying for better weather in the morning. About the same time, the leading Fords reached the college town of Lawrence, forty-five miles ahead, where they disagreed on whether to rest or keep going. The weather had turned especially foul, with a "whistling, moaning" wind that ripped away some shutters and shingles and stripped the ivy off the Lawrence National Bank, entangling it on telegraph wires, followed by thunder and lightning. The noise was so fierce that some feared "a sure-enough cyclone," in the words of the *Lawrence Daily World*. Harper and Kulick, utterly spent, voted to rest a few hours at the Eldridge House Hotel, where a crowd of spectators had gathered. Scott and Smith in the No. 2 decided to press on.

Facing down the storm's fury, they made it just ten more miles before Scott misjudged the road in the rain and the dark. Aiming for a small bridge, he toppled instead off the side of a culvert and crashed fourteen feet into a ditch. The men got tossed, and the rear axle and one of the wheels on the No. 2 got smashed and bent on impact. Shaken up, Scott and Smith waited out the worst of the night under the bridge. Accounts varied, but it seems they contacted Meade in Kansas City, and the Ford network sprang into action by morning, helping the No. 2 crew right the car, hammer the axle back into shape, and replace the wheel. The damage might have been worse if not for the strength of Ford's vaunted steel, though the selling point of the special alloy was muddled when a local reporter misheard "vanadium steel" as "Canadian steel."

That accident—misfortune, misjudgment—created an opening for the Shawmut, which also battled through the night, if at a modest clip. The

Boston car was first into Topeka on Wednesday morning, claiming a half-hour lead over the No. 1 Ford, which had gotten back on the road again from its rest in Lawrence by 4 AM. The No. 2, its lead squandered in the ditch, lagged some three hours behind, coming in about the same time as the Acme. The local *Capital* newspaper called them "the muddiest automobiles ever seen in Topeka. The roads they have encountered have been enough to break the heart of the average autoist. But the racers declare they will run out of the mud unless it keeps on raining ahead of them"—which is exactly what would happen.

The leaders peeled off to separate garages at the corner of Seventh and Quincy in Topeka. The Model Ts went to the Ford agency, in this case run by Charles Guild, a marble headstone and monument man who had branched out into automobiles; he had teased the coming of the cars in the local paper, inviting Topekans to visit the showroom or call for updates. The Shawmut hit the garage of Paul Mulvane, son of a prominent physician-rancher, who at twenty-seven had built a small bicycle shop into a three-story automotive retail-and-repair complex, boasting the only tire-vulcanizing equipment between Kansas City and Denver. Preserving first place, the Shawmut sped out of Mulvane's garage fifteen minutes before the Ford No. 1 left Topeka, but Kulick and Harper predicted they would retake the lead by Manhattan—the first of three checkpoints in Kansas.

Sure enough, the Shawmut punctured a tire around Wamego, forty miles out, giving the Ford side the satisfaction of being first by twenty-five minutes to that checkpoint, at Manhattan's three-story, mansard-roofed Hotel Gillett. The city of five thousand was equally abuzz over its brand-new streetcar system and the arrival of the racers. One reporter who watched the crews register thought the men "looked like road drags," those humble planks lugged behind horses to flatten dirt roads; indeed, the local commercial club had just handed out a raft of prizes, from $3 to $25, to farmers who'd done the best job of dragging the county's roadways that spring. Another reporter called the automobile men "the dirtiest, most disconsolate and utterly woe-begone individuals that ever struck Manhattan," while the cars were so caked in gumbo they looked like "a huge hog just out of a mud wallow."

Missing the chance to be first at the checkpoint because of that puncture stung for the Shawmut. While the race often drew small-town news coverage even without stopping, it was those thirty checkpoint locations where the crews stopped to register, refuel, and mail cards to Seattle that typically generated newswire dispatches dashed all across the nation—yielding headlines that favored whoever was winning at those very moments. The Shawmut crew sent a telegram back to Boston, acknowledging the heaviness of the roads but anticipating improved conditions, provided those rain clouds parted soon. "Will catch Ford west out of here. Have fine guide" in Gillmore from Kansas City, they wrote. "Car and crew in first class condition. Better roads later in West Kansas. Will make much better time and running night and day."

But the clouds did not part; the roads did not improve. A month's worth of rain fell in three days, with three inches measured across much of Kansas, and five or six inches in the wettest places. The race shifted into a brutal test of stamina, tire chains snapping, wheels alternately spinning or sticking, so much pulling and tugging and digging and shoving in the muck. The crews made the most of lulls when the rains stopped—though the sun remained mostly hidden—and patches where the ground was semi-firm.

The No. 1 Ford and the Shawmut scraped out forty-five miles in four hours, churning and straining in low gear, passing through Junction City—where two hundred people turned out in the sodden weather, even as they remained a little sore about losing out to Manhattan as a checkpoint—and reaching Abilene. That wheat-and-cattle community of four thousand was known less for the Eisenhower brothers (decorated scholar-athletes Dwight and Edgar had just graduated together from the local high school a few days before) than for America's youngest motorist, six-year-old Bessie Coulson. The apple-cheeked daughter of a local Buick dealer had been driving for over a year, a promotional stunt conceived by her father to demonstrate that people should not be intimidated by the training or skill needed to operate an automobile—so simple that even a child could do it, literally. When Bessie buzzed around Abilene with a car full of playmates, her father typically stood on the running board to monitor the proceedings. But when the little girl put on exhibitions at county fairs, she drove alone, tracing grooves around horse tracks largely by feel, unable to see much over the wheel.

The Shawmut nipped at the heels of the No. 1 Ford all the way to Salina, where Kulick was so fatigued—one paper described him as "nervous," another as "dazed"—that he failed to recognize local Ford agents he'd met multiple times before. Kansas City branch manager Meade had urged George Weisgerber, a watchmaker and jeweler who co-owned Ford's Salina agency, to order a stockpile of parts for the Model T racers, including four Prest-O-Lite tanks for the acetylene headlights. But Kulick and Harper hardly took anything, racing right back out of Salina to maintain their thin lead over Shawmut. The next checkpoint—the second in Kansas, and seventeenth of thirty overall—lay in Ellsworth, nearly forty more miles away. Kulick powered on through the exhaustion.

It paid off. At Ellsworth, the No. 1 Ford again checked in first. Instead of coming in on its heels, the Shawmut was nowhere to be seen. During a gap between guides, navigating in the dark, the men overshot Ellsworth and wound up in Black Wolf, a tiny village nearly eight miles out of the way—a staggering distance in gumbo over pitch-black prairie. Finally, the Boston boys clawed their way back to Ellsworth, an erstwhile Wild West town that had traded its rough edges for shade trees, tidy lawns, and other "smiling ornaments of civilization," in the words of a statewide gazetteer. They found their way after midnight to the checkpoint at the White House, a sturdy little hotel opposite the Union Pacific station. Lore had it that Wyatt Earp had gotten his start as a lawman on this same block thirty-six years earlier, arresting notorious fugitive gambler-gunman Billy Thompson and his brother.

As they registered, the Shawmut crew understood that their lost hours running to Black Wolf had surely cost them their cushion over the third-place Acme. But they also learned that the lead Ford had decided to hang up here until early morning. That would give Frank Kulick some recovery time while allowing the No. 2 Ford to catch up, so the Model Ts could again run in tandem. The second Ford, still worse for wear after its dive into that ditch the night before, had stopped in Manhattan for additional repairs and was now coming on strong once more.

If the Shawmut's Black Wolf mishap underlined the need for a guide at all times, at least the Boston crew was now picking up another good one: Nineteen-year-old Paul Warner, who in a few more years would become a prominent member of the Indian motorcycle factory racing team, alongside the famed Erwin "Cannon Ball" Baker and Paul "Dare Devil" Derkum. Indeed, Warner—who would become known to motorcycling-magazine readers as "Speck" and "The Kansas Cyclone"—would guide Baker across this same region during the latter's record-setting 1914 cross-country run, the first of several coast-to-coast sprints that would make Cannon Ball Baker the king of breakneck transcontinental journeys. Despite his youth, Warner was a rural-route postal carrier who had already discovered that he could make his job easier with a motorcycle instead of on horseback, and was so taken by his bike that he'd become a sales agent for Indian on the side. As he climbed into the Shawmut, he must have appreciated that Earle Chapin hailed from the same town as those Indian motorcycles, developed by a bike maker as a light but powerful "motor bicycle." And Warner's mail-carrying experience made him an expert at traversing the region.

The Shawmut set out in first, determined to extend a lead, but it was such hard going overnight that even with Warner they pulled off around Dorrance, less than twenty-five miles out, to rest for a few hours. The local motorcyclist had rarely seen conditions this bad. They fell into a deeper slumber than intended, awakening not at sunrise on Thursday but at the late hour of 7:30 AM, jolted by the unmuffled roar of the two Fords *rat-a-tat-tatting* past to retake the lead, the Acme right with them. So much for being in Colorado by now; it was June 10, and they were barely halfway across Kansas. The Shawmut trailed the pack another twenty-five miles or so to Gorham, where a modest creek had swollen into a river fifty feet across. The Fords and Acme were out of sight, after going way wide to try to skirt the creek or find an easier crossing. Gauging the depth, the Shawmut men with their forty-inch wheels decided to plunge straight through the water. The stream was three feet deep in the middle, at least. Water washed in, flooding the engine. The men waded into the current, fastening block and tackle, pulling the car across to the far bank. Chapin removed the carburetor and magneto, and they lost ninety minutes to cleaning and drying the parts before they could drive again. But the soggy shortcut paid off. The Shawmut was first into Hays City, where a local bank president waited outside of town with the big American flag he reserved for special occasions. Except the Boston car sputtered out of gas soon after, allowing the Acme and Fords to punch past again. The crew coaxed the Shawmut to the city's newest garage—Cox & Son's "Auto Hospital"—and stayed an hour, thoroughly washing away the gumbo from every crevice of the car and from their slickers, too, attempting to lighten their load before a hundred-mile run to Oakley, the third Kansas checkpoint.

By now the Itala was just leaving St. Louis, four hundred miles behind. Gus Lechleitner, the brawny driver with the racetrack record who claimed cowboy experience, had been struck out of Toledo with chills and fever so bad they feared he might have diphtheria. Bert Bellows and F. B. Whittemore fixed him up in back of the car, and Bellows took the wheel. That was just the beginning. Bellows knew cars as well as anyone, and in New York City he'd been impressed with the Itala's engine and construction. They had speed aplenty. But from his previous slog driving out west for Guggenheim, he could sense the Itala would be trouble. It was a car meant to dazzle wealthy motorists in Manhattan, at once low-slung and brawny, hanging just seven inches above the road. If the Itala "only had more clearance we could laugh at them all," Bellows had written from Buffalo. But on the rough roads of Indiana, they wrenched the rear axle. In Chicago, Lechleitner needed to be hospitalized; the axle required repairs. They eventually received a message to continue without him, but by the time they left Chicago, the Itala lagged nineteen hours behind the Fords.

Alone now with the younger Whittemore, Bellows needed to do all the driving. Demarest's Yale-educated grandson had studied the technical side of engineering, but in the age of chauffeurs he didn't have the driving experience to handle the big car in bad conditions. Not that it mattered. The Itala just wasn't built to plow over roads as rough as potato fields, regardless of who was driving. Fifty miles before St. Louis, they struck a rut at 2 AM and smashed the steering knuckle off the right front wheel. They needed to take the train to St. Louis, fix the part, take the train back, reinstall the knuckle, and start up again in the Itala. Naturally concerned, Egbert Lillie, the president of the import firm that brought in Itala running gear from Turin and partnered with Demarest to finish and sell the cars in Manhattan, traveled from New York to join them. He petitioned the referee and the other crews for permission to drive but was rebuffed as a late addition, allowed only to help with the mud and manage the process. Outwardly they vowed to catch the pack, but Bellows knew it was unlikely. "I wish I had the old A.K.," he wrote home, referring to Guggenheim's high-performance sports car. "I don't think we have a chance on earth with this car. It is too heavy, and it can't stand rough roads."

Out in Kansas, the four front-runners traded positions all afternoon, taking turns getting stuck in the mud and punching free, ruing the rich loam and clay that made this area so favored for farming. The Acme was first at Ellis, the Shawmut second, but the cars were so muddy again it was hard for locals to tell who was who among the big cars—unlike the little Model Ts, which stopped here at the Ford dealership of Henry Samuelson, also a trader in butter, eggs, poultry, hogs, and cattle, for minor repairs and a couple of tires. "The struggle for the honors promise[s] to be a thrilling one," one New York paper declared, taking a dispatch from Ellis. Back east, auto editors could scarcely believe the reports, four cars separated by mere minutes after eighteen hundred miles.

The Shawmut and Acme traded leads into the evening, charging toward Oakley (checkpoint number eighteen of thirty), each crew determined to beat the other but especially to deprive the Fords of claiming more checkpoint glory. Like everywhere, the Oakley area was getting drenched. By midweek, at two inches, farmers were talking about too much rain being too much of a good thing. Now past three inches, they were begging for it to stop. TURN IT OFF, a headline in the local weekly would cry the next day, near a story apologizing to the racers. "The roads have been in an awful condition for motorists," the paper noted. "Kansas was figured as a good roads state . . . but the Ocean to Ocean racers have had nothing but mud and water ever since they entered."

Here the muck proved too much for the Acme, which, unlike the other cars, featured chain drive, meaning engine power was transmitted to the rear axle not by one long jackshaft, or countershaft, running under the car, but by a shorter shaft connected to two bicycle-style chains. That chain-and-sprocket system transferred power more efficiently, but it was fussier for sure. A responsible motorist with a chain-drive car needed to periodically remove the chains, bathe them in kerosene, hang them to dry, then simmer them in tallow to keep them running smoothly. In time, the chains would cause trouble for the Acme crew. But here it was the jackshaft that broke, snapping off power to those chains and rear wheels twenty miles shy of Oakley. The Shawmut surged into the lead.

Finally, the Boston men hit Oakley, a wheat-belt community of roughly 680 people on the Union Pacific main line. It was 7:43 on Thursday night. Forty-six miserable hours into Kansas, and they'd gone only 425 miles. But they were first into a checkpoint for the very first time, allowing them to bask in the awe of local admirers and garner an achievement for the newswires. The crew walked into the Kauffman House, a three-story brick hotel known to traveling salesmen as a place with reliable rooms and steam heat for $2 a night. They'd barely handed over their racing passport at the desk when Kulick and Harper burst in behind them, trailing by just two minutes. Aided by separate pilots from local dealerships, the two Fords had again separated, with the No. 2—still a little battered from that accident outside Lawrence—nearly an hour behind.

"Oakley first. Ford two minutes [behind us]. Roads very heavy. Got into river but pulled ourselves out. No trouble. No [blown] tires. Made only one hundred seventy-five miles. Will drive tonight," the Shawmut team wired Boston, looking optimistically westward. "Deep mud. Car and crew in first class condition. Will make Denver tomorrow."

(Harper, from the No. 1 Ford, had sent his own optimistic wire to Detroit: "Race close. Four cars together all day. Shawmut ahead here two minutes. Our cars doing splendidly; crews feeling fine.")

Earle Chapin carried a couple of postcards he'd picked up at the Manhattan checkpoint the day before but hadn't had time to send. Now he drew his fountain pen and wrote a fatigued note in blue ink on one to Anita back home, a view from the Rock Island line. "Reached Oakley 1st car, but others right behind. Haven't heard from Itala since Monday. Mud all through Kansas."

Paul Warner, the motorcycling mailman who'd guided the Shawmut for twenty hours, signed off to take the Union Pacific back to Ellsworth. If he caught the 102 at 8:35, he could be home in under six hours, less than a third the time it had taken to drive through the mud. In his place the Shawmut team picked up an even younger guide, albeit to lead them a shorter distance: Walter Brown, a seventeen-year-old whose older brother ran the local roller rink and dabbled in auto sales. Their late father had operated a flour and grain mill, which meant they had relationships with farmers all around the county. Walter was tall and burly but dreamed of being a musician; in a few years he would go off to play lead clarinet in a big Denver movie house, accompanying the silent pictures.

Pressing on with the teenage guide, the Shawmut crew left Oakley around 10 PM, bracing for another miserably wet night. Though Harry Harper had claimed the Ford crews were feeling fine, they decided to hunker down at the Kauffman House, sleeping off the grind and hoping for better weather in the morning. Driving through a stormy night while the Fords rested could give the Shawmut a chance to extend the lead, but it could also mean disaster. The railroad traced a graceful curve for twenty-one miles from here to Colby, the next town of consequence. The route over the roads—if you could call them that—followed a dizzying zigzag for thirty miles, a series of right angles along the square-mile section lines that carved up Kansas townships. For three foul nights they'd tried to drive through Kansas; this was the angriest night yet. They made it less than halfway to Colby before seeking shelter at a farm just past the tiny village of Mingo, likely with a family that guide Walter Brown knew from the milling business.

Chapin pulled out another Manhattan postcard, this one a view of the Kansas State Agricultural College's green pastures, and wrote to Anita. "Have stoped at a farmhouse. Having a going hurrycane. Running into heavy rain the last three nights. Hard going."

In the morning, the Shawmut continued on without the young guide. The night before, a large collection of "sports" had sat up late in the center of Colby anticipating the autos, teased by word the Shawmut had left Oakley, not knowing the crew had hunkered down near Mingo. "About midnight the rain increased to a down-pour and it was evident that if any autos went through Colby that night they would have to be in boats," the local *Tribune* mused. When the Shawmut finally appeared the next morning, the car "was a mass of mud and the occupants were painted with Kansas soil from crown to toe." They plowed their way to a machine shop operated by Frank Louis, a blacksmith and small-town fix-it man—plumber, electrician, woodworker—who repaired everything from buggy shafts to windmill wrist pins. Seeing a market opening in the beginnings of Colorado-bound tourist travel, Louis had started advertising his shop more widely to automobilists; he even laid a cement floor specifically to handle the weight of motor cars. The Shawmut team picked up a shipment of supplies forwarded from Chicago and dashed another quick telegram to Boston, explaining why they'd advanced just thirty miles since their last message ten hours earlier: "Heavy thunderstorm. Stopped at farm house. Roads heavy again. Will try for Denver today."

A few hours later, Chapin penned one last postcard home from Kansas. The conditions, grim already, were only getting worse: "Hard going. Rivers and mud. Wont make 100 miles today." So much for that Kansas City vision of reaching Denver by Thursday or Friday. At this rate they'd be lucky to be there Sunday.

7

Captured in Goodland

Western Kansas, June 11, 1909

Goodland, Kansas, population nearly two thousand, matching the mileage to go in the race. When the first Ocean-to-Ocean cars splashed into town, T. E. Bateman happened to be around Main Street. A traveling salesman for a big plumbing-supply house in Kansas City, Bateman didn't usually venture this far west, practically the Colorado border. He'd been on the road seven years, covering a swath of north-central Kansas into Nebraska, calling on hardware merchants and pitching town officials on the right fixtures for that new jail or schoolhouse. For the first five, he'd been like any other traveling man, lugging sample kits by train. Then the W. B. Young Supply Company bestowed a 20-horsepower touring car on Bateman, making him one of the first commercial salesmen in the state to trade iron horse for horseless carriage. It also made him one of the first people with a car around his hometown of Concordia, grabbing the attention of the local paper. "The day is not far distant when most traveling men who cover a limited territory will be traveling by auto almost exclusively," Concordia's *Daily Blade* predicted.

A lean and youthful forty, Bateman was so enchanted by automobiles that he even built perhaps the first pedal-powered toy car anywhere, though he failed to patent his creation. He only happened to be in Goodland now temporarily, a way station on a nearly five-hundred-mile trip to

Colorado. Bateman and a group of modest investors—mainly in-laws and acquaintances—were considering buying shares of a mining proposition in the Rockies. It was the kind of thing many people plunged into on the basis of breathless brochures and newspaper ads alone, but Bateman wanted to vet it in person, wary of wildcat schemes. Naturally, they took the train; even for an auto lover, driving this far was out of the question. He'd brought his camera along, one of those popular pocket models that really only fit in the roomiest of pockets.

Around 11:30 AM, a roar like a machine gun drew Bateman and everyone else out onto the sidewalks. The weather had been miserable here all week, four inches and counting on the local rain gauge, more at some farms in the country. Up to that moment, talk in Goodland that morning centered on Mrs. Albert Patterson, the thirty-six-year-old farmwife northwest of town who'd braved the elements the day before, loading her buggy with eggs, chickens, and butter to come trade for supplies. When she reached a creek known as the Middle Beaver, it looked knee-deep to her horse, so she drove through. Then a jam of trash and thistles loosened around a bend; a wall of water slammed the wagon, overturning it in the river. Plenty of men might have drowned, especially if they were tangled up in a dress. But Mattie Patterson, who'd birthed eight children, six surviving, kept her wits, and kept her head above the chilly water. She swam the horse to a place where it could stand, though it remained hitched to the ruined buggy. So Mattie ran for help, rousing two men from a nearby farm. Refusing their entreaties that she stay and warm up, she took the lead back at the river, swimming to the wreckage, unbuckling the harness, and landing the horse safely. "She is the grittiest woman in Sherman County," one of the men said. "She's a brick," the other called her. Word reached Albert Patterson; reunited with Mattie, he beamed. "The chickens, the eggs, the butter, the harness and buggy have gone down stream," he said, "but I still have my plucky little wife and the colt."

In short, no kind of weather to be driving any contraption, auto or wagon. In Goodland, a county seat that had grown so fast they called it "The Metropolis of Northwest Kansas," they had recently added several blocks of proper sidewalks, but the downtown streets themselves were just dirt. Which meant they were now avenues of mud and muck—rivulets and pools of darkened water mingling with ankle-swallowing slop. The hundred or so feet between sidewalks across Main Street may as well have been a mile.

The two Model Ts burst in, loud as a stationary engine hooked up for threshing. They worked their way to Main and Tenth, heart of downtown, chained tires churning up the mire. There was no Ford agent in Goodland, not yet. So they jerked to a halt in front of William Hargraves's garage, a slender wooden storefront—converted bicycle shop—with AUTO GARAGE & LIVERY painted above the awning. When Bill Hargraves repositioned his business a year and a half earlier, not many here besides Hargraves himself owned a car, but like Frank Louis in Colby, he thought there might be work enough in serving the occasional motorists who stopped in town for directions, gasoline, or repairs, while awaiting the emergence of the local market. Then Goodland's doctor had gotten that urgent long-distance telephone call when a farmhand in the next county got pierced in the eye by a flying fragment while blacksmithing. Hargraves sped the doc and his sedatives twenty-eight miles out to the farm in just two hours, when a buggy would have taken half the day. That did its own advertising.

Now people crowded outside Hargraves's garage to get a load of the Ford racers. The cars looked less like they'd churned across the mire than tunneled up through it, nearly as battered and bedraggled as that Patterson buggy lost in the Middle Beaver. The crews themselves were equally drenched and ragged. Reporters from the two local papers tried to outdo each other with their synonyms for *muddy*. To the one from *The Goodland Republic*, the cars seemed fashioned from the "same stuff that Adam was made of." The men emerged in "rubber boots, rainproof caps, and rubber gowns with only a hole in the top for the neck. And as they peeked out from behind a thick layer of mud on their faces, it was a sight to make most sober men laugh, and to draw a few conclusions with regard to the wisdom of the continental chase." To the scribe from the rival *Sherman County Record*, the crew looked like "some unknown species of humanity more than just common American citizens."

The crowd hugged the sidewalk around the cars on both sides of the garage, from Lamberton's real estate office ("CHEAP LAND") to the shop of Joseph Kolacny, the first skilled tailor in western Kansas. Kolacny had followed the new railroad two decades back, arriving in a town so wild his best customers were gamblers asking for secret pockets in coat sleeves to stash extra cards or weighted dice. Now he cut smart suits to match Eastern styles for flourishing farmers and local merchants—men who were building fine houses on Goodland's avenues and considering their first autos.

Hargraves took a garden hose and hooked it to Goodland's city-water main. In suits and ties, in shirtsleeves, and in bib overalls, a collection of men and a few children watched as the garage man stripped the mud of the Plains from these Model Ts with the hose. Then Scott and Smith and Kulick and Harper bent over in their rain gear, and Hargraves turned the hose on them, too, rendering them human again.

Bateman, the traveling salesman who just happened to be there, captured everything with his camera. Working through a roll of postcard-sized film, he snapped the Fords up close on the east side of Main—from the front, from behind—and braved the muddy expanse to catch both in a row from across the street. The Ford crews crossed, too, to grab a bite at Al Roth's Bakery & Cafe, while Hargraves fueled up their cars. The rain cleared, if just for now. Harper walked to the Rock Island depot to send a telegram. The Fords were just about to head up Main again and leave town when the Shawmut rumbled in, approaching head-on.

Seven states, ten days, and over two thousand miles, and these three leaders were still separated by no more than a quick-service lunch. The big car from Boston, with its forty-inch wheels and substantial body, pulled beside the Fords at Main and Tenth, where the little Model Ts rested smack in the middle of the muddy intersection, amid a crowd of men and boys and a little girl with ringlets, no one worried about traffic. They were gathered in front of Goodland's Grand Opera House—humbler than the name implied, drawing the usual touring fare of minstrel shows and magicians, lecture-circuit speakers and local graduations. A hand-painted banner advertised Whitney's Celebrated Moving Pictures, in town for three days, offering TWO HOURS OF HIGH-CLASS PICTURES—reels of President Taft's inauguration, the Messina earthquake, balloon races, bullfights, and more—accompanied by music, starting at ten cents.

Bateman steadied his camera once more. He caught the Shawmut from behind, foregrounded in the frame, so muddied you'd barely know it was once white, tackle lines on the back obscuring the SEATTLE destination painted on the spare-tire cover. When Bateman developed the picture, he could see one of the rival Fords clearly beside the Shawmut. For thirty-three years these photos would reside in a box, in one home and then another, until Bateman's son James discovered them while visiting his father, by then retired in Missouri. Though the particulars had faded from the man's memory (*Was it 1906? 1908? Were those cars racing to San Francisco?*), the visceral thrill of catching the race in Goodland came flooding back. The Batemans mailed the pictures to Henry Ford, by then seventy-nine, hoping for a personal reply. For all the photos of the cars clustered at the starting line, and the others taken together after the finish in Seattle, the packet contained the first known photos of a Ford and Shawmut together in the same frame in the thick of the race. The family received a typed reply from Ford's secretary, polite if perfunctory. The Ford Motor Company would utilize Bateman's photos, if not necessarily the one foregrounding the Shawmut. Some things were better left forgotten.

8

Ford's Man in the Mile-High City

Colorado, June 12 to 13, 1909

Joined by reporters from Denver's leading papers, Charles Hendy Jr. sat up waiting for the race to reach the Savoy Hotel on the night of June 12. Ford's Denver branch manager, Hendy wasn't just hoping one or both Model Ts would be the first to eventually barrel down Colfax and turn up Broadway, passing his Ford branch a block before this hotel checkpoint. He was hoping they'd be first *that* night. It was late on Saturday, approaching deadline for the Sunday papers, biggest of the week. If the cars didn't show up soon, the stories would land instead in the Monday editions, when being first wouldn't carry the same punch.

Charlie Hendy had been plugging the Model T to the press all week, building on relationships he'd tended since opening the Denver branch at the end of 1907. He was thirty-three, a charismatic and classically handsome son of the West, with one foot in the old territory days and a long stride into the new century. Hendy had spent early childhood at a series of forts across the frontier before growing up in North Platte, Nebraska, where his father, Charles Sr., a federally pensioned "Indian fighter," settled into a comfortable second career as a cattle rancher and civic leader, a close friend of Buffalo Bill Cody. Charles Jr. was clean-shaven and lantern-jawed, with a sweep of dark hair and an outward geniality that belied a fierce competitive streak.

As a dynamo on Denver's Automobile Row, Hendy possessed the winning qualities of Ford's Eastern branch managers bundled into one: the bonhomie of New York's Gaston Plantiff, urbane impresario of the Broadway branch (who joined Ford at the starting line and helped secure the pace car); the hustle of Chicago's Tom Hay; the pluck of St. Louis's Fuzzy Anderson; the conviction of Kansas City's Charles Meade. Above all, Hendy was a kind of Ford's Ford, a natural at publicity, a true believer in the virtues of the lightweight, affordable car—and, like Ford, a man with a rigid outward ethic coupled with a personally flexible approach to the rules. If you believed unshakably that you were selling the right car, the car that deserved to reach Seattle first, then the ends would justify the means.

As a student cadet at the University of Nebraska, Hendy had relished the discipline and structure he found under the tutelage of Lieutenant John J. Pershing, before the future "Black Jack" Pershing got called to West Point. In February 1898, when Hendy was a second-semester senior, the USS *Maine* exploded in Havana, killing much of the crew. However murky the explosion's cause, the nation hurtled into war with Spain. Fifteen hundred miles from Cuba, Hendy volunteered for active duty. The state university was so new that no students had ever left for war before. The chancellor led a somber ceremony in the chapel, assuring the five dozen departing young men that they were each worth "a score of Spaniards." A professor hailed them as "defenders of the country"; a dean told them to "return with your shield or upon it." They rode off on a righteous wave of patriotism—making it as far as training camp in Georgia before the war abruptly ended. Forever after, Hendy would identify as a proud veteran of the conflict, organizing encampments and climbing the rungs of the United Spanish War Veterans.

Back home, he got "the Spanish out of his system" before enlisting in the Nebraska National Guard, becoming an officer and aide-de-camp to the brigadier general. By day he held down a white-collar job, initially as a timekeeper, with the Union Pacific, a professional association that would come to pay dividends here in the Ocean-to-Ocean Race. Hendy's hometown was a major center for the Union Pacific, with a big roundhouse and extensive blacksmith and machine shops. By 1904, when Hendy married a daughter of one of North Platte's other leading families, he'd been promoted to chief clerk of the master mechanic's office. But he itched for more than the city of four thousand could offer.

A boyhood friend, E. Linn Mathewson, had gone to Denver to sell bicycles in the 1890s and wound up becoming one of the leading automobile dealers and competitive drivers in the entire West. That sure was something. In 1905, Hendy joined him, as sales manager and righthand man. He took to it quickly, but eventually left to sell life insurance, perhaps chafing at being an old friend's understudy. Then he got his own chance to be in charge, winning the new Ford branch, a rare outsider at a company that had promoted most of its branch managers from within.

He quickly rewarded Ford's faith.

Denver now had full-blown automobile fever, and Charlie Hendy's sales feats had plenty to do with it. A city clerk had recently tallied the number of all-time auto registrations ($1, good forever) and discovered the figure exceeded three thousand, double what it had been two years back, and a sixfold increase in four years. That gave Denver one motor car for every seventy-five people, an astonishing per-capita figure, nearly ten times the auto-ownership rate of the nation. Soon a proud claim crystallized, touted in newspaper ads and relayed in boosterish letters mailed east: Denver boasted the most automobiles per person of any big city.

It was impossible to prove; registration requirements and recordkeeping practices varied widely. But it certainly *felt* true about Denver, a new kind of city, fundamentally Western, promoted as a crisply modern antidote to the creaky, claustrophobic, contagious urban centers of the East. Everything about Denver—"Queen City of the Rockies," "Queen City of the Plains"—was assuredly airier, cleaner, better, from the healthful breezes blowing in off the Front Range to the crystal tap water springing up from artesian wells beneath the city. Denver claimed *more sunny days, more buildings of "fireproof" brick and stone, more parks, more miles of streetcar lines, more "American-born citizens," and more good hotels than any comparable city*, among the superlatives that floated eastward, luring tourists and transplants alike. And now it boasted more automobiles and more paved roads, the two intertwined. Already 10 percent of Denver's 1,222 miles of streets were granite-block or asphalt.

Like other Western hubs, Denver was growing exponentially. Four decades back, it had been one-fiftieth the size of Boston. Now it was nearly one-third. In the fresh clay of this twentieth-century city, developers were shaping something new, abetted by those proliferating automobiles and an ample supply of outlying land: single-family homes on newly divided parcels, far from the dense blocks of the downtown core and beyond even the radial extension of streetcar lines. "House and lot hunger is growing. The fascination of a lawn to mow, and a flower bed to nurse, and the freedom of a man's own rooftree, is gripping the citizens of Denver," a *Denver Post* columnist noted, after an automobile tour of the outer rungs of the city.

That auto-loving Denver would expand outward instead of upward seemed abundantly beneficent when cars meant freedom and fresh air, not congestion and pollution. Denver the motoring city was Denver the healthful city, a rare metropolis where, as one promotional brochure put it, "lung diseases vanish, the chest expands, the heart enlarges, and health and strength replace invalidism and despair." And the urban-suburban expansion was just half of it. Someday all those tantalizingly close mountain resorts—still the exclusive dominion of the railroads, save for the boldest automobiles drivers, in good weather—would surely become accessible to motorists too.

Vigor, health, sensibility, modernity. That was how a man like Charlie Hendy sold automobiles, placing Fords in parades, promoting their capacity for "killing the hills" in this state where mountains met prairie. Determined to shake the stigma around low-priced cars, Hendy persuaded affluent men—the ones whose signatures he'd courted for Equitable Life insurance policies, and who already owned expensive motor cars—that the Ford's moderate price reflected a singular corporate focus on efficiency, making it an astute choice, affordable but not the least bit cheap. And if he could sell some Fords to these wealthy men, then surely he could move many more among the middle-class strivers eager to emulate the rich. Either way, "I don't care who buys them," Hendy said, "as long as they buy them from me."

In November he'd scored a big feature photo in the *Post*, ferrying three lovely young women in a Model K, his wife and sister-in-law included. That flanked a story he planted about passing twenty-nine struggling automobiles in the mud while returning from a big college football game in Boulder. The precise figure was Hendy's count; who could say if it was true? But it sure made great copy: "The performance of the Ford is one that will stand for endurance in the annals of Colorado motor history."

He did it again two weeks later, finessing the Ford into the story of the biggest sporting event to hit Colorado. Pop Warner's Carlisle Indian Industrial School football team, boasting all-around athlete Jim Thorpe and spiral-pass pioneer Pete Hauser, was in from Pennsylvania to play the ascendant University of Denver, best in the West. The game was so big, one wag claimed that Roosevelt would referee, Taft would assist, and the "crowned heads of Europe will be given sideline privileges."

The reality wasn't far off; Amos Alonzo Stagg, a father of modern football, came from Chicago to officiate. And there was Charlie Hendy, volunteering to zip the *Post*'s sports staff out to the stadium in a Ford and bring them back after, sparing them a sluggish streetcar commute. That act of benevolence just happened to secure him a big photo and favorable write-up alongside the game coverage. And never mind that the picture showed Hendy driving the scribes in one of those powerful—discontinued—six-cylinder Model Ks. The paper took his word that it was the new Model T: "Mr. Hendy says it can do most anything, and yesterday he had to be forcibly restrained from asking it to jump over the big touring cars that ploughed along through the slush and got in his way."

Naturally, Hendy was all in on the Ocean-to-Ocean Race, investing as much time and mileage on the ground in the spring as any branch manager, reflecting the sprawling nature of his "Denver" territory as well as his commitment. In May, he'd gone all the way to Pocatello, Idaho, 649 miles each way by rail. If all you did was ride straight there and back, it could be done in forty-eight hours, but Hendy stopped in seven cities to scrutinize the route and line up crack salesmen as guides. Along the way, he challenged big-car conventional wisdom and plugged the Model T to local reporters. "The light car will win," he said, simply, in Laramie.

Finally, the race itself neared. On Thursday, June 10, when the cars had yet to reach even Oakley, Hendy predicted a first-place Ford arrival in Denver by noon Friday, ginning up excitement among the city's "autocranks." When one harrowing telegram after another arrived, Hendy revised his prediction into the weekend. "I want to say," he told the *Post* on Friday, "that in making my estimate yesterday as to the arrivals in Denver, I overlooked that Colorado was suffering from Seattle weather." Still, he remained confident that one or both Fords would arrive first, whenever that might be.

Now it was Saturday night, clock ticking, deadline closing in for the big Sunday editions. No official word had come since the last checkpoint at Limon that afternoon, a hundred miles southeast, where the Shawmut had beaten the two Fords by fifty minutes. Though the No. 1 Model T had to pause there for repairs, the No. 2 kept going, determined to overtake the Shawmut and dash into Denver first that night. But eight and a half hours had elapsed since Limon, with no sign of the cars at the Savoy.

A roar snapped heads toward the street, louder than the usual purr and rumble of cars going by. The No. 2 was here, led by Stuart Alkire, one of Hendy's trusted pilots, a top mechanic from the Denver branch. They had passed the Shawmut, stuck in quicksand, about halfway from Limon. Three reporters clocked the Ford's check-in at 10:47 PM, a fourth at 10:48—enough time to dictate a story.

MUD-BESPATTERED OCEAN TO OCEAN RACERS ARRIVE, the Sunday *Post* headline would declare. FORD, NO. 2, FIRST TO REACH DENVER; OTHERS LAG BEHIND. MUD! MUD! THEY SAY. The ensuing report was dramatic—and dominated by the account of the newly arrived Ford team: "The mud-bespattered travelers had touching tales to tell—tales of anxiety and hardship, of hail and rain, of muddy roads—oh! such muddy roads." Curiously, the *Post* even claimed that the No. 1 Model T arrived close behind its leading sibling, giving Ford an emphatic one-two punch into Denver, while leaving the other competitors unmentioned. The paper must have taken the Ford side's word on deadline. In reality, the No. 1 T remained stuck far out in the mud with the Shawmut.

While that *Post* story ran inside, Denver's big *Sunday News-Times* reserved a page-one slot for the Ford arrival. That flagship paper, a joint Sunday edition of the daily *Rocky Mountain News* and *Denver Times*, treated Denverites to an exclusive interview with exhausted Ford driver Bert Scott, who "picked the cakes of dry mud from his hair, ears and neck" as he described that day's grueling run. Over a nearly sixteen-hour, 180-mile slog, Scott and Smith needed their block and tackle eight times to drag the car from the mire. They used six gallons of lubricating oil "to keep the machine in running order, the mud having penetrated to every portion of the engine"—an astonishing figure, equal to six full oil changes in a day.

With all that muck and quicksand, Scott thought the big cars would be in for trouble, and that they might not see any of them again before the finish line, if at all. The *Sunday News-Times* affirmed that prediction with a matter-of-fact declaration of its own, right there on page one: "The Ford No. 2 has been named by many as the probable winner in the big race and unless it meets with a serious mishap it will reach Seattle with a good lead." Never mind that fifteen hundred uncertain miles remained, or that the Shawmut might only be hours behind, no way to know. The "named by many" prediction had Hendy's fingerprints all over it.

Thirty-nine hours. That's how long it took the Shawmut to cover the 190 miles from the Kansas-Colorado border Friday evening to Denver Sunday morning, arriving to find those papers praising and predicting victory for the No. 2 Ford.

The Boston men had entered Colorado with a modest lead, squeaking ahead of the Fords by crossing a swollen stream on a low railroad bridge; one of the Model Ts got stuck in three feet of water, while the other tried the bridge but had to bail when a train approached. The bleak and boggy conditions of western Kansas carried over into Kit Carson County,

Colorado, no respect for state lines. With the sun dipping in the west, the Shawmut team stopped at the first town they reached: Burlington, the county seat, just a few miles in.

The 1900 census pegged Burlington at 183 people, but it had grown now to 300, with a solid new courthouse downtown, a couple of horse dealers, and two hotels that catered to railroad travelers and cattle traders. Still, the streets were dirt, and there was no electricity. The Shawmut stopped outside the Montezuma, a two-story lodging house with a porch in front and a privy out back. When Earle Chapin and his teammates had last laid their heads on hotel pillows, it was that nap at the Hotel Jefferson last Monday. They might have imagined driving straight through to Seattle, sleeping only in the back of the moving car. But the conditions in Kansas and Colorado had proven too brutal. Thursday night they'd been forced to stop at that farmhouse around Mingo, and here they were tying up again, twenty-four hours later.

Chapin drew two sheets of hotel stationery, unadorned save for the name of the Montezuma and its proprietor. He missed Anita dearly. Two weeks had passed since he'd seen her; next week would be their first wedding anniversary, and they'd be twenty-five hundred miles apart. "We have had hard plugging the last 3 or 4 days so we are going to have a good sleep, and hit out toward Denver to-morrow," he wrote. "Honey you don't know what storms are we hit one last night and you would think the house was going to go"—that rattling farmhouse—"but had we been 100 miles west we would have been up against a hail storm and they were as big as hens eggs, broke windows and came through some of the roof."

Neither of them had ever been anywhere remotely this far west before, a landscape so sweeping and unpopulated as to be unimaginable in New England, where the craggy farmland that existed had been pried from dense forest and rocky soil. He tried to convey what he'd encountered here, out on the treeless prairie, a land of homesteaders adapted to sod. "You ought to see some of the houses they are made of mud but are cozy as can be all plastered and papered," he wrote. "I sure will be glad when I'll be with you but dearie I think we will have better going from now on."

He told her they were in first, if only by a little, closing with a tender coda.

I am ever your sweet heart with all my love hugs and kisses.

Earle
Remember me to mother.

The Fords reached Burlington ninety minutes behind the Shawmut, making the same wise decision to stop for the night.

The Boston car departed first, leaving at dawn. The wagon roads were channels of muck, crossed periodically by railroad tracks, swollen irrigation ditches, and roiling streams. They churned onward toward the Limon checkpoint, covering the eighty miles in eight hours, no sign of the Fords behind them. Arriving around 12:45 PM, they stayed barely a half hour, just long enough to get their passports endorsed, sign the cards for Seattle, scrape off some gumbo, and wire an update to Horace Waite, the general manager in Boston. "Roads heavy. Are making good time. Fine guide to Denver. Car in first class condition."

They believed they held a two-hour lead. But just five minutes after the Shawmut left, the Fords roared in; they had plowed over the mud from Burlington to Limon much faster.

From there, the No. 2 left quickly to chase the Shawmut, while the No. 1 hung back to fix a broken spring. Hard as it was to believe, the conditions west of Limon were even worse. The Blue Book prepared by the pathfinder hinted at this, noting that the wagon roads leading to Denver could be "very muddy," while offering a nominally helpful tip: "There are, however, several cut offs across the open prairie, which provide better going in wet weather. These turns are hard to locate without a guide thoroughly familiar with the country." Typical.

That afternoon and the next morning, the crews would "borrow" more pigpen roofs and chicken-coop planks than they had salvaged even in western Kansas, wedging them under the wheels to nudge their cars through one mud pit after another, while relying heavily on block and tackle too. The No. 2 passed the Shawmut around the halfway mark, squirming ahead near Sand Creek, the Ford men leading the car through high water like a horse. Now in first, that Model T fought on toward Denver—toward Hendy and those waiting reporters—on Saturday night, while the Shawmut and the Kulick-Harper Ford spent the night out on the soggy plains, huddled under tarps as the mercury dropped into the forties.

Each crew waited until daylight to free their cars from the mire, and then the Shawmut and No. 1 Ford resumed the slog toward Denver, arriving around the same time, roughly 8:30 AM Sunday. There they could read in the *Post* about the No. 1's supposed arrival with the No. 2 the night before.

Adman Harper, the wordsmith of the Ford crew, gave an interview to *The Denver Republican*, calling the conditions the most horrific they'd encountered. "I don't see how they could have been worse. In places we had to literally pick up our car and carry it for several hundred feet in order to find ground sufficiently firm to admit of any progress by means of the engines," he said, though that beggared belief. With an automobile as light as the Model T, two men could typically raise one end with relative ease, but lifting and carrying a thousand-pound car the length of a football field was another matter.

But just to make sure Colorado readers weren't insulted, Harper praised the locals along the route for being welcoming, contrasting it with a Missouri farmer he claimed had pulled a gun on them after they spooked his horse some days back. "Even the Colorado horse seems to have more sense than the Missouri animal," he said, "and I wish that this dear old state extended West as far as Seattle."

Hendy was in charge now. He wanted each Ford fully overhauled and the crews rested before they left Denver. That meant the No. 2 would depart in a few hours, while the Kulick-Harper Ford would hang back until evening. Although there would be small-town dealers scattered the rest of the way, Hendy's showroom marked the final Ford branch house until Seattle—the last chance for factory-trained mechanics to comb every inch of these cars in a well-stocked company garage. That kind of care couldn't be rushed, a worthy investment even if it meant separating the two Fords, instead of the usual tandem travel.

The Shawmut team had no such luxury, determined to leave Denver as close as possible to the first Model T. They dashed off a message to Waite in Boston, their typically chipper-but-spare telegram voice tempered by losing the lead amid miserable conditions, though they anticipated firmer roads ahead on the way to Wyoming. "In second. Ford first. Got in quick sand thirty miles east. More muddy than ever. Better [to] Cheyenne. Other cars far behind. . . . Will keep right at it. Car in first class condition. Used chain [all] week."

Chapin penned a postcard to Anita. "Reached Denver all right. hard going," he wrote, with "mud and creeks all day." Rather than dwell on the quicksand, he told her he could see snow atop the Rockies from here, even in June. He thought the next stage of the race would be better. Denver had certainly become a big auto town, and the 120-mile route to Cheyenne had emerged as a popular recreational drive, a flat run due north along the edge of the High Plains that capable motorists could manage in a day.

The Denver Motor Club had even marked some of the route with signs. Last August, in a race sponsored by the *Post*, one daredevil covered the distance in just three hours and thirty-four minutes, shattering the previous four-hour record and rivaling the train time. The car that did it was a Chalmers-Detroit Forty, an automobile much more like the Shawmut than the Model T. Colorado had no speed limits—no motor-vehicle laws yet of any kind—making it easy to imagine the powerful Shawmut beating the Ford on this run by an hour or more. And the Shawmut had secured a good guide, an accomplished driver who had managed Denver's REO and Studebaker agencies, meaning they could open the throttle without fear of losing the trail.

Noon came and went. The No. 2 Ford rumbled out around 12:50 PM, guided by a pilot Hendy recruited from Cheyenne, with the Shawmut close behind. They made good time through Brighton, twenty miles out, passing so rapidly that a local paper said the cars left only "a cloud of dust and a strong gasoline [odor] in their wake."

But then another storm reared its head, hours of rain punctuated with hail so intense it brought down a hot-air balloon over Denver—the aerialist survived, plunging into a lake—and contributed to the death of a five-year-old girl along the corridor to Cheyenne. Just a few miles from where the Ford and Shawmut were being pelted, a homesteader caught out in the open in a wagon tried to race home while protecting his young daughter under a heavy blanket at his feet, a split-second decision that apparently caused the child to suffocate.

The Shawmut and No. 2 Ford crews pulled over for the worst of the hail and waited it out under rubberized blankets. When it passed, they made their way over messy roads that sapped the Shawmut's speed advantage. The Ford held a modest lead at the border, where they crossed into Wyoming by the expansive Terry Ranch, a cattle-and-sheep concern owned by multimillionaire U.S. Senator Francis E. Warren. The Civil War veteran had made his way to Cheyenne when it was still a shantytown where seemingly everyone slept with a revolver under the pillow, then rode savvy investments and good timing into a kingly fortune, amid Cheyenne's emergence as the "Magic City of the Plains," awash in livestock and mining wealth. In 1903, Warren's ranch hosted President Theodore Roosevelt for a five-course dinner that drew 125 leading citizens from around the area, converging by conventional horsepower. Just six years later, Cheyenne had become so auto-happy that if they did it all over again nearly everyone would have come by motor car except perhaps for Teddy Roosevelt himself, who made a habit of being photographed on horseback.

The No. 2 Ford reached the Cheyenne checkpoint fifteen minutes ahead of the Shawmut, a little after 7 PM. There at the Inter-Ocean Hotel, the crews agreed they would not set off again until 7 AM, resting overnight and preserving their tie until morning.

That same evening, Charlie Hendy boarded a Union Pacific train in Denver, bound for points northwest. Like many of the tourists at the Union Depot, he was—in a way—bound for Seattle and the fair, just not immediately. First he would make his way through Wyoming, to smooth the path for the two Model T Fords.

9

Beware the Unexpected

Wyoming, June 13 to 14, 1909

Shawmut driver Arthur Pettengill wasn't the epistolary sort, but from the high-altitude West he penned three hundred words to J. C. Kerrison of the *Boston Evening American*, one of the best-known auto writers in the East, who shared the letter in print. "This is the hardest kind of a hard run, and yet up to date we have had no great difficulties," Pettengill wrote, with small-town Yankee restraint, even as he alluded to the rain that pummeled them across Kansas and Colorado, and nodded now to the dramatic rock formations of Wyoming. He said they'd sweated out a few close calls, once skidding to a halt just inches from a sheer drop. "The boys crawled out of the car as best they could, and we pulled out in [an] easy manner."

Still, they were running neck and neck with the Fords. Other than tires, they hadn't changed so much as a spark plug since New York. Though the light weight of the Model Ts gave them an edge in the muck, Pettengill predicted that the power and durability of the Shawmut would see it through in the end, barring an accident.

"The car is good and true," he wrote. "It is the unexpected we are afraid of, and this unexpected will probably strike us in the dark hours of driving, when we cannot see more than ten feet in front of us."

Pettengill was right to fear the unexpected. But with Charlie Hendy coasting ahead by rail, an accident wasn't the only thing they needed to worry about.

The route across southern Wyoming unfurled over nearly five hundred miles, from Cheyenne to Cokeville, with three checkpoints along the way. The first was the most lavish, Cheyenne's Inter-Ocean, with signatures of multiple American presidents on the register, fresh oysters hauled in by rail, and rooms with bath starting at $3 a night. This was where the No. 2 Ford and the Shawmut agreed to hang up for the night, recuperating from that hail-battered drive from Denver, to leave together in the morning.

The Shawmut men could scarcely forget what happened the last time they went to bed with a similar understanding, six days back in St. Louis, only to be jolted awake at the Jefferson to the news that the Fords had raced off in the dark. That gave the Model Ts the edge to Glasgow, where that ferry took them across and never came back. *Hard to believe that was a coincidence,* the Shawmut men felt.

Two other things stuck in their craw, beyond the considerable advantage—unfair, if technically legal—that the Fords enjoyed from their network of garages and guides. The stripped-down nature of the Model Ts made it easy to get a good look at their axles. Pettengill thought that the axles on the No. 2 looked black in New York, only to appear light in Kansas City, then black again later, as if maybe they'd been changed and changed again, violating Rule 3. It was hard to prove, a question of impression and memory. But the other thing they were sure about: From glimpses they'd caught of the No. 1 Ford in that slog through western Kansas and eastern Colorado, they were convinced that star driver Frank Kulick had left the car at Oakley and returned at Limon, a gap of 180 miles over a day and a half. Under Rule 2, if a crew member left the car—like the Itala's hospitalized Gus Lechleitner, in Chicago—he couldn't return.

Chewing it over, they kept the axle part to themselves. But the Shawmut crew decided to blow the whistle on Kulick, sending a message to Guggenheim's office in Seattle accusing Kulick of leaving the No. 1 Model

T. And they resolved to give the Fords a taste of what happened in St. Louis, merely feigning that they would stay overnight in Cheyenne.

Both crews went around the corner to Frank Wright's Capitol Garage on West Seventeenth, ostensibly to rinse the mud, refuel and re-oil, and store the cars overnight. It was an impressive place, attesting to the rapid growth of motoring in the developed corners of the West. Three years back, Wright had opened the city's first small garage, as a bicycle repairman expanding to work on automobiles too. Cheyenne lay along the principal motoring route through the West, so he figured tourist traffic would only grow, especially as more decided to try automobile adventures from, say, Denver to Yellowstone or even California.

But motoring had exploded *within* Cheyenne too. Now the city of eleven thousand people boasted 127 automobiles and motorcycles. Copycat garages had opened, but Wright had expanded to remain the leader, with indoor storage for thirty-three cars, a battery-charging station, a drop pit for repairs, and even an outdoor tank for gasoline, with a special pump to funnel that fuel indoors while straining it to remove impurities, no need to ladle it from a barrel and filter it through a chamois cloth here. He'd become a dealer for three popular lines, too: Overland, Great Smith, and Ford.

That's right—this was one more place where the Model Ts would get kid-glove treatment, the No. 2 now and the No. 1 whenever it arrived from Denver. One of Charles Hendy's top agents, Wright made sure to capitalize on the race with advertisements in the local papers. "Watch the Fords Go By," his *Wyoming Tribune* ad boasted. "The Leading Cars in the New York to Seattle Race are Two Model 'T' Fords. Keep Your Eye on Them." He'd even gone down to Denver with one of his men to guide the Ford team back up over the border firsthand, piloting the No. 2 into Cheyenne in the lead.

For once this was a good thing for the Shawmut. If the No. 2 was about to get a stem-to-stern tune-up, it would be easier to make a nimble break and leave that rival car and crew flat-footed. The Boston men played it close to the vest, telegraphing word of their plan back home and quietly looping in their local guide, Will Barnett, president of the new Cheyenne Motor Club, who kept his car at Wright's Capitol Garage. "Will get a good lead," the men wired to Boston, adding that the bad weather seemed to be behind them, promising firm footing ahead in the dark.

Pettengill, Chapin, and Messer ate supper, fought the urge to sleep, and slipped back to the garage from the Inter-Ocean after 1 AM, convening with Barnett, a dynamic thirty-year-old dry goods retailer who'd made a small fortune selling corsets, cutlery, and chinaware to Cheyenne's burgeoning consumer class, but whose heart belonged to his big new Oldsmobile. Barnett wasn't the sort of pilot who was going to pile in amid the gear in the Shawmut. He brought his own car and chauffeur—Lial Branson, not yet twenty-one but already one of Wyoming's top mechanics and drivers—along with Branson's father, a rancher turned real estate agent.

The two-car convoy pulled out around 2 AM, aiming to make Laramie by daybreak, a sixty-mile run over mostly rolling grassland that included a sharp climb up remote Sherman Hill—highest point on the transcontinental railroad, more than eighty-two hundred feet above sea level—and an even sharper descent down the far side, where jagged rocks and sloping ranches would eventually give way to the Laramie Plains, a fertile valley amid the Rockies.

The roads were muddier than they'd expected, making for slow going over Sherman Hill, the Shawmut's headlights fighting the darkness. Beyond the western slope, the ranches included one in a place called Tie Siding, drawing fresh ire from Cheyenne and Laramie motorists alike. With the county road impassable due to spring flooding and mudslides, drivers had been cutting through the pasture of a homesteader named August Borgeman, prompting Borgeman to post hand-painted signs on both ends of his ranch: "NOTICE" ALL AUTOMOBILES GOING THIS ROAD TO CHEYENNE MUST PAY 50¢. Autoists blasted the "old German" in print as a luddite and profiteer. In fact, Borgeman was neither old (thirty-three) nor inherently anti-auto. He was simply worried about the safety of his five children and frustrated by shortcut-seeking drivers who'd snipped his barbed wire or left his gates open, allowing his cattle to escape. He was also fed up with the ones who'd gotten stuck in the mud and begged for help, only to roar off with barely a thanks when he used his horses to pull them out. The family kept watch during the day to collect the toll, but at night the ranch was quiet.

By sunrise the Shawmut had passed the last of the alfalfa and oat fields leading into Laramie, a city of eighty-two hundred that was equally rough-hewn and polished, a rail hub of stockyards and factories and a cosmopolitan college town. The Western humorist Bill Nye had called it a place where "a man with a $5 suit of clothes and a bobtail genealogy" was as good as anyone else—but it was also a city where people with money were now shelling out for motor cars, sixty automobiles and counting.

Except unlike the East, the car here was already less a status symbol than a practical tool. Rare for a city of its size and stature, Laramie lacked a streetcar system. "Thus it is that the ranchman and the real estate dealer, the professional man and the county official, the tourist and the pleasure seeker have found the automobile indispensable," a young Laramie lawyer had written recently in *The Horseless Age*, making the case that a moderately priced $1,800 auto could compete favorably with the $450 for a wagon, team, and harness, once you factored in feed, shoes, and veterinary care and considered it on a per-mile basis.

It was now 5:30 AM, an hour past sunrise. Though the Shawmut men had taken turns trying to nap on the overnight drive, they were surely too tired to gauge whether the air here was as "pure and filled with electricity and ozone, which give it a snap at once energizing and delightful," as Laramie's promotional brochures claimed. Any bite they felt was the cold, the early-morning mercury still below fifty, amid the chilly nights and hot days of high-altitude June. Will Barnett and Lial Branson in the Oldsmobile guided them up South Second past Custer Street, where brick storefronts replaced wood, toward their latest destination: Lovejoy Novelty Works, the unrivaled center of motoring in Wyoming.

Elmer Lovejoy, the thirty-seven-year-old proprietor, had a gift for breathing life back into the most benighted contraptions, revered locally for his ability to fix everything from broken wash boilers to balky phonograph players. He'd achieved wider renown over the last eleven years as the father of automobiling in Wyoming, after assembling the first functioning horseless carriage in the state—and one of the first anywhere west of the Mississippi. Early on, Lovejoy designed an ingenious steering knuckle that he traded to the Locomobile Company, though he parted with the rights for short money and the first factory-built automobile shipped into Wyoming. Later he would invent the first motorized garage-door opener. Already he'd founded the state's first motoring club, drawn its first reliable auto maps, and expanded his Novelty Works into Wyoming's first reliable garage, ahead of even Frank Wright in Cheyenne. He'd assisted the Thomas Flyer's pathfinding journey in the spring and guided the New York–to–Paris racers the year before. Long-distance motorists from Denver, Salt Lake City, and beyond routinely sought Lovejoy's guidance, whether they were aiming for Yellowstone or the coast.

As a Franklin dealer, Lovejoy had no allegiance in the Ocean-to-Ocean Race. But as a Diamond tire man, he signed on to help Shawmut. Though he didn't have the time to take them all the way to Seattle—they asked—he promised to guide them to Rawlins, 130 rough-and-tumble miles west. The drive would take all day. Then he could ride the train back and open the shop again in the morning. Any crew would have been thrilled to have him. After a shared breakfast, they set off before 7 AM on June 14, alone in the lead, Lovejoy on board. They must have felt their luck was picking up.

The telegraph and telephone lines paralleled the Union Pacific tracks. Word crackled in both directions that the Shawmut was on the move, stealing a march on Ford. In Cheyenne, Scott and Smith snapped into action, pushing the No. 2 T as fast as it could go, making hay in the daylight in a state with no speed limits, except in a few cities. Out west in Rawlins, Charlie Hendy got the news by phone from his dealer in Laramie. Ford's Denver branch manager had been working his way incrementally westward by rail, ensuring the pilots he'd lined up previously were properly in place. Now he turned back toward the coming cars, an ace up his sleeve.

Even with an overnight lead and an expert guide like Lovejoy, the Shawmut crew knew the day would bring a dogfight with the No. 2. The other cars were much farther back. The last reports had the No. 1 Ford still in Colorado. After lingering in Denver for an overhaul, that car got only halfway to Cheyenne amid the evening storm before stopping for the night in Greeley. The Acme was at least 250 miles behind, not yet in Denver, while the Itala journey had descended into full-blown disaster.

That star-crossed import had finally reached Glasgow, Missouri, the previous afternoon, five days behind the leaders. The Itala crew found the ferry was still out of service, whether or not it had broken down by coincidence or the ferryman had been persuaded it was time for an overhaul. Hearing about the Shawmut, they drove carefully across that towering railroad bridge. As the bridge crossed from the Glasgow bluffs to low-lying bottomland on the west side, it continued in elevated fashion for over a mile before finally giving way again to tracks on solid ground.

Bert Bellows had cleared the water and was nearing the end of the bridge when the boss of a Chicago & Alton section gang approached on a railroad handcar. He told him they had to "see" him before they could proceed. The Itala men said they'd gotten permission from the station agent across the river in Glasgow, and he should let them pass. That's when things got heated. It didn't help that they had ITALA splashed on both sides of their car, at a time when American newspapers bristled with alarming headlines about Italian anarchists and about emerging organized-crime networks employing the tactics of "the Black Hand," with an alleged plot to assassinate a Chicago detective broken up just days before. They were arguing so long that a freight train came up from behind, the Itala still on the tracks. Bellows, Whittemore, and Lillie jumped from the car, watching as the train slammed into the rear of the expensive automobile. The Itala skidded along the rails before tumbling down an embankment, with the force crushing the big gasoline tank mounted on the rear, knocking off a secondary tank, wrenching the front axle, and throwing the whole frame out of alignment. Hardly sympathetic, the section gang taunted the Itala crew as "dagos" and told them it served them right. Now the Itala was limping toward Kansas City, one of the men nursing gasoline into the engine from a can in his lap.

At the same time out in Wyoming, the Shawmut hurtled across wide-open country, jagged but unbroken by development, just a single town larger than 250 people along the all-day route between Laramie and Rawlins. Many of the names on the map were merely railroad stops, created for steam trains to take on fresh coal and water, with a telegrapher, a tiny depot, and a section house crammed with immigrant track workers.

The sun climbed higher and hotter, no shade in sight. The Shawmut passed Rock River, near where Butch Cassidy and his gang had used dynamite to pull off an outlandish rail heist a decade before, and Como Bluff, a ridge of variegated hues where a surprise discovery by railroad workers had revealed a bounty of dinosaur bones, scattered like matchsticks. It was around 11:30 when they reached Medicine Bow, an evocative name that resonated back East. The town had become famous as the setting for part of Owen Wister's runaway bestseller *The Virginian*, the 1902 cowboy novel that captivated city readers, tapped into a swirl of feelings around the vanishing frontier, and just about single-handedly created a new genre.

For all the book's conjured imagery—the stoic gunslinger, the sneering rival, and the prim schoolteacher, who eventually comes around and rides off with the cowboy after the gunfight—Medicine Bow turned out to be modest. The cluster of shops, saloons, and scattered homes near the depot housed an in-town population of twenty-eight families, sixty-six single men, and six single women, while supporting sheep and cattle ranches in the surrounding country as well. Still, a pair of developers were so bullish on Medicine Bow's literary fame, as well as the region's wool and mineral prospects, that they were erecting a massive hotel to be called The Virginian, its concrete shell already looming downtown.

The Shawmut stopped just long enough for Chapin to scribble a note to Anita, on a postcard of the Rockies he'd been carrying since Colorado:

All O.K.
better roads.
Earle.

The wires reported that the No. 2 Ford had left Laramie around 10, cutting the Shawmut's overnight edge nearly in half. At that pace they might slice the lead in half again by Medicine Bow, and catch them by Fort Steele, the last landmark before the Rawlins checkpoint.

They all had Steele in their sights, the Wyoming route's version of Glasgow, with a railroad bridge over a river. Here a decommissioned fort sat on a bluff above the west bank of the North Platte River, a remnant of what they called the Indian Wars, and of the protection the U.S. Army provided for the westward construction of the Union Pacific a generation back. The railroad now crossed the river on a modern steel-and-concrete span erected in 1901, more resistant than the previous timber bridge to damage from errant locomotive cinders or the powerful current of spring floods below. Because the wagon trail and the railroad followed the same general path, the automobile route across southern Wyoming also ran through Fort Steele, though the latest in a series of rickety wagon bridges there had washed away in May.

No matter; Shawmut guide Elmer Lovejoy knew the drill. Automobiles rarely came through Fort Steele. When the occasional car did appear, the station agent at the depot was fine with waving them across the railroad bridge, as long as no train was due.

But still the Shawmut had forty-five miles to cover from Medicine Bow to get there, and then another fifteen beyond Fort Steele to Rawlins, the checkpoint where Lovejoy would turn around. About halfway to Steele they would hit Hanna, a Union Pacific coal-mining city of roughly 1,000, where over 220 men had been killed in a trio of explosions and cave-ins in the past six years. As with many railroad havens, Hanna also had a reputation for attracting hoboes and tramps. When the Thomas Flyer stopped there in April, a clutch of men sleeping in the roundhouse so resented being displaced that they tried to attack the crew, who fought them off with wrenches. Fending for himself, the celebrity pedestrian Edward Payson Weston—now moving just a few days ahead of the Ocean-to-Ocean Race—feared the same might happen around Hanna. So the sinewy seventy-year-old started packing a revolver, though he acknowledged to *The New York Times* that the gun would most likely be turned on him in an attack. Deputies sent a protective convoy to encircle Weston, but not before he was assaulted by another Wyoming foe: the wind, which whipped so fiercely across the open range that a gale lifted Weston right off his feet, spilling him thirty feet down an embankment.

Little risk of that happening to the sturdy Shawmut, but the wind in the Hanna Basin surely contributed to feelings of isolation, just the four of them in the car—the crew and Lovejoy—churning across an expanse of brown, beige, and muted green. Occasional white patches interrupted the landscape, alkali deposits where even prairie grass and scrub cottonwood refused to grow. Mighty ridges hugged the horizon to the north and south, with snow-topped Elk Mountain rising 11,200 feet above sea level off to the left. This was sheep country—in a state of five million sheep and barely a hundred thousand people, both were concentrated near the Union Pacific rail corridor—but even the sheep were largely out of sight, grazing up in the mountains in summer, saving the sagebrush on the plains for winter. The only signs of civilization were the UP's steel rails and the telegraph and telephone lines beside them, winding close to the wagon trail in some places, bending away in others.

And yet: They couldn't shake the feeling that the Ford was breathing down their necks, even when it remained unseen behind them. The sun drifted into their eyes ahead, golden hour approaching. Finally, a band of deeper green broke the western horizon, the telltale grassy banks of a river in arid land. The North Platte.

The Fort Steele railroad bridge, for all its size, lay low on the horizon, a flush span carrying the tracks between the bluffs on both sides of the river, its superstructure entirely below deck. When they finally reached that bridge, they found a surprise waiting: two men who did not work for the railroad, one a Pinkerton type with a gun, the other Charlie Hendy. They weren't there to wave the Shawmut across.

10

"A Damned Crooked Deal"

Wyoming, June 14 to 16, 1909

Elmer Lovejoy had never seen anything like this before. Neither had the station agent, it became clear. Charlie Hendy—Ford man, former Union Pacific man—was determined to enforce an obscure regulation that no one could drive over the railroad bridge without official permission. And that permission couldn't come from the man at the Fort Steele depot, or the nearest dispatcher, or the railroad division point down in Laramie, but only from Union Pacific headquarters in Omaha. As for the armed guard, he was there to make sure "that Hendy's word went," Earle Chapin would remember.

Automobiles came through Fort Steele infrequently. There were just fourteen cars in all of Rawlins, the nearest city, and that was almost an hour's drive west. The shaky wooden Cosgriff Bridge nearby had finally given out in May, but wagons could reasonably ford the river here, anyway, except amid the worst swells. As for the occasional automobile, the railroad station man had been letting them use the Union Pacific bridge the last several weeks, just as he had before, given how infirm the wagon bridge was even before it washed away.

The same practice would hold true in another month, when Alice Ramsey and her pioneering party of "energetic young ladies" crossed Wyoming in their Maxwell touring car, "brown as berries" from the sun, as local papers put it. When Ramsey—that noted New Jersey chauffeuse, on an all-expenses-paid expedition conceived by her husband and backed by the Maxwell-Briscoe Company—reached the eastern bluff opposite Fort Steele in July, her companions walked across to ask permission, and then they waved back and she drove over the bridge. The hard part was all the thudding over the railroad ties, not the request.

How long could this take? the Boston crew wondered. They left the Shawmut on the eastern side, walking over the bridge toward the depot as dusk approached, mosquitoes buzzing along the banks. The station house was a little clapboard building nestled against the tracks; most trains came through here without stopping. The depot anchored the small community that persisted amid the remains of the fort, with a grocer, a baker, four saloons, and several rooming houses serving a mostly male population of cowpunchers, sheepmen, railroad section hands, and laborers at the nearby sawmill, which processed timbers floated down the North Platte from the mountains and milled them into mine props and railroad crossties.

The station agent was a thirty-five-year-old Kansan named Earl King, a career railroad man with a young family and an interest in English setters. He doubled as the local Pacific Express shipping agent and Western Union telegraph man, with a skill and sense of duty that would send him overseas in a decade as a wartime officer in the Army Signal Corps. Duty-bound here, the station man wired Shawmut's request to Omaha, 675 railroad miles away. It was past 6:30 PM, an hour to sunset on Monday, June 14. Then they waited.

The Shawmut crew had been going hard since 2 AM in Cheyenne, all day over rough country, only to get suddenly sidelined here. There was little alternative. About twenty-five miles south, the town of Saratoga had put up a rare iron bridge back in 1885, a long-term investment for wagons they were now trying to position as a lure for east-west autos, without much luck; coming from Cheyenne and Laramie, Saratoga was nestled on the far side of a daunting mountain range, no matter how sturdy its bridge might be. You could get there driving south from Fort Steele, but it was tricky in the dark. Plus there was a report the town might have been swamped by flooding. All of that made it too risky for the Shawmut to try for Saratoga at night, never mind the potential challenge of finding the route again on the other side.

So they stayed, watching their lead evaporate. The No. 2 Ford arrived and immediately crossed the bridge with permission Hendy had secured in advance, passing into first. If there was a mote of justice for the Shawmut, it was watching the pounding the smaller car took as it slammed up and down between the open railroad ties over the water, like a hundred unavoidable potholes. Eventually the Ford reached the western bank, wobbling off toward Rawlins.

Night fell, the Boston men marinating in frustration. In the morning, they learned that the No. 2 Ford was still only sixteen miles ahead, stuck in Rawlins. Clearly banged up by the bridge, the car had attempted to continue past that checkpoint city but lost a wheel another six miles out. It needed to be towed by a team of horses back to Rawlins, where it waited on supplies from Rock Springs, a bigger city four hours west by rail. To the east, the trailing No. 1 Ford had stopped for the night in Medicine Bow, meaning it should close in on Fort Steele at any moment.

The Shawmut crew sent a Western Union message to Boston, a pay-per-word telegram stripped of emotion: "Delayed at Fort Steel[e] waiting for permit to cross R.R. bridge. Wagon bridge washed away. Ford got permit last night. Guide crossed before. No permit [needed]. Wired for one last night. Will get across this morning. No [car] trouble. One tire. Roads very bad. Awfully hot in foot hills."

But when Earle Chapin sat down to write to Anita, he didn't hold back. "The Ford people put a game on us," he wrote on a postcard of a Wyoming cowboy and a bucking bronco. "They have done it all the way along."

In the same blue ink, he scrawled a second postcard, this one a black-and-white photograph of the very railroad span that taunted them over the North Platte. "Was ahead up to this bridge," he wrote, "but was held up, no permit to cross."

Americans were mailing nearly a billion postcards a year, using them mainly for quick messages—*you'd love it here; meet me at the station at 3; I ran into your cousin; I promise to write later*—that could be sent for a penny, a cheap alternative to pricey telegrams or exorbitant phone calls. But real writing meant one thing: a letter in an envelope, mailed with a two-cent stamp. With plenty of time, Chapin drew two sheets of cream paper, ruled with baby-blue lines. It had been nearly three weeks since he'd heard Anita's voice or gazed into those eyes. He'd received just two letters from her this whole time, forwarded through the Diamond tire network, each one mailed many days before. They both felt the distance and separation acutely, with their first wedding anniversary on Thursday.

Missing it was hard to justify, but the race had seemed the last, best chance to prove the Shawmut's worth and revive the business, with a nice purse in it for the crew. How naïve they'd been. Now he just ached to be back in Stoneham with Anita. He dipped his pen in the ink, pressing hard at times: "This is the first chance I have had to write you for some time and dearie it is a time when we ought to be on the road. We are at Fort Steel Wyo. held up from crossing the river on account of the Ford Co. having the Union Pacific R.R. Co enforse a law stopping cars crossing without a permit, which comes way from Omaha," he wrote, calling it "a damned crooked deal."

He told her he longed to "be back in my own Morris chair saying wait a little while before we go to bed, yes?" Though the Shawmut itself was holding up just fine—despite being "too heavy for these roads," compared with the Fords—"win or loose I don't give a dam," Chapin wrote, in thwarted exasperation. "I want to be home more than I ever did."

Chapin wasn't the only one who considered it a "damned crooked deal." Receiving only the slimmest wire update from remote Fort Steele, the national press glossed over the episode, ascribing it to bad luck on Shawmut's part and smart planning by Ford. But locals who witnessed the scene understood this for what it was, foul play by Hendy to derail the leader. Fort Steele had no newspaper, but the *Laramie Republican* reflected the mood two days later, after Elmer Lovejoy returned home: "The efforts of the Ford agent in preventing the passage of the Shawmut car over the railroad bridge at Fort Steele brought down upon his head the condemnation of many residents of that place, who considered the trick not good sport."

Charlie Hendy could weather the disapproval of the locals in a far-off town with no newspaper. He needed to impress one person—Henry Ford—and didn't need to linger in Fort Steele. Once the No. 1 caught the Shawmut, he took off for Rawlins too. But first, there was the matter of crossing that bridge, no picnic even with a permit.

"Crossing the ties was fierce," Hendy would write, describing how they "bounced and lurched around over the ties until we thought every wheel would break." The wheels on the Model T were thirty inches in diameter and three inches wide in front, and the same diameter but half an inch wider in back. Compared to wheels of the future, those T wheels were roughly twice as big in diameter but less than half as wide, making them more like skinny wagon wheels. Even at that circumference, they were still not long enough around to avoid plunging into the gaps between the ties on the bridge. New Jersey chauffeuse Alice Ramsey would describe the experience of crossing that bridge even more vividly than Hendy. "Feed a little gas! Let in the clutch! BUMP! Touch the brake, so the bump isn't so great it throws you out of rhythm. Repeat the process. BUMP! BUMP! BUMP!" Ramsey's Maxwell had thirty-two-inch wheels, just slightly bigger than those on the T. Confoundingly, the crossties seemed perfectly spaced to "hold the wheels as in a cradle and prevent moving ahead, unless the auto was kept in motion," Ramsey wrote. "By the time I had reached the end of the bridge I was in such dreadful pain from the jarring that I would not have been surprised to have developed appendicitis right straight off."

Here the Shawmut's larger size would provide a rare advantage, with those extra-large forty-inch wheels better suited for the bridge gaps. Finally word came back from Omaha, after about sixteen hours of waiting.

In third place now, the men darted over the bridge and started up the car, jostling over the ties and off toward Rawlins.

Checkpoint 22: The Ferris Hotel. Not long ago, Rawlins was one of the roughest "Hell on Wheels" towns that followed the advancing end of the railroad, bristling with gambling houses, saloons, and brothels, "a man for breakfast every morning" and all that. Now it was a burgeoning city with a hint of refinement, as a bustling Union Pacific repair hub, wool-and-livestock clearinghouse, and regional mining center, noted especially for nearby iron deposits that made "Rawlins Red" the paint color of choice for the Brooklyn Bridge and so many barns. An imposing but handsome $100,000 state prison, a sandstone castle topped with turrets, also put Rawlins on the map. Now the city boasted several fine Victorian homes, a Richardsonian Romanesque railroad depot, and that first-rate Ferris Hotel, with its lace curtains and electric lights. Still, the automobile hadn't really penetrated, with just those fourteen for a population of four thousand. Mainly they belonged to wealthy sheepmen, whose thousands of heads were scattered among camps far beyond Rawlins. With a car instead of a horse, they could inspect all their sheep bands in a mere day or two, instead of a week.

The Shawmut had driven on without Elmer Lovejoy, who had to turn back amid the Fort Steele holdup. Reaching Rawlins at eleven, they registered and met a new pilot, a complicated sheepman named Jack Booth who had come in off the range and was about to enter the horse barn, feed, and livery business amid a grim opening in Rawlins: The previous proprietor had accidentally shot and killed himself while trying to extricate a Colt pistol that had gotten tangled up in straps and string in a dresser drawer. Booth was a skilled bucking-bronco rider with a mustache as big as a prairie dog, and strong opinions to match. He'd once protested when he thought his taxes were too low, eager to critique local government and proud of the value of his ranch. Four years back, Booth and a brother had so objected to the looming nuptials of their kid sister—who at nineteen needed family permission under Wyoming law—that they fired several shots with their Winchesters in the direction of her suitor, after warning him to stay away. Nobody got hurt, the brothers got hauled into court, and the couple eloped to Colorado anyway, hard feelings persisting. The next year Booth ran for sheriff, albeit unsuccessfully. Somewhere along the way, he'd also invented a fence post that he insisted couldn't be pulled from the ground, but a dishonest patent lawyer had apparently stolen his idea, sold it to a corporation, and absconded to Canada. And yet whatever you might say about Jack Booth, he sure knew the Red Desert, an area nobody wanted to cross without a good guide.

The Shawmut took on fuel, oil, and water, and then they took off, eager to reclaim the lead, knowing both Fords were now tied up here in Rawlins for repairs after that pounding over the bridge. The roughly 130 miles ahead to the city of Rock Springs were as unforgiving as any on the continent, across that Red Desert and its Great Divide Basin, where the wind howls over a nearly treeless landscape, and where the scant rain that falls simply evaporates off the alkali flats or collects in bitter little creeks, instead of flowing toward the Atlantic or Pacific. Some found the wild beauty enchanting, but the charm eluded Robert Louis Stevenson, who had crossed by train a few decades back. Exhausted and lovesick at the time, the Scottish writer rued the view as "sage-brush, eternal sage-brush; over all, the same weariful and gloomy colouring, grays warming into brown, grays darkening towards black; and for sole sign of life, here and there a few fleeing antelopes."

Between Rawlins and Rock Springs, the scattered names on the map were mainly railroad coal-and-water stops that made Medicine Bow seem like a metropolis. In Wamsutter, roughly a third of the way, the Shawmut crew stopped and sent a late-afternoon telegram to Boston, letting Horace Waite know they'd regained the lead and were now "way ahead," with the car in good condition and a plan to make Granger tomorrow, the twenty-third checkpoint, another forty-five miles beyond Rock Springs. The Shawmut executive relayed the word to Boston auto writer J. C. Kerrison at the *American*, who reprinted the good news without aid of a

Wyoming atlas, situating the action in far-off "Waumsetter" and "Rollis." At Tipton, the next telegraph station down the line, a railroad operator clocked the Shawmut about five hours ahead of the two Fords, relaying the news that night to the Associated Press desk in Salt Lake City.

The long Ford layup for repairs in Rawlins at least meant Hendy could send those two cars out across the desert in a convoy with one good guide, while riding ahead himself by rail. He turned to D. V. Bell, a waterworks superintendent who helped direct the pumping system that supplied the Union Pacific with water along the parched corridor in between the North Platte River at Fort Steele and the Green River in Rock Springs. Before he turned his engineering expertise to water, Bell had come out from Pennsylvania in the early 1880s to assist with the drilling of some of Wyoming's first oil wells, when crude was prized as a source of illumination and lubrication. Gasoline then was an unloved byproduct of distillation—noxious, dangerously combustible, used mostly for cleaning. It had come into its own over the last decade as a motor fuel, boosting the demand for petroleum; for the first time, Wyoming in 1909 was on track to produce twenty thousand barrels. Still, at that level it scarcely factored into the state's identity or economics. But not for much longer; over the next decade, Wyoming would transform into a petroleum pump for the nation, producing nearly fourteen million barrels a year by 1919, for an America in thrall to the auto.

Blistering heat gave way to the chill of night. The three leaders drove on across powdery sands and "soda," the dried salt beds left behind by a vanished prehistoric ocean. The light Fords made better time over the shifting terrain, even as the No. 1 was hampered by a radiator leak. The Shawmut still held the lead around the halfway point, between Table Rock and Bitter Creek, near where the Thomas Flyer had gotten swallowed up amid the April thaw by a sinkhole of massive proportions. That forced the pathfinder crew to walk several miles, to recruit a railroad gang to try to dig out the car and lay wooden ties for traction. Even then, it took twenty men all day to liberate the Thomas and get it rolling: the pathfinder crew, the Swedish section boss, and a team of fifteen Japanese and Italian section hands—plus Guggenheim himself, an unlikely millionaire muck-shoveler. He happened to be passing by in a Pullman sleeper, on his way to Idaho to meet the governor and greet the pathfinder. He got off, doubled back, and delighted in lending a hand, despite plunging multiple times into the mire.

The Shawmut pressed on. Rain struck, as it sometimes does in the desert, an intense burst that can bring flash flooding. The two Fords sought shelter at the railroad section house at Table Rock. The Shawmut must have camped just down the line. In the early morning, the Boston car encountered its first mechanical trouble of the race. A minor engine problem forced a stop around Point of Rocks, about thirty miles before Rock Springs, near the ghostly remains of a sandstone-block and chinked-mud stagecoach station on the Overland Trail, the route that preceded the railroad. They got the Shawmut humming again in short order, but not before the Fords surged past to regain the lead.

Point of Rocks had a telegram station, and they sent another message to Waite. The engine might be working now, but the clutch was wearing out, and probably wouldn't make it to Seattle. They asked for a replacement, thinking about the time for an express shipment and calculating where they might be four or five days down the line. "Send disc clutch, spring, flywheel bolts Baker City," they wired, referring to a point 725 miles out in Oregon. "One bolt holds." They didn't mention the engine hiccup. "With Fords. One tire [replaced today]. Roads rough. Very hot."

Those Model Ts reached Rock Springs around 10:45 AM on Wednesday, June 16, about seventy-five minutes ahead of the Shawmut. The city was a commercial haven on the far side of the Red Desert, a mining and railroad hub of roughly five thousand people, the fourth largest city in Wyoming. The mines yielded nearly a million tons annually of high-quality coal, drawing workers of forty-one nationalities. That diversity had become a point of pride in promotional literature, but Rock Springs remained notorious for an 1885 massacre, when European miners who thought they were being undercut by Chinese workers torched the community's densely settled Chinese quarter. Coal wealth had given Rock Springs an array of fine homes, two banks, two newspapers, four schools, and a downtown aglow with electricity. The railroad defined the contours of the city, with the main tracks of the UP splitting the bustling shopping district; manicured lawns framed the depot, and a pedestrian bridge straddled the tracks, connecting the two sides of downtown. A few blocks southwest, the railroad operated a massive freight yard.

Hendy was here, waiting. When the Fords arrived, he guided them down to that freight yard, where the Rock Springs Lumber Company waited to provide a proper tune-up. Much more than a lumberyard, the company served as the community's leading general contractor, wholesale and retail supplier of building materials and hardware, and purveyor of farm implements and wagons. The big firm had branched into Fords about a year earlier, after the owner fell in love with his bright red touring car and became an agent for Hendy, with a proper garage too. This was the dealership that had shipped those parts to Rawlins for the repairs the day before.

Just before the No. 2 entered the garage, a photographer captured the scene, with a crowd of two dozen gathered in the dirt around the car. The Ford's undercarriage provided the only shade in sight, and a dog lazed beneath the chassis. Grit, sand, and soda covered almost every inch of the car's surface, encrusting even Bert Scott and Jimmie Smith's goggles. Hendy stood erect at the far end of the gathering in a suit, tie, and high collar, hat cocked low, mouth set in a firm line. He studied the car, not the camera. "The crews were tired," he would write, so he decided to let them rest well into the afternoon, along with the tune-up. His presence caught the notice of a local reporter: "Hendy, the Ford Auto representative, is doing the trip in the train and stops off at each place to send his wires, and to see that the machines are in good shape. He is much interested in the race and is sanguine of the Fords winning out."

With those Fords at the garage, the Shawmut barreled into town three blocks over, stopping on North Front opposite the depot, along a block that included the post office and a theater. The crew ducked into a soda fountain called Peterson & Lerch, gulping some refreshment. Perhaps the bonbons beckoned—our candies *make the ladies bless the donor at every mouthful*, the confectioner boasted—but they'd be a melted mess by the time Earle Chapin reunited with Anita. They took off again quickly, riding west still with Jack Booth, who would take them all the way over the border to Montpelier, Idaho.

That was 160 miles away, impossible to make by nightfall, with some of the most daunting "roads" of the race in between: faint wagon trails that wandered far from the railroad for long stretches and zagged eventually through steep Nugget Canyon, a death trap in the dark. They would try instead to get halfway, aiming for Green River, Granger (the twenty-third checkpoint), and a little railroad town called Opal.

Hendy released the No. 2 Ford to chase the Shawmut around 2:40 PM, while the No. 1 stayed in the lumber company's garage until well after four. The two guides leading the Model Ts out of Rock Springs could not have been more different, but both knew the terrain—Dr. William C. C. Freeman, a University of Toronto–educated physician accustomed to making wide-ranging house calls, and Sam McCourt, a twenty-four-year-old coal miner whose older brother had just been elected sheriff. McCourt was tenacious, a prizefighter and sprinter who would later go to superhuman efforts to survive, after crashing through a dark bridge onto a frozen river in 1923. Regaining consciousness beneath the car with his leg broken, his shoulder blade fractured, and his face frozen to the ice, he would squirm and twist to fish out his pocketknife and hack himself free, nearly severing an ear, before crawling up a forty-foot embankment and collapsing at the threshold of his home.

The Shawmut held the lead to Green River, covering sixteen wagon-trail miles in a brisk hour. If not as bustling as Rock Springs, this was still a real town, a railroad division point with three hotels, two banks, a movie theater, and electric lights—amid a valley surrounded by jagged shale-and-sandstone cliffs that had captivated the pioneering Western painter Thomas Moran. One formation resembled a teapot; another, known as Castle Rock, loomed above downtown like a guard tower. In half a century, a double-barreled interstate tunnel would punch through the bottom of Castle Rock, carrying automobiles at speeds these 1909 motorists could scarcely imagine. As it was, the Shawmut—and the Fords a few hours behind—impressed the *Green River Star* by "getting over the ground at a lively clip."

Up next, thirty or so miles out, Granger was no Green River, an old stagecoach stop with a population of just a few dozen. But it had struck the pathfinder crew as the right distance from Rawlins (180 miles) for a checkpoint. And it had nice symbolism as the place where the railroad split, with the main line of the Union Pacific continuing southwest toward California, and the subsidiary Oregon Short Line peeling off toward Idaho and Oregon.

To reach Granger from Green River, the cars would need to cross Marston Wash, a normally dry gully that ruptured the landscape about two-thirds of the way out, roughly thirty feet deep and sixty feet across. The road between the two communities ran straight through the gulch as if someone had simply forgotten to build a bridge. If you were crazy enough to drive it, you dropped down one steep and sandy embankment to a bed a few feet across, then immediately needed to scramble up the other side. The alternative was little better: a long detour around that gully that led to a river known as Blacks Fork, often too deep to be forded this time of year. No wonder tourists wealthy enough to own a car often shipped them across Sweetwater County by rail.

The Shawmut crew made it, but it apparently cost them a tire. They reached Granger around 5:45 still in the lead, but they must have felt the little Fords pressing in from behind, scrambling down and up across the gulch with comparative ease. On the racing passport, the pathfinder men had misspelled the name of the checkpoint here, leaving off the "s" in Hotel Antlers, but the Shawmut team had no trouble finding it. The tiny downtown contained just two modest hostelries, one run by the deputy sheriff (the Antlers), the other by a justice of the peace who also oversaw the school board, sold insurance, drove a livery wagon, and dealt supplies to sheepmen.

Determined to make Granger a quick stop, the Shawmut crew stayed long enough to change a blown tire and send a telegram to Boston—and to see the No. 2 pull in beside them. "In first," the men reported to Waite. "One tire. Clutch paid. Will go on tonight. Crew in fine condition. Road dry but not dangerous."

Chapin glanced at the postcards, the town too small for a published scene that might show Anita what Granger looked like. He settled on one with embossed flowers around a blank box that someone had localized with glue and glitter, so that it read *Hello: From Granger Wyo.*

"Will try and make Opell tonight," Chapin wrote, meaning Opal, an equally small town another twenty-five miles out. That covering the distance might even be a question at 6 PM—this far west, at this time in June, with two more hours to sunset—spoke volumes about the terrain. But no need to worry Anita. "All O.K."

Mulling his guides like a hand of cards, Charlie Hendy was especially keen on one of the men he'd lined up in Granger, a feisty, angular forty-five-year-old cowboy named Edwin J. Thomas, known to some as "Skinny." The gunplay in his past made the shots that Shawmut guide Jack Booth had fired around his future brother-in-law seem like an innocent prank.

Thomas had run a big ranch of his own outside Rock Springs until 1904, when he got into a scrape with a sheepherder named John Alameda way out near Rawlins. Thomas opened fire, killing the horse underneath Alameda (whom the newspapers identified as "a Mexican," though he came from the Azores). The sheriff brought an attempted-murder charge, and Thomas bolted; during a long period on the run, his wife filed for divorce, seeking the ranch as alimony. Finally caught in Idaho in 1905, Thomas defended himself on extraordinary grounds. He was known to be such a crack shot—picking off rabbits on the run with a revolver—that if he'd really meant to shoot Alameda, he would have killed the man, not the horse. He got off with a fine, plus court costs, then staked out a new homestead near Granger.

The No. 1 Ford wasn't even in yet. Hendy sent the No. 2 off to the races with Thomas, the car getting out just ahead of the Shawmut. The other Ford rolled in over an hour later, turning around quickly to chase the two leaders. None made it farther than Opal, that little livestock-shipping town twenty-five miles past Granger. Going all the way to Nugget Canyon was too risky, though they might have tried to at least drive thirteen more miles to Kemmerer, the next town past Opal. But a flash storm hit, and all three agreed to tie up for the night. The Acme was stuck way back in northern Colorado, not yet even in Cheyenne; the poor Itala was just now entering Kansas. And yet sixteen days down, the three leaders remained knotted in a little town on the far side of Wyoming, altitude sixty-six hundred feet, population maybe fifty. It was the last night they would all be together.

11

Broken Down by Bancroft

Wyoming and Idaho, June 17 to 18, 1909

On the morning of June 17, the Shawmut would be first to falter, but not the last. The Fords got a fast start out of Opal to Kemmerer, the last supply point before a nearly fifty-mile stretch of open range. Kemmerer was another town built up by coal and defined by the railroad, booming from nonexistent to nearly a thousand people in twelve years, with a little bandstand opposite the depot and a grid of streets named for precious stones. Just sixteen days earlier—the same day the race started—a shopkeeper named James Cash Penney had left Kemmerer for bigger things in Salt Lake City, placing his Golden Rule store in the hands of an assistant, intent on growing the chain that would become J. C. Penney.

The two Ford crews sat down together to eat, likely at Tom Ming's Kemmerer Hotel Café, a rare all-hours dining room anchoring a downtown otherwise jammed with saloons, run by a popular Chinese cook who never let anyone leave hungry. It wasn't yet 8 AM. The Ford guys were just finishing breakfast when the Shawmut crew entered with Jack Booth, as if the three cars remained connected by invisible thread.

The Shawmut team ate quickly, determined to follow the Fords out through the sparsely populated corridor from Kemmerer to Cokeville, an L-shaped route over the rugged terrain where Wyoming hits Utah and Idaho. Crossing Rock Creek on a wagon bridge, the two Fords worked carefully through Nugget Canyon, with advertising man Harry Harper grateful that Frank Kulick was still handling the wheel beside him in the No. 1; evidently nothing had come of the Shawmut crew's complaint. "If you want any excitement, try that run . . . after a heavy rain," Harper would write, crafting copy for Ford. "There are down grades there, several of them up to 1,000 feet in length, averaging 30% where the roadway in places is six inches wider than the car tread and a slip means dashing hundreds of feet onto the rocks below. But don't do it unless you have a good driver, a cool, steady, level headed man, for the excitement may be too great."

The Shawmut ran aground near the canyon, busting one of the car's two steering arms, a small metal part near each front wheel essential to steering. Under an unrelenting sun, Earle Chapin spent three hours laboring before they could get rolling again. The car seemed to be all right, but the Fords were long gone.

It was deep into the afternoon by the time the Shawmut reached Cokeville, Wyoming, an Oregon Short Line Railroad community of about five hundred at the confluence of two rivers, which had made it a stopping point for wagon trains since the 1840s. Though the name nodded to the coking qualities of the coal in the area, mining ran a distant second to sheep interests.

The Boston crew discovered that the No. 1 Ford had come and gone a few hours back, no surprise there. But they did not expect to learn the No. 2 was stuck here still, indefinitely at that. The car had limped in with engine trouble. As the Shawmut team heard it, the No. 2 had suffered a broken piston; a brief news report down the line would simply deem it an unspecified breakdown. An account years later would clarify it as a broken connecting rod, a related woe that can be even more catastrophic. In the engine, the connecting rods serve as the essential links between each piston and the crankshaft. The pistons fire up and down, but the rods connect them to the crankshaft, turning it to convert the engine's power into rotational motion. If you imagined the engine like a bicycle, the pistons were the cyclist's thighs pumping up and down; the shin bones were the connecting rods, making sure all that pumping turned the pedals.

The four-cylinder Model T had four pistons and four connecting rods, so you could technically run for a bit if one of those rods broke, drawing reduced power from the three connected cylinders while that busted fourth rod flopped around wildly on the crankshaft. Maybe you'd get one more mile out of it, maybe a hundred—no way to know. If you were unlucky, the broken rod would punch a hole through the engine block, draining the coolant and grinding the motor to a halt. You might crack a piston and not even know, a subtle problem that can go undetected without opening the engine. But if you bust a connecting rod, you're liable to hear a racket. They had no choice but to stop.

With the No. 2 Ford stranded, the Shawmut regained second, leaving Cokeville at 4:45 PM to drive thirty miles to Montpelier, the twenty-fourth checkpoint of the race. They must have been grateful that their engine was working just fine, and figured they wouldn't see the No. 2 Ford again for a while, if that. Even for an expert mechanic like Jimmie Smith, replacing a connecting rod would take several hours, requiring complete disassembly and reassembly of the engine, all to swap out a simple, wrench-sized piece of steel. (In 1911 Ford would add a little access panel to the oil pan, or crank case, making it simpler to replace a connecting rod.) Except even the Jimmie Smiths of the world could only do it in that time if you had a spare part in hand already. Cokeville didn't have an automobile garage yet of any kind. The nearest Ford agency was in Montpelier, a branch of Consolidated Wagon & Machine, a Salt Lake City wagon-and-buggy chain that Hendy had lined up to sell Fords in parts of Utah, Idaho, and western Wyoming. But that agency was brand-new; they'd just received Montpelier's very first Model T last Friday, selling it Monday, three days back.

Henry Ford and his deputies envisioned a near future when there would be tens of thousands of Model Ts across the country, served by a network of professionalized dealerships with trained service mechanics, too, placing a reliable and predictably priced repair in reach of most drivers. But that day wasn't here yet. They were building the Ts as fast as they could in Detroit, and had just shipped their five thousandth that week. Those cars were scarce in the rural West, spare parts even scarcer. Maybe Consolidated

Wagon in Montpelier had a connecting rod, but it was highly unlikely. The same would have been true even for a more established dealership like Rock Springs, at this early date in Model T production. The nearest new part may have been all the way off in Denver at Hendy's factory branch—maybe all the way out in Detroit—a delay that could put the No. 2 out of the running for good. It would be faster to cannibalize a connecting rod from another car, and the Montpelier dealer had a couple more Fords, one of them apparently still unsold. If you got word there right away, you'd still have to wait for that spare car—or its parts—to arrive. Even then you were just getting started, needing to first sink as many hours into removing the connecting rod from that donor car as you would then need to invest in reinstalling it in the No. 2 racer. It would be far faster to swap out the entire engine, disconnecting and reconnecting it using just a few wrenches. But that was forbidden under Rule 3 of the race, as the engine block and cylinders had been stamped in New York with that telltale pattern to be inspected at the finish. Broken rods or pistons could be swapped, but not an entire motor.

Anyway, that wasn't the Shawmut's problem. The Boston team drove on toward Montpelier, crossing the Idaho border.

The race was the biggest thing to hit Montpelier in thirteen years, since Butch Cassidy and two associates waltzed into the Bank of Montpelier without disguises, wielding six-shooters and making off with about $7,000 in a sack. They'd rushed off on horseback, hastening their getaway by picking up fresh horses near the Wyoming line. Deputy Sheriff Fred Cruikshank, a slender young man with a bright smile, pursued them in vain that day by bicycle. At least, that's what people remembered.

In fairness to Cruikshank, he'd only used the bike for part of the chase. Hardly a steely-eyed lawman, he was a twenty-five-year-old general store clerk saving up for marriage with two jobs on the side, one selling bicycles and the other serving papers as deputy. In this tranquil Mormon village, he didn't carry a gun. When he heard what happened at the bank, he rushed over by bike—then grabbed a horse, riding out with a growing posse.

A lot had changed since then, with Cruikshank at thirty-eight now a pillar of this community of nearly two thousand, a multi-term mayor, real estate man, furniture dealer, church leader, and partner in that general store—as well as the owner, since Monday, of Montpelier's first Model T, about the tenth or eleventh automobile in town.

He'd bought it right on Washington Street from Consolidated Wagon, a block from the Ocean-to-Ocean checkpoint at the Burgoyne Hotel, two blocks from that bank Butch Cassidy had robbed. Montpelier had been buzzing about the race ever since the pathfinder crew stopped here in April, followed by a visit from Ford's Denver manager, Hendy, to make pilot arrangements. The city truly crackled now, with word that the leader was close.

In three days of automobile ownership, Fred Cruikshank had not done more than nose around town, trying to get a feel for the controls, with three foot pedals, two hand levers—spark and throttle—and a gooseneck emergency brake beside the driver's seat that doubled as a clutch release, putting the car in neutral. But with the No. 1 Ford approaching, Cruikshank decided to put his new Model T to the test. He loaded the car with friends and drove toward Cokeville. The party made it about four miles when they saw a cloud of exhaust approaching amid a wild racket. Next thing they knew, the No. 1 Ford blew past at what must have been twenty miles an hour, Kulick driving and William Bourne hanging on as pilot, a Cokeville laborer who normally operated a steam plow.

Cruikshank threw his new car into gear and charged back home, making "a great reputation as a speedy driver, keeping close behind the racing machine," the *Montpelier Examiner* would note. Arriving a little after four, the No. 1 Ford stayed in town until 5:50, replacing a front wheel and springs. Then the No. 1 raced off again, with its broken-down sister still stuck back in Cokeville.

Fighting through mud in a few places, the second-place Shawmut arrived at 7:05, impressing locals with its power and heft. Jack Booth, the rough-hewn forty-one-year-old sheepman who'd guided them since Rawlins, parted ways here after fifty-five hours and three hundred miles. The new guide they picked up cut a different figure: John J. Jones, the trim, diligent thirty-one-year-old owner of a first-rate clothing store for men and boys. A father of three, he was married to a daughter of Mormon pioneers that Brigham Young himself had sent to settle the area. Though Jones didn't own an automobile yet, he was keenly interested in them, on top of being an expert on the route to Pocatello; he loved to go out riding with his fine team of horses.

One other thing about Jones, which would matter more than the Shawmut team could possibly know: He was a crack investigator, having spent several years working for the Oregon Short Line, vetting claims of accident, injury, and loss against the railroad for any hint of fraud. It ran in the family. Jones's father was a law-enforcement legend, the chief special agent for the entire OSL. He ran the railroad's detective squad, which meant protecting passengers, crew, and property; investigating crimes; and bringing fugitives to justice across the Short Line's twelve hundred miles of track, from Wyoming to Oregon, Utah to Montana. And the elder Jones did it with a flourish, a raconteur with a voluminous mustache and diamond-studded badge. As one guide to the leading men of Utah put it, "The name of Joseph Jones, chief special agent for the Oregon Short Line railroad, is a terror to box-car thieves, bandits and other evildoers." In other words, if something fishy was about to happen along the Oregon Short Line, the Joneses would eventually find out.

The Shawmut crew felt good about John Jones and their chances, even setting off in the dark at 8:20 PM. The day had started with a three-way tie. Although they had lost time for that busted steering arm, they were only a few hours behind the No. 1, which had stopped for repairs of its own. The No. 2 was stalled behind them in Cokeville, hung up because of that broken connecting rod. It now felt like a two-car race, with the lead attainable.

For thirty miles they plowed ahead toward Soda Springs, a community of about eight hundred boasting underground springs (bottled as Idan-ha Natural Mineral Water, "The water that is making Soda Springs FAMOUS!") and a hotel called the Stock Exchange, nodding not to Wall Street but the local livestock trade. At Soda they learned they were running the same pace as the lead Ford, making up no ground. Midnight loomed. Their aching bodies must have begged them to stop. Other long-distance motorists had been plagued here by altitude sickness, describing aches, chills, fever, difficulty breathing, and even gushing nosebleeds, starting in Wyoming and worsening with the western climb into Idaho.

But the Shawmut crew was running on adrenaline, no time for fatigue to catch them lingering in Soda Springs. They knew the Fords tended to stop at least a few hours every night—in those stripped Model Ts, you couldn't get even the meager rest possible reclining in back of the Shawmut—so they vowed to keep going, at least until they caught the No. 1. Chances are it was stopped at Pocatello, the twenty-fifth checkpoint, another seventy miles out.

They wired Boston, telling Waite they were one hour behind. That wasn't quite true, but they planned to be caught up by the time he got the news in the morning anyway. They told him about the broken steering-knuckle arm but assured him the repair was holding up all right. Still, just to be safe, it might be a good idea to send a couple of spare arms down the line for the home stretch. Too late to get them to Baker City with the clutch shipment; better to send them off to Walla Walla.

They also told Waite about the No. 2 Ford's busted piston, while affirming their own steady state, even if it meant shelling out for a longer telegram. "Machine and crew in first class condition," they wrote. "Will go after Ford [No. 1] tonight."

The next town, Bancroft, lay about seventeen miles off. Night driving was slower, but they might reach it in an hour, moving steadily through the dark. Suddenly the car shuddered, one of the front wheels crunching into a deep rut. Inspecting the damage by lamplight, they discovered that the impact had smashed a ball bearing inside that front wheel, meaning the circular metal housing in which steel balls roll between two tracks known as races, essential for the wheel to rotate smoothly. It was terrible luck, a casualty of driving with only gas headlights and a searchlight to illuminate the ink-black range.

Pettengill, their steady captain, had been prescient. "It is the unexpected we are afraid of," he'd written, in that letter home to the *American*, "and this unexpected will probably strike us in the dark hours of driving, when we cannot see more than ten feet in front of us."

Chapin considered the hour. The night had rolled over into June 18. His wedding anniversary was over. They'd been going so hard he hadn't had time to write to Anita.

In Seattle that night, Robert Guggenheim was racing along in his Allen-Kingston, the muscular two-seat roadster that Elbert Bellows had brought out for him in the spring. Under other circumstances, Bellows might have been behind the wheel of that mighty roadster. Instead, Guggenheim's favored chauffeur was just then passing through central Kansas, finally picking up the pace in the doomed Itala after a dreadful two weeks. So the twenty-four-year-old millionaire was driving himself.

The speed limit in Seattle was twelve mph, restricted to four at intersections. Guggenheim came tearing down Queen Anne Avenue going at least fifty, slicing through one intersection after another without slowing—though to be fair, you could hear the warning roar of the A-K's engine far in advance. Two patrolmen tried chasing him down, catching up only after Guggenheim stopped to pay a social call at Queen Anne and Galer. The officers arrested him, hauling Guggenheim to police headquarters, where he cheekily told the booking sergeant that his name was "John Doe."

Faced with the customary choice for a motorist caught speeding—post bail or sit in jail awaiting a hearing—Guggenheim opted for the $25 bail, more than most families earned in a week. He produced a roll of bills. The smallest one he had was twice what he needed. "Well, it may as well be fifty dollars," he said, handing over the deposit.

Broken down four miles before Bancroft, the Shawmut team had few options. A smashed bearing wasn't something you could fix in the field, not without a replacement. And wiring Horace Waite to express one from Boston would take the better part of a week, out of the question. The part itself wasn't unique; Shawmut used high-end DWF races from Germany, imported by the Philadelphia firm Hess-Bright, the same found in other top-of-the-line automobiles, like the Mercedes, Züst, and Pope-Toledo. But it wasn't as if the Shawmut crew had a Charlie Hendy waiting in the wings to bail them out with a spare. The fastest alternative would be to cast a replacement—not the same as new, but good enough.

That kind of casting would require a skilled machine shop, not just a local blacksmith. They would need to go nearly sixty miles to Pocatello, home of the biggest shops complex on the Union Pacific system west of Omaha, a twenty-four-hour hive employing a thousand workers. The Pocatello shops had bailed out the Thomas pathfinder back in April, casting a replacement for a snapped steering arm too broken to fix by welding. Three passenger trains a day ran westbound along this corridor, one leaving Montpelier at 2:15 AM. It would hit Soda Springs behind them at 3:04, and Bancroft up ahead at 3:30. If they missed that, they were in trouble.

They split up, Pettengill staying with the car, Chapin and Messer hoofing it alongside the tracks in the direction of Bancroft. Years later they would recall flagging down the train in between stations, the fireman wielding a shotgun, wary of robbers. Whether that happened or they walked the four miles to that next station, they made it to Bancroft, where they sent a telegram to Boston before continuing by train all the way to Pocatello. That meant when Horace Waite awakened in the East, he would have two telegrams waiting—one from Soda Springs claiming they were just an hour behind the leader, and a superseding message from Bancroft, telling Waite the car was now stranded. "Fifty-five miles from Pocatello. Broken inside front wheel bearing. Will repair and continue on," they wrote, trying to end with a few positives. "Second car now. Roads better. One hundred sixty miles today. No [blown] tires. Crew in fine shape."

They disembarked at Pocatello's depot, a long clapboard building adjoining a Union Pacific–built hotel right along the tracks. With roughly nine thousand people, Pocatello was Idaho's second-largest city, owing its growth entirely to the railroad. The main branches of the Oregon Short Line crossed here, making it a natural center for both heavy maintenance and administration. As a result, a few thousand OSL workers called the city home, from salaried office types to refrigerator-car "icers" and dining-car cooks.

The depot hotel was dated, and the pathfinder crew had set the race's twenty-fifth checkpoint instead at the more modern Bannock Hotel two blocks southwest. The Shawmut crew had been exactly right about the No. 1 Ford crew, who had reached that checkpoint with a lead at 2 AM and turned in for the night. In a city with round-the-clock workers, Pocatello was buzzing about that begrimed Model T. "It is a very light looking machine to make such a hard trip, but is standing up under the strain remarkably well," the local *Tribune* would report, contrasting it with the lovingly tended Ford owned by a leading merchant. "It is not a very attractive looking car, with its coating of mud and dust, and makes as much noise as a threshing machine owing to lack of a muffler."

Arriving with no car, Chapin and Messer weren't bound for the Bannock checkpoint, not yet. They needed the shops complex northwest of the depot, the swarming hive charged with building, servicing, and fixing the engines, coaches, and freight cars for the entire Short Line railroad. The yard's biggest building spanned almost two acres under one roof, a brick behemoth with central skylights sixty-three feet high and a crane inside strong enough to easily lift locomotives. The machine shop boasted just about every type of lathe, drill, shaper, cutter, and press imaginable.

A facility like this could easily cast a serviceable replacement for the bearing race, and they agreed to hurry the work. But that was just the halfway point for Chapin and Messer. Now they had to dash back to the station and catch the *No. 8* eastbound at 11:30 AM, return to Bancroft, and hike out again to the stranded car.

Chapin worked as fast as he could, but not fast enough to make up for all that time trekking to Pocatello and back. As he toiled in the sun, the No. 2 Ford suddenly blazed past, with Smith and Scott hooting, waving their caps, and calling to the Shawmut to "hurry up."

They meant it as jocular razzing. As much as the Shawmut men might seethe over the Ford organization, burning up about Fort Steele and Glasgow, their quarrel was with the higher-ups, not their counterparts in the race. They had developed a shared respect across so many checkpoints, a competitive but friendly rapport; just like Chapin and Pettengill, Scott and Smith were automobile factory men grinding their way through a nearly impossible journey. But to see that pair buzz past again was as surprising as it was deflating, given that the No. 2 had been mired all the way back at Cokeville. The Ford crew must have performed a nimble repair, then made excellent time over the route through Montpelier and Soda Springs, driving the light car faster by daylight.

Finally, the Shawmut got moving, nearly sixteen hours after running aground. The remaining route to Pocatello was brutal, full of ditches and washouts, slippery sands and jagged lava beds, winding finally through canyon land where three separate mountain ranges from the Rockies converged. They reached Pocatello—this time with the car—at 7:20 PM June 18, handing over their passports and signing the cards at the front desk of the Bannock.

The first Ford was long gone—10 hours ahead at least—and the second Ford had come and gone that afternoon, too, several hours ahead of the Shawmut. This was disappointing news to more than just the Boston crew or its backers at home. In Washington especially, people rooting for a down-to-the-wire finish lamented this update from Pocatello, hoping the Shawmut might bounce back yet. The *Seattle Star* called the Boston car's Bancroft breakdown an unfortunate turn "for the interest of the sport."

Before heading out again at 9:40 PM, the Shawmut changed guides.

John Jones signed off, though this wouldn't be the last they heard from Montpelier's leading men's clothier. In his place, J. B. Trist and Theo Turner got in. Turner was a real estate man, so he knew the region as well as anyone. Trist was a forty-one-year-old hardware-store tinsmith, but that didn't cover the half of it. Julius Brutus Trist—named with the weight of Caesar and his betrayer, both—had become Pocatello's top bicycle repairman, while running a shop selling sporting goods and fixing typewriters and sewing machines too. Then he got auto fever. He didn't have his own car, but he made himself handy as a chauffeur and freelance expert when the first automobiles appeared in town. He left with a splash in late 1906, bound for LA or Denver, determined to make it big there in autos, only to return just a few weeks later. After an attempt at farming and sheep-shearing in Blackwood, he'd settled back into Pocatello as a tinsmith at the hardware store. But not for long—his hardware boss liked cars, too, and they were preparing to open a dealership.

With these two aboard, the Shawmut made fast time, covering twenty-six miles to American Falls in just seventy-five minutes at night. The city of one thousand sat along the Snake River near a waterfall so powerful that Oregon Trail emigrants used to hear it well before they could see it, and it was admired now by Oregon Short Line riders who rushed to the observation car while passing by along a towering railroad bridge. Beside the falls, the pride of town was the $30,000 Hotel Remington, a three-story manse with a broad porch. The Shawmut men considered the circumstances, debating whether to continue. They were probably five hours behind one Ford and ten behind the other. But they'd been going hard for forty hours straight, from daybreak in Opal yesterday to near 11 PM now in American Falls. And last night's midnight drive had backfired. They booked rooms at the Remington, with electric lights, running water, and private baths, starting at $2 a night.

Before turning off the bulb, Chapin wrote to Anita, apologizing for not sending a letter on their anniversary. "Would have wrote you yesterday but it was a hell of a day," he began. "I hope you celebrated better than I but never mind dearie we will celebrate it to-geter next year you bet."

Using two pages of lined stationery (THE REMINGTON—ONE OF THE FINEST HOTELS IN THE STATE), he told her how the broken steering arm cost them three hours, but how they still felt good after that, especially going out at night to chase the No. 1 Ford with a strong guide out of Montpelier in John Jones. Except then they'd smashed a bearing race in the middle of nowhere and burned up over fifteen hours, *so you see the Ford cars have quite a lead.*

He said they would chase those leaders again in the morning, but he sounded disillusioned. "Win or loose I don't give a dam. I'd give all I got to see my honey and steal some besides, but we will be to-gether soon and here is hoping my sweetheart is well and happy," he wrote, closing it "with all my love hugs and kisses."

Saturday morning they started early. On the way out, Chapin bought a postcard of the Remington for Anita, scratching another quick note. He conveyed some of what he'd written in the letter, not sure which would arrive first:

> *Stopped here last night. mishap put us back 15 hrs but are on the road again nearing the end*
> *Earle.*

12

No. 2 to the Fore

Across Idaho, June 18 to 20, 1909

The Shawmut crew was right to be surprised by how quickly the No. 2 Ford rebounded from that breakdown in Cokeville, given the need to track down a distant part and perform time-consuming engine surgery. But the truth was, the Ford side hadn't removed and replaced the busted connecting rod at all. Instead, they simply pulled out the entire engine, replacing it with a new motor from another Model T, to get the car back on the road as fast as possible. That was a clear violation of Rule 3:

> The Technical Committee of the Automobile Club of America will stamp the car before departure as follows:—The side members of the frame, front and rear axles, engine base and cylinders, transmission case and steering gear. The winning car must bear the stamps on arrival at Seattle. All other parts can be changed at will. Any contestant having to replace any of the above parts can continue in the contest and on arrival at Seattle will be awarded a certificate of performance. He will not be eligible for the prizes, however.

If you wanted to stay in the running, you could remove and replace a broken rod or piston, but not an entire engine. Except the Ford team had no interest in settling for a certificate of performance. Rather than own up to the swap, they did it on the sly. With the No. 2 racer back on the road powered by a replacement engine, they could take their time with a complex repair to the original, then ship that stamped engine ahead by rail to be swapped back in before the finish-line inspection.

For now, no one outside the inner circle was any the wiser. Maybe they figured it would stay that way, with less scrutiny on the No. 2 than on the front-running No. 1 Model T, especially with that Scott-Smith Ford trying to claw back from third at the time. To be sure, both of the company's entries were in it to win, but the No. 1 was clearly first among equals in Ford's eyes, between the hood number and the duo assigned to the crew, with superlative driver Frank Kulick accompanied by in-house copywriter Harry Harper. That made the No. 2 a kind of understudy or wingman, assigned to flank the leader, assist it, pace it—and serve as an insurance policy if the No. 1 should falter. If everything went according to plan, those two cars would cross the finish line in succession, the No. 1 and No. 2 Fords first and second, irresistible ad copy awaiting Harper's pen. Except the engine trouble in the No. 2 Thursday had disrupted that plan, separating the sibling Model Ts and miring the No. 2 in third. If it managed to regain second, who would ever know that part of the run had been powered by a replacement engine? Except on Friday, the fate of the two Fords would flip.

Armed with that illicit new engine—all four pistons pumping, connecting rods moving the crankshaft in harmony—the No. 2 crackled back to life, scooting out of Cokeville at 5 AM Friday, some fifteen hours behind the No. 1 Ford and twelve hours back of the Shawmut. To Charlie Hendy's delight, Scott "drove like a demon," passing that stalled Shawmut and cutting the gap with the No. 1 Ford in half by Pocatello, that railroad hub known as Idaho's "Gate City." Not that the No. 1 was sitting around waiting.

Hendy's sprawling Denver-branch turf had always included Cokeville, though initially it hadn't gone much farther, stopping at the border with Idaho. When the company planted those stores in Denver and Seattle at the end of 1907—its first two branch houses in the West—the sales team originally assigned all of Idaho to Seattle. But Hendy was irrepressible, manifesting his own destiny, swallowing up more turf for Denver. Back in Detroit, the company had big registers that listed every town in the country with a population of five hundred or more, marking branch-manager terrain and recording any local agents that had been signed up beneath them. The Idaho pages were now full of cross-outs for the branch in charge, reflecting Hendy's westward expansion.

Not that R. P. Rice, the Seattle man, was any slouch. At thirty-five, he had a showman's streak and a breezy charisma, coupled winningly with dark suits and Republican politics that made him a business leader in wildly mushrooming Seattle. Unlike Hendy, Roland Preston Rice had been promoted from within, picked for Seattle after serving under Tom Hay in Chicago, where he'd climbed quickly to assistant manager of that powerful Ford branch. At first glance, the clean-shaven Rice might blend into a crowd, with his average build, round face, and soft features, a minister's son who initially studied to be a pharmacist. But Rice's father was a tent-revival preacher, and Rice himself had a taste for speed and the good life, becoming a daredevil bicycle racer and crackerjack bike salesman. His knack for closing deals swiftly extended to romance, when a Sunday excursion on Lake Michigan with his sweetheart in 1899 turned into a sudden elopement—albeit one intertwined with tragedy. When newlywed Georgia Mae Rice wired her father with the news ("Roland and I were married to-day. Tell mamma"), her mother ended her life by swallowing carbolic acid.

The marriage held, despite that trauma. With Georgia beside him, Rice sailed for Liverpool as a representative of Chicago meatpacking giant Armour, returning in 1904 with a fine British wardrobe and a keen interest in autos. Among branch men, Rice developed a reputation for solicitousness toward existing customers. He understood that an ongoing relationship with Ford—for repairs, for quick questions, for a spirit of camaraderie among fellow Ford owners across their city—could pay dividends, yielding repeat business and word-of-mouth referrals.

With the Idaho dividing line a tad amorphous, and with Hendy and

Rice both determined to impress Henry Ford and secure Ocean-to-Ocean victory, Rice had dispatched one of his top men deep into Idaho, reaching Pocatello by train two days ahead of the leading car. From there, the man was supposed to turn around and work backward, making sure the guides were in place over the final eight hundred miles of the race. Hendy, meanwhile, kept pressing westward.

Even careful plans can falter. After the No. 1 Ford raced into American Falls on the morning of the eighteenth, the crew couldn't find their next guide. Apparently Kulick came in so fast that the new pilot wasn't there yet, though maybe the guide had gotten mixed up. The duo started asking around. Feeling antsy, not wanting to cede their lead, Kulick and Harper took on a local who swore he knew the way to Twin Falls, the next checkpoint.

Idaho was a state with unforgiving topography and very few roads, mainly old trapping routes and wagon trails that dated back generations. Between the leading cities of Pocatello and Boise, there were two established routes, each running roughly 275 miles, neither one a picnic. One curved south, down past American Falls and along the Snake River, the timeworn path of the old Oregon Trail. The other banked sharply north, an Oregon Trail offshoot known as Goodale's Cutoff. Either way, crossing the Idaho Territory by covered wagon had been a hardship for settlers trying to reach Oregon's fertile Willamette Valley beyond. The northern route remained unforgiving. But the southern route had become relatively inhabited, with large-scale irrigation along the Snake River turning swaths of desert into farmland, yielding agricultural tracts sprinkled with hamlets. Twin Falls, midway down the Snake, anchored that route.

To the pathfinder crew, the choice had been obvious. They wanted as many eyeballs on the race as possible, plotting the route through county seats and newspaper towns, places with garages or stores to stock gasoline, not to mention a good checkpoint hotel. They planted the twenty-sixth checkpoint in Twin Falls, following the southerly curve of the Snake.

Still, you could find certain people in Pocatello convinced that the northern route to Boise was faster, notwithstanding the need to hit a southerly checkpoint. What no one advised was to go due west. But that's exactly where the No. 1 Ford headed.

American Falls to Twin Falls, halfway to Boise. When the No. 2 Ford arrived at 10 PM on June 18, Scott and Smith discovered they were in first. That couldn't be right. What had happened to the No. 1, with its half-day lead out of American Falls? They hadn't passed it on the way, and there were no telegrams waiting at the Perrine Hotel checkpoint clarifying its progress either. A mystery, for now, and one that meant the No. 2 Ford had vaulted from third to first in a single day. The Shawmut crew was a hundred miles back at American Falls, bedding down at the Remington.

In the morning, the No. 2 Ford tore out of Twin Falls, while the Shawmut left American Falls with a new guide: Lorenzo Lloyd Evans, a fifty-one-year-old bank president with a carefully trimmed goatee and a tidy shirt and tie, topped with a pristine duster and unblemished hat, making him a vision of crisp haberdashery amid the begrimed car and crew.

Here was a guide they could count on, an eminent citizen of the Snake River Basin, involved in stock raising and the mercantile trade as well, deeply familiar with the territory as the brother of a former Idaho House speaker and a soon-to-be state senator himself. Their mother, recently deceased, was one of the last of the "Welsh Saints," those pioneers from Wales who so embraced the message of Mormon missionaries in the 1840s that they sailed the Atlantic and trekked west by wagon and on foot seeking Latter-Day Zion, enduring cholera outbreaks and unimaginable hardship. Now the family flourished.

With Pettengill driving and Lorenzo Evans in back beside Earle Chapin, the Shawmut crossed sand and sagebrush that seemed to stretch forever, twenty-five miles at one point between ranches. Eventually they reached the "Magic Valley," half a million acres newly transformed by irrigation—"a mighty victory over Nature," in the words of *The Pacific*

Monthly, that popular magazine of the West. "It is as though some good fairy had waved a magic wand over the land and said, 'Sagebrush, begone. I bid come forth grains, grasses, fruits, flowers, and a great splendid people.'" Soon they hit Twin Falls itself, hub of this Magic Valley. In five years it had grown from two lonely buildings to a city of five thousand, fifth largest in the state.

The Perrine Hotel checkpoint was a $100,000 stunner, the kind of stately three-story hotel you might find anchoring a mill city of fifty thousand back in New England. Except Twin Falls wasn't like anything the Shawmut men had seen before, more like a moving-picture set. Despite the substantial brick and stone buildings on the two main blocks downtown, the rest of the considerable Twin Falls street grid contained far more empty lots than actual structures. And all those platted streets were simply dirt roads for now, in a pop-up city with big dreams on the horizon.

At the Perrine, the Shawmut crew learned they'd retaken second, with a picture now emerging of the fate of the No. 1 Ford. That afternoon, Kulick and Harper made their first of two grudging appearances in Shoshone, twenty-five miles north as the crow flies. It may as well have been two hundred. They'd been out a day and a half and still hadn't hit the Twin Falls checkpoint.

If they'd followed the official route from American Falls, the prescribed hundred miles should have taken roughly eight hours. Instead, by the eight-hour mark, their odometer showed just thirty-two miles, excruciatingly slow over the sands. And those miles didn't even mean progress, just circular motion. They'd gotten lost, and lost again, seeking a missed cutoff southwest to Twin Falls. Finally, their guide persuaded them he'd found the route. Plowing ahead with more confidence, they pressed into the night, believing at 1 AM that just a dozen miles remained. Conceding to exhaustion, they stretched out to sleep on the ground, saving the last bit to Twin Falls for sunrise. Except when they got their bearings in daylight, they realized they were at least fifty miles off, with just a few drops left in the tank.

They hiked six miles to railroad tracks, borrowed a handcar, pumped to Dietrich, and picked up a passenger train to Shoshone. There they bought gasoline and oil and borrowed a car to return to the desert. After refueling, they drove back through Shoshone, where a road would meander down to Twin Falls. A photographer caught the misplaced Ford in Shoshone, an unexpected thrill for the town, less so for Harper and Kulick. The only consolation was knowing that they'd ditched their pilot—a man Harper deemed "that American Falls Greaser"—in a place where he had to wait eighteen hours for the next train home.

Alone in Twin Falls, the Shawmut was the talk of the town, drawing a huge daytime crowd outside the Perrine, where the lead Ford had come and gone by morning, and the other remained missing. The Boston crew stopped for gas around the corner at the Hall garage, amid dozens of onlookers. Like so many of the garages sprouting on America's Main Streets, Hall's—technically on Shoshone Street, around the corner from Main—occupied a modest storefront, in this case between a milliner and a motion-picture house. They kept the gasoline in an underground tank in the back alley. Upstairs, the office windows were plastered with dazzling posters for the coming Sells-Floto Circus, one of Ringling's rivals, teasing its thirty "Champion Aerialists," "Double Herd" of giant elephants, and "Band of Sioux Warriors."

Making the most of the afternoon, a hustling photographer named M. B. Martin scurried to snap the Shawmut for prints he could sell as postcards, catching it outside the garage and across from the hotel, the crowd watching with awe and apprehension, the car so dirty and tattered it was as if it had burrowed up through the soil. In back, there were enough tackle lines wrapped around the tonneau to lasso an elephant. In one of the resulting postcards, more than sixty people squeeze within an arm's length or two of the car, keeping one side clear as they look toward the camera. In another, Ira Perrine himself—a visionary hailed in *Harper's Weekly* for creating "the largest irrigated tract of desert land in the world"—glances at the Shawmut with his hands in his pockets.

As the Boston car drove off, Martin scrambled to capture one more photo, a rare action shot of the Shawmut charging down Shoshone Street on its way out of town.

Filer to Buhl to Hagerman—across the Snake on a little cable-guided ferry—to Bliss to Mountain Home and then to Boise. The No. 2 Ford churned through them all, nearly 150 miles from Twin Falls in a day, undeterred by a burst of rain. They even beat their own pilot, mired in the sands somewhere on the Snake River Plain, but Scott and Smith had little trouble finding Idaho's capital. A convoy of enthusiastic motorists from the new Boise Automobile Club met them outside town, ushering the Ford crew in for a surprise ceremony. They rewarded the duo with five $20 gold pieces for being the first car to reach Boise.

Around 8 PM, the men registered at the twenty-seventh checkpoint, in the gilded lobby of the Idanha Hotel, a six-story, turret-topped temple of splendor at Tenth and Main. Just three more checkpoints to go between here and the finish.

The Idanha buzzed on Saturday nights, its dining room the finest in Boise, sixty feet long and anchored by a big fireplace. To the exhausted Ford pair, the scene—right down to the gold in their pockets—must have felt like a mirage. They told reporters they would indulge in a bath, a hearty meal, and a few hours of rest in one of the 140 rooms upstairs, then get on the road by 3:30 AM, no time to waste. "We have had little sleep and are not looking for sleep," Scott said. "We will sleep when we get to Seattle and plenty, too."

But oh, those Idanha beds. Even as Scott said it, a wire went out to waiting Ford dealers anticipating a more realistic 6 AM departure. Sure enough, it was well after sunrise when they got going. No matter; they still had a big lead on the other Model T and the Shawmut, while the fourth and fifth cars might as well have been all the way back in Manhattan. The unlucky Acme was stuck in Laramie for repairs, after twisting its jackshaft again. And while the Itala was finally humming for a change, only now was it even entering Colorado.

Scott and Smith pressed westward, meeting the Snake River again where it curved and danced north along the border with Oregon. Here they found a fertile valley, about two thousand feet above sea level, with apple orchards, hayfields, and strawberry farms. They passed through Weiser, a muscular railroad-junction city of about two thousand, then crossed the Snake at Olds Ferry, aboard their second rickety, cable-guided raft in twenty-four hours.

From there they began crossing the northeast corner of Oregon, a 170-mile slash through all kinds of terrain in short order: sand flats, river valleys, canyons, even a mountain range (the Blue), though the road across was rumored to be reasonable. Then they would reach Washington, the twelfth state of the race, closing in on victory.

At 3:45 that Sunday afternoon, the leading Ford hit Baker City, a wealthy mining hub of six-thousand-plus people, the biggest city in eastern Oregon, rivaling Spokane, Washington, as the self-styled "Queen City of the Inland Empire." Scott pulled up at the twenty-eighth checkpoint, the Geiser Grand Hotel, an opulent palace crowned by a corner clock tower. A familiar figure greeted them with a cheer: Charlie Hendy, out far past the bounds of his Denver turf.

It had taken Scott and Smith two and a half days to get here from Cokeville, after they'd jackhammered out of western Wyoming into Idaho with that new engine at 5 AM on Friday. Hendy had leapfrogged them in the meantime, a 505-mile, eighteen-hour rail journey, not counting the hour saved when the clock rolled back at the Oregon border. All told, he was over a thousand miles away from his home branch. Whether Hendy had intended to come this far all along, or had jumped back on the train after the American Falls fiasco, he had no plans to turn back now.

13

The Shawmut Charges Back

Idaho into Oregon, June 19 to 21, 1909

Still guided by Lorenzo Evans in his cream-colored attire, the Shawmut rolled out of Twin Falls on Saturday in second place, trailing the front-running Ford by about eight hours. A substantial but not insurmountable gap, with four checkpoints and 675 miles to Seattle. The Boston men knew their ability to "sleep" in the car—taking turns stretching their legs in the tonneau, at least—could be crucial for gaining time over the No. 2 Ford, with Scott and Smith's tendency to stop for a few hours each night. And their powerful motor was churning right along, if only they could find some firm roads and straightaways.

They made fair time to Buhl, sixteen miles west, stopping in a hard rain for an hour to change guides and dry just a little. The little farming town was buzzing over the arrest of the alleged leader of a gang of masked highwaymen who'd brazenly robbed the Union Pacific's Overland Limited near Omaha in May; Pinkerton detectives combing the West had traced the man all the way to one of Buhl's two hotels, where converging deputies found him writing a letter with a six-shooter by his side. After they cuffed him, he managed to shove the letter in his mouth and start chewing. (Eventually identified as William Matthews, he would be convicted with four accomplices in a sensational trial and sentenced to life at

Leavenworth, though President Woodrow Wilson would commute that sentence a decade later.)

Buhl was the end of the line for an Oregon Short Line branch that ran back through Twin Falls on the way to the trunk line, making it the turnaround point for businessman Lorenzo Evans. In his place the Shawmut picked up a Mormon pioneer of a rougher-hewn sort: Seymour Fairchild, a forty-eight-year-old farmer and gold prospector who had been indicted in the 1890s for "timber depredations"—plundering public forest—with the government contending that Fairchild laid waste to valuable trees "out of pure spite, in order to inconvenience a rival." Later he would draw more legal heat for selling questionable "subscriptions" to a melon farm he claimed would provide free watermelons "for the delectations" of servicemen returning from the Great War. But Fairchild contained multitudes. He drove the local horse-drawn school wagon, helped other settlers put up "prove-up" shacks to secure homestead claims, and tenderly and diligently worked with a young son—one of his dozen children—for two years to regain the use of his damaged leg after the nine-year-old was burned and thrown in an explosion while playing with abandoned black powder.

The Shawmut team engaged Fairchild for just a short distance north toward the Snake River, to a viable ferry to cross to the far side. They were advancing through a broad wedge, with the Snake River on one side and a major tributary known as Salmon Falls Creek to the other. Long ago, this had been the edge of the continent. By the time of the Pliocene, it had become the edge of a vast inland lake instead, a lush landscape home to saber-toothed cats and mastodons, giant otters and an equine ancestor dubbed the Hagerman horse. Now it was arid hills and sagebrush scrub, jagged lava rock and dramatic canyon walls. No bridges crossed the fiercely flowing Snake anywhere near here, but there were a few modest cable ferries, and they would need to pick one to cross over, to pass through the Hagerman Valley on the far side and hit Bliss, Mountain Home, and Boise.

The guidebook that the pathfinder prepared suggested the Riverside Ferry, run by a man named Newt Uhrlaub, which plied the Snake about a dozen miles northwest of Buhl. The Shawmut's guide instead recommended a ferry just half that far, going due north to an area known as Clear Lakes, beside the dramatically named Devil's Washboard cascade. That ferry was run by a practiced bronco buster named Otis Syster, whose spread included an irrigated orchard so prosperous that he'd recently bought a Winton auto, a rarity on the north side of the river.

Maybe Syster wasn't home to operate the ferry, or maybe they ran into trouble with that fading clutch. They might have gotten delayed by illness, struggled to climb the edge of the canyon rim, labored through the notoriously sandy and rocky stretch beyond Bliss, or wandered off course without a guide when Fairchild signed off. Or they might have been waylaid by the unforgiving latticework of irrigation ditches that carved up the orchards and farmland approaching Mountain Home, some of them still under construction—ruts that would be harder on a big car than a small one, especially a small one with the Model T's flexible three-point construction. Possibly the Shawmut crew rested for a spell and overslept. Whatever the reason, it took them twenty-two hours to go eighty miles between Buhl and Mountain Home, a pedestrian pace that would go unexplained in the day's newspaper coverage, which focused on the front-running Ford and that $100 surprise at Boise. Earle Chapin kept his pen dry. And either the team sent no telegram home to Horace Waite or it was lost later. But the eight-hour gap between the Shawmut and the lead Ford out of Twin Falls had yawned into a twenty-six-hour chasm by Mountain Home.

Whatever befell them, it was now in the rear. They made fine time from there to Boise, fifty miles in roughly five hours—nothing like what they could have done on the roads around Boston, but leagues faster than the horse-drawn homeseekers who still followed this rutted section of the Oregon Trail corridor by wagon.

Finally, the Shawmut reached Idaho's capital, a fast-growing city of seventeen thousand, buoyed by mining and agricultural wealth, with tree-lined streets, a comparatively mild climate, and eighty miles of streetcar track already. They found their way to the Intermountain Auto Company garage and registered at the nearby Idanha checkpoint at 8:45 PM that Sunday, June 20. In the process, they discovered that they'd been passed by

Kulick's No. 1 Ford, the rival that had gotten so lost trying to find Twin Falls. That Ford had reached Boise around 2:30 PM, bolstered by the guiding hand of Sherman Johnson, a twenty-year-old mechanic at Boise's new Ford dealership, which was operated by Johnson's father, a successful gold miner and banker. Even with a four-hour stop for repairs, the Kulick Ford left Boise before the Shawmut arrived. Still, the third-place Boston crew had gained some ground on the overall leader, owing to Scott and Smith's overnight stay at the Idanha.

That rested Ford duo had told Boise reporters they were confident of reaching Seattle first, with a solid lead and 525 miles to go. The Shawmut men tried to project a similar confidence, an hour or two back of the Kulick Ford and thirteen or fourteen hours behind the leader. They "assert that their car is in fine condition and that they will catch the Fords before the destination of the journey is reached," the *Idaho Daily Statesman* would report.

Resolving to drive straight through to the finish, the Shawmut crew left Boise at 10:15 PM on June 20, pointing their lights along the bank of the Boise River and beginning their journey toward Oregon. They drove all night through the blackness, showing what a good car and crew could do with fair conditions and a good guide—in this case Allen G. Randall, a thirty-six-year-old Buick, Thomas, and Pierce-Arrow dealer. A former bank clerk and real estate man, Randall had arrived from the East just a few years back, but he'd made an immediate impact with Boise's first automobile livery service and full-fledged car dealership and garage, commanding a market previously occupied only by a bicycle man dabbling in autos. Now Randall had six competitors, including the big Intermountain garage and the new Ford agency run by J. C. Johnson (Sherman's father), but Randall considered himself the dean of Boise auto men. He loved a good long-haul drive—especially with something at stake—and had helped in May as a Thomas dealer when the pathfinder came through. That none of the models he sold were entered in the race didn't mean he had no dog in the fight; as a Buick dealer, he was determined not to cede prestige or sales to Ford.

The Shawmut rolled on, chewing up the miles over rough roads, passing through New Plymouth, Payette, and then Weiser in early morning, sending Randall back to Boise by train. They crossed the Snake once more by ferry, the current lapping the timbers of yet another cable-guided raft, and disembarked into Oregon, curving away from the Snake for good near the aptly named Farewell Bend of the Oregon Trail. They churned on over sandy but fair roads nearly thirty miles to Huntington, then a dozen more clenched miles through Burnt River Canyon, with serpentine curves, sudden climbs, and short but steep drops. Finally, they eased into Pleasant Valley and found a fast, smooth road over the last fifteen miles to Baker City.

They hit checkpoint No. 28, the Geiser Grand Hotel, before 9 AM—a remarkable overnight pace, eclipsing 130 miles in less than eleven hours, regaining second place. But the No. 2 Ford remained fifteen hours ahead, and the Boston men had a new problem, beyond the usual throbbing and fatigue of endless hours in the car: Earle Chapin, trusted mechanic, was hunched over in agony. He needed a doctor, stat. And with the clock ticking, his teammates would need to decide whether to wait in Baker or press on without him.

14

A Case of "Auto Intoxication"

Baker City, Oregon, June 21, 1909

Baker City was a bustling burg of sixty-seven hundred that boasted three banks, a brewery, and a bevy of stone buildings in a downtown wired for electricity. In this city with two daily papers, the morning broadsheet was especially bullish about automobiles in general, as well as about Baker City's inclusion in the Ocean-to-Ocean Race, putting it on the map for automotive tourists.

"Some day there will be a real highway across this continent—roads for the use of autoists and used by them but not more so than by the farmers and the people themselves and when that day comes the fact that Baker is on the motoring line between New York and Seattle will mean much to this city," the Baker City *Morning Democrat* opined, with more gusto than punctuation. That was in May, with the pathfinder approaching. As the racers themselves neared, the paper served up more affection for the motor car that Saturday, June 19. "Very few industries throughout the United States have grown to so large proportions during the past decade as has the manufacture of automobiles," the *Democrat* wrote, in an unsigned item on the editorial page. It was not original copy but instead a widely circulated press release from the American Motor Car Manufacturers' Association; in keeping with the fuzzy standards of the day, it ran most places without a byline. "This modern method of transportation and pleasure riding is becoming popular with all classes, and it is believed that nothing can be invented in the future that will displace the use of the automobile."

The paper reflected the automotive enthusiasm of Baker City officials. Back in May, a farmer outside of town had been so rattled over the roaring speed and *rat-a-tat* combustion of Elbert Bellows in the Allen-Kingston that he appealed to the police to arrest Guggenheim's chauffeur. The chief busied the farmer with paperwork to fill out, then gleefully shook hands with Bellows, wishing him luck on the way to Seattle.

Now the racers arrived: first the No. 2 Ford, in and out that Sunday afternoon, followed by the bigger Shawmut, No. 5 on the hood, as Monday dawned on Baker City. At the hotel checkpoint, the talk was all Ford. Charlie Hendy from Denver had held court in the lobby the day before, regaling reporters with predictions of Ford victory. "There is little doubt that No. 2 will arrive in Seattle first," he told the *Baker City Herald*, with high hopes that the No. 1 Ford would finish second. "The Shawmut is coming along and will finish third in my opinion. Yes, there were eighteen starters from New York. Only the three cars mentioned have gotten west of the Rocky Mountains. Two other cars are now in the vicinity of Denver. We are trying to demonstrate that the light car is the one for all kinds of travel and I believe we will do it."

Hendy knew full well that eighteen cars hadn't gone anywhere near the starting line. Never mind that. It sounded good, made the Ford achievement seem even more impressive. Then Hendy was gone, back on the train to leap the No. 2, only his bravado remaining in Baker City. When the Shawmut arrived on the morning of June 21, the men understood they had no time to spare, the lead Ford fifteen hours ahead, the next one closing in from behind. And yet, there was Chapin, reeling, in little condition to continue. If he left the car, that would be it; under the rules, he couldn't rejoin the crew, a month of his life sunk into a journey ending abruptly in Oregon. But if they waited for him to be treated by a doctor, any remaining chance of catching the leader would vanish. They might even cost themselves a shot at second, with the No. 1 Ford just forty minutes back and closing.

The day clerk at the Geiser Grand was a young man named Robert Armstrong, one of three round-the-clock employees authorized to endorse the racing passports. The Shawmut crew learned that Baker City had a fifty-bed hospital and fifteen doctors in private practice, including one in an office behind the hotel: Dr. Carl G. Patterson, a well-regarded generalist who doubled as official city physician.

At thirty-one, Dr. Patterson was a snappy dresser with a carefully trimmed Van Dyke beard. He was a practicing "eclectic"—meaning he had studied at the Eclectic Medical Institute of Cincinnati, one of many proprietary medical colleges of varying quality and divergent approaches that educated most of the nation's physicians, far removed from the few university-based, research-driven medical schools open mainly to the elite. Amid these many institutions training homeopaths, hydropaths, physio-medicalists, electrical healers, botanics, and more, Patterson's alma mater was a leader in eclecticism, which drew a little from everything but mainly blended modern medicine with plant-based treatments.

His office occupied a suite on the second floor of Baker City's Kennedy Building, with a small but comfortable waiting room, and an exam room accented with lace curtains, a potbellied stove, and a porcelain sink, along with a case of medical texts. A reclining examining chair anchored the room, with upholstered armrests and metal stirrups.

Dr. Patterson examined Earle Chapin and rendered a diagnosis: "Auto Intoxication," as he would write in slashing cursive on a medical note. It would be tempting to assume this was an illness du jour ascribed to extreme motoring conditions and prolonged exposure to exhaust, much like the dreaded "automobile face"—also "auto face," or "motoring face"—that had gotten considerable press of late, with magazine wags and medical doctors warning that the nerves, muscles, and skin of the face were not meant to be thrust into the wind at high speed atop a vibrating contraption for long periods, with supposedly telltale effects. Instead, autointoxication—as it was more commonly spelled—was a popular theory, not yet discredited as quackery, that the body was prone to poisoning itself. By this thinking, a wide variety of ailments could be pinned on internal putrefaction from microbes in the digestive system. The remedy? A robust colon cleanse.

No question, Chapin would need to remain for the night under Dr. Patterson's care and observation—"much against his wishes," *The Seattle Daily Times* would report. For the first time in the journey, Arthur Pettengill and Bob Messer climbed into the Shawmut without their mechanic, pressing toward Washington without him.

15

Henry, Edsel, and the Crack Train of the Northwest

Rolling, June 19, 1909

Henry Ford had made it clear in the spring that he was in it to win, and now he punctuated that announcement. On Saturday, June 19, he wired R. P. Rice, Seattle branch manager, that he was coming west for a reason: to see the two Model Ts in the race claim first and second in person.

Ford was then in Indiana, watching the state's first major automobile races—though not in Indianapolis, where workers were still putting the finishing touches on the motor speedway that would open later that summer, as America's first purpose-built automobile track. The Chicago Automobile Club had staked out a road course in a place called Crown Point, in northwest Indiana, investing heavily in grading and paving a panhandled loop running 23.27 miles, gravel treated with liquid coal-tar pitch. Tired of seeing New York get the attention, the Chicago swells were throwing what the press dubbed the "Western Vanderbilt," to rival the Long Island racing spectacle that drew hundreds of thousands of motoring fans annually. They sprinkled grandstands around the route, ran an abundance of special trains, and brought in the National Guard to keep crowds from spilling onto the road course.

The Chicago club organized two races for stock cars, with the Indiana Trophy for smaller entries on Friday, followed by the Cobe Cup for heavyweights in a longer race Saturday. Initially, Ford showed little interest. For one thing, he was no fan of separating stock cars into categories like weight or price, believing his cars could take on all comers. Besides, he'd sworn off racing—sort of—after Frank Kulick was nearly killed twice in the fall of 1907. He meant he opposed racing with speed-freak creations, their engines too powerful for their slender tires, tearing around cramped, unpaved horse tracks in uncertain conditions. He remained open to pitting custom racers on a new generation of longer, banked tracks specially designed for speed—Brooklands in England, the Indianapolis speedway—as well as to contests among actual stock cars with real road conditions.

But Ford was focused on the Ocean-to-Ocean Race, anyway. Still, amid a relentless drumbeat of local coverage for the coming Crown Point affair, Chicago branch manager Tom Hay persuaded the boss to enter a Model T for the Indiana Trophy race, submitting the $500 entry fee a day before the June 5 deadline. The press speculated on the potential driver, with the famed Kulick and the seasoned Scott both engaged in the New York–Seattle contest. A few days later, Ford tapped Frank Dunnell, an experienced part-time racer who had sold the first Ford in New York—the fifth anywhere—in 1903 as a twenty-year-old bicycle mechanic turned salesman for initial Ford dealer C. A. Duerr. The kid had stayed on as a "demonstrator" when the Ford agency for New York transferred from Duerr to Wanamaker's department store and then to the factory branch on Broadway. Now Dunnell was based in Detroit, traveling the country to show brand-new dealers how to operate and maintain an automobile.

Ford brought along his fifteen-year-old son Edsel, out on summer break, to watch the Crown Point contests before taking the boy to Seattle for the Ocean-to-Ocean finish and the World's Fair. But at the last minute, the Ford team withdrew. Tom Hay told a reporter the car hadn't reached the course in time for Dunnell to get in enough practice runs and tune it up properly. Later they would claim the car hadn't gotten there at all, that two weeks simply wasn't enough time to build another stripped-down body like those two Model Ts now bound for Seattle. That strained credulity. Just as likely, Henry Ford sized up the situation and realized they didn't stand a chance to win.

Though the press called Friday's Indiana Trophy contest a "lightweight" race and a "small car" affair, both were misnomers. It was open to stock cars of any size and weight so long as their engine-cylinder displacement did not exceed 300 cubic inches. (The bigger Cobe Cup race Saturday had a minimum weight—2,250 pounds—along with a maximum engine displacement of 525 cubic inches.) That meant even in Friday's small-car race, many entries boasted engines that dwarfed the 177 cubic inches of the 20-horsepower Model T, coupled with stripped bodies in an assortment of sizes. In a true stock-car contest with real-world conditions—like the Ocean-to-Ocean Race—Ford had supreme confidence in the power-to-weight superiority of the lightweight T. But some of these Indiana entries seemed to stretch the definition of stock car. To qualify, a company simply had to pledge to build ten copies of the car in the race for sale to consumers by late 1910. That was supposed to make it easier for tiny automakers with modest production capacity to enter. Instead, it opened the door to big firms gaming the system, building special racers with maximally powerful engines on long, lean bodies—more than anyone but a professional racer could handle—and then producing nine duplicates to claim stock-car status. One look at the test runs and it was clear these "small" cars were flashing by as fast as or faster than the big racers slated for Saturday, obliterating the Model T's top speed.

Henry Ford hated frittering money, but he hated losing even more. They pulled the Model T entry from the lineup, eating the $500.

Henry and Edsel stayed anyway, joining friend Harvey Firestone in the grandstand, as Joe Matson won the lightweight race in a Chalmers-Detroit (covering ten laps at an average 51.46 mph) and Louis Chevrolet claimed the seventeen-lap Cobe Cup in a Buick, indeed running a slightly slower 49.29 mph. *The Automobile* called Ford "a keen-eyed though quiet observer of the racing."

As soon as it was over, Henry and Edsel hightailed it for Chicago, on one of the special express trains spiriting spectators the forty miles back from Crown Point. At the Union Passenger Depot, an antiquated brick station on Canal Street, the Fords boarded an overnight train for the Twin Cities and Seattle beyond, $62 round-trip apiece, plus Pullman sleeping-car charges.

Until that summer, traveling between Chicago and Seattle required a transfer, even with a bundled ticket. To speed service to the World's Fair, James J. Hill's two transcontinental lines—the Great Northern and the Northern Pacific—began offering through trains, with the Chicago, Milwaukee & St. Paul Railway nipping at their heels. That line (the "Milwaukee Road") had just completed an extension from the Twin Cities to the Pacific Northwest, operating as the Chicago, Milwaukee & Puget Sound, though it was only running local service for now. A consortium fixed long-distance rates to prevent price wars, but the lines competed to lure travelers other ways, with those three plus the big southerly railroads—for those who might head to Seattle by way of Denver or California, on the Union Pacific or Rock Island—dangling enticements that included complimentary clothes pressing, female stenographers, fresh eggs stamped with "birth" dates, and even a loss-leading table d'hôte meal for a single dollar, starting with a cocktail and ending with a plump Perfecto cigar.

For a man seldom concerned with blandishments, Ford's choice was practical: the train that would reach Seattle fastest, preferably while passing part of the race. That meant the Northern Pacific, which had cut stops and sped up its signature *North Coast Limited*—"Crack Train of the Northwest," they called it—to reach Seattle in seventy-two hours.

For the Eastern press, this was a marvel that made it possible to pare mail time between the World's Fair city and New York down to just four days, with the Northern Pacific's *North Coast Limited* and slightly slower *Exposition Special* trains aligning nicely with the fastest Chicago–New York trains of the Pennsylvania Railroad. Transfer that same mail to a fast steamer and you could theoretically send a letter from Seattle to London in a week and a half.

For Ford, the *North Coast Limited* appealed because it would trace the race's route in Washington between North Yakima and Cle Elum, then reach Seattle in time for him to turn around and usher those Model Ts home to the finish.

At the far end, R. P. Rice wasted no time after getting Ford's telegram. He turned to Harry Disher, at twenty-three already a Ford veteran. Disher had worked with Rice in Chicago, following him as head mechanic when Rice got tapped to open the new Ford branch in Seattle covering the Pacific Northwest. A daring racer and dashing dresser with a taste for life above his pay grade, Disher had a dark streak yet to fully reveal itself. For now, when the press wrote about him, it was automotive fodder. In time, he would make the news as a uniformed Army aviator with a habit of wooing vulnerable heiresses, culminating in tragedy in 1923, when Disher would kill his third wife before turning a Colt .45 on himself.

Already Rice had primed the route by sending assistant manager John Lund, a former Chicago bike racer, out by train to line up guides and nail down details all the way from Oregon west to the finish. Now he told Disher to drive east from Seattle, toward the Cascade mountains, and to keep going until he saw that familiar Ford signature on a radiator grille coming toward him. Then he should turn around and lead that car—the No. 2, or possibly the No. 1—home to victory.

16

"The Greatest Thrill of My Life"

Crossing the Blues into Washington, June 20 to 21, 1909

Even with a sixteen-hour lead and just four hundred miles remaining, Scott and Smith felt the pressure to keep plugging out of Baker City. The final stretch would subject them to two mountain ranges and a wind-whipped steppe—the Blues and the Cascades, with the Horse Heaven Hills in between—as if the continent was taunting anyone who dared make it this far. If the Blue Mountains were less severe than the Cascades, they were still daunting enough that locals disagreed about the best way to surmount them while driving from Baker City to Walla Walla, connecting the twenty-eighth and twenty-ninth checkpoints and bringing the racers into Washington.

In May, both Bellows in Guggenheim's Allen-Kingston auto and the Thomas pathfinder had gone up through the city of La Grande, on the western side of the fertile Grande Ronde Valley, then ascended the Blues over a northwesterly course to Pendleton, before tacking back to Walla Walla, a 140-mile trip. On that drive, Bellows encountered snow near the summit at Meacham, a railroad outpost, and journeyed twenty-five miles at one stretch between houses; with fallen trees blocking the road and forcing long detours in multiple places, he had to stop periodically to seek directions from inhabitants of the Umatilla Indian Reservation, each side eyeing the other apprehensively. A few days later, the going was similarly rough for the Thomas, prompting the crew to recommend in the Blue Book that the racers follow a course the pathfinders hadn't even tried, tracing the eastern edge of the valley before climbing the Blues over the Toll Gate Road, a shorter but steeper journey.

That sounded smart to L. C. Smith, a Ford dealer in La Grande, even if it meant bypassing the two biggest cities in the region—La Grande and Pendleton—for a route through a lightly populated farming corridor. That didn't just mean fewer eyeballs on the cars themselves; it meant missing a chance to drive through two cities with daily newspapers and to parade past Smith's own newly expanded garage, the only Ford agency in the region. The *La Grande Evening Observer* called it "quite a disappointment to the local automobile enthusiasts that La Grande was not on the route as it would be quite a treat to view the famous cars." But sacrificing local publicity or ruffling a few feathers to save twenty miles and preserve the lead was an obvious choice for the Ford side.

Smith had moved around a bit, coming west after working for an engine manufacturer in Kansas City. Eleven months back, he'd evidently spotted an enticing REPRESENTATIVE WANTED ad amid the small-print classifieds of the *Evening Observer.* "Live hustler, with or without previous experience, can easily clear $2000.00 in season," the ad read, one of many that Ford had placed in similar papers all over the country, seeking to grow its dealer network before the launch of the Model T. "Write, with references at once. Ford Motor Co., Dept. H, Detroit, Michigan."

Well, Smith surely met both requirements. For one thing, he was still alive, having just survived a pipe wrench to the head in an attempted robbery, his thick leather cap absorbing most of the blow. And he was a hustler, never letting grass grow underfoot as a mechanically minded entrepreneur. After coming to La Grande to manage a bicycle shop around 1903, Smith split off to open his own business, offering to repair guns, sewing machines, scissors, roller skates, umbrellas, typewriters, or anything else that needed mending. He did well enough to buy a big lathe powered by a gas engine, at which point he declared himself La Grande's first automobile mechanic too. When he committed to the role by painting GARAGE over his door, the term was still exotic enough in eastern Oregon that Smith had to search for the word in several national magazines to make sure he spelled it right. Soon he was running an auto livery—twenty-five cents a ride, anywhere in the city—and dabbling in new and used car sales too. After grabbing the Ford rights, he sold six Model Ts to people in and around La Grande in quick succession in early 1909, numbers to rival a big-city dealer. Now he was moving into larger quarters. "If the present automobile craze continues," the *Evening Observer* noted, "the horse will see his finish in Union county."

Preparing for navigation duty, Smith went down to North Powder, a small town nestled in the hills south of the Grande Ronde Valley, to await the No. 2. He would guide the leader about seventy miles toward the Toll Gate, high in the Blue Mountains, an afternoon's journey into night. Even here there were no straight lines, and they set out over a rolling route to the northeast, coming down over those hills into Telocasset, at the corner of a fertile valley roughly twenty-seven hundred feet above sea level, hemmed in by the Wallowa Mountains to the east and the taller Blues to the north and west, the highest peaks scraping seven thousand feet. They drove up through Union, Alicel, and Summerville, where the No. 2 Ford stopped to repair a spring. The village of two hundred had retained its population even after being bypassed by the OR&N railroad, thanks to a 3.5-mile stagecoach line that ran regularly for twenty-five cents. The community included a soda jerker named Walt Witherell who'd been beaten by a minister in nearby Wallowa in 1908—reportedly with brass knuckles—for operating a soda shop and pool hall on Sundays. Doing business on the Sabbath wasn't Witherell's only vice. He smoked a hundred cigarettes a day, a habit still legal in Oregon—but not up the road in Washington state, where activist lawmakers had just banned the sale and public use of those so-called "coffin nails." That the legislature targeted cigarettes while giving a pass to cigars and pipes was no accident; reformists viewed cigarettes with particular loathing—cheap, machine-made, and spreading rapidly among the masses. Witherell would succumb to a bronchial attack the following week. That the controversial cigarette could be blamed made his death news beyond Summerville.

From there, the Blue Mountains loomed so large across a high ridge sweeping from the west that it was almost as if you could reach out and touch them. For thirty-five years, a private route known as the Summerville and Walla Walla Wagon Road had cut over those mountains via a comparative gap east of the summit known as the Toll Gate—later called Tollgate, a mere five thousand feet above sea level—linking the Summerville side of the Grande Ronde Valley with the Wallowa Valley farther east and booming Walla Walla to the north. Most people simply called it the Toll Gate Road or the Woodward Road, after the homesteaders who collected the toll at the top, starting at three cents for a sheep, a quarter for a saddled horse. The seasonal flow of traffic included fruit growers and sheepshearers, loggers and stockmen, as well as emigrant families still traveling with six-horse teams, small children poking their heads out from the wagon sheet. The forest around the summit had also become a popular recreation area, with the original Woodward cabin growing to include an eight-room inn and feed barn favored by fatigued travelers and fervent fly fishermen alike, with a store and dining room serving the broader campgrounds as well.

Climbing from Summerville, the toll road cut a narrow path through lush forest, amid crystalline streams and tempting huckleberries, but danger seemed to lurk too, and not just where the trail danced above a sheer drop. Thirteen years back, paterfamilias Dave Woodward had disappeared while trekking home from the valley in winter with provisions loaded on a hand sled; extensive searching in the months that followed yielded only his snowshoes, one of them broken, scattered a quarter mile apart. And three years ago, a four-year-old boy named Cecil Brittan wandered off while camping with a party near the summit, never to be seen again. Despite a search that included 150 men, the state-prison bloodhounds from Walla Walla, and the promise of a $1,000 reward, involving detectives and clairvoyants, no one found any meaningful trace of the boy, leaving authorities unsure if he'd been kidnapped or killed by a cougar.

Scott and Smith nosed the No. 2 uphill, fighting their way in the dark along a trail salted with occasional boulders—fine for a sidestepping horse and tolerable even for a wagon, but trouble for any automobile, even the comparatively high-riding Model T and its flexible suspension, especially at night. They straggled in at the summit after midnight, sinking into a few hours of sleep at the little hotel, where "Ma" Woodward's "bounteous table [had] become famous for its excellent mountain fare," in the words of one regional magazine. Four guides from Walla Walla were already waiting for the Ford, and they wasted little time in setting out again after the sun rose at 4:15 AM.

Not that they needed much help now. It was thirty downhill miles to Walla Walla, an auto-crazy city whose commercial club and automobile club together had been posting directional signs all over the region to blaze the trail for the racers and for summertime tourists—the sort of thing the Ocean-to-Ocean organizers had hoped would happen everywhere, mostly without success.

On the way, they passed the twin communities of Milton-Freewater in early morning, driving through wheat farms and fruit orchards toward Walla Walla. Just shy of the border, in an unincorporated place called Ferndale, the distant machine-gun snarl of the No. 2 Model T startled a slender boy named Oland Hubbs, out hunting rabbits with older brother Romeo. The worldlier fifteen-year-old Romeo suspected what they might be hearing was an automobile. Soon they could see it coming—the mud-caked Ford, a *2* barely visible on the hood, rumbling toward Walla Walla with a few pilots. The boys waved wildly. Bert Scott waved back. Olie Hubbs was not quite twelve. Already he had seen some things, meeting Buffalo Bill as a small child, and traveling west in a wagon train from the Tennessee hills at seven. In his long life ahead, he would become a leading apple grower, improving the color of the Red Rome Beauty and developing an enhanced variety of Red Delicious. In his eighties, writing to Bert Scott's son, he would call that surprise glimpse of the No. 2 Ford exiting Oregon "the greatest thrill of my life."

17

Going on Nerve Alone

Eastern Washington, June 21, 1909

Even with that catnap at the high-altitude Woodward ranch, the shortcut over the Toll Gate Road saved so much time that Scott and Smith surprised the people of Walla Walla when the No. 2 Ford eased in around 6:45 AM on Monday, June 21. Many still figured they were coming via Pendleton, and wouldn't arrive until late morning at least. The crew registered at the Hotel Dacres checkpoint—No. 29 of 30—and brought the car to the Inland Auto garage, one of the best-equipped in the Northwest, for a tune-up and new tire. Cut off from communication with the cars behind them, the men thought they might now be a full day ahead of the next car, maybe more, inside three hundred miles to go.

A scribe from the local *Evening Statesman* was one of the few to catch the arrival. "Travel-stained, bent and broken, with temporary repairs showing on every line of its frame work, with driver weary and soiled, mechanic greasy and black, the little Ford car, No. 2, which started from New York June 1 on its record-breaking New York–Seattle race . . . puffed exultantly into the Garden City at least 24 hours in advance of No. 1, its nearest competitor for the honors," the reporter would write—accepting the Ford estimate at face value, while assuming the Shawmut had slipped to third.

Word spread across Walla Walla, and soon hundreds of people had gathered at the corner of East Alder and Spokane, craning for a glimpse of the No. 2 through the big plate-glass windows of Inland Auto. After all, Walla Walla wasn't about to be caught napping for the race. This city of under twenty thousand punched above its weight as an agricultural hub, industrial center, and rail crossroads, taking pride in being the largest community in any direction for two hundred miles. Home as well to a substantial Army cavalry post, this was a mature city by West Coast standards, with a population that had first swelled amid an 1860s gold rush. Walla Walla had blossomed since into a place with broad boulevards, lush lawns, and ample shade trees, the kind you couldn't fake in a railroad town newly platted. Brochures boasted of New England–style charm, noting that President Theodore Roosevelt himself had claimed "Walla Walla made the pleasantest impression upon my mind of any city I visited in the Northwest," indelibly charmed by the "sweet perfume of the thousand locust trees."

Naturally, Walla Walla was all in on autos. "Every where is heard the warning honk! honk! of these machines of pleasure and gasoline," *The Evening Statesman* declared, describing a place swept up "by the merry sport of 'chuffing.'" And that was two years back, when it boasted just a few dozen automobiles. Now there were well over a hundred cars in the city limits, and several dozen more in the surrounding county. WALLA WALLA THE "BUZ WAGON BURG," the *Sunday Morning Bulletin* declared, deeming Walla Walla second only to Los Angeles in "number of 'whizz-wagons' in proportion to its population," among cities and towns of the West.

That was because locals had money to spend, between the might of the river-powered mills and factories in Walla Walla proper and, especially, the production of the wheat farms in the wider county. For 1908, Walla Walla County rated as one of the richest in the nation in per-capita agricultural production, at $200 for every man, woman, and child. And just one pass around the area this season made it clear the "stand is thick and the wheat has headed well," as Walla Walla's *Up-to-the-Times Magazine* put it, anticipating a 1909 yield of over $5 million for wheat alone—never mind apples and hops. That meant one thing, post-harvest: "The automobile agents will have another active season in Eastern Washington." The magazine made no apologies for that agrarian embrace of the auto, even if farmers in some other places still viewed cars as horse-spooking abominations. "Farmers have more use for a self-propelled vehicle than any other class of people. They travel oftener and go farther than many of their professional brethren; they have journeys to go and goods to deliver that call for speedy, reliable locomotion," *Up-to-the-Times* opined. That season alone, one Walla Walla wheat king bought three White steamers—a touring car for his family, a roadster for himself, and a runabout for his grown son—at $10,000 combined.

Amid that car-loving culture and civic pride, Walla Walla expressed as much enthusiasm for the Ocean-to-Ocean Race as any place on the route. Locals knew it meant one day "this whole stretch of country from New York to Seattle, via Walla Walla will be one long macadam road, suitable for automobiles or teams," the *Bulletin* wrote. "And when this day comes it means that Walla Walla will be on the direct line of pleasure seeking parties of easterners who are seeing the country by easy stages in automobiles." Car owners contemplating a motor club for outings and advocacy finally made it happen in the spring, motivated to put up those directional signs and send out a welcoming party for the pathfinder. When Elbert Bellows came through in Guggenheim's Allen-Kingston, preempting the official Thomas Flyer, nearly a dozen Walla Walla autoists met him twenty miles out, and several more fell in along the way. A week later, fully fifty automobile owners from Walla Walla drove all the way to Pendleton—forty miles—to escort the battle-scarred Thomas pathfinder to town for a royal reception at the Hotel Dacres. "If the president had been making the trip more anxiety and ado could not have been manifested by the motorists of this city," one paper said.

Even now, a month later, people were still mentioning that tremendous Thomas, its capacious rear covered with stickers and graffiti from around the world, and thunderous Allen-Kingston, sleek and muscular at once. So when they finally caught a glimpse of this vaunted first-place

Ford—well, they were a tad underwhelmed "at the size of the buzz-cart, as they had looked for a machine of greater dimension," the *Statesman* noted.

Part of it was they just hadn't seen many Fords, let alone a stripped-down one. For all of the company's inroads elsewhere, Ford had scarcely scratched Walla Walla. Twice the sales team had false starts lining up agents, once with a twentysomething student named Archie Henderson, attempting to sell Fords through a couple of failed partnerships while also working as a timekeeper for his father's construction firm, and then with the Walla Walla Motor Company, an actual brick-and-mortar dealership, though that outfit mainly focused on selling Reos—an accessibly priced Ford rival, backed by Ransom Eli Olds—before going under. Mostly people here drove what was on offer, meaning mid-priced Franklins, purchased from established dealer Inland Auto, or powerful but expensive White steam cars—like the ones President Taft favored—from rival dealer McBride three blocks over.

With the race looming, R. P. Rice in Seattle had lined up Henderson as a Ford guide—both in and out of Walla Walla—and booked him for a second try as local agent, though Henderson put up the deposit to order just two Model Ts for the entire season. Maybe this wasn't yet the place for lightweight cars. "For extended touring the light car can no more do the big car's work than a race horse can do the work of a draft horse," the *Morning Union* had noted that very weekend the racers approached, reprinting an anonymous car-buying guide that ran in several papers.

Charlie Hendy had other ideas. This wasn't even his territory—it was Rice's, of course—but when he rolled in by train a little behind the No. 2 he sang the praises of the lean car, at least as manufactured by Ford. "This race has demonstrated I think conclusively, the superiority of the light-weight car for touring purposes. Weighing scarcely more than 1200 pounds, the Ford cars have made their way over places where the heavier cars have stuck," Hendy told the *Evening Bulletin*.

By then the No. 2 was gone. Scott and Smith bolted west around 8:15 AM, hoping to hit the finish line inside forty-eight hours, depending on how they fared crossing the Cascades. Armed with updated information,

Hendy predicted the No. 1 Ford would reach Walla Walla by nightfall, just twelve to fourteen hours back of the leader. He said nothing of the Shawmut.

Forced to leave Earle Chapin behind, the Shawmut managed to get out of Baker City ahead of the No. 1 Ford that Monday morning, but fell back again into third inside twenty miles, in the hills approaching the Grande Ronde Valley. From there, Kulick in the No. 1 Ford pursued the same route that the leader had taken the previous afternoon, up the eastern edge of the valley, aiming for the Toll Gate Road. The Shawmut went the same way. The two cars battled all the way to the little town of Alicel, roaring at a speed rarely witnessed in these parts, until the Shawmut clutch gave out near a ranch belonging to James McKenzie, a fifty-year-old cattle and fruit man who'd come to the valley as a boy in a wagon train with his Scottish parents. Pettengill and Messer nursed the car up the road to Summerville, where they stopped for repairs.

Back in Rock Springs, Wyoming, they had telegraphed Boston to ask Horace Waite to ship a replacement clutch ahead to Baker City. Whether or not Waite followed through would become a matter lost to history, though the crew felt increasingly untethered from corporate support the farther west they drove. New clutch or old, the Shawmut duo managed to fix the problem in forty-five minutes, even without Earle Chapin's expertise. Soon they were off again, clawing up and over the Blue Mountains with surprising agility for a car that size.

The Shawmut reached Walla Walla just after 7 PM, an hour behind the second-place Ford. Locals had turned out in big numbers to watch "the battle scarred benzine carts ramble through the streets," as the *Statesman* put it. Pettengill and Messer stashed the car at Inland Auto and headed to the Hotel Dacres a few blocks west, to register at the checkpoint and get some sustenance. From the outside, the three-story Dacres looked like a generous wedge cut from a frosted cake, simple brick along the sides but heavily adorned along its Main Street front, with an incandescent overhanging sign and a whitewashed Italianate façade on the upper stories, decorative columns between every window. Inside, the Boston men ventured to the desk, amid potted palms and polished-brass spittoons, opposite a dining room where a four-piece orchestra performed nightly. As they handed over their racing passport for endorsement and received the cards to sign and mail to Seattle, the Shawmut men learned that the No. 1 Ford crew was dining at the Dacres at that very moment.

The begrimed motorists greeted each other warmly. The evening papers were already out, with stories about the No. 2 Ford's success splashed across the front pages of both the *Statesman* and *Bulletin*. The latter at least had been topped off with a note about the imminent arrival of the Shawmut and the No. 1 Ford, after their dual departures from Baker City in the morning. But to read the *Statesman* was to think the Boston entry had vanished outside Boise the night before, a distant third: "The Shawmut car, one of the racers, has not been heard of in this section, and it is thought has been delayed for a considerable length of time by accident or break."

The *Statesman*'s man on the scene made up for it now, interviewing Pettengill. The Shawmut captain said they were all going on "nerve" alone, and if they had to drive any farther than Seattle he wasn't sure any crew would finish. After this meal, he and Messer would try to push straight through from the Dacres to the end without a break. They were glad to be dining at an established hotel with transparent pricing, and told of being charged exorbitant sums at some stops. One man who furnished a meal initially refused to take their money, seeming to signal it was an honor just to feed them; only afterward did he hand over a folded paper requesting \$5—an extraordinary bill, equal to a dinner, a show, and a moderate hotel on Broadway. (Auto writer J. C. Kerrison in the *Boston Evening American* predicted as much, warning in May about the considerable premium imposed on motorists at some rural hostelries: "In general, the sentiment toward the automobilist is much improved, but there is still a widely spread notion that they are all very wealthy sports and legitimate prey for mulcting.")

As for all the crews going on "nerve," well, the Fords had that, but it wasn't nerve alone, not with a network of helping hands laid out from New York to the finish. That the Shawmut had made it this far, still in the running, was an achievement not lost on a local *New York Times* stringer, rushing to compile a race dispatch with the hour growing late back east. Soon, that feed from Walla Walla flashed across the continent toward Times Square as a succession of telegraphic pulses, annihilating the distance in an instant. At the end of its journey, the signal darted in via copper cable under the Broadway side of the New York Times Building between Forty-Second and Forty-Third, where 162 bundled telegraph wires lay buried beneath the very pavement that the Shawmut and Fords had driven over twenty days earlier. From there the pulses climbed through fireproof ductwork to the newspaper's telegraph room, where a dutiful corps of men listened fastidiously to the *click-clack-clack* of their respective sounding boxes and transcribed the audible dots and dashes into text, hammering out thirty-five words a minute on typewriters—a torrent of daily wire copy from all points, coordinated and sifted by the telegraph editor, and sent from there to the proper desk in the newsroom.

They slotted this story on the sports page, between the baseball scores and the latest feed from seventy-year-old pedestrian Edward Payson Weston, now crossing Utah. FORD NO. 2 LEADING NEAR END OF RACE, they headlined it. SHOULD WIN VERY EASILY. But they also gave credit to the oft-overlooked Boston entry: "The performance of the Shawmut car has been remarkable, for throughout the long and trying journey the car has labored under the handicap of being without adequate equipment. Any sort of serious accident would put the Shawmut out of competition, for it has not had the support of a factory such as the Ford, Acme, and Itala cars have had. When the Shawmut left New York automobile experts prophesied that it would be the first car to drop out of the contest."

According to that *New York Times* dispatch, the neck-and-neck No. 5 Shawmut and No. 1 Ford had reached Walla Walla faster than expected, then left again quickly, "after being oiled and gone over." That line did some heavy lifting for a correspondent on deadline. The Kulick Ford was in rougher shape than the Shawmut, needing repairs to its gas tank as well as an axle—presumably the rear one, notoriously problematic on first-generation Model Ts. Ford had used simple sleeve bearings on the sides of the differential, made from soft Babbitt metal prone to stretching out from pounding on rough roads, requiring regular replacements during the race.

Inland Auto was not technically a Ford shop, but the garage managers had a relationship with Archie Henderson, the on-again, off-again Ford agent in Walla Walla, and they had helped guide the No. 2 that morning from the Toll Gate. Now in the evening they had pulled the No. 1 Ford into the rear repair room at Inland. More than half of the big garage was taken up by an open space for washing, oiling, and storing twenty-four automobiles, but the rest of Inland Auto had been carved into smaller warrens, including an office, a bunk room for overnight workers, and a thirty-five-by-fifty-five-foot repair shop laden with equipment for heavy work. That the No. 1 Ford had not yet reappeared from that repair room gave Pettengill and Messer some confidence that they might leave Walla Walla in second, with a little breathing room on the Kulick T.

They had picked up a new guide, Dick Tyson, a twenty-five-year-old who lived on a ranch thirty miles west with his widowed mother, just the two of them now, after his father had died suddenly and a brother got crushed working on the railroad. Tyson had helped the pathfinder in May, after it got marooned amid high water near his home in Wallula, making him a good candidate for the Shawmut. Around 9:20 PM, the Boston men were preparing to depart when they learned that the No. 1 Ford had already left, ducking slyly out the side door of the repair room instead of coming back through the garage. The Shawmut bolted, ten minutes behind.

In the lead, Scott and Smith felt constant pressure, knowing the faster Shawmut might charge from behind. Nothing would be a given until they got over the mighty hump of the Cascades, another two hundred miles off, and could coast the final fifty miles to Seattle. Out of Walla Walla, they would first need to cross the Columbia River by ferry at Wallula, then skirt the Horse Heaven Hills to Prosser and trace the Yakima River—a tributary of the Columbia—northwest to the mountains, deep into the geographic center of the state.

That first leg started with a fine drive among fertile farmland west for ten or fifteen miles, roughly following the westerly course of the Walla Walla River toward the Columbia, the largest river in the American West. Then the conditions became unforgiving, wheat fields and orchards giving way to sagebrush and sand, the treeless hills laced with jackrabbit trails, the dusty roadbed whipped by more tumbleweed than traffic. It took the No. 2 over two hours to reach and cross the river at Wallula, as even the light Ford spun out and struggled for traction.

That was just a taste of what was to come. The mighty Columbia curved like a hairpin at Wallula so that upstream it banked northwest, while downstream it flowed three hundred miles southwest toward Portland and the ocean. Known for its massive width as well as its length, the Columbia ran a mile wide here—comparatively narrow—hemmed in by a cliff formation known as the Wallula Gap. The region lay in the rain shadow of the Cascades, hotter in summer and substantially drier than the coast, deprived of the temperate air known as the Japan Current; as an arid shrub-steppe, it received less than a foot of rain annually. Across the river, the west bank boasted a rugged, foreboding beauty that matched the east side in treelessness but far exceeded it in expanse. Although irrigated farmland and scattered communities clung near the river going northwest, the vast land to the west climbed swiftly to form the sparsely populated Horse Heaven Plateau and adjoining Horse Heaven Hills, a rolling region ribbed with gulches and canyons, where wild horses still roamed, feeding on bunchgrass and coming down to the river to drink. The wind blew strongest this time of year, whipping the thin, loose topsoil into dust storms that could last for days, shaping dunes to rival any beach or desert.

Once across the river from Wallula, most travelers traced the irrigated, inhabited edge of the Columbia twelve miles northwest to Kemmerer, either by stagecoach or a relatively new railroad, and from Kemmerer headed due west to Prosser, even then a rough ride winding across a mesa. The

Ford men, guided by Archie Henderson, attempted a far more strenuous shortcut from the ferry to Prosser, slicing directly over the Horse Heaven Plateau. The Horse Heaven crossing should have been the worst part. But that route first brought them across the southern end of a recently expanded irrigation system known as the Kennewick Canal, presenting the sort of ditch the Model T could typically drive through, especially with water flowing well below the rim. But this canal was especially prone to seepage, and that morning the surrounding area had become a mess. For a time Bert Scott thought they might be trapped amid high water, but they eventually worked their way through.

From there they fought for seven hours across the Horse Heaven Hills, covering barely thirty miles, scraping over sagebrush and jouncing among deep ruts. Sand whipped their faces beneath their goggles; their wheels spun in the dunes with so little purchase at times that Scott worried they might get stuck there. Jimmie Smith was so tired he would doze off, snap awake to help, and then promptly fall asleep again, upright in the passenger seat, immune to the jolting and bumping, the roar of the engine and the howl of the wind. Crouching in back, guide Archie Henderson from Walla Walla could scarcely believe it.

At 6:20 PM they reached the tiny community of Horse Heaven, which shared its name with the wider plateau, sustained in this spartan region by a well sunk a thousand feet down. It was less a town than a post office locale, twenty miles southeast of Prosser, the city of twelve hundred where Henderson planned to leave them. Mail reached Horse Heaven just twice a week, but a barbed-wire telephone network connected the homes here to Prosser. One rancher who saw the little Ford go by called ahead to the city, the line crackling with excitement. Five leading citizens piled into a car belonging to a wealthy real estate man and drove out to the base of the hills beyond Prosser to greet the leader.

Around 7:30 they saw the No. 2 tearing toward them, kicking up dust. The quintet guided the Ford into downtown Prosser, a small but thriving county seat nestled into a cove between those Horse Heaven Hills and a bend in the Yakima River, with municipal water, electric lighting, and two weekly papers, its tidy downtown bisected by the Northern Pacific. They pulled up outside the Prosser Hotel, a two-story frame structure with a broad porch and columns that looked suitable for tying up a horse, the sun dipping low over town to the west. It seemed like half of Prosser was out, hundreds of people crowding for a glimpse of the Ford.

This wasn't a checkpoint, but Scott and Smith planned to stop here to change guides, refuel, and revive themselves a bit. They were famished and fatigued, going eleven straight hours since Walla Walla, nearly all of it through hostile conditions. Sitting down to eat, they chatted with reporters, Scott explaining that his division of labor with mechanic Smith had blurred, each of them taking turns at the wheel, driving until they could no longer keep their eyes open. They scarcely had time to rest here. They got a message from R. P. Rice, Seattle branch manager. He had telephoned long-distance from Ellensburg, ninety miles away. That daring driver he'd sent eastward to greet them, Harry Disher, had needed the better part of two days to clear the Cascades. The situation was so urgent that Rice had evidently gotten on a train and come east to help, before doubling back to await Henry Ford in Seattle. He urged Scott and Smith not to linger. They needed to keep driving through the night, pressing on for North Yakima and Ellensburg.

At that moment, the other Ford and the Shawmut were both in Walla Walla, about eighty-five miles back. Scott and Smith hustled out of the hotel, stopping for gasoline before cranking up again. They moved quickly, nerves strained, a large crowd around the car. You had to lift the passenger seat to pour gasoline into the tank. Some of it sloshed, spilling onto blankets and gear amid the seat and footwell, the pungent smell of gas vapor hanging in the air. As for what happened next, even onlookers couldn't agree. Did *Prosser Republican-Bulletin* editor Halsey Watson accidentally lean in with his cigar, or had someone else foolishly struck a match? Did the splattered gasoline ignite, or just the vapor? Because all of a sudden, flames enveloped the cab. For a heart-stopping moment, people thought they were witnessing the demise of the front-runner, right here in Prosser. But Bert Scott and Jimmie Smith sprang into action, along with some onlookers, to smother the fire with coats before dousing the car thoroughly with an extinguisher rushed over from the Prosser Hotel. By the time the city's volunteer firefighters had retrieved the department's fifty-gallon, horse-drawn chemical engine, the drama was over. A conflagration that might have consumed Ford's shot at victory instead ended with the No. 2 T simply scorched—looking more bedraggled than ever, but still drivable when Scott and Smith departed around 8:45 PM, crossing the bridge over the Yakima River and pointing toward Sunnyside, barely two hundred miles to go.

18

Clawing Through Central Washington

June 21 to 23, 1909

On the flat road west from Walla Walla, the Shawmut thundered into the night, gunning for the No. 1 Ford. The big car seemed made for stretches like this, making up time with its muscular engine and sixty-five mph straightaway speed. But as solid ground gave way to basalt sands moving westward, it was the lighter Model T, not the Shawmut, that ran into trouble. Roughly halfway between Walla Walla and the Wallula river crossing, multiple parts on the No. 1 broke down. Grounded, Kulick and Harper had to send back to Inland Auto for repairs. Now it was the Shawmut's turn to pass a Model T in the night, Pettengill and Messer wondering how long this rival might be stalled.

Continuing toward the river, the Shawmut was moving at a good clip, twenty miles down in barely half an hour, when the car punctured a tire in the black of night. Of course their good luck couldn't last. Laboring in the dark, they chewed up at least two hours struggling to fix the stubborn shoe. It must have felt like the Ford would catch them again at any moment. Finally, they got the car moving, rolling into sleepy Wallula at 12:50 AM. Here they were at the mercy of yet another ferry, the *Elsie May*, docked at a lonely slip on the river a mile west of town. They would be forced to wait until dawn to cross—an unwanted respite, with the No. 2

Ford surely gaining ground ahead, and the No. 1 likely to creep up from behind at any moment.

What a place to be stuck. Wallula (population 350, maybe) had known more drama in its history than most places ten times its size—bearing the hallmarks of how a railroad could make and break a town, and a river before that, here where the Walla Walla River met the mighty Columbia, just downstream from the Snake. Lewis and Clark had stopped here on their way out in 1805 and again coming back in 1806, receiving such a generous welcome from the local Wallulapum that Meriwether Lewis deemed them "the most hospitable, honest, and sincere people that we have met with in our voyage."

In 1818, the river bend became the site of a massive fur-trading post—first called Fort Nez Percés, then Fort Walla Walla—so fortified that some called it "the Gibraltar of the Columbia." For decades, a mountain of pelts passed through here, loaded onto boats floating down to Fort Vancouver and the Pacific, to feed London's hunger for beaver-felted hats. After the second of two forts here burned in the Yakima War in 1855, the Hudson's Bay Company abandoned the post; at the same time, the U.S. Army built an unrelated Fort Walla Walla thirty miles east, near what would become the city of Walla Walla.

That might have doomed this old locale, but the rise of steamboats caused a boomtown to sprout at this convenient bend in the river. The town—now dubbed *Wallula*—mushroomed into a rough-and-ready outpost for cattlemen and traders, miners and teamsters, serving as a junction between Columbia steamboats and inland wagon routes. Then railroads supplanted river and wagon trade, initially ignoring Wallula. The town withered, amid sand dunes inhospitable to farming. Just when Wallula seemed written off, an entrepreneurial doctor tied it to Walla Walla in 1875 with a narrow-gauge railroad fashioned from wooden boards and strap metal, sustaining Wallula until larger railroads arrived as well. Except when they did, both major players here—the Northern Pacific and the Oregon Railway & Navigation Company—bypassed Wallula by laying rails a mile inland. Instead of folding, the town carted itself toward the tracks and started over. The railroads rewarded the relocated community with roundhouses and machine shops; the new Wallula flourished, with the population exceeding a thousand by the late 1880s, buoyed by railroad laborers and their families. But those railways were fickle, and both eventually moved operations elsewhere, leaving Wallula a husk of a city by 1890, with ranchers carting off abandoned buildings to homesteads outside of town. A grand depot remained, two hundred feet long and finished with oiled hardwoods, a bittersweet reminder of that brief second ascendance.

And yet: Just a few years ago, Seattle investors had revived a dormant private irrigation scheme, bringing a trickle of settlers back. Now Wallula had a three-teacher school, a weekly newspaper, a town band, two general stores, and a hotel. (All of it would be doomed in 1953, when the Army Corps flooded the region, forcing Wallula to move once again.)

At least the overnight here for the Shawmut would be short, the sun rising at four this time of year, not seven. While waiting, they picked up a new pilot, Ive Doak, a twenty-seven-year-old day laborer who had done time for highway robbery when he was just a teenager.

Finally, 3:30 came around; they set out with Doak for the ferry landing. No sign in town yet of the No. 1 Ford. They had the boat to themselves. The *Elsie May* was a stern-wheeler, though with none of the grandeur that might convey, just a flat-topped barge with a pilot house. Its captain, Robert Pitman, was a retired railroad section foreman from downriver with the good timing to buy the sleepy ferry in 1904, just as canal projects on both sides of the Columbia were about to draw new settlers and cause traffic to pick up. At first Pitman operated with no license and no foghorn or bell. When the feds got word, they sent a series of letters. When those were ignored, a customs inspector visited Wallula, only to slip and scald his hand on the *Elsie May*'s steam pipe. Infuriated, the agent issued three fines totaling a staggering $780. Pitman resisted, but after lugging the inspector to see his lawyer, he acquiesced, while insisting the government agent accompany him by horse another few miles to his home for payment. There, the ferryman drew a weathered billfold—and extracted a thousand-dollar bill, attesting to the *Elsie May*'s profits. The agent's jaw dropped. He had nowhere near the cash to return $220 in change. They tried working it out with money orders at the post office, but Wallula's postmaster didn't have enough on hand either. When the government finally knocked the fines down to $150, the tale made news across the state.

The *Elsie May* puttered across the Columbia with the Shawmut, sun peeking up behind them. On the opposite bank, they disembarked near a little town called Hover, named for a wealthy Washington land speculator leaving his own mark on the auto world. The year before, Herbert A. Hover and his wife, Mata, had completed a seven-month, seven-thousand-mile journey from Tijuana up to Washington and across the country to New York, with just a modicum of railroad assistance. That made them the first known motorists to traverse the nation both south-north and west-east, and they were just getting started. Hover was a self-made land baron with an eighth-grade education; he yearned to see the world with Mata from behind the wheel of their Maxwell. They planned a four-year, seventy-five-thousand-mile trek around the globe, intending to ship their car from continent to continent in between. That worldwide journey wouldn't quite work out as planned—they survived the sinking of the White Star Line's RMS *Republic* in January, but it put a damper on that trip—though by 1949 they would be profiled in *The New York Times* for their decades of prolific motoring. By then they were believed to be the first married couple to log one million automobile touring miles, Herbert still doing all the driving into his eighties.

With Ive Doak as guide, the Shawmut headed up from Hover along the northwest curve of the Columbia, a less direct but smoother route than the sand-swept, sagebrush-trampling journey of the No. 2 Ford the day before. Breezing through Kennewick sometime before 6 AM, the big Shawmut caught early risers by surprise. "The people of Kennewick have been seeing things," the local *Twin City Reporter* would write. Not "those fly-by-night airships, such as wafted across the borders of Germany recently . . . but racing devil carts which are here today, there tomorrow, and leave behind but a fleeting memory and a smell." If locals blinking sleep out of their eyes missed the NO. 5 on the hood or the SHAWMUT on the side as the car raced by, they could tell what it was from the words stenciled on its vanishing rear, as the auto "whizzed through town at a breath taking clip."

From there it was nearly forty miles to Prosser, where the Shawmut stopped briefly at 9:20 AM to change guides. Dropping Doak, they picked up Alva McLane, a thirty-four-year-old optician, city councilor, and bank vice president who had been part of the welcoming party that greeted the leader the night before, shortly before the No. 2 Ford caught fire. That was almost thirteen hours ago. The Shawmut was firmly in second now, but they'd made up no time on the leader since Walla Walla.

Up ahead, in that flame-scarred No. 2, Bert Scott had fought the urge to fall asleep with every fiber of his being. If he and Smith stopped to rest, the Shawmut could cut the gap to just a few hours before they even reached the Cascades, where anything might happen.

From Prosser to North Yakima, fifty miles off, they followed a team of guides in their own car, not just one man hanging on in back of their Ford. These four men had come from fifteen miles up in Sunnyside, a "Christian Cooperative Colony" that had grown into a bustling town of a thousand in a decade, drawing transplanted Midwesterners looking for a place where alcohol, gambling, and prostitution were not just banned but would cause property forfeiture, written into the deeds. The crew included one of the colony's founders, Christian Rowland, a former Illinois bank president, with his son Joy, an aspiring doctor, at the wheel.

The convoy passed through Sunnyside well after dark, no real time to stop. And yet, decades later, a Sunnyside fixture who became a prolific chronicler of the Northwest would write with aplomb about sneaking away from work as a twenty-year-old hardware clerk to await the lead racer. Roscoe Sheller recalled joining the throngs on Sixth Street, watching for a telltale cloud of dust to appear in the distance, a "*Here she comes!*"

cry electrifying the crowd when it arrived—a daytime scene laden with details that popped in his memory.

Plastered with mud, the crew asked for a pail of water, washing themselves, "exposing brown, leathered faces below the goggle-protected white skin," otherworldly in appearance. With heavy gloves, Bert Scott removed the radiator cap carefully, the car emitting a "wrathful 'hiss-s-s.'" Fed water from the pail, the little Ford sprayed steam over the crowd, a scalding souvenir "for folks to boast about to their unborn grandchildren." Then "Smitty" *glug-glugged* motor oil from a can into a breather pipe under the hood until it flowed from two petcocks sticking out of the crankcase beneath the car, indicating it was full.

"Sure takes a lot of oil," a kid said.

"You would, too, if you'd been through what this car has," the mechanic replied.

Maybe, maybe not. But the seeds of truth in the scene surely grew in Roscoe Sheller's mind, after that young hardware clerk became a Ford salesman himself.

Another ten miles past Sunnyside, still with those guides, the No. 2 reached the village of Granger around 11:15 PM. Scott went to the telephone and asked to be connected with the Yakima Hotel in North Yakima, the final checkpoint of the race. A man named Guy C. Williams had come down from Ellensburg to wait for them there. When Seattle branch manager R. P. Rice and assistant manager John Lund had lined up guides across the state in the spring, they lacked the luxury of their counterparts back East, in populous states with scores of Ford dealers. In all of Washington, besides the big Seattle branch, you could count the state's Ford dealers on two hands—and none of those agents operated along the route. That was part of why Rice had sent experienced mechanic and driver Harry Disher out from Seattle, to keep going until he met the lead racer coming the other way. Rice and Lund had been forced to get creative, shaking the trees. In Walla Walla that meant reengaging on-again, off-again dealer Archie Henderson. In Sunnyside, it was the Rowlands. In Ellensburg, it was Williams, an especially good catch.

It wasn't just that Williams, at twenty-seven, was an influential local businessman, involved in real estate, lumber, insurance, and agriculture, or even that he would sign on as a Ford agent, trying his hand at selling a few Model Ts around the small but growing Kittitas County seat, giving him some skin in the race. His father was none other than H. R. Williams, president of the Chicago, Milwaukee & Puget Sound Railway—the man in charge these last four years of developing the massive extension that made the Milwaukee Road a true transcontinental line, and who now oversaw fourteen hundred miles of track and operations from the Dakotas to the coast. The son didn't quite hold an official role, but last year he'd turned the partial completion of the line into a chance for a party, throwing a dinner-dance for fifty in a railroad warehouse, followed by a christening ride on a pair of specially outfitted flatcars. Not a bad friend to have if the race's final hurdle would take you over remote Snoqualmie Pass, where the Milwaukee Road boasted a small army of railroad section hands.

On the telephone line from the hamlet of Granger, Bert Scott informed Williams about the fire in Prosser. He was exhausted, not sure how much farther he and Smith could make it. But he agreed to keep plugging for North Yakima, trying not to fall asleep at the wheel, understanding the top-down imperative to continue no matter what. Grinding out the distance at less than ten miles an hour, they passed Toppenish around midnight, finally reaching North Yakima at 2:30 in the morning. Despite the late hour, two dozen people waited to glimpse the leader in front of the Yakima Hotel, a handsome three-story building with a broad balcony and tiered roofline, on busy East Yakima Avenue. They gaped at Jimmie Smith, somehow asleep even as he sat upright in the stiff passenger seat of the Model T.

North Yakima was a bustling place with Walla Walla energy, though here they would have said it the other way around. This city of nearly fourteen thousand also punched far above its weight class, as the largest community in any direction for more than a hundred miles, similarly bolstered by river and rail and flush with agricultural profits—in this case apples, as well as hops and potatoes, cherries and grapes, dairy farming and poultry, if not Walla Walla wheat. Despite the relative lack of rain, the soil here proved a supple gift to farmers, responding handsomely to private irrigation efforts that preceded a massive federal Reclamation Service project now in the works. "Yakima valley is a land of marvelous fruit stories, of big ditches, of plenty of sunshine, of activity . . . in building. Everybody has money, and public sentiment ostracizes the man who complains of hard times," *Pacific Builder and Engineer* magazine recently put it. The local press estimated there were even more automobiles here per capita than in Walla Walla. And all those cars—gleaming from the factory or dusty from the farm—conjured a cheeky line on many a mind: "Who'd a thought it? Apples bought it."

Another thing about North Yakima, which would drop the *North* in another decade: Charlie Hendy was here too. Already far beyond the boundaries of his Denver-branch territory back in Walla Walla, he'd kept right on going deep into Washington, plunging into Seattle-branch turf. That was the kind of tenacity Henry Ford appreciated.

Scott and Smith scraped themselves from the car and entered the hotel, to register at the checkpoint and meet Williams, the next guide. As Smith waited to sign the card for Seattle, exhaustion overtook him again; he dropped to the counter, suddenly asleep. Hendy sized them up and "permitted the boys" to nap ninety minutes, matching the time for a brief tune-up.

After a couple of recent closures, North Yakima had two bona fide garages, typical of the shuffle and growing pains that accompanied the automobile's emergence in communities like this, where entrepreneurial dreamers and enterprising mechanics sometimes got ahead of their skis. One garage sat a block from the hotel, in a retrofitted Methodist church. The other, half a mile west, occupied a purpose-built automotive building, though that wasn't the only thing it had going. The Yakima Auto Company was less than a year old, but the partners behind it—one a former drugstore man, the other a rancher and real estate investor—had jumped in big, acquiring the vacant brick garage of the similarly named Yakima Garage & Automobile Company, a failed outfit organized by relatives of a major hops broker.

From the get-go, the new Yakima Auto advertised storage for fifty cars, plus repairs, vulcanizing, and battery recharging, but they were already running out of room as they matured into a sales agency too. Soon they would build a bigger space on the east side, picking up Ford rights for the area; within a few years, lead partner Fred Chandler, the former druggist, would own five Ford dealerships up and down the valley. For now, they remained officially unaffiliated. But two of their mechanics had worked at the Ford factory back East.

They evidently oversaw the tune-up, and then Hendy roused Scott and Smith at the Yakima Hotel. Word spread, and by the time the No. 2 had pulled out of the garage again onto West Yakima Avenue, a phalanx of local auto owners had lined up to escort them out of town, even though it was 4 AM. It was enough to give even the most exhausted crew a jolt of adrenaline.

The breakdown for the No. 1 Ford, in third place, out of Walla Walla set that car back more than either of the first two crews realized. The Kulick Model T didn't reach Wallula until 1 PM that Tuesday, June 22, half a day after the Shawmut's sunrise departure and a full twenty-seven hours behind the first Ford. (At that moment, the Acme had not yet reached Idaho, while the Itala was somewhere between Denver and Cheyenne.)

Forced to improvise, they picked up a seemingly knowledgeable guide, Ernest Swauger—a forty-year-old Wallula laborer, a hardworking family man who had driven teams, worked on the railroad, and dug canals. He said he could take them to Prosser. Evidently he knew more about the east side of the Columbia River than the west. After crossing on the ferry, they got lost going over the Horse Heaven Hills. Just a few miles in, the crew began to worry, as they bumped over bunchgrass ridges far from anything resembling a landmark, not even a tree. The region had been formed by ancient lava flows that cooled into solid basalt, several thousand feet thick. With nothing to break the wind, the decomposing top layer had been whipped into a chalky sand, as if they were stuck in an endless golf trap.

"The road was entirely lost in the sand," Harper would write. "In that country the sand drifts and blows with every puff of wind—a sand storm that was a veritable blizzard of sand had raged around us for hours. To have stopped anywhere on that desert for the night would have meant being buried in the sand. In places it had blown in piles as high as a three story building."

Around 9 PM they finally came downhill toward something resembling civilization: a lone turkey ranch, framed by railroad tracks and a river. But this was not their destination of Prosser, on the Yakima River. Instead it was a place called Mottinger, along the Columbia—about fifteen miles downstream from Wallula. If the Horse Heaven region was a clockface, they had started at three o'clock, needing to go northwest to Prosser, beyond ten o'clock. Instead, they'd gone inland and out again, somehow ending up around five o'clock on the dial, meaning they made *negative* progress over a brutal seven and a half hours. Prosser lay thirty-five miles off as the crow flies, a grim drive back again over the Horse Heaven country.

Mottinger wasn't even a town; it was just this ranch, where George Mottinger and his family let turkeys roam during the day, feeding on stubble and grasshoppers, herding them into pens at night before the coyotes started to howl. He also served as one-man postmaster and meteorological observer. Two years back, the first phase of a new railroad came through and broke up the isolation—the Spokane, Portland & Seattle Railway, which hugged this side of the Columbia, built by rail tycoon James J. Hill to link the two transcontinental railroads he controlled, the Great Northern and Northern Pacific, with Portland. Scattering stops along the way, the SP&S placed one here and named it after the rancher as a courtesy, putting Mottinger on the map.

George Mottinger was overjoyed by the surprise. No automobile had ever visited before. Less charitably, Harper would deem it "a place where no automobile has any moral right to be," describing the mixed-up guide who got them there as a "road juggler" to rival the man who lost them in the middle of Idaho. They had to stifle the urge to ditch him at this ranch.

But they would need Swauger's help a little longer. Mottinger told them there was a slightly larger place called Plymouth nine miles west along the rails, still unincorporated but sitting opposite the Columbia River from Umatilla, Oregon, a bona fide town. You couldn't get lost if you simply rode the tracks, but the route would end with a claustrophobic tunnel. Plymouth had been named for a big rock jutting into the river, and the railroad burrowed through it with an eight-hundred-foot tunnel—though it was so cramped and devoid of light that it felt far longer. Kulick and Harper bounced along the ties to the mouth of that tunnel, then made the guide get out and walk clear through to the other side, so he could flag down any train that might approach while they made their way through the inky interior of the rock.

At Plymouth they dropped Swauger and hired a fresh guide, trying for Prosser anew. By the time they reached the destination at 9 AM Wednesday, they had fallen some twenty-four hours behind the Shawmut and thirty-six hours behind the No. 2 Ford.

It was now a two-car race.

19

Bearing Up Under the News

Washington's Yakima Valley, June 22, 1909

Bolstered by that 4 AM convoy out of North Yakima, Bert Scott aimed the lead Ford toward Ellensburg. At least the sun was up, because the drive was about to become mountainous, here among the eastern foothills of the Cascades. Ellensburg lay twenty-seven miles north as the crow flies, thirty-seven by rail, with the Northern Pacific following the jagged course of the Yakima River through a dramatic canyon path of basalt ridges and folds, ninety minutes on the train. A lone rider on horseback could make a fairly straight shot, but getting to Ellensburg with a wagon team or an automobile meant an indirect trip. There was no natural room for a road in the narrow river canyon, and the state wouldn't blast out space for another decade and a half. The primary wagon route wound for forty-five miles, swinging west toward the Wenas Valley, where you could follow a more manageable incline over the Umtanum Ridge, then descend Shushuskin Canyon into Ellensburg, a city of four thousand nestled in a valley along the river, surrounded by lush timothy grass.

It was nearly eight o'clock by the time Scott pulled up in front of Ellensburg's Hotel Antlers, a three-story brick hotel at the head of Pearl Street, steam heat and running water in each of its ninety-five rooms. He and Smith hadn't gotten a real night's sleep since Twin Falls, three days back, rarely even stopping for a few hours. They went inside the Antlers for breakfast, sitting for perhaps a half hour, going through the motions of being human. Guy Williams, the guide who'd ushered them from North Yakima, son of the influential railroad executive, apparently dropped out here. He'd been on high alert since the previous afternoon, then pulled an all-nighter, as much as most ordinary people could take. Joseph Steiner replaced him, a twenty-seven-year-old who ran the Antlers with his father, a veteran hotelier and caterer who'd worked in hospitality since before Washington was a state.

According to the Blue Book prepared by the pathfinder, Ellensburg was where you needed to telegraph ahead forty-five miles to Lake Keechelus, via the station at Martin, to alert Patrick Flanagan that you would need his ferry across the lake, a remote, crystalline body of water nestled amid the mountains right before the climb up Snoqualmie Pass. Otherwise, you might really have to wait. Flanagan was a colorful miner and lumberman who operated a small barge on the lake to serve his own businesses and bring occasional travelers across, mostly teamsters and families with wagons, for a tidy fee. He could afford to name his price, especially when it came to the odd automobile that attempted to venture this way. The old wagon road around the lake had been flooded out two years back by a temporary dam, making Flanagan's ferry the only way to get from one side to the other.

The Ford left immediately for Cle Elum, nearly thirty miles off to the northwest, the last big town before that daunting climb over Snoqualmie Pass. One hour bled into the next, as they ground out ten miles an hour on a meandering wagon road. The established Northern Pacific and the newly transcontinental Milwaukee crossed at Ellensburg, and the two railroads danced close to the Yakima River from there all the way to Cle Elum, with the Milwaukee mainly hugging the south side and the NP the north. The wagon road wandered in and out of view of the river and rails on the southern side of the valley.

At 11 AM the Ford reached Cle Elum, a coal town of nearly 2,750 that had grown tenfold in a decade. As *The Coast* magazine put it, this was a place of beauty and grit, of breathtaking mountain vistas and cool-running streams, soot-covered men and frugal cottages, "the accent of foreign tongues" echoing up and down First Street. It was undeniably "sprightly and thriving," with two hotels, five churches, and a substantial schoolhouse, all sustained by pick-and-shovel labor and blasts of black powder to extract ever more coal—that "one great commodity which with food and clothing and shelter man requires." As with most coal towns, Cle Elum wore its prosperity unevenly, and bore the scars of danger; the previous summer, seven men had been killed by an explosion while unloading black powder mixed with dynamite, a blast that also claimed the lives of a woman and her young daughter living in a nearby tent.

On this Tuesday in June, Cle Elum was on edge even more than usual. For weeks the annual warm-weather trickle of tramps and hoboes along the Northern Pacific had become a full-blown stream, with World's Fair tourist traffic drawing in its wake a surfeit of shiftless hangers-on, part-time pickpockets, harmless loafers, and hardened opportunists. The night before, an auto coming from Roslyn—a sister coal-mining community four miles north, away from the railroad and reliant on automobile stages—had barely managed to barrel past three bandits determined to rob the car at gunpoint. Those foiled bandits apparently turned their attention next to downtown Cle Elum, breaking into three saloons and a general store over the next four hours. At 4:30 AM, the local deputy tracked them to the overgrowth behind the freight depot. When one of the trio turned and aimed a revolver, the marshal drew and shot the man through the neck, as attested to by two railroad workers. The stranger bled out, carrying a cash register pouch and a pry bar, but the two men with him fled to the hills. Amid praise for the deputy, there was talk of rounding up a posse, of shooting the men on sight.

That talk got put on hold for a moment with the roar of the No. 2 Model T, which charged down East First and pulled in front of the Cle Elum State Bank, one of the sturdiest structures in town, a two-story brick edifice topped with a line of chimneys resembling the battlements of a castle. A crowd surged around the car. The building also housed the local Pacific Telephone and Telegraph office, and Bert Scott and Jimmie Smith went in to try to get a bead down the line on the Shawmut. In a trance, they retreated to the bank lobby to await an answer. Fully fifty people surrounded them, straining for a glimpse of this duo who had driven all the way from New York in just three weeks, fording rivers and scrambling over mountains. But even as the people of Cle Elum peppered them with questions, Scott and Smith offered nothing but the occasional twitch, sound asleep in their chairs. Finally, word came back. The Shawmut was getting closer, reportedly just seventy miles off.

That message snapped the Ford men from their trance, "and the way they turned on the juice was something worth seeing," the *Cle Elum Echo* would note. Though "both men were almost dead for want of sleep, they braced themselves in the seat, threw the lever and with a snort not unlike a grizzly bear, the machine bounded into the air and made a white streak in the atmosphere as it rushed through the city."

The paper called this "the greatest automobile race ever run for both time and distance." To the crowd left behind in the vapor trail, the little Ford seemed to touch only "the high places" as it flew west along First Street, disappearing beyond the hospital hill a mile down the line.

Seventy miles wasn't quite right, more like a hundred, but the truth was undeniable: The Shawmut was narrowing the gap, charging up the Yakima Valley. It had taken the No. 2 Ford nearly six hours to go from Prosser to North Yakima—not quite sixty miles—last night and early this morning. In the prime of day, the Shawmut chewed up that same stretch in barely half that time. When the big car pulled up at the Yakima Hotel at precisely 1 PM on June 22, the men received their biggest cheer since the start of the race: Fully five hundred people lined the sidewalk in front of the hotel, crowding the corner of East Yakima and South Third.

Who didn't love a tightening race and an underdog? It helped that the Shawmut had picked a popular local guide too. North Yakima's Harry Tucker had gone down to Wapato, thirteen miles south, to bring the Shawmut here to the checkpoint and stay on to the finish, no matter how long it might take. Only twenty-three, Tucker was a sharp dresser with a dimpled chin and hair parted just left of center. His father had been North Yakima's first liveryman, a popular figure whose horses everyone knew by name. A Civil War veteran who had fought under Grant and survived Vicksburg by inches—haversack blown right off his shoulder—Henry Tucker had migrated west to work railroad construction. After trying his hand at mining, he set up a pack train between Yakima and The Dalles, then opened a livery barn and hack service too. In time, he became a sheriff and city councilman, with a fine home in town.

It figured that Henry Tucker's boy would be a natural with horses as well. For his tenth birthday, Harry got a Shetland pony and a sporty little phaeton carriage, cutting a nimble figure as he dashed along North Yakima's roads. He even took over the family business for a time, running the livery and stables across from the Northern Pacific depot, perfect for ferrying passengers to and from the station. But by 1907, Harry was more in love with horsepower than horses. The family sold the venerable H. L. Tucker & Son operation, and Harry Tucker became a full-time chauffeur and auto mechanic, hired out to a couple of different garages already.

After Tucker guided the Shawmut to the Yakima Hotel, Messer and Pettengill registered at the front-desk checkpoint and hit the washroom to clean off some of the alkali and grime, then sat down in the lobby restaurant. Ravenous, and knowing they might not eat another real meal until the other side of the Cascades, they polished off an entire fried chicken and a massive sirloin steak between them, plus trimmings. Outside the hotel, people who'd been awake early enough to see the fire-scarred No. 2 Ford expressed the opinion that this big Shawmut was in better shape, while the Boston crew—able to take turns stretching out in back—also seemed fresher, if only by comparison. The crowd debated whether the powerful car would have enough running room to catch the Ford, with just 160 miles or so left until the finish. Messer seemed discouraged, but Pettengill told a reporter he thought they could prevail. They might make up time while the Ford tried to hack through the snow-crusted, boulder-clogged wagon trail over Snoqualmie Pass, then benefit from the road-breaking work of the leader. After that, on the far side of Snoqualmie Pass, their power and speed would serve them well on the home stretch to Seattle. Of course, the question remained whether any of them would make it up and over Snoqualmie Pass at all, given the fate of the pathfinder and the Allen-Kingston.

At two o'clock, while the Shawmut men were still dining at the Yakima Hotel, the *North Coast Limited* blew into town, smoke billowing, whistle sounding, following the tracks along South Front Street toward the depot, a handsome half-timbered station flanked by a manicured lawn and a fistful of sidings. The train carried a line of first-class Pullmans finished in mahogany and accented with gold and green, ending with a striking observation car. Henry Ford was on board, one passenger among many. In a few more years he would be too famous and too rich for the plush but crowded accommodations of these Pullman sleepers—each with one private drawing room followed by twelve or fourteen sections, meaning sets of convertible seats that turned into berths at night, separated by drapes—and would instead traverse the country in an entire customized Pullman all his own, built for a whopping $159,000 and dubbed Fair Lane. For now, he was still just another Midwestern businessman, riding to the coast with his son.

The Northern Pacific had a policy of not attaching private cars like that to its flagship *North Coast Limited*, so as not to mar the view from that trailing observation car on the "Crack Train of the Northwest." A jewel box of smartly apportioned space, the observation car contained men's and ladies' toilets, a buffet, a barbershop, a bathroom with full tub, writing alcoves, and sequestered smoking rooms—no plumes of cigar smoke here to spoil the trip, as the railroad put it, "for women and for those who do not care for tobacco," Henry Ford among them. The final third of the car offered an airy viewing room with wicker chairs and broad windows, ending with an open observation deck, the railing adorned with the Northern Pacific's telltale yin-yang logo, in dramatic red and black.

The *North Coast Limited* stopped in North Yakima briefly, not long enough to risk getting off. The two ex-Ford employees who worked at

Yakima Auto had rushed over to greet the train. "Mr. Ford!" they must have called, spotting a trim figure on that panoramic platform at the back of the observation car. The men called out to tell Henry Ford that the No. 2 had come through town that morning, leaving about nine hours ago, a comfortable lead.

With humor, Ford said he would "try to bear up under the news."

20

Snoqualmie Pass

The Cascade Range, June 22 to 23, 1909

Of all the woebegone wagon trails and misbegotten byways that qualified as public roads in 1909, Washington State Road No. 7—the Snoqualmie Pass Wagon Road—may have been the worst in the country. On paper it had seemed a tempting shortcut for generations, the lowest-lying pass over the Cascade Range, that north-south mountain barrier running from British Columbia to Northern California and bulging down the center of Washington like a high spine. In reality, the pass was torture for anything on wheels, automobiles especially. Imagine a path cut through a primeval forest with so little wiggle room that you often couldn't fit two cars side by side between the walls of trees. Now salt that path copiously with stumps, boulders, and fallen timbers in various states of decay, requiring you to dig them out or lay planks to surmount them, no room to go around while hemmed in by those evergreens. Add to the difficulty by burying the area in so much snow—as much as five hundred inches over a winter at the summit, and three hundred at the base—that several feet still clogged much of the trail in June, concealing many of the stumps and boulders. To make it even more interesting, coat that melting snow with a spring crust of ice strong enough to support the weight of an automobile in some places but not others. But be careful what you wish for; in parts of the trail exposed to the sun, the ground in June is soft and muddy, laced with rushing

The aftermath of an early-morning fire on November 13, 1908, which gutted the factory of the nascent Shawmut Motor Company. The company occupied a wooden former tannery complex in Stoneham, Massachusetts.

(Courtesy of the Stoneham Historical Society & Museum)

Ford entered two Model Ts, identified as Nos. 1 and 2, seen here at the starting line on June 1, 1909. Henry Ford stands in the background before the tree, visible beyond the hood of the No. 2 (dark derby, left elbow cocked); he is chatting with race sponsor M. Robert Guggenheim, the bearded figure to his right. Bert Scott sits at the wheel of the No. 2, Jimmie Smith beside him.

(From the Collections of The Henry Ford)

Crews could replace parts subject to wear and tear, but if major components broke, they could only be repaired, not replaced. To verify that those same parts remained in the car at the finish, the Automobile Club of America used a stamping hammer to mark the components with a distinct pattern before the race began, as seen here on the No. 3 Stearns.

(Courtesy of the National Automotive History Collection, Detroit Public Library)

The No. 4 Acme at the starting line, with all three crew members wielding Barney Oldfield–style cigars. George Salzman is at the wheel, at left; Jerry Price sits beside him; and James Hemstreet is in back, speaking with a reporter. A sliver of the Shawmut is visible at left. *(From the Collections of The Henry Ford)*

President Taft sent a signal to start the Alaska-Yukon-Pacific Exposition in Seattle and the Ocean-to-Ocean Race in New York by pressing a telegraph key adorned with some of the first gold nuggets from the Klondike, set on a base of white Alaska marble. The key lever was walrus ivory. This composite photo ran in *Harper's Weekly* on June 19, 1909. *(Courtesy of the author)*

New York City Mayor George B. McClellan Jr., son of the Civil War general, fired the starting gun on the steps of City Hall after receiving the signal from Taft. Race sponsor Guggenheim, newly twenty-four, is at left in the straw boater, right arm bent, with his wife, Grace, beside him. Industry titan Daniel Guggenheim, his father, stands in the rear at the center of the frame.

(From the Collections of The Henry Ford)

The No. 5 Shawmut on the road during the first day of the race, with lead driver T. Arthur Pettengill at left; mechanic Earle Chapin, center; and backup driver Robert Messer at right in the rear.

(Courtesy of the National Automotive History Collection, Detroit Public Library)

The No. 6 Itala moments after pulling into the Poughkeepsie checkpoint on the first night of the race, June 1, 1909. Gus Lechleitner is at the wheel, with F. B. Whittemore Jr. beside him. Elbert Bellows sits in the rear.

(From the Collections of The Henry Ford)

Though not visible in the photo, Henry Ford was here for this scene, as the two Model Ts prepare to exit a small ferry after crossing the Missouri River from Glasgow to West Glasgow, Missouri; Frank Kulick is at the wheel of the No. 1, about to drive off. The ferry suffered a mysterious breakdown after taking the Fords across, stranding the Shawmut and Acme on the opposite bank. *(From the Collections of The Henry Ford)*

Torrential rains slowed the crews across Kansas, including this scene showing the Shawmut in water over the hubs. A 1909 caption identified this locale as Ellsworth, but it is more likely Gorham, nearly fifty miles west, where the Boston crew tried to cross a creek that had swollen considerably. The two men standing beside the Buick in back hold a tackle line, ready to help pull the car out.
(Courtesy of the Stoneham Historical Society & Museum)

Many Ford dealerships and agencies updated the company's progress and touted its success in the race with showroom-window displays, including maps, news clippings, and telegrams, as with this scene outside the flagship Manhattan branch at 1721–1723 Broadway.
(Courtesy of the National Automotive History Collection, Detroit Public Library)

As a pricey, low-slung import better suited to improved roads, the Itala struggled with the nation's unforgiving terrain as well as with bad luck. Here Bert Bellows (in suspenders, leaning on the radiator cap) works to repair the car, likely after it was struck by a train amid a dispute with a railroad crew west of Glasgow, Missouri. From a comparison photo, the smiling figure with the tire appears to be Itala importer Egbert Lillie, who accompanied the crew after Gus Lechleitner fell ill. *(Courtesy of Janice Bellows Feaman and Sarah Bellows Upbin)*

By western Kansas, the race had turned into a dogfight between the two Fords and the Shawmut. Though the crews crossed paths on their way in or out of a succession of towns, surviving photos are rare. Here the Shawmut can be seen arriving in muddy Goodland, Kansas, with one of the Model Ts partly visible at right, facing the opposite direction.

(From the Collections of The Henry Ford)

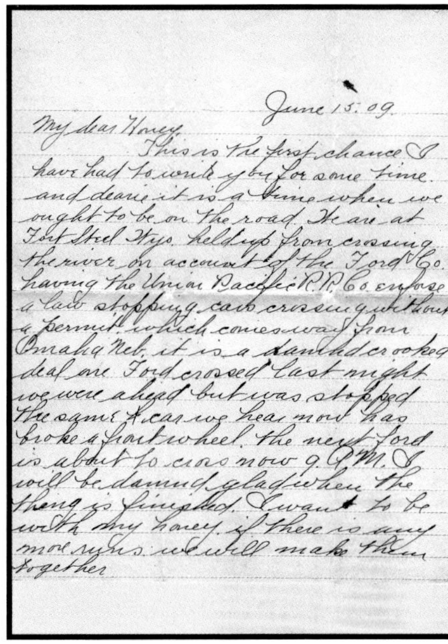
June 15. 09.
My dear Honey.
This is the first chance I have had to write you for some time. and dearie it is a time when we ought to be on the road. We are at Fort Steel Wyo. held up from crossing the river on account of the Ford Co. having the Union Pacific R.R. Co. enforse a law stopping cars crossing without a permit which comes way from Omaha Neb. it is a damned crooked deal. one Ford crossed last night we were ahead but was stopped. The same car we hear now has broke a front wheel. the next Ford is about to cross now 9 P.M. I will be damned glad when the thing is finished. I want to be with my honey. if there is any more runs we will make them together

At Fort Steele, Wyoming, the local Union Pacific station agent typically allowed the occasional autos that came through to cross the railroad bridge over the North Platte River, provided the tracks were clear. But when the Shawmut arrived in the lead, Ford's Charlie Hendy was there with an armed guard to enforce an obscure rule requiring the Shawmut crew to secure permission from railroad headquarters. The Shawmut was forced to wait overnight for a permit. This letter from Earle Chapin to wife Anita calls it a "damned crooked deal." *(Courtesy of Bruce Chapin)*

Stuck at Fort Steele, Chapin wrote two postcards as well as a letter to his wife, including this card showing the bridge that the Shawmut had been denied permission to cross. *(Courtesy of Bruce Chapin)*

A portrait of Caroline Wright, the future Caroline "Anita" Chapin, from 1901. *(Courtesy of Bruce Chapin)*

The Shawmut speeding out of Twin Falls, Idaho, on June 19, 1909. The photo was taken and sold locally as a "real photo" postcard by photographer M. B. Martin. The hand-drawn *x* marks the spot where an architect watched the car pass by from his office window; he later mailed the card to a young woman in Chicago. *(Courtesy of Linda and Ralph Allen)*

THE SEATTLE POST

HENRY FORD, WHOSE CAR WON GUGGENHEIM TROPHY, IS LED TO WATER AT SNOQUALMIE

Mr. Ford and His Party, Former Drinking Water, at Snoqualmie Pass, Where They Went to Meet the Ford Car No. 2, Which Won the Ocean to Ocean Race

After a seventy-two-hour train ride from Chicago to Seattle, Henry Ford and fifteen-year-old son Edsel immediately drove up into the Cascades with Seattle branch manager R. P. Rice to greet the leading Model T coming down the remote Snoqualmie Pass road. Here Ford can be seen drinking from a trough in a picture that ran after the race in *The Seattle Post-Intelligencer.* *(Courtesy of University of Washington Libraries)*

Bert Scott and Jimmie Smith in the No. 2 Ford about to break the tape —a red ribbon, faintly visible here coming from the chest-high right hand of a uniformed gateman standing near the Ford's left front tire—at the entrance to the Alaska-Yukon-Pacific Exposition fairgrounds in Seattle, June 23, 1909, at 12:55 PM. *(University of Washington Libraries, Special Collections, Nowell x2203)*

Robert Guggenheim poses with the crew of the victorious No. 2, an exhausted Scott and Smith, in the Mines Building at the World's Fair on the afternoon of June 23, 1909. *(University of Washington Libraries, Special Collections, Nowell x2192)*

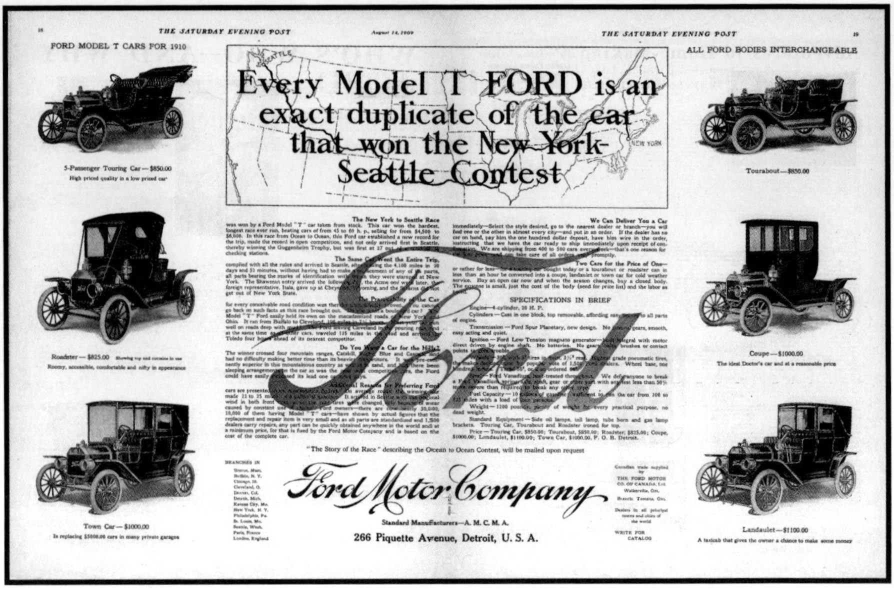

Though Ford preferred to pass on the cost of advertising to dealers in local newspapers, the company proclaimed its apparent triumph with a two-page ad in the widely read *Saturday Evening Post* that summer. "Every Model T FORD is an exact duplicate of the car that won the New York–Seattle Contest," the ad boasted, calling it "the hardest, longest race ever run." *(Courtesy of the author)*

In 1945, the Shawmut crew (from left: Robert Messer, Earle Chapin, and Arthur Pettengill) reunited at a meeting of the Stoneham Rotary Club, where Pettengill, who had become a local auto dealer, was a charter member with perfect attendance.

(Courtesy of the Stoneham Historical Society & Museum)

A grinning Bert Scott (left) and Jimmie Smith during their Detroit homecoming in September 1909 after a summer-long victory tour visiting dealerships across the country.

(From the Collections of The Henry Ford)

snowmelt streams. For the crowning obstacle, impose a grade of 20 percent or more in some places, with slopes best suited for hooves.

No wonder one motorist of the era called it "the hardest test that man could invent." Some would later claim to have surmounted Snoqualmie Pass by auto as early as 1905, but there was little evidence to support it at the time. As of early 1909, locals on both sides of the mountains had witnessed just a handful of cars try, typically requiring rescue by horses and completing the journey by freight car. As far as anyone knew, only one auto had ever made it fully over the pass by its own power, and that was in late August 1908, the warmest and driest time of year, after the snow melted, the mud firmed up, and the freshets receded to a trickle.

But the Ocean-to-Ocean Race couldn't wait until August. Naturally, the matter of Snoqualmie Pass in June was a touchy subject for the Seattleites who persuaded Robert Guggenheim to throw his money and name behind the race. They yearned for a "highway" running straight across the state—nothing like the multilane freeway the word would later evoke, but the suitably ambitious 1909 goal of a continuous, clearly marked road grubbed, graded, and surfaced with gravel or asphalt, open for seasonal travel. They hoped within a few years that this same Washington-spanning roadway would connect to a succession of similar ribbons running all the way to the East Coast. But you couldn't build that road across Washington without clearing the Cascades, presumably over Snoqualmie Pass.

Oregon offered alternatives that were a tad better. You might go west from Boise across central Oregon, on the old Willamette Valley & Cascade Mountain wagon road, via Prineville and Albany, before running north through Portland and continuing another 180 miles up to Seattle. Or you could try going all the way up to the Oregon-Washington border, near Walla Walla, before tracing the southern bank of the Columbia River west to Portland, then on to Seattle. Being new to the Northwest, Guggenheim thought these routes sounded fine. Sure, they would pad the mileage some, but they would bring the race through another major city while avoiding the most brutal obstacle—and the potential embarrassment of seeing every competitor stymied by Snoqualmie Pass, failing less than seventy miles from the finish.

Except Seattle's swells and stalwarts weren't about to cede anything to Portland, proud at having recently surpassed that rival city in population and, they firmly believed, influence. Routing the race through Portland would mean conceding second-class status; they would sooner call off the whole affair. Besides, they felt strongly that a cross-country race ending at the Alaska-Yukon-Pacific Exposition—Washington's first World's Fair—should traverse Washington, not tiptoe in from Oregon.

After all, they had two overriding goals for the Ocean-to-Ocean Race: publicize this World's Fair for readers across the country, and shine a light on the slipshod condition of the nation's roads, to stir some action. Ratcheting up the drama by threading the race over the roughest road imaginable, right through the center of Washington, could serve both ambitions.

Of course, the difficulty posed by reaching the pass meant few in Seattle had actually seen it, despite the summit lying "less than 45 miles from Seattle as the pigeon flies," as one city lawyer put it in a letter to *MoToR* magazine, trying to reassure readers that the race would indeed conclude over Snoqualmie Pass, not via Oregon. Yet even that writer assumed the published snowfall figures must be a typo—"Blittzens! how cold!" he wrote—given Seattle's mild winters.

Even among civic organizers who did have a clear sense of the difficulty, some hoped or imagined the Snoqualmie Pass road might be mashed into shape by June through force of will or wishful thinking. After all, these were the same pioneers turned urbanites who through grit and providence had seen their Seattle grow nearly a hundredfold in a generation—who cut down the city's most imposing hills with mighty hoses and steam shovels, who were carving a ship canal to link Lake Washington and Lake Union with Puget Sound, who dominated the Alaska trade, whose streetcar system boasted 180 miles of track, whose new Carnegie library contained a hundred thousand volumes, whose port cleared $140 million a year in Pacific commerce. Now they were applying their capital and enterprise to the World's Fair, hurtling with power and precision toward an opening date calibrated two years precisely from the ground breaking. They were determined to be the first host city to meet the target on time, with none of the usual punch-list details still needing paint or polish when the gates opened—an achievement that spoke volumes, at least to them. It was why their brochures boasted that the A-Y-P would not just be "The World's Most Beautiful Exposition," but also "The Fair That Will Be Ready."

In February, with the June exposition deadline looming, and with the planning for the Ocean-to-Ocean Race heating up, Washington Highway Commissioner Joseph M. Snow offered a clear-eyed assessment. It "would require the energy of Hercules" to get Snoqualmie Pass into drivable shape by June, though he believed it could be done with enough money and men.

Snow had taken office in 1905, after Washington's part-time, biennial legislature recognized the shortcomings of leaving road construction and maintenance to county and local hands. State legislators identified ten existing or planned inter-county routes that would benefit from a jolt of funding, coordination, and expertise, putting $100,000 seed money into a highway fund to be fed subsequently by a twenty-five-cent tax on every $1,000 of taxable property. When the legislature met again in 1907, lawmakers doubled the tax and added a few more roads to the list. So far, $37,000 had been set aside for State Road No. 7, which would connect Easton (and Kittitas County) east of the Cascades with North Bend (and King County) on the west, via Snoqualmie Pass. The redesigned road would run about forty-seven miles—roughly half on each side, with the hardest ten miles ribboning the summit—though they wouldn't know the precise distance until they finished ironing out the slopes with long switchbacks. Still, only a bit of that money had been spent by early 1909, and then only on surveying, not anything a motorist would recognize as improvements.

As a footpath, the Snoqualmie Pass trail predated recorded history, embraced by the Indigenous groups who lived on both sides of the Cascades—and who traveled up the mountains seasonally to hunt, fish, and collect huckleberries—as a link for trade and social connections. Still, the future Civil War general George B. McClellan and his men got lost trying to find Snoqualmie Pass in 1853 while surveying a possible transcontinental-railroad route.

After the government persuaded the Yakama Nation to give up most of its land and resettle on a reservation southwest of the Yakima River in 1855, homesteaders from the East began arriving. They used Snoqualmie Pass for cattle drives, as a cheaper and more direct route to coastal meat-packing houses than shipping livestock by steamer down the Columbia River, though the bite and sting of flies, mosquitoes, and thorny devil's club added to the agony of the shortcut over the pass. When the railroads arrived and claimed that cattle-shipping traffic, Snoqualmie Pass receded into a seasonal route of necessity used by hardy locals and by emigrant families with little alternative, their wagons straining over the summit, their high axles at least better suited to boulders and stumps than the automobile.

And now the railroad had finally reached Snoqualmie Pass too. The pioneering Northern Pacific had crossed the Cascades in the 1880s using Stampede Pass to the south, going to Tacoma first, then Seattle. The Great Northern followed in the 1890s, pursuing a northerly route over Stevens Pass to Everett, and then down to Seattle. But Seattle's leaders clamored for an even more direct link, and the newly arrived Milwaukee Road had delivered, stringing a "high line" up and over Snoqualmie Pass as a prelude to tunneling beneath it, a beeline to Seattle.

But back to that wagon road of last resort creeping through the forest beyond those new Milwaukee tracks: It remained no place for an automobile in 1909. When Washington's lawmakers convened for a new session that winter, press clippings were starting to pile up about the coming Ocean-to-Ocean Race. They voted to double the tax for roads again while designating a headline-grabbing $120,000 for State Road No. 7, to improve that Snoqualmie Pass road and extend it in both directions so that it ran all the way from Seattle to the Idaho border. That sounded great when Guggenheim sat down at the White House to pitch President Taft on pressing that golden telegraph key; between this Washington appropriation and $50,000 pledged in Idaho, he could tout the demonstrable effect the race was having already on the Good Roads cause in the West.

The reality was that little of this money could be spent in time to provide any benefit by June. Simpler but more immediate improvements would need to come from county commissioners, local road districts, and commercial clubs, as with most of the route across the country. That was part of the pathfinder's job, with the Thomas Flyer's four-man trailblazing crew—and their attendant publicity—encouraging officials along the way to pitch in and improve their share of the course. But by April, with that pathfinder limping badly, the civic leaders in the Seattle Automobile Club could no longer wait for the Thomas to do that work in Washington.

The local auto club, which served as the organizing body through which Guggenheim sponsored the race, worked in hand with the Alaska-Yukon-Pacific Exposition board on race planning. (The lofty Automobile Club of America in New York lent its official sanction to the contest, and hammered the telltale stamps on the components of each car that could not be replaced, but had little other work to do besides validate the outcome.) The Seattle Automobile Club's influential members persuaded the commissioners of King County—which stretched from Seattle to a dividing line atop Snoqualmie Pass—to put up $1,000 for immediate pick-and-shovel labor to improve the road coming down the west side of the pass.

For the east side, Seattle Automobile Club president J. T. Ronald, a former mayor and newly appointed judge, called on H. C. Henry, one of Washington's leading capitalists and philanthropists. Henry's contracting firm was just finishing the three-year, $20 million job laying the 450 miles of rail that brought the Milwaukee Road from western Idaho to Puget Sound, a massive feat of rock-blasting, tunnel-digging, and bridge-building that included laying those tracks over Snoqualmie Pass. Henry was also a vice president on the Seattle World's Fair board. He promised Ronald he'd send men out to improve the roughest few miles of the wagon road on the east side of the summit at no charge. And Clarence Hanford, a member of the Seattle Automobile Club's race-planning committee, set off from Seattle to supplement the mission of the stalled pathfinder, asking local officials to help improve roads while nailing down details about directions and checkpoints for the race's final stages, all the way to Wyoming. No mere junior motorist dispatched to the hinterlands, Hanford was a silver-haired business leader from a pioneering Washington family.

Despite all that effort and attention, by the time June rolled around you'd be hard-pressed to notice a whit of improvement on what passed for a road over Snoqualmie Pass.

As Scott and Smith pressed on in the No. 2 Ford, Charlie Hendy was riding with them now, folded onto the little platform in back. Around 11 PM Tuesday, they buzzed into Easton, a rough-hewn little railroad town that managed to sustain ten saloons and one church. This was where the Northern Pacific and the new Milwaukee Road extension crossed for a second time, after sticking mainly to the opposite sides of the river since Ellensburg. For the next few miles, those two railroads danced so close that the firemen on one line could have lobbed coal at the other. Up ahead, at a place called Martin, the Northern Pacific would bank sharply southwest to cross the Cascades in that tunnel under Stampede Pass. That would leave only the Milwaukee rails and the forlorn wagon road continuing toward Lake Keechelus and Snoqualmie Pass just beyond it.

Keechelus glistened as the westernmost of three pristine lakes nestled close together on the eastern slope of the Cascades, fed by the spring freshets that raced down the mountains. Together on the map, the lakes looked like a swipe taken by one of the mountain lions that roamed the forest at night, a set of gashes on a northwest-southeast axis. On its own, Keechelus resembled a four-mile-long club; at the wider southeast end, it trickled out into the start of the 214-mile Yakima River. Near that end, a couple of bachelors lived off the land amid small clearings. Otherwise, heavily timbered mountains shot up in every direction, rising quickly from 2,500 feet above sea level at the lake to 5,500 feet or more. On the northwest side, the comparative dip of Snoqualmie Pass beckoned among higher peaks at just 3,127 feet. Hidden by dense Douglas fir as well as cedar, pine, and hemlock, the rising slopes concealed a few tumbledown cabins and the entrances to mines for gold, silver, copper, and quartz.

The railroad and the wagon road split at the lake, with the Milwaukee following a path hard by the southwestern side of Keechelus and the wagon road tracing the opposite shore. Or rather, they were *supposed* to diverge. That wagon road simply stopped. The seven-year-old United States Reclamation Service was just beginning an ambitious project to dam these lakes as part of a massive effort to irrigate the Yakima Valley. The region held two advantages over most of the arid West. For one thing, the soil here had proven to be a waiting gift for farmers, rich and supple, if they could just get a steady supply of water. For another, they actually had an ample water source here with the snow on the Cascades, but no natural way to store that annual snowmelt and sustain the long growing season.

The reservoirs planned by the federal government would change the equation, capturing a million acre-feet of mountain runoff to irrigate the Yakima Valley. Most of that work lay ahead, including plans for a massive earthen dam curving across the southeast end of Keechelus—ultimately over 6,500 feet long, with a structural height of 128 feet and a 20-foot width across the top, increasing the lake's capacity tenfold. As a prelude, the government had completed a small wooden dam in 1907, running 240 feet long and 15 feet high. That temporary dam had raised the water level enough to submerge the wagon road that hugged the northeast side of the lake.

In other words, if you weren't planning to take the train or swim to the other side, you were captive to Patrick Flanagan's ferry, pricey and unpredictable. Equally restless and entrepreneurial, Flanagan had been a florist in Akron, Ohio, when he picked up a second job with the United States Postal Service, during its rapid expansion in the 1880s and early 1890s, as free delivery expanded from a big-city perk to a benefit available to most Americans. One Monday in 1898, Flanagan failed to show up for his postal route, abruptly closed his greenhouse, and ran off to the goldfields in the Klondike, leaving behind a wife and five children. Unlike the many who would fail, or the few who would become wildly rich, Flanagan achieved reasonable success, earning several times his previous income in one hard season while becoming a folk hero in Akron, the papers carrying stories of his exploits in the "frozen northland" and of the gold dust he sent home.

When that rush subsided, Flanagan still had the itch. Seattle matured both as the jumping-off point for miners to purchase provisions and sail to Alaska, where they could trek to the Yukon goldfields, and as the clearinghouse when they returned. Like some other returning miners, Flanagan turned his attention to the Cascades, securing a few claims on the north side of Lake Keechelus. Yet again he did well enough to impress people back in Akron, this time with greater ambitions. After discovering gold and other minerals, he incorporated a company to sell shares back home and pay for his vision—sinking shafts and building crushers and concentrators, to reduce the weight of raw ore and make it easier to haul from the remote lake. He also operated a sawmill, to clear timber and cut props. To facilitate everything, Flanagan and his men built wood-rail tramways to connect their mines and sawmill to the wagon road and railroad. He also connected his interests around the lake with that barge towed by a one-cylinder launch. If travelers caught his attention—by flashing a light, or firing a gun, or telegraphing in advance—he took them across at steep prices, typically \$3 for a horse and buggy or \$10 for an auto, for a sluggish ride lasting forty minutes to an hour.

The No. 2 Ford reached the lake somewhere between 2 and 3 PM. Decades later, Jimmie Smith would recall that the ferryman wanted to wait for the Shawmut, to minimize the number of trips. In Smith's retelling, they secured a sheriff to insist the ferry take them across immediately. That seems unlikely, unless they had already squeezed the lawman into the back with Charlie Hendy and arrived with him from Cle Elum or Easton. Otherwise getting a message to the nearest county deputy, and bringing him out to the lake, would have consumed a few hours at least. Other accounts alleged that the Ford side not only crossed immediately but made it worthwhile for Flanagan not to rush back. Either way, it's hard to imagine Hendy sitting on his hands during a delay.

They reached the far side in late afternoon. There the flooded-out wagon road picked up again and began a four-mile ascent toward the summit, crossing Rocky Run, the toe of Rampart Ridge, and Gold Creek. Shaded by hulking evergreens, the narrow trail wound up the woods on the east side of a cascading stream known as Coal Creek, while the railroad followed a wider man-made clearing several hundred feet west. Though less steep than the wagon trail, the railroad route was still steep enough that the Milwaukee needed to attach helper engines to push the train up Snoqualmie Pass coming from either direction. At the summit, where the Milwaukee had carved out a tiny station called Laconia—to decouple those helper engines and tend to the trains and tracks—the wagon road and the rails would cross twice in quick succession, before diverging again for the western descent.

Precisely what happened next—who helped, and in what way—is a matter the Ford team would keep close to its vest. They clawed their way up at a rate of about one mile every hour. Partway up, they encountered snowpack chest-high. The crust on top held them until it didn't. From there it was all hands in the mix, shoveling, pushing, pulling, pressing, digging, and willing the car inch by inch through the snow and muck, uphill amid and around the rocks and fallen timbers. Hendy was there with Scott and Smith, along with—almost certainly—Harry Disher, the Ford mechanic from Seattle who'd been dispatched to drive east over the mountains until he found them. Joe Steiner, the guide they picked up in Ellensburg, may have been there too.

Eventually they heard pounding in the distance, the sounds of a Milwaukee section gang, Smith would recall decades later. That meant they were nearing the summit. They recruited the railroad workers to help them shovel and push the car through the snow.

They reached the top somewhere between 8 and 9:30 PM, just as dusk was enfolding the mountains, late on the summer solstice. Traditionally, the summit of the pass in summer was a marsh where the trees parted to offer a view of higher peaks, the gnarled ridge of Snoqualmie Mountain and jagged point of Guye Peak among them. Already the railroad had laid rudimentary infrastructure, including a small depot and telegraph station—little more than a shack, with LACONIA marked on the side. There was also space for decoupling the helper engines (known as Mallet locomotives) that pushed the trains up the mountain.

In the spring of 1910, the census taker would count fifty-four people here, mostly Greek and Bulgarian railroad laborers, and the summit would include a water tank, coal tower, covered turntable, beanery to feed the workers, and a bunkhouse known as Holden's Hotel, destined eventually to become a mountaintop inn. For now it was a work in progress, and the section gang lived in converted boxcars known as outfit or bunk cars, a charmless staple of life for many a rail gang.

Scott and Smith were as starving as they were exhausted. It was now late Tuesday night. Going back to their few hours of sleep at the Toll Gate in Oregon Sunday night, they had rested for ninety minutes just twice, in Walla Walla and North Yakima, and not eaten since 4 AM that morning. They scarfed food at the railroad camp and napped in one of the bunk cars for somewhere between two and five hours, Hendy's account differing from Scott's.

What remained unsaid is whether the No. 2 Ford kept moving in the meantime. The Shawmut team would later contend that an unnamed Ford employee from Seattle—Disher, presumably—worked the wheel and the throttle while Scott and Smith rested, as those railroad workers helped hack at the snow and rocks and push the car up and over the summit. Extra hands digging and pushing were legal within the rules, but it would be disqualifying for anyone but Scott or Smith to sit in the driver's seat and advance the car toward the finish.

Whether they all stopped when Scott and Smith rested or whether they kept pushing and the two men instead caught up again—easily hiking faster than a car could be shoved up and along the clogged mountain trail—the No. 2 Ford began its descent early on June 23. From the summit it was about twenty-five miles to North Bend, the first community in the western foothills. The final few miles would bring a properly graded road. Until then, the way down would be little easier than the way up, featuring the same travel-thwarting, tire-and-chain-chewing mix of boulders, stumps, and rotting timbers, with massive snowdrifts in some places, muck in others.

They had gone only a little way when they met another Ford coming the other direction, headlights apparently meeting headlights in the darkness. It was a runabout from Seattle—out surprisingly deep in the Cascades, far from any form of communication. That the car and its occupants had made it this far up the pass wasn't the only surprise, though. It carried R. P. Rice, the Seattle branch manager, along with Henry Ford and his son Edsel, who had willed themselves up into the mountains to greet the lead racers and help them on to the finish.

"When Mr. Ford saw us coming through," Smith would remember, "he was tickled to death to see we were the first."

21

Breaking the Tape

Central Washington to Seattle, June 22 to 23, 1909

Charging up the Yakima River corridor at thirty miles an hour, the Shawmut reached Ellensburg around 5:15 PM Tuesday, putting the big car roughly fifty miles and one ferry ride behind the lead Ford, which at that moment was just a little up the trail beyond the lake. Not that Pettengill and Messer or guide Harry Tucker had any precise way to gauge the gap. They knew only that the Ford preceded them here in Ellensburg by eight hours and fifteen minutes. That meant the Shawmut had taken a bite out of the lead since North Yakima, and the update dancing over the wires gave sports editors laying out their pages a jolt. AUTOS EXPECTED IN SEATTLE TODAY, the *Oregonian* would tell Portland readers, for one. SHAWMUT CAR MAY YET WIN. But to the crew in second, eight hours was still a considerable gap. They would need to scorch from Ellensburg and hope for the best over Snoqualmie Pass. They stayed just a few minutes, long enough to replenish oil, glug some more gasoline into the tank, and, evidently, send a telegram requesting that Flanagan ferry.

Then they plowed on toward Cle Elum, halfway between Ellensburg and Keechelus. Two main roads ran through the heart of that coal-mining town before diverging on the west side, with First Street banking southwest and Second Street veering gently northwest. It was reasonable to assume the northwest road was the right one, that being the compass direction of

Lake Keechelus, Snoqualmie Pass, and Seattle. Guide Tucker was doing his best, sixty miles from home. But rushing off, they missed the fact that the southwesterly road was the right one, and would eventually swoop around toward Easton and Snoqualmie Pass. The road they picked led instead to Roslyn—Cle Elum's sister city in mining—before dead-ending at Cle Elum Lake. Only in Roslyn, where they surprised the locals, did they understand their mistake. They backtracked, burning seven miles and precious time.

Take two from Cle Elum: Now they barreled along the right road, toward Easton and Keechelus beyond it, reaching a clearing before the lake where a rough-and-tumble twenty-nine-year-old named Les Reinovsky had built a small house and was raising chickens and some crops—rent-free and unauthorized, on federal land doomed to be cleared for that massive dam. Reinovsky wasn't a full-blown hermit, with relatives in settled corners of the county and designs on getting married. True seclusion belonged to the weathered figure just around the final bend on the wagon road, hard by the shore where Keechelus spilled into the Yakima River, inhabiting a cabin that looked like it might collapse into kindling with a stiff breeze: Christian Hansen, or maybe Christopher or Cris or Christ, and possibly Hanson, a solitary Dane in his mid-sixties. Even the federal government that was both fighting and paying him was unsure how to spell his name, let alone what to make of him.

The lakeshore was so remote that it hadn't even been surveyed yet when Hansen arrived around 1891, let alone been opened up for homesteading claims—meaning the process, going back to the Homestead Act of 1862, through which the nation deeded millions of acres of undeveloped land for free (mostly in 160-acre parcels) to citizen-farmers, provided they had never taken up arms against the country, paid a filing fee, and then lived on and improved that land for at least five years. It wasn't unreasonable for Hansen to think the lake would eventually open to homesteading, and that he might even get first crack. Except now his remote idyll was destined to be condemned for the big Reclamation Service dam. Despite viewing Hansen as a squatter, the feds offered him $500 to relocate. The hermit, who stashed his cash under his pillow and led a life devoid of creature comforts, dug in and demanded $20,000. Upping the ante further, Hansen connected with a high-profile lawyer, who elevated the simple ejection case of an eccentric loner in the Cascades into a constitutional challenge of the Reclamation Act itself, threatening the future of irrigation across the entire West. "The old fellow is a peculiar character and will not listen to our arguments," Frederick H. Newell, founder and inaugural director of the Reclamation Service, testified in Congress.

Hansen even managed to prevail in federal district court, but the government successfully appealed. The old trapper's lawyer talked about challenging the ruling all the way to the Supreme Court, but the Department of the Interior placated Hansen by letting him stay for now—the real work wouldn't begin for a few more years, anyway; he would be dead by 1910—and putting him on the payroll as a watchman, keeping an eye on the temporary dam and the vacant construction camp beside it.

So this was the scene the hard-charging Shawmut men encountered at water's edge as night approached, pulling up where Keechelus sloshed out over the temporary crib dam and formed the start of the Yakima. Hansen's tumbledown cabin sat to the right, the dormant construction camp to the left. What they did not find was Flanagan's ferry. They waited one, two, three hours. As a chill descended over the inky lake, visions of Fort Steele and Glasgow must have swirled in their heads. Finally, after four hours, the ferry arrived to tote the Shawmut across in the darkness. By then the men figured their chances were finished.

Two travelers, heading in unequal and nearly opposite directions late on June 22, 1909, each with mechanical minds but modest formal educations—boys who had loved to pick apart clocks, and who had grown into wiry and energetic men at ease in machine shops: Henry Ford, speeding from Seattle as fast as he could in an automobile bearing his own name on the radiator, and Earle Chapin, barreling toward it by train. He was frustrated and homesick, carrying a note from Dr. Carl Patterson of Baker City, Oregon.

Earlier that night, the *North Coast Limited* had steamed into Seattle's King Street Station at 8:15 PM, depositing Henry and Edsel Ford after a seventy-two-hour ride from Chicago, nearly six times faster than the Ocean-to-Ocean racers. The duo went straight to the Rainier-Grand Hotel, a venerable institution near the waterfront where Henry Ford's idol, Thomas Edison, had stayed the previous fall, during a rare vacation taken in part so Edison could witness the monumental regrading of Seattle's Denny Hill firsthand. Ford had no time to rest, or to take in the fine ceramic tile work in the Rainier-Grand rotunda. He claimed his reservation and dropped his bags, telling the desk clerk he would not need the room until tomorrow. Then Henry and Edsel jumped into a three-seat runabout with R. P. Rice and raced off toward the Cascades.

Anyone still out when that Model T passed through North Bend that night, nearly forty miles off, might have scoffed at the sight of a car going east. It was foolhardy enough to try driving Snoqualmie Pass during the daytime in the dry heat of August; this was June in the dark, with mud, snow, and crusted ice waiting to thwart them. But sure enough, that same Ford came roaring back into town a few minutes before ten the next morning, with a stripped-down, battle-scarred sibling rumbling beside it. A crowd gathered to gawk in downtown North Bend, a modest mining and sawmill village nestled below craggy Mount Si.

People wanted to know how the No. 2 had done it, conquering Snoqualmie Pass so briskly. The Ford team had picked its way down the first ten miles of the western slope in the dark at about one mile an hour. Sure, they might have driven over the railroad bed for some of that, but nothing disqualifying there, as long as they didn't use flanged wheels. Once they hit the Fifteen Mile Bridge over the Snoqualmie River—a toll bridge operated by a man who also maintained a few cabins for weary wagon travelers—they found a good road and cruised over the final fifteen miles to North Bend in an hour. They stopped just long enough to replenish fuel and oil and "to tighten a few loose bolts," in the estimation of a correspondent for a nearby paper.

They were cooking now, and burst through Issaquah around 10:50 AM "going like blazes," per one witness, finding another big crowd cheering them on with less than thirty miles now to the finish. When another car rolled in just twelve minutes later, an overeager correspondent mistook it for the Shawmut and relayed the news to Seattle, sending a shudder of excitement down the line, triggering false reports of a near-deadlocked finish in the earliest afternoon papers.

In another thirty-one years, the largest floating bridge in the world would shoot motorists directly across Lake Washington to Seattle, but in 1909 you needed to drive down and around the lake or take a ferry. With a small convoy of cars waiting to escort the leaders over the city limits for a sensational parade to the finish, the choice was predetermined. Soon they encountered Guggenheim's raucous, racetrack-ready Allen-Kingston, carrying the millionaire, his wife, and his personal secretary, Larry Walker, a dutiful twenty-four-year-old from the Canadian Maritimes who had tallied and tracked all the signature cards mailed from the checkpoints these last three weeks.

A little before noon, this cacophonous convoy hit the southern end of the lake and buzzed through Renton, a lumber-and-coal town and railway center a dozen miles southeast of downtown Seattle. Then they curled up through a thousand acres of bottomland that a swashbuckling and ultimately crooked developer named Clarence Hillman had recently purchased and dubbed Earlington Gardens, intending to transform it into a new suburb, advertising empty lots for $125 or a seven-room house for $550, on installment plans at $5 a month. It was here on the countrified outskirts of the expanding city that a farmer apparently reached out with a long fishing pole, dangling a wreath over the road that he'd prepared for the victors. As the No. 2 Ford raced past, Bert Scott thrust a hand in the air and speared the wreath on his arm, nabbing it without slowing down.

The roads were exceptionally dusty, ever more grit clinging to the cars and occupants with each revolution toward Seattle. For all the excitement in the city over the race, the regional water and lighting superintendent had refused to budge and allow the customary road sprinkling, part of a broader water-usage clampdown amid a concern over reservoir levels. That had less to do with drought than with pipeline ruptures in Seattle's vaunted water-supply system, normally so robust as to afford locals a seemingly limitless supply of gravity-fed hydration from the foothills of the Cascades. The water was such a point of pride that A-Y-P organizers advertised it as a free benefit at comfort stations around the fair. ("No grafter will be found selling the drinking water which the Creator gave so liberally to Seattle. . . .") To run out now, with Seattle hosting a record number of tourists, would be a black eye for the city.

So the dusty convoy plowed northwest toward the city limits, taking a plank road over tidal flats and marshland. Near Seattle's expanding border, between the recently annexed Columbia neighborhood and soon-to-be-annexed Georgetown, Fire Chief Harry Bringhurst swooped ahead of the pack, his warning siren blaring. Or rather, Bringhurst's personal chauffeur swooped in, a skilled twenty-three-year-old motorist from Boston named B. Dean Kuhn, who last year had beaten out an army of daring drivers applying for a rare job giving a chauffeur a free pass to speed as much as possible. He sat beside the chief in the pride of the department, a custom-built 1908 Autocar with a top speed near sixty miles per hour and a turning radius designed for cutting and darting, outfitted with bucket seats in front for the chief and chauffeur and a little railed cushion in back where a few firefighters could squeeze in and hold on. (That car put the fire department on equal footing with Seattle's police force, which acquired its sole patrol automobile—a wagon-style Knox with room for twelve prisoners—the year before.)

The No. 2 and the victory pack slashed across Seattle toward Yesler Way, the once-greased "skid road" that sliced east-west and sloped down toward the waterfront, where pioneer Henry Yesler had built the village's first sawmill fifty-six years back. As they approached the business district, they could hear the tolling of the modern city's fire alarms, a gonging that would normally telegraph the location of an emergency, but was now telling people instead to prepare for the approaching leader.

The crowds grew larger by the block, but nothing could prepare the Ford crew for the crush waiting once they turned right from Yesler onto Second Avenue. At least seventy-five thousand people had crammed onto the ten blocks of Second from there to Pike Street, where the route would bank inland again from the waterfront commercial district. A brick-paved thoroughfare through the heart of downtown, Second was so broad that wagons, pedestrians, and automobiles could normally weave easily in and around the double-tracked streetcar lanes down the middle of the avenue, with a wide margin of concrete sidewalk on each side as well.

Now, though, you could hardly see a speck of that pavement from above—and there were indeed many watching from above, in a commercial canyon lined with muscular mid-rises and soaring skyscrapers, anchored at one end by the Alaska Building (fourteen stories, the tallest tower in the Northwest) and at the other by the bountiful Bon Marché, the self-styled largest department store on the West Coast. They looked down not just from windows but from telephone and telegraph poles, too, where some had shimmied to try to spot the approaching cars. When Robert Guggenheim had persuaded the mayor to close this half mile of Second Avenue to traffic, stationing police officers at every corner, the young millionaire with a taste for speed naïvely imagined the winner sailing through at forty miles an hour. Instead, this corridor was now one thicket of humanity, elbow to elbow, sleeve to sleeve. From above it was all derbies, boaters, and fedoras, accented by the occasional bright, broad-brimmed lady's hat.

Excitement had been building all week. Since Saturday, the gleaming Guggenheim Cup had drawn a stream of admirers to Second and Madison, where it reposed in a window of upscale retailer Frederick & Nelson. That was the day the trophy arrived from San Francisco's venerable Shreve & Company, winner of a design contest that attracted 116 entries. No mere loving cup, the trophy with base stood over four feet high and weighed as much as a small child, a towering heap of precious metal and rococo adornments; the value in silver and gold alone could have paid for several houses. At the top, Winged Victory mounted a half globe that showed the northern hemisphere, centering on North America. Polar bears as big as a man's thumb protruded incongruously around the equator. Below that, the cup featured four photorealistic engravings of New York and Seattle: the start of the race, the Gotham skyline, Seattle's Second Avenue, and the Court of Honor at the World's Fair. Despite Guggenheim's professed modesty about preferring a background role in the race's planning, his full name gleamed around the midsection in giant capital letters brazed with gold nuggets. Even with all that ornamentation, sufficient room remained between there and the base to include the entire mouthful of the race's title, "International automobile contest for the M. Robert Guggenheim transcontinental trophy. Under the auspices of the Alaska-Yukon-Pacific exposition and of the Automobile Club of Seattle with the sanction of the Automobile Club of America." All over, the trophy was sprinkled with gold leaves, gold nuggets, and gold-embossed cactus dahlias, the official flower of the fair. At the bottom, the cup widened out again with still more engravings—smaller scenes from the race route—above four busts of Chief Seattle.

Four blocks north at Second and Union, crowds hungry for race updates had clustered outside the Times Building since Monday morning, when the No. 2 Ford first crossed the state line and hit Walla Walla. *The Seattle Daily Times* had adorned a plate-glass window on the ground floor with a big map of Washington, charting the positions of the crews with stickpins connected to colored ribbons and streamers bearing the name of each car, updated as reports reached the newsroom by telegraph and telephone. Meanwhile, uphill on Seventh Avenue, switchboard operators at *The Seattle Star*, a workingman's penny paper known for punchy headlines and plentiful illustrations, had all they could handle fielding calls from people seeking information on the race between editions.

When word came that the Ford had passed North Bend, doors seemed to spring open across Seattle all at once, never mind that it was unusually cool, mid-fifties, rain threatening. "Men would have simply lost their positions rather than miss that one exciting moment's pleasure," noted *The Seattle Republican*, the city's African American weekly, calling it a thrill with universal appeal. "All America is always interested in the outcome of an exciting game of chance and the powers of endurance on the part of the human family," the paper wrote, likening it to a championship prizefight. "For more than an hour the good-natured crowd, which extended from the South end of Second Avenue to the exposition grounds, watched and waited for the flash to go by, and when it did young and old America was not slow in letting the 'boys,' who had made the hard trip almost at the risk of their lives, know how they appreciated their manly struggle and their powers of endurance."

The convoy was deafening enough, between the unmuffled rumble of the No. 2 Ford, the peal of the fire chief's whistle, and the roar of Guggenheim's equally unmuffled Allen-Kingston. But when those cars rounded onto Second Avenue from Yesler, all that mechanical racket was drowned out by a cascading cheer as loud as anyone in Seattle could remember. As the cluster of cars lurched forward, the crowd parted enough to let them through, a plume of exhaust rising from the No. 2, Scott and Smith as begrimed as a couple of coal miners emerging into daylight at Cle Elum. A tourist from California's San Joaquin Valley who squeezed to the front wrote home about the "mass of surging humanity. Every man and woman seemed to want to caress the little machine and its driver."

Scott banked inland, with Smith beside him and Hendy hanging on in back, to follow the final four miles to the finish line, up mostly paved Eastlake Avenue and across the Latona Bridge that connected the core of Seattle with the university district and fairgrounds. The nascent University of Washington occupied a smattering of buildings on a small clearing in the forest beside Lake Washington, in what had been a remote corner of Seattle, though neighborhood development had followed the construction of the fairgrounds the last two years. Below that original clearing, the A-Y-P utilized a wooded 250-acre promontory that belonged to the university, framed by Lake Union and Portage Bay to the southwest and Lake Washington's Union Bay to the east, offering a sweeping view over the water to the distant Cascades. School regents endorsed the plan, and state lawmakers put up $1 million toward the anticipated $10 million

A-Y-P construction costs, with the understanding that the transformed fairgrounds—designed by Boston's esteemed Olmsted Brothers, in a way that accentuated the natural setting and preserved fir groves amid a radial layout of paths, circles, and fountains—would provide a picturesque expanded campus for the maturing university.

On the northwest side of the promontory, the A-Y-P Exposition's main entrance faced the T-shaped intersection of Fifteenth Avenue and Fortieth Street, where the perimeter wall of the fairgrounds opened to an inviting plaza and a three-arched French Renaissance gateway, sixty feet high and nearly two hundred feet across. Here the crowd awaiting the racers gave Second Avenue a run for its money, with fifteen thousand squeezed along the final few blocks, many of them there since mid-morning. People crammed around the plaza on the street side and congregated inside the fair's entrance as well, before a monumental sculpture of George Washington, the first erected anywhere west of the Mississippi.

The crackle of anticipation sent people scurrying out of the open-air cafés and unofficial souvenir stalls that had popped up across the street; some climbed to rooftops. When the convoy appeared, a long cheer erupted. The other cars pulled aside, letting Scott and Smith—and Hendy—in the No. 2 turn into the fairgrounds and cross the finish on their own. They could not drive through the stunning main gate, connected to an unbroken semicircle of forty-two entrance turnstiles, but were guided instead to a gap beside that arched gateway, where fair officials had swung open a hinged wall that contained a row of full-height exit turnstiles. Across that opening, one of the gatemen strung a red ribbon, clutching it tightly in his right hand. A southerly wind snapped the flags at the top of the wall, the forty-six-star standard of the United States and the blue-on-gold banner of the A-Y-P.

The little Ford rumbled right through, exhaust billowing from those snubbed pipes jutting from the hood. Guggenheim had abandoned his Allen-Kingston and rushed over with his pocket watch in hand. (With all eyes turned to the finish line, an errant gateman couldn't resist swiping the official referee's pennant from the back of the millionaire's A-K; he was caught and fired the following week.) Guggenheim declared an official time of 12:55:36 PM. Giving President Taft credit for a precise 3 PM Eastern start on June 1, that meant twenty-two days and fifty-five minutes since the opening gun.

The car stopped, briefly. William M. Sheffield, the ex-newspaperman who helped conceive the fair and who shrewdly planted the idea for the race in Guggenheim's head, stepped forward as secretary of the exposition, a round-faced man with a bold mustache. He pumped the hands of Scott and Smith, on behalf of other officials around him, A-Y-P President John Edward Chilberg included.

But the winning Ford did not linger. It picked up again at a trot, the other automobiles falling in behind, destined for the exposition's far southeastern corner—for five prescribed victory laps around the track of the A-Y-P stadium, nearly three-quarters of a mile from the entrance. This may have sounded good in planning, but it now seemed like an anticlimax, because the crowd had to choose, and most favored the finish line at the entrance. When the No. 2 and the accompanying cars finally reached the stadium, only a small group greeted them there, and Scott and Smith must have wondered why they needed to do five laps when one would have been plenty. By the time they finished, though, scores of people had sprinted across the grounds all the way to the track, hoofing past the Exposition Monument—an eighty-foot-high shaft accented with gold, topped with an American eagle, and surrounded at the base with a ring of swastikas, still a good-luck symbol associated primarily with Asia—down the Cascade Court, around the Geyser Basin, along Rainier Vista, past the Versailles-style gardens, and out to the lawn by the stadium. Scott rounded the last lap, swung back to the stadium entrance, and stopped the car. People swarmed the little T, some hopping or straddling the stadium gate.

Guards cleared the way for the fair's official photographer, an exposition force deputized with police powers inside the grounds, 150 men of mostly military background drawn from 10,000 applicants, all enticed by the thrill and privilege of patrolling a World's Fair in a pearl-gray uniform with gold braiding. Guard Fred Bloom towered over everyone at six foot seven, an ex-military officer and champion wrestler from Finland, then a duchy of Russia. He'd even been a bodyguard for Czar Nicholas II, before fleeing when it emerged that Bloom was involved in activity opposing increased Russification of Finland. With the massive guard holding back the line, Henry Ford stepped forward, in a long chesterfield atop the three-piece suit he'd been wearing since last night's arrival by train. Ford adjusted his derby as he took his place beside Bert Scott on the driver's side, allowing a little grin before tightening his look for the camera. Guggenheim strode up to the other side of the car, rakish as ever: plaid driving cap; double-breasted motoring coat with contrast buttons; pinkie ring; stovepipe pants. His wife, Grace, flanked him in a modishly patterned blazer and skirt and a jaunty bowtie, clutching flowers and a handbag, her fair skin cloaked by a gauzy veil.

Guggenheim clapped a hand on Jimmie Smith's knee, then leaned on the weary mechanic like an armrest. Ford reached out for Charlie Hendy, his do-what-it-takes Denver branch man, contorted in back amid coils of rope and supplies. On the far side of the Ford, Seattle branch manager R. P. Rice occupied a front-row position just past Grace Guggenheim, with fifteen-year-old Edsel Ford peeking up behind Rice in a matching short-brimmed driving cap. Beyond the wind-whipped wreath fastened to the radiator grille, the winning car and crew looked like they'd been chewed up and spit out, with car, clothing, and skin all mud-caked and mottled. Where a proper side lamp had once been mounted beside Scott's seat, now a battered lantern and tin cup dangled from a strap, adding to the coal-miner effect. What appeared at a glance to be gauntlet gloves on Bert Scott's hands were just his actual hands, casualties of an unrelenting open-air odyssey in all weather.

The photographer got his shots. Even now, Scott and Smith were not done. They drove to the Mines Building, where every car that completed the race would be displayed alongside the trophy, livening up an exhibition hall full of raw ore and assorted minerals. Other than the daily demonstrations of rescue techniques, the Mines Building had a hard time competing with the attractions on either side of it—the mighty Forestry Building, with a colonnade of soaring columns fashioned from 124 unfinished fir logs that weighed fifty thousand pounds each, and the fortress-like Battle of Gettysburg rotunda, which paired a life-sized cyclorama painting with sound and special effects.

Scott drove right up the front stairs, no match for this little car that had summited mountains. Only when reaching the landing did they discover that the door was not wide enough to accommodate an automobile, so they backed down and went around to the side, this time successfully. Some of the crowd had rushed over from the stadium, and others filtered in from the manicured paths nearby. Once more Fred Bloom—the towering Finn, who would remain a university fixture for decades after the fair as the most recognizable guard on campus—cleared the way, ushering the No. 2 behind the ropes in the sunlit, bunting-draped exhibition hall. The official photographer again set up his tripod, this time with just Scott and Smith in the car and Guggenheim beside them. The throng, mostly men at the stadium, now included a number of small children and a line of women on a riser in festive headwear; rarer still for the fair, the crowd included a few people of color.

Autograph-seekers thrust pencils and notebooks toward Scott and Smith, who smiled wanly but were too exhausted to sign. Before they could be released to the Rainier-Grand—to be "turned over to the tender mercies of barbers, tailors and other artisans of a kindred sort," in the words of the *Post-Intelligencer*—they needed to make one more stop. Richard Eskridge, a young lawyer whose grandfather had been the Washington territory's first governor, held the role of reception chair on the Seattle Automobile Club's contest committee. A formal banquet would follow in a few days, but for now he ushered the crew and an assortment of officials to the A-Y-P president's office for a light gathering honoring the Ford win.

Bert Scott mustered the stamina to speak with reporters, alongside Henry Ford. He shuddered to describe Snoqualmie Pass, shook his head over the gumbo muds of the Great Plains, and recounted all those days when the Nos. 1 and 2 Fords and the Shawmut had scrapped for the lead, trading places over and over.

Guggenheim was so moved he pledged to sponsor the race again next year. Scott was sure the roads by then would be better.

"We were well received at all points," the Ford driver said. "Where roads were bad the sentiment of regret prevailed, and the desire and promise was for improvement. 'When you come this way again you will find better roads,' was the remark that we heard all along the line."

Henry Ford called the race "one of the greatest boons to the cause of motoring and good roads in the history of the automobile." He lamented that AAA and the manufacturers' alliance had fought so hard against the contest, shrinking the field. But whether it was five cars or fifty, he'd always known a Model T would break the tape.

"The result of the race," Ford said, "is just as I predicted."

Finally free, Scott and Smith declined invitations to dinner parties, the theater, and still more receptions, desperate to wash up and reclaim lost sleep. Seattle's two afternoon papers rushed out editions with full coverage of the finish, the *Star* splashing a FORD NO. 2 WINS RACE / MAKES GREAT TRIP ACROSS THE AMERICAN CONTINENT headline across page one, *The Seattle Daily Times* giving it similar treatment.

In their haste, neither the *Star* nor the *Post-Intelligencer* the next morning got Henry Ford's name right, as he appeared on the jump pages inside. To the *P-I* he was "Harry Ford," to the *Star* he was "J.C. Ford"—"the happiest man of all" in Seattle. His car might now be a household name in Seattle, but he could still slip quietly through a hotel lobby.

22

A Scrap in Seattle

June 23 to 29, 1909

After arriving by train from Baker City, Earle Chapin took a room at the Hotel Savoy, a stolid skyscraper overlooking Second Avenue, squarely amid the straightaway that would fill wall-to-wall with people cheering on the No. 2 Ford. The Shawmut mechanic endured the indignity of witnessing the Model T's "victory," giving a polite but disappointed interview to a local reporter. Then he trudged back out to the fairgrounds early the next morning to await his teammates, finding the previously boisterous plaza around the A-Y-P entrance now quiet and deserted.

Out in the Cascades, Pettengill, Messer, and guide Harry Tucker had finally crossed Lake Keechelus in the Shawmut, then persevered up and over Snoqualmie Pass in an anticlimactic slog. For all the boulders they encountered, they had to wonder if somebody had rolled them back into place after clearing them for the Ford. Counting several hours waiting on the ferry, it took the Shawmut twenty-four hours to traverse the thirty miles from the southeast end of the lake to the summit and back down again to North Bend, that first sign of civilization on the home stretch to Seattle.

By then, millions of Americans had already learned of Ford's triumph in their evening papers, with millions more about to discover it over breakfast. Brutally exhausted, and knowing that the No. 1 Ford was in no danger of overtaking them for second, the Shawmut crew stopped at

North Bend's Home Hotel for a late supper. The rest of the way was supposed to be easy, but in their fatigue they drove off the road in the dark and tumbled down a steep embankment along the Snoqualmie River, on the way to the town of Snoqualmie Falls. No one got hurt, but they weren't able to shove the Shawmut back up onto the road themselves. Eventually a wealthy logger from the coast happened past in a Stoddard-Dayton, on his way to visit family nearby. Promising to get help, he roused the local liveryman and returned with a team of horses, hauling the Shawmut back up as midnight neared.

The Shawmut crew finally reached the outskirts of Seattle in the early morning. Instead of end-to-end cheering and a long convoy to lead them, just a single car waited. Robert Guggenheim, who rarely needed encouragement to stay out late, had driven out in his Allen-Kingston to greet their arrival. Together they crossed the city line at 5:18 AM, the bedraggled Shawmut giving the millionaire's A-K a run for its money even after four thousand miles on the road, both cars speeding freely with Seattle mostly asleep. With the Shawmut sticking close, Guggenheim let out his roaring automobile, leading the way up Fourth Avenue South, a long causeway over marshland filling in with scattered industry. They met a car of waiting newspapermen, and then the three autos rolled together to the fairgrounds, the Shawmut hitting forty mph with little strain.

The Alaska-Yukon-Pacific Exposition opened for the day at eight. It was 5:33 AM when the little convoy arrived, with just Chapin and a few overnight guards waiting for the second-place Shawmut at the gate. At the sight of the car, Chapin gave his teammates a cheer. At the hushed edge of the fairgrounds at daybreak, a couple of the guards joined in, clapping for the Shawmut.

They were about sixteen hours and forty minutes behind the Ford, almost exactly the amount of time they'd lost waiting on the bridge permit at Fort Steele, never mind everything else that had transpired. The Boston crew drove the requisite laps around the empty stadium, and then they deposited the car in the Mines Building, the big No. 5 Shawmut looming beside the No. 2 Ford. With none of the ceremony that had attended the winner, the Boston crew retired swiftly to the Savoy. Pettengill, the taciturn lead driver, wrote a brief postcard to his wife and children—blue cursive in a cramped hand, on the back of a view of the A-Y-P Administration Building—before collapsing at the hotel:

finished second
will write more
about it later
glad it is over

It was still morning when twenty-four-year-old Bob Messer emerged and spoke with a *Star* reporter. Six days had elapsed since he'd last seen a bed—"and he looked it," in the eyes of the newsman. "Every feature in his face showed the terrible strain which he had been put to and the lack of sleep." For all that the Shawmut men had endured, Messer singled out that moment in Idaho, when they'd been far ahead of the broken-down No. 2 Ford and were closing in on the resting No. 1—only to smash that bearing in the wheel by striking a rut in the dark, in the middle of nowhere.

"It was just a case of luck and that's all," he said.

Except it wasn't "just a case of luck," not to the Shawmut Motor Company's backers in Boston. Already the company had engaged a prominent Seattle litigator, James Blake Howe, to prepare an appeal. Howe came from Yankee stock and had contacts in Massachusetts as lead Washington counsel for Stone & Webster, the Boston engineering, electric-utility, and streetcar giant with interests across the country. Blake contacted Guggenheim to ask him to hold off on awarding the trophy, and to signal that formal charges would follow.

That same day, the third-place No. 1 Ford finally reached the Snoqualmie Pass summit, striking a boulder around the start of the descent. The rock tore through the underside of the car, snapping the front axle and mashing the transmission so badly that the flywheel wouldn't turn. Instead of mending that axle high up in the Cascades, Kulick evidently extracted the part they needed from an accompanying Model T—a violation of the rules, but by now they just wanted to be done—and resumed the journey, stopping for a long dinner in North Bend with Henry Ford and R. P. Rice. Reaching Seattle early Friday morning, the No. 1 crew didn't even bother driving to the finish line. Instead, Kulick and Harper pulled up at the Rainier-Grand and went to sleep. They picked up again in late morning, rolling to the fairgrounds around noon.

In their initial coverage of the fanfare at the finish, Seattle's dailies had emphasized the impact of the race on the millions of Eastern readers who, while tracking this sporting contest, also learned about the A-Y-P Exposition itself, the shortcomings of the nation's road network, and the rapid growth of the West. But when the latest *Seattle Republican*—the city's African American weekly—emerged that Friday, its editors clearly understood the paramount importance of the race for the victor: "The Ford cars won the trophy, which means millions for the concern that build them in the way of sales." Indeed, Ford and his dealers were already striking with the irons hot, placing newspaper ads in big weekend papers from Seattle to Sydney, Australia, touting the triumph of the No. 2 Model T.

By the time the trailing Ford crossed the finish that day, five formal charges had materialized from Shawmut's lawyer:

First, that the Shawmut had reached the railroad bridge at Fort Steele, Wyoming, one hour before the No. 2 Ford and sixteen hours before the No. 1 Ford, only to be "refused access to the bridge" for lack of a permit.

Second, that the Lake Keechelus ferryman had been "seen" by someone "anxious to get the Ford in first," who persuaded him to keep the Shawmut waiting for four hours.

Third, that a Ford employee from Seattle who was not part of the coast-to-coast crew had taken the wheel of the No. 2 in the Cascades and driven part of the way over Snoqualmie Pass, while the crew rested.

Fourth, that the No. 2 Ford had changed axles partway through the race and arrived in Seattle with a new axle, not the original stamped in New York.

And fifth, that the ferryman at Glasgow, Missouri, had been compelled to "break down" after taking the Fords across, stranding the Shawmut on the approach.

The Shawmut side had no idea yet about the most explosive violation, that Ford had *changed the entire engine* on the No. 2 Model T to keep it moving at Cokeville, rather than repair the busted connecting rod in the original as required. The Acme team knew of the subterfuge as a side effect of running so far behind, having picked up all the local scuttlebutt while passing through one town and then another after the dust had cleared from the Fords and the Shawmut. That was the main reason they kept plugging; they believed both Fords could be disqualified for multiple infractions, which would vault the Acme from fourth into second, if they could just reach Seattle.

But the Shawmut team itself had no inkling about Ford's motor swap.

In a canny move, Ford and his allies openly confessed that the No. 1 Model T had changed axles after striking that boulder atop Snoqualmie Pass, disqualifying that car from an official third-place finish—though it could still receive a generic "certificate of performance" and be displayed in the Mines Building. Ford's gesture seemingly signaled a commitment to transparency and sportsmanship. In fact, it made no difference. Victory was what mattered, though a one-two finish together would have been nice. There wasn't even any prize money for third. The trophy plus $2,000 cash had been guaranteed to the winner, along with $1,500 guaranteed for second, but the lesser purses for third through fifth were contingent on a field of ten cars.

That technical disqualification of the third-place Model T did nothing to deter R. P. Rice, who booked big FORD—WINNER OF THE O. TO O. CONTEST ads for the weekend in all three of Seattle's dailies, claiming a double triumph for Ford anyway:

"First and Third Places [in] the race from New York to Seattle have been secured by Ford cars. That's the biggest demonstration of car superiority ever offered—the greatest proof of genuine automobile merit that could be secured. In the hardest, longest race ever pulled off, a Ford car secured first place and a second Ford car third place, winning from cars which sell for from five to ten times the price. It's a significant fact that of the three cars to finish, two of them are Model T Fords."

Out in New York, the nation's media and automotive-sales capital, the narrative crystallized quickly. That Sunday's *New York Times* hailed the Model T's "splendid showing," noting the importance of its horsepower-to-weight ratio: "The little cars could push through the tangled vegetation of the plains more easily than the heavier cars, and when it came to traveling over rough roads the small cars again had the advantage of lightness and power." The rival *New York Herald* ran a SEATTLE CONTEST A TRIUMPH FOR FORD headline, calling the Model T's victory "the most remarkable triumph ever scored by a small car." In the *Sun*, a delighted Henry Ford offered to pit either or both the No. 1 or No. 2 Model T against anyone who might now dare to challenge Ford in a return race to the East. And in the *New York American*, John Gerrie—the ACA's pacemaker from New York to St. Louis—lavished praise on the runabouts that he'd casually dismissed back at the starting line, saying that the "tenacity of the little Ford contestants was an eye-opener to me."

In Seattle, Ford and his allies brushed off the charges of foul play, attributing victory to the Model T's lightness coupled with its strength. Rice insisted only one of the five claims had an inkling of truth—the Fort Steele delay—but framed it as savvy "generalship" on Ford's part, not a violation of any of the fourteen official rules of the race. The Ford side muddied the waters with whataboutist claims that the Shawmut wasn't flawless, either, contending without evidence that the Boston car had left one or more Eastern control points before the full twelve hours had elapsed.

Henry Ford himself pretended to take the high road. He defended the sanctity of the No. 2 Ford and praised the performance of the Shawmut, even as he tut-tutted the Boston company—desperate for survival, and with genuine grounds for appeal—for making such a fuss with what he considered sour-grapes allegations.

"It is not necessary for me to say at length," Ford said, "what I think of the Shawmut car. My testimonial rests in the fact that after the demonstration it has made across the continent I intend to buy one when I get back to Detroit."

Of course, there were no new Shawmuts to be purchased, not in Detroit or anywhere, not after the factory fire last November. Henry Ford knew that for sure.

"I am very much surprised," he added, "that the Shawmut should have entered the protest, for the winning car has in no way violated the rules governing the contest. I will admit that Ford No. 1 was disqualified, and such statement, together with the reason, was given to the referee immediately upon its arrival, which will allow the Acme car third place. I would under no circumstances accept the cup had my car been guilty as the protest alleges, but knowing, as I do, that the car came through with a 'clean bill,' I will not under any condition surrender the victory it has legitimately won."

Despite Henry Ford's outward confidence, Edsel was circumspect in private. The fifteen-year-old boy—showing signs of the thoughtful, if tragically overshadowed, adult he would grow into—wrote a postcard to his mother. "The fair is just fair," he began, playfully. "We are having a nice time but wish you were here. Burt arrived last Wednesday and was cheered by 150,000 people. The streets were packed. Mr. Guggenheim is a fine fellow and the cup is great but im afraid we wont get it," Edsel wrote, in looping cursive on a Rainier-Grand Hotel postcard, explaining that "there is a scrap on."

Guggenheim had little appetite for delay, eager to hold a banquet and award the towering trophy to the Ford team, but he granted a hearing for the Shawmut appeal and Ford's countercharges. Even the local press seemed to be rolling its eyes over the kerfuffle, with the *Star* opining, "In the matter of protest, both the Ford and the Shawmut appear to possess marvelous powers of endurance."

The papers were more interested in the travails the racers had encountered across the country, and the dazzling account of Ford's triumph. Scott and Smith had become instant celebrities in Seattle. Here was a story bursting with too-good-to-be-true yarns from their adventure (an old

Kansas farmer who wielded "a blunderbuss" and threatened bloodshed when they bumped his horse; a Wyoming sheepherder named "Alkali Ike" who demanded they slug "squirrel whisky" when they stopped briefly for refreshment at a place called the "Mountain Dew"). There was a feature photo of the boys with Ezra Meeker, the grizzled seventy-nine-year-old who had become a national icon as the embodiment of the movement to preserve the vanishing Oregon Trail, and who ran a pioneer exhibit-restaurant at the fair.

The Shawmut crew was an afterthought, a squeaky wheel. Homesick, exhausted, the Stoneham trio just wanted to get on the train and return to Boston. But the company's backers pressed on with the appeal.

Guggenheim gave them the weekend to try to gather witnesses and evidence, with the understanding that they now needed to delay the banquet anyway to accommodate the persevering Acme, once it became clear that distant crew was determined to finish. Still in Idaho when the third car reached Seattle, the Acme had seemed a sure candidate to drop out, just as the Itala had. Guggenheim, who bankrolled that international entry, pulled the plug on the fifth-place car as soon as the No. 2 Ford broke the tape. Out in Cheyenne, Bert Bellows was game to continue, but the two with him were spent, their wind-whipped, sunburned skin peeling and bleeding. And their young benefactor saw no value in sinking more money into the misadventure; beyond the $25,000 or so Guggenheim had spent to underwrite the race and then purchase the Itala, he'd burned $700 on repairs and crew expenses since June 1.

But the Acme men kept going, wielding that explosive charge about the engine swap in the No. 2 Ford. They weren't even quiet about it. In eastern Oregon, Acme's George Salzman—a con man, his teammates must have understood by now, yet still a skilled and daring driver as well—told *The Baker City Herald* about Ford's illegal engine swap, among other alleged misdeeds. He was confident that the winning Ford "would be disbarred . . . for several reasons and that the honors would go to the Shawmut car which Mr. Salzman believes is honestly entitled to them."

Unaware of what the Acme team knew, the Shawmut side raced before the hearing to secure evidence for the charges their lawyer had levied. They hired a premier Kansas City private detective to go out to Glasgow and try to pin down proof that the Missouri River ferryman had been bribed. They attempted to round up witnesses from Lake Keechelus—where that elderly hermit named Hansen might validate their claims about the thwarted ferry there too—and up in Snoqualmie Pass, where someone from the railroad might verify the assertion that Scott and Smith had rested while the car kept moving. Except the hearing came up quickly, and it was just Shawmut's word against Ford.

Held in Guggenheim's office at the Lowman Building, the proceedings had a courtroom feel, crowded with Ford and Shawmut crew members, lawyers for each company, an A-Y-P official, a notary, and a stenographer to capture the proceedings for the record. Testifying under oath—at least to the extent that one could in a sporting affair, on the witness stand in a private office—Chapin described the scene with Hendy and the armed guard at Fort Steele, where the hamstrung station agent said he'd never had to close the bridge to any automobile. But Guggenheim heard nothing in that incident that violated the rules, while the rest of the charges to him amounted to matters of hearsay and speculation; he dismissed them all. DECIDES FORD CAR WON TROPHY, the headline declared in that evening's *Seattle Daily Times*, even as the story noted that Guggenheim was not empowered to make the final decision, and that all testimony and evidence would be relayed to the ultimate authority, the Automobile Club of America.

Still, at the banquet that night in the exposition's New York Building—modeled after the stately colonial of former Empire State governor and senator William H. Seward, who negotiated the purchase of Alaska as America's secretary of state—Guggenheim could barely mask his eagerness to award the trophy to Ford. He poked fun at the appeals process, drawing laughs by reading a fake telegram supposedly sent by Oscar Stolp, ill-fated owner of the No. 3 Stearns, the car that had started late and never made it out of Westchester County. According to the bogus missive, Stolp remained determined to reach Seattle eventually, convinced that every car ahead of him would be disqualified for cheating, making him the winner.

Clarence Hanford, the Seattle business leader who had laid out the route from western Wyoming to the finish, predicted the time would come when Snoqualmie Pass would be a pleasure to drive. Judge Ronald, the former mayor serving as president of the Seattle Automobile Club, rapped the many automakers who had backed out of the race but said the contest did yeoman's work for the Good Roads cause even without them. "I expect to live to see the day when 50,000 people travel yearly from New York to Seattle and make the trip in fourteen days, and I believe that such a highway will be the first national one in the country," he said, even "before one from New York to San Francisco."

Although no one had come forward to accept Henry Ford's challenge for an eastward rematch, he announced at the banquet that he would send the No. 2 with the same crew out again anyway to conquer the continent anew in the opposite direction—"without change of apparatus, and with the same parts that were stamped in New York." And Guggenheim declared his intention to start the second annual Ocean-to-Ocean Race on July 4, 1910.

Then they all retreated for a night of merriment along the Pay Streak, a candy-colored midway teeming with carnival barkers hawking rides and amusements, where visitors could watch a troupe of "Royal Pekin" acrobats perform in the pagoda-capped Chinese village, admire the scientific marvel of the Baby Incubator—where nurses in crisp whites cared for newborns under glass—or stroll through the Streets of Cairo, where hieroglyph-covered gates gave way to a crowded bazaar of donkey drivers, camel rides, and theaters "where the women dance the couche-couche." As with other expositions of the day, fairgoers flocked especially to the so-called "educational" exhibits that amounted to a human zoo. The A-Y-P's Eskimo Village, frosted with fake snow, showcased more Indigenous people from around the Arctic and subarctic than had ever been glommed together at any other World's Fair, forced to don furs all summer. Farther down the line, the Igorrote Village—or Igorot, a term applied to multiple ethnolinguistic groups from the mountainous northern Luzon region in the Philippines—featured fifty nearly nude "head hunters" and "dog eaters" living behind a fence in thatched-roof huts, making traditional crafts and performing dances for spectators, opposite kiosks selling Coca-Cola and waffles with whipped cream.

As a stunt, the best-known member of that Igorot group—Antero, who had wowed the crowd as a boy at the 1904 St. Louis World's Fair with his command of English and sung "My Country 'Tis of Thee" for President Roosevelt at the White House—would be called on to visit the automobile display at the Mines Building. The Igorot practiced a traditional form of metalwork known as the lost-wax process. Race and fair officials seized a cross-promotional opportunity by inviting Antero to make wax impressions of the stamps on all the parts covered by Rule 3, with a reporter and photographer capturing him at work among the cars in his loincloth. Antero found no signs of foul play—because the swapped-out Ford engine had of course been put back in before the finish. But the resulting dispatch generated free publicity for the fair, with the story running under sensational headlines, like CIVILIZED MAN CALLS UPON HIS SAVAGE BROTHER.

On July 8, Scott and Smith set off again in the purportedly victorious Model T, with Guggenheim wielding the starting gun. The car had now been decorated on both sides to read FORD NO. 2 / WINNER / NEW YORK TO SEATTLE RACE / NOW RETURNING TO NEW YORK.

Unhurried this time, they followed a zigzagging route to expose the fabled little car to as many people as possible while underscoring its vaunted durability, drawing crowds to local dealerships and attracting rhapsodic press clippings in small towns and big cities. They hit all the major hubs of the Pacific Coast—Portland, San Francisco, Los Angeles—before mounting what Ford claimed was the first successful automobile crossing of Death Valley in summer, venturing cautiously over the scorching sands at night with deflated tires and a handsomely compensated guide. Retracing part of the race backward, they visited Cheyenne's Frontier Days extravaganza—where Charlie Hendy had arranged to display the car near the grandstand at an auto-racing carnival that had been added to the annual rodeo and Wild West programming—on the way to Denver.

Scott and Smith were still in Wyoming when the August 14 issue of the *Saturday Evening Post* came out, three million copies circulating to the newsstands, homes, libraries, and waiting rooms of the nation, this one bearing a cover story about a "Reformed Suffragette." In the center of the magazine, a two-page spread opened from the Ford Motor Company, with a big map of the race and illustrations of six Model Ts, the same chassis with six different bodies and seating configurations, from roadster ($825) to landaulet ($1,100).

"Every Model T FORD is an exact duplicate of the car that won the New York–Seattle Contest," the ad boasted, in big print sweeping across the centerfold. It was a rarity for the Ford Motor Company, which preferred to earn free coverage and leave the work and cost of advertising to local dealers, providing them with sample copy and illustrations but giving them wide latitude. Of the hundreds of papers that had carried localized ads touting the victory so far, some indeed ran polished text verbatim from the desk of H. B. Harper in Detroit. But many put their own spin on it. NEW YORK TO SEATTLE! FORD WINS! a dealer in Cairo, Illinois, announced, in a box framed by bullet points. Some added gimmicks or attacked straw men. "It has been reported to us that the cars entered in this contest were not the same model T cars such as we offer for sale at $850," agent C. S. Sands noted gravely in his THE FORD WINS! ad in Kirksville, Missouri. "To anyone substantiating such a statement we will gladly pay $100." There were local ads in foreign languages (FORD VINNER STÄNDIGT TERRÄNG, dealer Hagstrom Brothers declared in Kansas's Swedish-language *Lindsborgs-Posten*, detailing the all-terrain victory of "Bert Scott och James Smith"), local ads with poetry, local ads with typos.

But this *Saturday Evening Post* spread was something else entirely, a broadside direct from headquarters—shouting the victory from the rooftops, lionizing the achievement of the little Model T—in a magazine reaching every corner of the nation, at a time before radio, let alone TV. It boasted all the hallmarks of the automobile advertising of the future.

Want a car for cruising on smoothly paved roads? The Fords dashed from Buffalo to Cleveland in just seven and a half hours. Stuck in the mud? They outran the competition by four hours in the rain on the way to Toledo. Worried about hills? "The winner crossed four mountain ranges, Catskill, Rocky, Blue and Cascade and had no difficulty making better time than its heavier competitors."

Still not sold? How about fuel economy of twenty-two to twenty-five miles a gallon on average roads, or the reassurance of knowing you're never far from an agent or dealer if you need to obtain repair parts, backed up by an automaker that has produced thirty thousand cars in six years—nearly ten thousand of them Model Ts just like the winner. "**The Same Car Went the Entire Trip**, complied with all the rules and arrived in Seattle . . . without having had to make a replacement of any of its parts, all parts bearing the marks of identification with which they were stamped at New York," the ad insisted, the real truth still concealed.

In the ad, which echoed the "hardest, longest race" superlative of Rice's Seattle newspaper spots, Ford also invited readers to send for a free copy of *The Story of the Race*, a pocket-sized, lavishly illustrated thirty-two-page booklet recounting the "victory" and doubling as a Model T brochure, with a textured cover and cream pages. Thousands more copies waited to be handed out at dealerships, along with the fortnightly *Ford Times*, which found new ways to celebrate the Ocean-to-Ocean achievement with each issue.

Scott and Smith returned to Detroit in the third week of September, greeted on the outskirts in Dearborn by a reunion with Henry Ford and other executives. Kulick and Harper even trotted out the No. 1 again to accompany the victors in tandem. Ford advertised the occasion with a call for everyone in the city "who appreciates courage, pluck and energy and who has a warm spot in his heart for a winner" to join a parade ending at the magnificent Hotel Pontchartrain, where two thousand people waited to cheer the No. 2 and hear Detroit's mayor toast the seemingly victorious car and crew.

In an era of long exposures and unsmiling photographs, someone snapped Scott and Smith close together at that homecoming, each one beaming majestically. Harper would feature it in the next *Ford Times*, with the headline HOME AGAIN and the caption *Are we glad to get back?* "Bert Scott and Jimmie Smith have secured the champion belt of the smilers class," he wrote. "The smile they wore going down Second avenue, Seattle, as winners of the New York to Seattle Race was nothing in comparison."

By now they had driven nearly ten thousand miles since June 1, and they weren't done yet. Ford sent them on for one last leg to New York, to complete this second transcontinental journey and to place the No. 2 on display at Ford's big Broadway branch. The timing mattered, with Gotham about to begin the Hudson-Fulton Celebration, two weeks of pageantry and parades commemorating the history of New York and three centuries of progress, timed to the three hundredth anniversary of Henry Hudson's arrival and the hundredth anniversary of Robert Fulton's Hudson River steamboat. Finally, after four months on the road, Scott and Smith were allowed to go home. But the little No. 2 kept on going, a high-mileage meal ticket that continued to appear at scattered showrooms into 1910.

And yet: On August 2, October 25, and October 28, the Automobile Club of America's five-member contest committee met to review Shawmut's appeal in an opulent hall at the Ernest Flagg–designed clubhouse of the ACA, around the corner on West Fifty-Fourth from the flagship Ford showroom on Broadway.

Robert Lee Morrell, the committee's chairman and elder statesman at forty-three, was a "gentleman lawyer" who retained the boyish features and elfin build of his days as a five-foot-three, 104-pound coxswain at Exeter and Columbia, if now with a feathery mustache and a tad more padding about the middle. A godson of Robert E. Lee but a proud Union League member as well, Morrell was a fourth-generation New Yorker who'd been raised amid servants in a Fifth Avenue townhouse. He had a small, round head with slicked hair parted left of center, and cheeks that swelled like billiard balls when he laughed, which was often. He enjoyed performing in amateur theatricals, but mostly he devoted his energy to motoring, logging fifteen thousand recreational miles a year when even one thousand was tremendous, almost always with his wife, the former Anita Hetherington Haggerty, whom he'd married across class lines, drawn to her intellect and beauty. A locksmith's daughter, she had graduated near the top of her classes at Vassar and NYU Law, becoming one of New York's first female attorneys, though she rarely practiced.

The leading figures of motoring respected Morrell as a man of intellect and backbone. Before the rift between the two leading automotive associations, he had served as ACA-appointed chairman of the AAA Racing Board, running the tightest ship the big Vanderbilt Cup race had ever seen. Later, he'd been the driving force behind Briarcliff, the first major road-circuit stock-car race in America. Now he was lead judge in a sporting dispute handled with judicial gravitas: "The matter of the appeal of the Shawmut Motor Company against the decision of the referee, Mr. M. Robert Guggenheim, rendered on the 29th day of June 1909, awarding the first prize in the International Contest from New York to Seattle to Ford Car No. 2, and rejecting the protest of the Shawmut Company." In other words, Ford vs. Shawmut, Shawmut vs. Ford.

Unlike with the rapid sessions held in Seattle, Shawmut now had sufficient time to gather evidence. They only needed to prove one of the charges, and the unassailable one was the newest, regarding that sly engine swap. The smoking gun came in the form of sworn affidavits and duplicate shipping receipts for the removed-and-repaired Ford engine, procured by John Jones—the guide for the Shawmut and then the Acme out of Montpelier, Idaho, the men's clothier who had previously worked as a fraud investigator for the Oregon Short Line railroad, and whose father was the chief special agent for the entire OSL. This was clear proof that Ford had pulled out the engine on the No. 2 after the breakdown at Cokeville, sent the car on its way with a replacement, repaired the extracted motor, and then shipped that original stamped engine west on the Oregon Short Line, to be swapped back in discreetly before the finish-line inspection.

In defense, Ford sought to pursue a mutual disqualification of the Shawmut, claiming the Boston car had left the Chicago control station sixty-five minutes shy of a full twelve hours. But the ACA's pacemaker, John Gerrie, verified that he'd given the Shawmut permission to leave then, as an equal adjustment after he'd previously delayed the car for official purposes. The contest committee rejected that Ford charge, unanimously finding in favor of the Shawmut. The men ruled:

> That it was proven to the satisfaction of the Committee that Ford Car No. 2, in the New York to Seattle Contest was guilty of a violation of Rule III . . . in that it traveled a part of the distance between New York and Seattle with an engine which was submitted in place of the engine stamped in New York by the Technical Committee of the Automobile Club of America, and is therefore disqualified.
>
> The decision of the Referee in awarding first place in the contest to Ford Car No. 2 is hereby reversed and Shawmut Car No. 5 is declared the winner, and it is hereby directed that the M. Robert Guggenheim Trans-Continental Trophy and Prize be awarded accordingly.

The news landed with a whisper. Even Guggenheim, who was bear hunting at the time with another Seattle millionaire, didn't catch up to the telegram until the next morning. He instructed his secretary to send the trophy and a note of congratulations to the Shawmut Motor Company in Boston. With no showroom and no factory, Shawmut's general manager, Horace Waite, lent the cup to *The Boston Herald*, the favored broadsheet of the city's Brahmin gentry, to display in a window of the newspaper's stately headquarters opposite Boston Common. But even the *Herald* ran the story of Shawmut's redemptive victory on page eleven. Across the country, scattered papers carried a wire brief about the ACA ruling against Ford, buried in blink-and-you-miss-it fashion deep inside. Most outlets simply ignored it entirely.

For its part, the Ford Motor Company ignored the ruling as well. At the corporate level, official organs like *Ford Times* quietly—if suddenly—stopped mentioning the race. But nearly all the advertising that Americans saw for the Model T came from independent dealers, anyway—and those decentralized ads continued to trumpet "victory" in the New York–to–Seattle race long after the ACA's damning decision against Ford. That all added up to a mountain of advertising column inches in big-city dailies and small-town weeklies, seen by thousands upon thousands of potential car buyers well into the new year. The FACTS FROM FORD ad placed in December 1909 in Pennsylvania's *New Castle Daily Herald* by local dealers Patterson & Emery was typical, enumerating six detailed "facts" (quality, weight, tires, horsepower, brakes, and precision engineering) that were key to the Model T becoming "the WINNER of the hardest, toughest, and most grueling contest ever run." In January, Portland's Ford dealer invited *Oregonian* readers to buy a "Duplicate of New York to Seattle Race Winner." And in February 1910, Pensacola's Ford agent—a music dealer who sold Model Ts alongside player pianos—continued to boast, "A Ford won the New York to Seattle race, defeating all the high-priced cars." That was eight months after the race, and four after the ACA had declared Shawmut the winner.

The Ford victory slipped as well into end-of-the-year almanacs and became an entrenched fact in the era's automotive zeitgeist. In April 1910, a *Washington Post* auto column included a gem from the other Washington, where Ford's new North Yakima agent, Fred Chandler, had gotten a call from a farmer enjoying a bountiful year. "Say, do you sell the Ford car?" the farmer asked, receiving an affirmative answer. "It's the same car that finished first in that race from New York to Seattle?" the man asked next. Again hearing yes, the farmer asked Chandler to bring one out for a demonstration ride. When he did, the farmer was so tickled that he asked Chandler to wait there with his wife, then went behind the barn with a shovel and dug up enough cash to purchase the car in full. Seattle branch manager R. P. Rice loved that tale, which ran in big-city papers around the country.

The following month, when a man named Fred Sweeney drove a Ford 450 miles from Oakes, North Dakota, back to his old hometown in Iowa, *The Oakes Times* reported that local hardware merchant Jut Bush was hardly surprised to get a note saying his friend had arrived safely, without any trouble from his Model T. "That's nothing, Jut says. Isn't it a matter of record that the Ford won the race from New York to Seattle?" A matter of record, indeed.

The beat continued. By then, with the first anniversary of the race just days away, Ford had produced a cumulative total of more than twenty-five thousand Model Ts, making it the bestselling car of all time already, though they were just getting started. And the Shawmut, little remembered nationally even by the spring of 1910, had faded out already.

23

Carrying On

With all the publicity around an unambiguous first-place finish in June, the Shawmut Motor Company almost surely would have attracted the capital needed to start over, allowing the Shawmut brass to complete a purchase option on a big new factory site in South Boston (an old cordage works) and pursue an ambitious growth plan. In the three years before the fire, the small company had sold $47,900 in stock and traded other shares in-kind for machinery, but Shawmut had mostly been floated by favorable loans from its own deep-pocketed directors. The lion's share had come from Quincy Adams Shaw Jr., the dashing clubman who had contributed materially to the design of the Shawmut engine. Shaw had infused the business with well over $220,000, the equivalent of $7 million in 2025, with and without formal notes.

After the fire, the company effectively had nothing. Even if men like Shaw erased those debts, they weren't about to sink even more money into starting over from scratch. The prepared plan would formalize the company and prepare it to significantly increase production at the converted cordage plant, with a larger workforce and substantially higher capitalization. Shawmut lined up a venerable Boston banking house to underwrite it all, provided the company sold a certain amount of stock first. With only a battered car on display in Seattle as a seeming second-place finisher, that task became a lot harder than it would have been with an avalanche of international press clippings touting the Shawmut's underdog victory. So the company turned to Boston's chamber of commerce, asking the chamber's research staff to prepare a thorough report on the prospects of the auto industry as a whole and the viability of Shawmut's blueprint for rebuilding and expanding in South Boston. They did so with the understanding that the report would be dispassionate and objective, but that if it came back with favorable conclusions the chamber's leaders would allow Shawmut to solicit stock subscriptions among its three thousand rank-and-file members, from East Asia importers to neighborhood florists and tailors. The report came back in late October, right before the ACA's pro-Shawmut ruling. By all accounts, it was "most flattering." But then, for complex reasons, things ground to a halt. In a looming winter mayoral race between chamber president James J. Storrow, a standard-bearer of Boston's Brahmin banking elite, and the charismatic Irish American pol John F. Fitzgerald—the future President Kennedy's maternal grandfather—ethics became Storrow's watchword, in a reformist campaign against patronage and corruption.

The chamber swallowed the report whole, for Storrow and his upright associates to avoid even the slightest hint of playing favorites with an individual business. (Unstated: In addition to queasiness around the chamber's wealthy board allowing any one company to invite middle-class members of the chamber to make an uncertain investment, the banking firm prepared to underwrite Shawmut's rebirth was presumably Lee, Higginson & Co., where Storrow was a partner.) So the chamber stashed the report, allowing members to come to the office and review it in person—but only if they knew about it and so desired. The report was otherwise embargoed, with Shawmut or anyone else prohibited from circulating it, quoting from it, or even summarizing its conclusions, as a means for soliciting investment or otherwise. Small-town chambers of commerce might trip over themselves to lure or retain individual businesses and even dangle financial incentives, but that sort of activity was unbecoming of proper Boston.

When word leaked, the people of South Boston were apoplectic. For a time, the controversy became a combustible political issue, drawing huge crowds to neighborhood meeting halls, and serving as one of many cudgels by which "Honey Fitz" hammered Storrow and the city's elite bankers for being out of touch with the employment needs of the working class. Fitzgerald won by a point and a half. But far too much time had elapsed. As Shawmut's Horace Waite put it, a buried report—after a "three months' thorough investigation," no matter how favorable the conclusions—that chewed up the calendar and could not be used to solicit investment was far worse than no report at all. With the purchase option on the factory set to expire, the plan to restart the Shawmut Motor Company withered and died.

In an unlikely outcome, some of Shawmut's directors also held an interest in a small candy-making venture in Boston's Charlestown neighborhood. Unable to raise the capital needed for Shawmut, they eventually purchased the cordage plant anyway, to retool it for their expanding candy operation, which required less capital. In April 1911 they ran a classified ad offering two Shawmut roadsters and one touring car, "slightly used but in fine condition." They may not have had any takers. The following year, a final sprinkling of Shawmut classifieds ran in the Boston papers, this time offering some "excellent bargains in built over second-hand automobiles for sale."

Arthur Pettengill, Shawmut's lead driver, went to work after the race for that candy firm, National Wafer, as a chauffeur and machinist. When the ACA awarded Shawmut the victory, even the local weekly paper in Stoneham hardly noticed. But Pettengill's sister, Grace Leacock, wrote a five-stanza poem celebrating the car and crew. "Many a line could we write here / For faith in the Shawmut car is sincere, / An honest car, and an honest crew, / A fine combination, I think, don't you?"

An honest car and an honest crew—scattered to the wind, at least locally. In 1911, Pettengill opened a modest auto garage and service station in a cinder-block structure behind his home. Over time, he expanded it to eight bays, dispensing Socony gasoline, performing all manner of repairs, selling auto parts and accessories, and "putting up" cars for the winter, when motoring was still a three-season activity in New England. Eventually Pettengill became a dealer too, ultimately selling Nash automobiles.

Robert Messer, the backup driver who had joined the crew as a third member, the auto-loving son of a popular funeral director, returned to Stoneham right after the Ocean-to-Ocean Race and got into the garage business with a partner. By late 1909, the duo had added a second location ten miles away in Lynn, so they invited Earle Chapin to join their partnership and run the initial Stoneham garage. He ended up buying the place from them, and in time opened a second garage in neighboring Reading as well. He did everything—washing, polishing, storing, repairing, scraping carbon from cylinders. For several years he even sold Fords. If you were going to sell any car at all in the 1910s, you were crazy not to make it the Model T. Chapin had to admit, it was a reliable car for a good price, a car people wanted. But that didn't mean he had any fondness for Henry Ford. Earle Chapin made that much clear while taking his grandsons on fly-fishing trips around northern New England in his own car much later in life, a beautiful blue 1948 Chrysler Business Coupe, with an engine so smooth you could balance a quarter on it.

"Paps was not afraid to let you know where he stood on issues, or if he thought somebody was a shitheel," grandson Craig Chapin would recall. "He had no good words for Henry."

Had the Shawmut crossed the finish line first and gotten the publicity and the capital to rebuild, Chapin and Pettengill surely would have stayed on. But the future of a company like that would hardly have been guaranteed. The E. R. Thomas Motor Company of Buffalo produced handsome, expensive, powerful automobiles in the Shawmut vein, and they did it in much larger numbers, selling 700 cars in 1907, then 817 in 1908—the year they basked in abundant glowing publicity, winning the New York–to–Paris Race—and more than 1,000 in 1909, when that same car became the pathfinder for the Ocean-to-Ocean affair. But they rested on their laurels, turned out some clunkers, succumbed to management squabbling, and fell to the auction block by 1913.

The Acme, which appeared to struggle to a fourth-place finish—but was eventually elevated to second, after the disqualification of both Fords—survived only until 1911, when it was sold to a successor company, S.G.V., for $250,000. (The "S" in the acronym stood for Sternbergh, the nut-and-bolt-manufacturing heir who had previously owned Acme outright and who had enthusiastically entered the Ocean-to-Ocean Race in 1909.) The S.G.V. paired advanced engineering with luxury finishes and soon landed a place in the garages of the elite, but a failed foray with a push-button electric gear-shifting system mounted in the middle of the steering wheel led to one of the industry's first recalls. By 1915, S.G.V. was on the auction block too.

And yet, the Shawmut, given its consummate attention to detail, might well have flourished without any of the same production miscues or managerial missteps—and lasted two more decades into the Great Depression, when the death knell largely sounded for the remaining Brass Era survivors that had built their reputations on hand-turned luxury, produced at a smaller scale.

Ford was selling something altogether different, in type and in quantity. Within five years of the race, the company would be shipping nearly a quarter million Model Ts a year, with the price by then at $550 for a touring car and dropping. Henry Ford would become one of the most recognizable men in the world, never again mistaken as "Harry." In the 1913–1914 production year, he would introduce both the moving assembly line for mass production (December 1913) and the fabled $5-a-day wage (January 1914), an act of calculated necessity—desperate to attract reliable workers who could keep cranking out Model Ts for an insatiable public—celebrated as corporate benevolence. By the early 1920s, Ford would produce well over one million Model Ts a year, with the company and the man both the subject of endless fascination.

"More was written about Henry Ford during his lifetime, and he was more often quoted, than any figure in American history," the venerable automobile historian James J. Flink would write in 1975's *The Car Culture.* Ford died in 1947. Considerably more has been written about him since.

The Model T changed everything, ushering the automobile from its uncertain adolescence into an essential feature of American life and an indelible shaper of the landscape, for good and for ill. The ten millionth Model T rolled off the assembly line on June 4, 1924—fifteen years and three days after the start of the Ocean-to-Ocean Race—with a celebratory paint job. Frank Kulick, still a favorite of the mercurial Henry Ford, drove that car cross-country on the nation's first true coast-to-coast roadway—albeit not to Seattle, as Guggenheim had been rooting for in 1909. Kulick took the Lincoln Highway, connecting New York and San Francisco. By then Ford had shaved the Model T's price down to a truly affordable $290, where it would hold nearly until the car's retirement in 1927, by which point over fifteen million had been manufactured. The United States had become a nation of white lines, service stations, and traffic lights, with social scientists studying "automobile psychology" and planners beginning to draw the car-centric suburbs and interstates that would define twentieth-century living. "The saturation point in the automobile industry is always being predicted but never coming," *The New York Times* opined in 1925. "I'll go without food before I'll see us give up the car," one Muncie woman said, in the famed Middletown study of mid-1920s Middle America. Will Rogers, sage of the heartland, would sum up Henry Ford in 1929 like this: "It will take a hundred years to tell whether you have helped us or hurt us, but you certainly didn't leave us like you found us."

In hindsight, the Model T—the most influential car in history—might seem predestined for significance, equally inevitable and irrepressible as the first lightweight, moderately priced, mass-produced car that managed to be durable and reliable too. In other words, the car the world was waiting for. It very well might have taken off even without the Ocean-to-Ocean "victory" boost out of the gate. But its fate was far from certain in the spring of 1909. And the race is an inseparable part of the Model T's origin story—not to mention a long-underexplored and underappreciated one at that.

With so much advertising handled by local dealers, it was easy to miss the full extent of the campaign to capitalize on the race, before the recent widespread digitization of old microfilm; now it's clear just how relentless and pervasive the messaging was. Touting the victory was an easy way for independent dealers to cut through the clutter of competing boasts and declare exactly what the Model T could do. That drumbeat continued long after Ford had been stripped of the title and the company itself had stopped mentioning the race.

By 1944, around the thirty-fifth anniversary, enough time had passed for the contest to become something for Ford Motor Company itself to celebrate again. A watercolorist rendered the 1909 starting scene at City Hall with a panoply of straw boaters and Gibson-girl types, for a then-and-now advertisement about "the inventive genius and the precision skills" associated with the company, in wartime and in peace. Headlined PRESIDENT TAFT GAVE THE STARTING SIGNAL, the ad ran far and wide, from *Life* to *Look* to *Popular Mechanics*, from *The Boston Globe* to *The B'nai B'rith Messenger.* It offered a dramatic recounting of the race capped with a visionary—if likely apocryphal—quote from Robert Guggenheim, supposedly delivered at the 1909 post-race banquet: "I believe Mr. Ford has the solution of the popular automobile." Naturally, the ad made no mention of the embarrassing epilogue to the race for Ford.

Fifteen years after that, when Ford Motor of 1959 was a billion-dollar behemoth—with Robert McNamara heading the car and truck divisions, and young Lido A. "Lee" Iacocca managing car marketing—the company threw its weight behind a celebration of American motoring, past, present, and future. As it happened, the fifty millionth Ford was due to come off the assembly line that spring within weeks of the fiftieth anniversary of the Ocean-to-Ocean Race. Seizing the fifty–fifty synchronicity, Ford assembled a national tour to retrace the four-thousand-mile route between June 1 and June 23 of 1959, mounting a "caravan of progress" that included that fifty millionth car (a Galaxie, with Michigan license plate *50 000 000*), an original Model K (the pace car from 1909), and an authentic Model T stripped and painted to look like the original No. 2 racer, as well as a space-age vision of the 100 millionth Ford that they imagined producing in the 1970s—the hovering "Levacar," a "wheelless vehicle that glides on a film of air."

The caravan included a museum exhibit pulled in a trailer by a Ford truck, featuring a sixteen-foot display telling the story of the race overlaid on the route map. Stopping in eighty-three cities and towns that had witnessed the original contest, the publicity-rich convoy was greeted by state governors and small-town mayors who read proclamations and handed out keys to the city. At each stop, an all-American cavalcade unfolded—parades, cookouts, ice cream socials, meetups for regional Model T clubs—and the local press loved it. Old-timers who remembered seeing the original race come through turned out to swap stories. Ford dispensed safety belts for local police departments to install in cruisers. And at the end of the line, Henry Ford's grandson, William Clay Ford Sr., would greet the caravan in Seattle, with that Ford fanfare incorporated into the groundbreaking—or, rather, the rocket-launching—festivities for Seattle's second World's Fair, the coming Century 21 exposition. (Washington's governor would push a button to launch the first shovelful of dirt into space.)

In preparing the caravan's exhibit and a related national media campaign, Ford corporate researchers spent months mining the story of the 1909 Ocean-to-Ocean Race, identifying four hundred communities bisected by the route, and writing to small-town newspapers and local historical societies to amass reams of microfilm prints and typewritten memories, in a pre-internet age. Amid a flurry of "Intra-Company Communication" memos and binders full of information, they even engaged a rare-books dealer in Massachusetts to try to discreetly track down the missing Guggenheim trophy. They unquestionably knew the true story of the race.

And yet, for all the breathless copy that resulted ("In bringing the farmer to the city and enabling the city dweller to enjoy country nature, the automobile produced another change. The two migrations somehow met head on to create that miracle of modern living—the suburb"), Ford made no mention of the contest's incriminating epilogue. For fifty cents they even sold thousands of unaltered copies of *The Story of the Race*—"a collector's item reprint of the original story of the 1909 Transcontinental Contest for the Guggenheim Trophy which was won by a Ford car"—lavishly reproduced on cream-colored paper.

Never mind that the first volume of a landmark history of Henry Ford and his company by Columbia University historian Allan Nevins—funded by a grant from Ford Motor, but produced with academic independence—had clearly stated the facts already, with Nevins capping a brief account of the race in that 1954 opus by noting the "cruel anticlimax" of the forfeited victory. ("Nevertheless," he wrote, "the Ford had amply proved the possession of special virtues in this punishing contest.") Where the race occupied two pages in that thoroughly footnoted 688-page volume, the historian Philip Van Doren Stern gave it a full chapter the following year, in his whimsically illustrated *Tin Lizzie: The Story of the Fabulous Model T Ford.*

In one of scores of oral histories recorded for the company archives in conjunction with the Nevins project, C. J. "Jimmie" Smith—the mechanic on the No. 2—had maintained in 1951 that "there was nothing to the charges; we had the same engine all the way through." But in a subsequent interview for Stern's book, Smith acknowledged that the engine "might have been changed without his knowing it while the car was overhauled en route by one of the many Ford dealers who were eager to see it win."

In other words, the Ford executives behind the 1959 caravan knew what really happened. But as far as the company was concerned, the race remained a landmark victory to celebrate.

Livid over the erasure of the real story, the son of the late Shawmut driver Arthur Pettengill—Gordon Pettengill, who'd followed his father into automobiles and continued to run their Nash dealership—wrote a strongly worded letter to Ford Motor emphasizing the truth. Replying to him privately, Ford's public-relations office sidestepped the known outcome ("The emphasis is not so much on who won the 1909 Race, but on the fact that there was a race and that it was a pioneering effort in terms of the interest and need at that time to focus attention on the possibilities of the automobile as a practical means of transportation") while buttering up Pettengill: "I am sure you must be rightfully proud to be the son of someone who was so prominently associated with the automobile industry in its early days. . . ."

To get out ahead of any rumblings, Ford issued a press release acknowledging a vague "controversy," as if the matter remained forever unsolvable, lost to the mists of history. "Many of the old-timers will tell you that there were so many protests, nobody really won the 1909 ocean-to-ocean endurance race. But perhaps fifty years later, it really isn't important," the company began, emphasizing that a Model T had crossed the finish line first, that Henry Ford demonstrated that his car could go the distance amid hellish conditions, and that this "harrowing endurance contest helped open up to automobile traffic the increasingly important Pacific Northwest, and pointed up the urgent need for better roads across America."

Richly, Ford Motor patted itself on the back for owning up to the axle replacement that disqualified the No. 1 Model T from collecting official third-place status, an admission in 1909 that amounted to something between an afterthought and a smokescreen. But the company reiterated Guggenheim's June 29, 1909, decision in favor of Ford without mentioning that the ACA had overruled Guggenheim four months later, after a careful review of evidence confirmed that secret engine swap in the No. 2. *Nothing to see here,* in Ford's retelling.

"With his promotion of both the race and the exposition a success, Guggenheim lost interest in the post-contest bickering. The Shawmut car driven in the race was the last one ever built by the company, which went out of business in the fall of 1909," Ford declared.

"So today, as Ford Motor Company re-stages the historic cross-country run, nobody seems to know who technically won the race. And for that matter, probably, nobody cares."

Except Pettengill's family cared, as did Earle Chapin, by then the only surviving member of the three-man Shawmut crew. If there was an accidental benefit to Ford shining a light on the forgotten 1909 race, it was that a *Boston Globe* auto columnist, Arthur Kelley, connected with Chapin that June. Earle Chapin had gotten out of the garage business in 1923 and started a successful home heating-oil company. By then seventy-six, he still had a gleefully colorful way with the English language, and he hadn't appeared to gain an ounce. He enjoyed fishing, tinkering in his basement shop, plinking squirrels with a .22, and making his own sauerkraut. Most of all he loved spending time with Anita; the year before, they had celebrated their fiftieth wedding anniversary with a road trip to Maine, then returned to the Boston suburbs to cut into a three-tiered cake at a party with seventy relatives and friends.

Reflecting on the race, Chapin delighted the *Globe* man with vivid memories of that long-ago "fight for survival," when you "needed a man who could find a way through when no roads existed, a man who could make major repairs with baling wire and had the direction sense of a carrier pigeon." He recalled seeing the Itala hung up on a tree stump, "with all four wheels off the ground"; being wined and dined at an Elks convention during the twelve-hour layover in Toledo; and getting lost amid the stockyards in Chicago, while trying to make their way at night with only that meager Blue Book. Kansas was one long "sea of gumbo mud," and the hail approaching Wyoming turned the road into "a bed of greased ball bearings." He made no mention of having to drop out for illness in Oregon, and—curiously—the *Globe* skipped the part about Ford getting caught and Shawmut receiving the honors in the end. Maybe that was for lack of space on a page flush with automotive ads, maybe for other reasons. No surviving Shawmuts were known to exist; the trophy had long since vanished; Ford was an American giant.

Across the decades, a few of Earle Chapin's memories had become interwoven, and some had become a little or a lot embroidered—celebratory cowhands shooting up Medicine Bow about the time of their arrival; an anxious fellow trying to unload a cache of cigarettes with them in Hays City, to avoid the wrath of Carrie Nation—but he crisply summoned a couple of notable numbers. "We used up fourteen tires and forty-two tubes, but strangely enough the left front tire never went and we still had New York air in it when we got to Seattle," Chapin recalled.

"We couldn't have worked harder," he added, "if we carried the car across the country on our backs."

EPILOGUE

In June of 2023, on a research trip to Seattle, I borrowed a friend's Volkswagen Tiguan and drove fifty miles east on Interstate 90 to Snoqualmie Pass, to retrace the final leg of the race. If I'd kept on going, I could have followed I-90 for another 2,962 uninterrupted miles without the aid of a map or an app, taken the Allston-Brighton/Cambridge exit on the Mass Pike—as I-90 is known in Massachusetts—and navigated the final mile and a half home in my sleep.

Instead, I followed the fast-moving highway—three lanes in each direction over the Cascades—only as far as Lake Keechelus, just beyond the eastern slope of Snoqualmie Pass, and took Exit 62 for the lake. For about a mile, I followed a bona fide road paved with asphalt amid towering evergreens, and then I turned right onto the kind of gravel way where Google Street View abruptly stops.

In short order I found myself weaving over and amid ruts on a "road" improved with just a smattering of crushed stones on top. I passed a sign advertising sled dogs and another warning what might happen if I followed a driveway (TURN AROUND HERE . . . WE DON'T CALL 911), as the road became truly cratered. Even at a cautious pace, the car bounced and jostled in a way I'd rarely experienced, even as a reporter in small-town New

Hampshire early in my career. For barely a mile, I had a taste of America's roads in 1909, and it was more than enough.

Finally, I reached the turnoff for the earthen dam that arcs along the southeastern end of Keechelus, where the lake flows into the start of the Yakima River. Hiking beyond that dam to the undisturbed edge of the lake, I looked out across the lapping water, the sloping shoreline enveloped by forest on each side, the snow-dusted peaks looming in the distance. All I could hear were the birds, the wind, and the distant rumble of the interstate. Minus the cars moving along that far-off ribbon of highway, the view remained unchanged from the one the Ocean-to-Ocean racers had encountered near this very same spot in the very same month, well over a century before. Back then, you needed Patrick Flanagan's expensive and unpredictable ferry to cross the lake, after which the climb up and over Snoqualmie Pass posed the hardest test of the entire race, a brutal ordeal along a snow-choked, boulder-clogged mountain trail that could take twenty-four hours, if you succeeded at all.

I stayed for a bit, contemplating the scene. Then I got back in the VW and retraced the route to the exit for the summit. In twenty minutes I had surmounted Snoqualmie Pass; the hardest part by far was the first stretch going back over the rutted trail from the lake, not the climb up the mountain. In place of the scrubby clearing and railroad camp of 1909, the summit is now a long-established ski resort and recreation area.

I found my way to the Firehouse, where an old fire station had recently been saved from demolition and given a mountain-chic makeover, with a coworking space, a Forest Service visitors' center, a gear outfitter, and a boutique grocer and café, Laconia Market, named for the vanished railway outpost. Eating a Tips Up Turkey sandwich—artisanal ingredients on ciabatta—and sipping a cold-brew iced coffee, I couldn't help but think that even if this was not the simple fare that Henry Ford favored, this was the world he made. With no mechanic beside me and little technical know-how, I'd ascended the mountain without cursing or breaking a sweat. There was a through-line from the first appearance of the No. 2

Model T atop Snoqualmie Pass in June 1909 to the opening of a properly graded road here in June 1915 to the six-lane interstate sweeping over the mountain in that June of 2023. ("King Gasoline's mighty army is now ready for the triumphant march across the mountains," the *Seattle Sunday Times* had crowed back in 1915, when that dazzling new road was a sixteen-foot-wide gravel byway zigzagged with switchbacks, open only in warmer months.)

On the way back to Seattle, I stopped in North Bend, where the logging hamlet of 1909—last stop for the racers—had grown into a thriving bedroom community and picturesque pilgrimage site for fans of David Lynch, whose *Twin Peaks* was partly filmed there. Even then, I still reached Seattle in plenty of time to return the car to my friend before he punched out at work.

I drove cross-country twice in my twenties, long before I had an inkling of this project. My wife and I mused about trying to follow the full course of the race in a camper while stopping all along the way to research this book, but the realities of life with school-age children made that impossible; I did the bulk of the research and reporting remotely, augmented by two trips to Detroit and one to Seattle. That ride from Keechelus to Snoqualmie Pass to North Bend to Seattle was the closest I came to driving the route, even as I methodically traced the four-thousand-mile course in my mind over the last several years.

A story is only as good as its characters, and here I consider the Shawmut and the Model T to be main characters as much as any individual. But I'm equally fascinated by the people who populated this tale—the crews and their guides, the impresarios and the investors, the folks of all stripes who brushed up against the race at this inflection point for the automobile and America. I can't resist a *what-happened-later* montage amid the rolling of the credits, so what follows is a collection of post-1909 portraits of some of the characters who populated this narrative. But first, one more word about the race: Beyond helping to launch the Model T and giving Henry Ford a jolt when he needed it—in September 1909, a federal judge would rule against Ford in the Selden lawsuit, but he would persevere and win on appeal in 1911—the Ocean-to-Ocean Race has lived on in a way in every cross-country speed challenge and endurance contest since. Acknowledged or not, the race's DNA suffused Cannon Ball Baker's captivating runs in the decades before World War II; the unsanctioned, unofficial, but widely recognized "Cannonball Runs" of the 1970s (the Cannonball Baker Sea-to-Shining-Sea Memorial Trophy Dash); and the equally outlaw Cannonball revival in the twenty-first century. At saner speeds, dozens of Model T enthusiasts retraced the Ocean-to-Ocean Race for the 75th, 100th, and 110th anniversaries. And the Ford Motor Company itself revisited the race again in 2021, sending an all-electric Ford Mustang Mach-E from New York to Seattle, accompanied by an original Model T (decorated like the No. 2) in a trailer towed by a Ford pickup. Just as the original Ocean-to-Ocean Race served as a showcase to prove that a lightweight Model T could genuinely withstand a transcontinental trip, the 2021 tour—dubbed "Ocean to Ocean Reimagined" by Ford—demonstrated that a Mach-E could easily hit enough charging stations to cross the country without trouble. Like the "winning" Model T in 1909, the electric Mustang wore the number *2* on its sides, along with the words *New York to Seattle.*

Now, back to the characters from the Ocean-to-Ocean Race:

The No. 1 Ford

Though his near-fatal 1907 crash forced Frank Kulick to wear a brace into 1909 and caused him to limp for the rest of his life, he yearned to return to driving high-powered racers, and Henry Ford soon granted his wish. Manning a specially built Ford racer in 1910, Kulick narrowly defeated an iceboat at seventy-five miles per hour in a two-mile-long contest on frozen Lake St. Clair, then delighted a crowd that included Teddy Roosevelt with his feats of speed around the track at the New York State Fair. In 1911, he beat the world-famous Blitzen Benz in a racetrack exhibition in Detroit, running off a blistering fifty-second mile around the oval from a standing start. Henry Ford rewarded Kulick with a thousand-dollar bill on the spot. (By one account, it was offered with the hope he would quit racing.)

After setting more records in 1912, Kulick retired from competitive motorsports and assumed an executive role as a Ford confidant, understated and reliable as ever. In 1924, he drove that ten millionth Model T across the country, giving a ceremonial ride to Hollywood's Douglas Fairbanks and Mary Pickford near the end of the journey. In 1927, Kulick was one of the eight longstanding employees who each stamped a digit on the serial number for the fifteen millionth Model T.

Kulick left Ford abruptly the following year, going into construction and real estate. He held no grudge, and in 1944 he enjoyed an unexpected phone call from Henry Ford, with the two reminiscing at length and Ford's grandsons listening to the conversation. By 1959, Kulick was the only living member of the four Ford crew members in the Ocean-to-Ocean Race; the company tracked him down at age seventy-six for a feature photo atop the reconstructed No. 2 racer. Just as in the old days, he clutched the wheel easily, cradling it underhanded at eight and four—not ten and two—for easy access to the spark and the throttle.

H. B. Harper, the advertising man sitting in as "mechanic" in the No. 1 Ford, got promoted the following year to run the entire foreign department, a New York–based position that put him in charge of international sales. He lasted about a year, jumping in 1911 to automaker Willys-Overland. Aside from a foray or two out of the industry, Harper would spend most of his career as an auto executive, focusing on merchandising, sales, and advertising. He served as sales director for Studebaker in the early 1920s and spent a year as president of the National Automobile Dealers Association.

The No. 2 Ford

Bernard W. "Bert" Scott stayed with Ford until 1911, leaving to join Studebaker, initially in engineering, though he continued to drive in exhibitions. Studebaker sent him to Australia for a stint as general sales agent and demonstrator. When the Great War broke out, he returned to Ford as chief inspector on the Liberty aircraft engines being built under contract by Ford and other automakers under the auspices of the federal government. After the war, he became an executive with a wholesale oil company, active in the Rotary Club and Boy Scouts in Marine City, Michigan. Scott died at fifty-six in 1940, when his only child, Jack, was twenty. Jack would become fascinated by his father's automotive feats, particularly the Ocean-to-Ocean Race. Irrespective of the controversy around the end, nothing could diminish the familial pride in the fact that Bert Scott had driven a car cross-country amid brutal conditions, stayed up for inhuman stretches, and broken the tape first. While working in communications for the Air Force, Jack wrote an article about the race for the Air Force's traffic-safety magazine. In 1984, when he learned that Model T enthusiasts were crossing the country for a seventy-fifth anniversary "Re-Run," he greeted them in Kansas City. The president of the Model T Ford Club International gave him a ride in a carefully reconstructed 1909 racer and called that surprise meeting with Bert Scott's son "probably the highlight of the entire trip." Jack went on to write a hundred-page account about the No. 2's experience in the race, gathering material long before the internet, and trying to make sense of photos he'd never gotten the chance to ask his father about. Though Jack Scott died a few months before the centennial, his own children celebrated with the Model T enthusiasts on the hundredth-anniversary tour. (The organizers dedicated the "Triptik" directional booklet for participants to Jack Scott, as well as to Bert Scott and Jimmie Smith.) Bert Scott's grandchildren take pride today in a gold pocket watch that Henry Ford presented to Bert, as well as in a trophy awarded for being the first to reach Walla Walla in 1909.

C. J. "Jimmie" Smith, mechanic on the No. 2, stayed in Ford's good graces for the duration of his career, working in the experimental department under the direct supervision of Henry Ford, retiring in 1949. He contributed to the development of the Fordson tractor and the first Ford airplane, and he personally accompanied Ford on some of the legendary camping trips he took with Thomas Edison and Harvey Firestone in a heavily laden Model T, including one with President Harding.

Later Smith repaired classic cars for the museum that became The Henry Ford. In 1938, he served as Henry Ford's driver, in a vintage Model T, around the State Fairgrounds coliseum at a seventy-fifth birthday celebration for

Ford in which thousands of Detroit schoolchildren serenaded the auto magnate. In 1942, when Smith was part of the oldest cohort of men required to register for the World War II draft, he still weighed just 135 pounds at the age of fifty-seven. He passed away in 1955.

The Ford branch managers

Several of the branch managers who served as Henry Ford's field lieutenants in the race and provided the essential logistical support for the company's "first-place" finish—through savvy "generalship," outright rules violations, or otherwise—were rewarded with even larger assignments, particularly as Ford Motor grew and the branch work came to include oversight of regional assembly plants as well.

W. C. "Fuzzy" Anderson, the St. Louis branch manager who drove Ford across Missouri and was photographed beside him on the bank in a companion photo to the one in this book showing the fateful Glasgow ferry crossing, became the manager of the powerful Chicago branch in 1918, then got sent overseas in 1919 to oversee sales in Western Europe. He resigned in 1921, with European sales slumping amid boycotts of Ford Motor Company, after Henry Ford used his *Dearborn Independent* to publish anti-Semitic conspiracy theories. Anderson's life took several colorful turns after that. A friend of circus impresario John Ringling, he became a part-owner of the St. Louis Cardinals, a Florida land speculator, and a bank executive, only to die penniless after the Great Depression.

R. P. Rice ran Ford's Seattle branch until 1916, when he was transferred to Kansas City, an important post for its vast, fruitful territory—it was second then in wholesale business, selling to dealers and subagents—and as the site of one of Ford's largest assembly plants outside of Detroit. In time he decided to go the independent route instead; he ran one of Kansas City's most profitable auto dealerships for many years, first selling Fords, then Chryslers. Just before switching, in the mid-1920s, he pitched Ford on a visionary idea, a dedicated plant to tear down and rebuild preowned Model Ts and recondition them for like-new resale. Active in Republican politics, he died in 1948.

If Shawmut had a bête noire in this story, it's Charlie Hendy, Ford's Denver branch manager, the omnipresent fixer who worked to secure Ford "victory" by every means at his disposal. He hauled that armed guard to Fort Steele and imposed the obscure permit rule, barring the Shawmut from crossing; he was in charge when the No. 2 broke down at Cokeville, with the illicit engine swap occurring on his watch; he climbed on board the No. 2 itself in Washington and rode along all the way to the finish, never mind that it was Rice's territory. Beyond the race, Hendy continued to travel regularly to visit his scores of dealers across the West. On a 1912 trip to Kemmerer, Wyoming—one of the stops in the 1909 contest—the local paper referred to him simply as "the gentleman who won first prize with a Ford machine in the race between New York City and Seattle," as if Hendy had done it all himself, which in some ways he had. (Never mind the actual outcome.) Within four years of the race, Hendy was selling $2 million worth of Model Ts annually. In 1913, he oversaw construction of a big Model T assembly plant and distribution center in Denver. In 1919, he got promoted to succeed Anderson as head of the powerful Chicago branch.

Hendy left Ford in 1921 to become vice president and general manager of an anti-theft auto lock company, receiving an equity stake, then seized an opportunity the following year to become exclusive Kansas City dealer for the Wills Sainte Claire, a luxury car company started by former Ford executive C. Harold Wills, who had contributed substantially to the design of the Model T, pushed the development of vanadium steel, and even created the iconic Ford script logo. Unexpectedly, Wills left Hendy high and dry; he retreated to the West with his tail between his legs.

Discovering that a Denver junk dealer named Jacob Abraham Hayutin owned a rare—but decrepit—Ford Six-Forty roadster (the muscular sibling to the 1906 Model K touring car), Hendy tried to get back in Henry Ford's good graces by purchasing the car for him, without tipping his hand. Ford indeed wanted the roadster, but at no more than $500. Hendy spent months circling Hayutin, to no avail. But the surviving letters and telegrams between Hendy and Ford's personal secretary drip with anti-Semitic disdain for the junk dealer, with Hendy ruing that the car remained "in the hands of the Jew."

Soon after, Hendy became a Denver distributor for the Gray, a car of substantial promise backed by millions in venture capital and organized by former Ford treasurer Frank Klingensmith. Billed as the "Aristocrat of Small Cars," the $500 Gray intended to challenge the Model T head-on, with similar size, power, and weight, and better fuel economy. (That the Gray is not a household name today tells you how that went.) Hendy spent the rest of his life focusing on real estate interests and United Spanish War Veterans activities, dying in 1954 with a substantial estate.

The No. 4 Acme

The Acme was an also-ran that encountered a slew of problems, but by being first to hear about Ford's engine swap, it's essential to this story. Its crew was unusually colorful, even by the standards of the race, from that first photo of the group at the starting line with cigars dangling. In streamlining the story, I lost all mention of one crew member, James Hemstreet, but as a fellow newspaperman he intrigued me. Sometimes referred to as team "manager," Hemstreet was a former penman—a calligrapher—and schoolteacher from a literary family who became a *New York Times* adman and sometime reporter. After Hemstreet wrote an early dispatch about a novel vacation by automobile, he jumped into the auto industry full-time, with his Acme role just one of many gigs. He eventually served as tour director and general manager of AAA. When Hemstreet died in 1935, one obituary credited him with "knowing as much about the country's roads and travel accommodations as any other man in the United States."

Fay Sheets, the backup driver arrested for speeding in Erie, got recruited for the race from Acme's San Francisco dealership after they heard about his performance at a fifty-two-miler in Santa Rosa, where he blew out a tire with sixteen miles to go but still managed to grit out a fourth-place finish on three wheels and a white-hot rim. He spent the rest of his career selling cars in California, making the news again in 1928 when he flipped while driving in rural Tulare County, found himself pinned beneath his auto, and eventually got free—before driving himself thirty-five miles to the nearest hospital with a broken collarbone, broken ankle, and assorted cuts and bruises.

Jerry Price, the factory foreman who served as elder statesman and brought substantial racing experience to the crew, got into aviation after the Acme's demise. In 1914 he became vice president of the pioneering Curtiss Airplane Company. In 1919 Price returned to automobiles, spending five years as "works manager"—head of factory production—for Willys-Overland, followed by five more in the same role for Durant Motor. He spent the remainder of his long career as works manager for Mullins Manufacturing, a pressed-steel giant that was an autobody pioneer, in addition to manufacturing kitchen cabinets, sinks, and washtubs. With that considerable responsibility, an employment contract saved by his family shows Price was paid $15,000 for 1931, a towering sum in the Depression. Already thirty-three during the race, he had a wife and four children at home in June 1909, including a young daughter, the future Florence Price Dwyer, who would become a progressive Republican congresswoman from New Jersey, a champion of civil rights, women's rights, and anti-poverty programs and a critic of the Vietnam War.

George Salzman, the con man/driver, is a beguiling enigma. Even if he wasn't *the* George Salzman—while trading on the good name of that famous driver—he seems to have genuinely been *a* George Salzman. At least, that's the name he used throughout his life, and the name on his death certificate. After the race, he lingered in Washington, surfacing the next winter in Spokane, claiming again to be *the* George Salzman while partnering in an automotive business that never got off the ground, and may have been a sham. Even claiming to be that George Salzman was not enough, as he added fake credentials there to the real man's impressive automotive résumé, claiming to be a graduate of Princeton and MIT as well—and forcing the real Salzman to circulate yet another round of letters in the trade press trying to clear his name. And yet: This George Salzman possessed skill and daring at the wheel too. In 1911 he raced pioneering aviator Lincoln Beachey in an exhibition at Elmira, New York, tearing around a field at sixty-five mph while trying to match Beachey's Curtiss biplane overhead; he lost, but the local paper credited Salzman with an electrifying performance, leaning out over the running boards to keep from skidding or flipping on turns. He stayed in and around Elmira and Hornell, New York, as an automobile dealer, marrying in 1912; unbeknownst to his wife, who would later seek an annulment, he had already spent time in prison.

When the real George Salzman—former star racer and executive of the Thomas and Simplex car companies—became factory manager for the promising new Grant Motor Company of Ohio in 1913–1914, the lesser Salzman seems to have struck again. At least, a man claiming to be *the* George Salzman, with the same old modus operandi, got arrested in Detroit on fraud charges, after running up a huge hotel tab in the good man's name; when police caught him, he tore up two fraudulent checks and shoved them into his mouth, but they pried out the soggy bits and pieced them back together.

Whether out of bravery or simply to escape, he enlisted in the British Royal Navy early in World War I, before American involvement, serving as mechanic on a series of ships. That may not have seemed exciting enough, because in a series of letters back to Hornell he regaled recipients with tales of being the most celebrated daredevil in the British flying force, promoted to lieutenant and known as the "suicide pilot." Major papers in Elmira and Buffalo breathlessly reprinted these exploits and celebrated his 1919 return, reporting that Salzman had been shot down a preposterous thirteen times, wounded seven times, and received virtually every honor for bravery imaginable, including the Victoria Cross. He claimed to be contemplating a record-setting transatlantic flight, but of course nothing came of it. In 1921, he posed as a federal agent while marrying again. In 1924, while operating an auto garage and body shop in Canisteo, Salzman was arrested for running an elaborate stolen-car resale ring and sent back to state prison. He died alone in 1962.

The No. 5 Shawmut

Earle Chapin, Arthur Pettengill, and Robert Messer all ended up in the garage business, as noted in the previous chapter, with Pettengill making it a career. Messer's family had been undertakers in Stoneham since 1843. He promised his father he would succeed him in running the family funeral home when the elder Messer could no longer continue, and he made good on it in 1937. Before that, he had a successful career in life insurance, largely on the West Coast. On a trip to Seattle in 1923, he marveled at being able to drive over Snoqualmie Pass with ease.

Chapin remained a lively character to the last. His oldest grandchildren, Craig and Bob, still cherish the memories of taking road trips with him in the 1940s and early 1950s in that big, beautiful 1948 Chrysler Business Coupe of his, and before that in a Packard convertible. "Paps had some really neat cars," Craig remembered. They both spoke often with him about the race, and the old days: "We would jabber with him whenever we had the opportunity." Earle and Anita resisted getting a television; they would listen to the radio, and Anita would play a baby grand piano, Bob said, recalling sleepovers fondly. "They did a good job spoiling us." His grandfather had no tolerance for cheating, in the 1909 race or anything else: "That was just a no-no."

When Chapin died in 1964, his successor in the oil business published a remembrance for customers, many of whom knew Earle as a vivid character. "His tall, almost scrawny figure was topped by a face that, once seen, couldn't be forgotten. Invariably it was wreathed in smiles and his laugh made everything seem all right. He was a person who called things as he saw them, good or bad," the eulogist wrote. "Profanity rolled off his tongue with great regularity"—in a colorfully emphatic way, never crude or gratuitous. "It was impossible to meet him and not remember him." As a man with immense technical know-how but little formal schooling, Chapin was proud of his two children, Ross and Jack, who became a physician and an MIT-educated chemical engineering professor, respectively.

Pettengill, a man of quiet dignity, was known during his decades running a garage and auto dealership in Stoneham for the same reliability and steadiness he displayed in the Ocean-to-Ocean Race. He served on the town finance board, was a director of a local bank, and was active in youth-recreation programming. A founding member of the Stoneham Rotary Club, he kept a streak of perfect meeting attendance for thirty-one years before falling ill in 1954.

It was at one of those meetings of the Stoneham Rotary Club that Pettengill, Chapin, and Messer got back together for a reunion in 1945, regaling the club with tales of that transcontinental race—the conditions nearly impossible to imagine already after just thirty-six years. "In summing up the trip the trio stated it took 22 days of grueling driving to cover the 4106-mile trip," the local paper wrote. "And by mutual agreement once was enough."

The vacant site of the Shawmut factory, scarred by fire, was deeded to the town in the 1920s and became a park and playground. In 2021, the Stoneham Historical Commission erected a marker there noting the history of both the Shawmut and the race.

The No. 6 Itala

Gus Lechleitner, the would-be cowboy driver who fell ill and dropped out in Chicago, moved to Australia in 1913 to start a new life. He made a genuine splash in the auto business there, while claiming to be the son of a San Antonio rancher—instead of a German-immigrant engineer on Manhattan's East Side—and adopting the nickname *Tex*.

Mechanic F. B. Whittemore Jr., a grandson of storied coach-builder Aaron T. Demarest and the snappiest dresser in the race—with his corduroy suit, lace-up boots, and hat accented with a feather—had a career in the auto business that outlasted the family coach-building firm and the Itala automobile as well. He spent many years as an automotive engineer with Mack Trucks and remained a sharp dresser to the end. "He was just a really gentle, kind man," granddaughter Linda O'Connor recalled. Living until 1969, Whittemore was the last survivor of any of the crews in the Ocean-to-Ocean Race. As for the striking headquarters at Fifty-Seventh and Broadway that the Demarest firm was building on

Automobile Row in 1909, it is today a New York City Designated Landmark that—along with its adjoining sibling, the old Peerless automotive building—has housed a panoply of notable tenants over the years, including General Motors, Hearst Magazines, and George Soros's Open Society Foundations.

Elbert Bellows, who handled the wheel after Lechleitner's exit, had little desire to relocate to Seattle and resume working as Guggenheim's driver. Known to his family as Bert or E. E., he contemplated moving to Boise to open an automotive business but ultimately stayed in the East. After a few more years as a mechanic and chauffeur in Manhattan, Bellows relocated his family to Saranac Lake in New York's Franklin County, a summer-resort community that had charmed him when he was driving for Guggenheim.

In 1914, Bellows partnered in an auto garage and dealership there, the Gray-Bellows Motor Company, catering to locals as well as seasonal tourists, and providing automotive service, storage, and sales in a two-story building erected on a hillside, allowing them to avoid installing a costly elevator or ramps; in 1915, the business was featured in a laudatory three-page feature in *Motor World* as a portrait of a well-run small-town garage and dealership. Selling air-cooled Franklin automobiles and later Hudsons and Chevrolets, they expanded to encompass a network of regional sub-dealers.

For many years, Bellows also operated a coach line, the Adirondack Motor Bus Company, providing service between Saranac Lake, Lake Placid, and other North Country locales. A Spanish-American War veteran who was in his mid-forties when the U.S. entered World War I, Bellows organized a Saranac Lake home-defense unit that became part of the Fifth Battalion of the New York Guard. When the unit deployed overseas, Bellows remained stateside because of his age and family responsibilities, but he continued serving for twenty more years as a respected captain and drill instructor.

Though his own formal schooling had been limited, Bellows prized education, serving as president of the local school board; he sent his daughter to Vassar and his two sons to St. Lawrence, with both young men serving as naval officers in World War II. Though Guggenheim pulled the plug on the Itala crew in Cheyenne, one of Bert's granddaughters, Janice Feaman, retraced the route on her own in 2016, making it all the way to Seattle.

Robert Guggenheim

By the winter of 1909–1910, M. Robert Guggenheim had become a subject of mockery in Seattle, retreating cross-country to the St. Regis Hotel in New York with a supposed case of the mumps, amid a cloud of bad press clippings, a slew of failed promotional ventures, the specter of lawsuits, and a litany of arrests for speeding. "Ever since his advent in Seattle society the young man has stood in the spotlight, in various phases, almost continuously. In almost every instance disaster and discredit has been his portion," *The Seattle Daily Times* noted, ticking off his overruled decision in the Ocean-to-Ocean Race, his ham-handed effort to purchase victory for his wife in a charity dance competition, his fiasco of an attempt to organize a world-class marathon footrace—when he may have been played as a mark by a slick San Francisco sporting promoter—and his utterly ill-fated attempt to raffle off the star-crossed Itala automobile. So many people complained that the ticket sales and the drawing itself were not on the level—on top of potentially running afoul of state and federal law—that Guggenheim's father had to bail him out and reimburse everyone who bought a ticket. The following fall, in late 1910, Robert tried to unload the Itala again, this time for $2,500 trade-in credit toward a new car in Portland, transferring it to a dealer who, in a pinch, quickly resold it for $2,200 and some telephone bonds of possibly manipulated value. That resulted in a legal tangle before Daniel Guggenheim again intervened and seized the car by replevin, with newspapers joking that he planned to promptly ship his son's "hoodoo" automobile cross-country and "dump it into the East River."

And that was just two years in the life of a young playboy who would go down as "one of America's most charming wastrels," in the words of John H. Davis, author of *The Guggenheims: An American Epic.* Robert married four times and owned five successive seagoing yachts dubbed the

Firenze, named for his beloved mother, Florence, who retained a special affection for her mischievous son long after he'd been dismissed by his father, bought out with a trust to keep him from working in the family business and from embarrassing them by failing at a job elsewhere. Robert Guggenheim did find a place for himself as an officer in World War I, an aide and confidant to generals away from the front, where he befriended a young lieutenant named Dwight D. Eisenhower. Decades later, after Guggenheim donated substantially to the Eisenhower presidential campaign, Ike rewarded him with the ambassadorship to Portugal—an epically abbreviated assignment that ended when Robert playfully flipped a spoon into the air at a state dinner, then fished it from the cleavage of a Portuguese grande dame with his bare hands. He was who he was, in 1909 and 1953.

In the 1950s, young grandson Dan Guggenheim visited the aging Robert in Sun Valley, Idaho, fishing for bass and learning to shoot skeet with him. He told me he savored that time with his grandfather—"he was just a great guy, a fun guy, to be with"—but understood early on that Robert's life was a cautionary tale. Dan grew up with some privilege, but owing to divorce he lived largely outside the gilded Guggenheim circle, mowing lawns and gardening in junior high, and spending summers in high school working in a noisy machine shop and in a blazing-hot foundry. The summer Dan was sixteen, his grandfather couldn't understand why the boy was working, offering to match his hourly wage to abandon the job and join him in leisure. But Dan liked the machine shop, with none of the men around him knowing he was a Guggenheim. Then one day the anonymous teen exited work to find a waiting gift from his grandfather: a gleaming Ford convertible, with the boy's initials, DGIII, emblazoned on the side.

Say what you will about Robert Guggenheim; he loved a good car to the last.

AFTERWORD

I spent years dreaming of writing page-one stories for my hometown *Boston Globe*, and for over a decade I was lucky enough to do it. This book grew out of the first of those A1 bylines, indirectly and by chance. In 2007 I was a new reporter in a suburban bureau, keeping an eye on several communities northwest of Boston, hoping to get the attention of the city desk. That spring, Stoneham faced a budget crisis so severe that the town eliminated high school sports (temporarily, at least), a move dramatic enough to land on A1. While covering that story, I signed up for a Stoneham email list, but by 2009 I had moved on to other beats, and those messages went unread. Then one day I randomly clicked on one; scanning the latest Select Board agenda, I saw only the usual fare—until the last item, which recognized something called the Shawmut Motor Company, once the pride of Stoneham, the rightful but forgotten winner of a cross-country auto race in 1909. The hundredth anniversary neared. I snapped to attention.

That June, I wrote a *Globe* feature about the Ocean-to-Ocean Race and the Shawmut, with Model T enthusiasts retracing the route for the centennial, much as they had for the seventy-fifth. This time they'd extended an olive branch to Stoneham and connected with descendants of True Arthur Pettengill, Shawmut's lead driver. I spent hours at the Stoneham Historical Society & Museum, guided by volunteer curator Mary Marchant, who at eighty-three remembered Pettengill from her Depression-era childhood as a quiet man with hands blackened by automotive grease. I also traveled to Lang's Old Car Parts in Central Massachusetts, a family-run mail-order supply house revered by Model T restorers, where Don Lang gave me my first ride in a T. The story stayed with me. I thought it might make a great book, maybe even a movie. But time passed, and I did little else with it.

Seven years later, a colleague introduced me to agent Wendy Strothman. We met for coffee at the Boston Public Library. By then I had a few more ideas. Before I'd even taken a sip, Wendy—brilliant, experienced, no-nonsense—dismissed each of those, deeming one a magazine article, the other two nonstarters. She asked if I had anything else. I gulped, then offered my sole remaining idea, about a cross-country auto race that Ford cheated to win to promote the Model T. "Now *that's* a book," Wendy said.

I'd love to tell you I took off with a jolt, but four years passed before I dug into the proposal. Wendy helped me shape it into a package that coupled an approximation of this book's opening chapter with crisp jacket copy and a reasonable outline. Charles Spicer saw potential and acquired the book for St. Martin's Press in 2021.

Time passed before he received any pages. Life happened, but so did my propensity for diving down rabbit holes. Probably I spent too much energy researching arcana or going deep on characters who might only merit a sentence. But I would burrow so often into something wonderful that it was tempting to keep digging. I knew the nuts and bolts of the race would come from newspaper coverage, but enlivening the story would require much more. I built dozens of family trees to track down descendants, hoping to find people keeping faith with their forebears via passed-down anecdotes or preserved materials that could pop off the page—the joyful detective work at the intersection of journalism and genealogy.

It's one thing to email people out of the blue about a 1909 auto race and a long-ago name in their family tree. Cold calls are another matter. Some direct them to voicemail, never to call back. A few engage warily, suspecting a scam. Many are vaguely aware of the name but don't know much about family history. Occasionally they have a portrait that can help with a visual detail, or they know a cousin who might know something. In the rarest cases, you connect with someone who seems to have been waiting years for this call, versed in the story of the Ocean-to-Ocean Race and possessing a trove of materials that, until now, no one has asked about.

To that end, I'm grateful to the many descendants of crew members, automotive pioneers, race organizers, guides, and others who responded warmly, but I'm especially indebted to the families of Earle Chapin and Elbert Bellows, without whom this would be a diminished book. In Chapin's case, his grandson Bruce harbored a passed-down collection that included three dozen letters and postcards Earle mailed from the race, an assortment of transcribed telegrams that the Shawmut crew sent to the company's general manager, a scrapbook of clippings kept by Earle's wife, multiple Shawmut brochures, and assorted snapshots affording a glimpse of life in and around the Chapin home and Shawmut factory.

On Ancestry.com alone, I reached out to two hundred people who had built publicly visible family trees that included someone connected to this story. It was a low-yield game. So I got chills when Bellows's great-granddaughter Sarah Upbin wrote back immediately—late at night, from an apartment a mere hundred blocks south of where I was living at the time, during a foray in New York—to say she could "provide some information." That was an understatement. Once she'd established that my interest was sincere, Sarah introduced me to a cousin—Janice Bellows Feaman, Bellows's granddaughter—and the two shared a digitized trove that included over thirty letters and postcards from Bellows's prerace Western journey and the race itself, snapshots showing the travails of the Itala car, and what may be the only surviving copy of the passport carried by every crew, which was supposed to be endorsed at the checkpoints along the way and turned in at the finish. (That Itala passport survived in Bellows's hands because they dropped out before Seattle.) Janice was so drawn to her grandfather's story that she had retraced the route in 2016, keeping a journal and taking hundreds of photos along a fifteen-day drive.

As a postcard collector, I love real-photo postcards, meaning genuine photographs developed onto light-sensitive paper with postcard backs, not mass-produced using a printing press. These were the smartphone snapshots of the early 1900s, a way to easily capture and share images from everyday life. I wrote an essay about their popularity as a form of small-town photojournalism—recording a fire on Main Street or, say, a coast-to-coast automobile coming through—for a book, *Real Photo Postcards: Pictures from a Changing Nation*, that accompanied a 2022 exhibit at the Museum of Fine Arts, Boston. I figured local Kodak enthusiasts must have snapped cards like this of the race in 1909. Sure enough, some of the most intriguing photos I found at The Henry Ford's Benson Ford Research Center (BFRC)—the set from Goodland, Kansas—were real-photo postcards. Still, they were outliers. Most of the known images of the race were professional shots taken around big cities like Cleveland, where the cover photo for this book was captured.

Surely other photo postcards of the race must exist—or existed at one time—stashed in albums or cigar boxes, cherished in private collections or overlooked in attics, misidentified or never identified at all. I set some eBay alerts and waited. Eventually, a stunner popped up showing the Shawmut racing out of Twin Falls, Idaho, but I just missed it. Hoping to ask the buyer or seller for a scan, I struck out internally but eventually reached the seller, a semi-retired Montana antiques dealer named Colleen Rooke, after buying an unrelated card and sending a snail-mail letter to her return address. She was unable to contact the winner of her Shawmut listing, but something about my story spoke to her, and she took my breath away by mailing me a separate card showing the exhausted Acme crew in Twin Falls—as a holiday gift. I framed it for display. The next year a different view of the Shawmut in Twin Falls popped up. Though I got outbid, this seller connected me with winner Ralph Allen—who also owned a copy of the card I'd previously failed to track down. He let me reproduce it in this book, and he put me in touch with another collector, Idaho historian Ron Yates, whose extensive insights—in detailed emails, with annotated maps and images—enriched my writing about the race from Pocatello to Boise.

One other word about this latter-day shoe-leather reporting, a century out. With Ford-affiliated families, I anticipated that the outreach might be complicated, given what really happened. I had polite exchanges with several descendants who were interested but had no material beyond what I could gather elsewhere. Bert Scott's grandchildren were an exception, and I'm grateful for the stories, photos, and artifacts they shared. Their grandfather died relatively young, and their father—Jack Scott—a World War II B-29 instructor pilot who had a long and varied career—dedicated considerable time to studying the Ocean-to-Ocean Race and connecting with the Model T community, honoring his father's legacy. Until 2009, Jack's children knew the tale of the No. 2 as an unqualified point of family pride. Only with the centennial did they learn of the ruling that stripped Ford of the title. Bert Scott's grandson, Jack B. "Burt" Scott II, acknowledged the complexity. "I grew up knowing that my grandfather won the race, and then in recent years just discovered the other part," said Burt, whose nickname nearly echoes his grandfather's. He considered everything that the No. 2 crew endured and achieved up to Cokeville, and the tenacity required to keep going after breaking down, irrespective of the epilogue. "To me, it's still the story," he told me. "They didn't quit."

Scott and Smith certainly had grit; they all did. In time, I amassed a hundred-plus images from the race itself, and scores more from the daunting pathfinder expedition and Ford "victory tour" at the other end. I've spent hours scrutinizing them, and I remain transfixed. Here in late 2025, toting my kids around in a new family car with touchscreen display and lane assist, I'm struck by the audacity and fortitude—and the mechanical know-how—of these competitors who climbed into open-air automobiles and barreled across the continent, whether they broke down in Tarrytown, withdrew in Cheyenne, or made it all the way to Seattle.

ACKNOWLEDGMENTS

I'm grateful to everyone who made this book possible, starting with my agent, Wendy Strothman, and my editor at St. Martin's Press, Charles Spicer. Wendy elicited the idea and guided me through the proposal, while Charles believed in it enough to take a chance on a first-time author.

I feel kinship with those who wrote about this race previously, especially Curt McConnell, who studied microfilm and corresponded with historical societies for his *Coast-to-Coast Auto Races of the Early 1900s: Three Contests That Changed the World*. He was gracious when I contacted him while hunting for elusive photographs, delighted to discuss the race and learn I had connected with descendants, aided by the internet.

I confess to being a mediocre driver who started with a love for good stories and history but little auto expertise. Enter Henry Dominguez, a retired automotive engineer who has restored antique Fords and written ten books on Ford history. With patience and humor, Henry spent many hours answering questions and providing a technical read. Trent Boggess, an academic who specializes in early Ford history and collects Model Ts, also graciously fielded technical questions.

I'm indebted to numerous librarians, archivists, and experts from New York to Seattle, but Lauren Brady from The Henry Ford's Benson Ford Research Center (BFRC) stands apart. Even as the BFRC remained outwardly closed after the pandemic, Lauren nimbly responded to dozens of emails, tracked down rare photos and documents, and helped facilitate an in-person visit for me to the archives.

Also in auto circles, I'm grateful to Carla Reczek and Mark Bowden of the Detroit Public Library's National Automotive History Collection; Ryan Bollinger, then librarian at Philadelphia's Simeone Foundation Automotive Museum; and the late Chris Ritter, librarian of the Antique Automobile Club of America, widely appreciated for his generosity to researchers.

Close to home, the Stoneham Historical Society & Museum welcomed me for multiple visits, while board members Dolly Wilson and Joan Quigley spent hours corralling materials. With yet-to-be-digitized newspapers, I borrowed microfilm through interlibrary loans facilitated by the Boston Athenaeum. Special thanks to Hub Town Tours, where I've worked as a part-time guide, for the perk of that Athenaeum membership.

Along the race route, generous help came from (among others): Orton Ortwein of the Chicago Public Library; Preston Petermeier, St. Louis Public Library; Vickie Johnson, Missouri's Marshall Public Library; Samantha Windle, the High Plains Museum, Goodland, Kansas; Suzi Taylor, Wyoming State Archives; Jennifer Messer, Wyoming's Rock Springs Historical Museum; Evie Hergenrather, Idaho State Archives; and Steve Wadner and Josh White of Oregon's Union County Museum. Wanting the book to end vividly in the Washington of 1909, I faced a challenge as a New Englander with a limited travel budget and no time machine. The Snoqualmie Valley Museum's Cristy Lake, Milwaukee Road experts Allen Miller and Andrew Craig Magnuson, and Bureau of Reclamation historians Kate Hovanes and BranDee Bruce provided considerable help.

Researching in Seattle, it was electrifying to walk the University of Washington campus where the race ended, anchored by what's now Drumheller Fountain, centerpiece of the fairgrounds. I mainly dwelled in UW's Special Collections but also spent time at Suzzallo Library, where librarian Jessica Albano surprised me with original 1909 newspapers—a thrill for any journalist, especially one straining over microfilm.

Early on, I received generous encouragement from Bob Goetz, a veteran *New York Times* editor, and his friend Bill Vlasic, former Detroit bureau chief for the *Times*. I also connected with a thoughtful coach, Kyle Fabel, who helped me manage the tasks that coalesced into this book, while providing narrative feedback too. In later stages, it was a pleasure reconnecting with my former *Globe* colleagues Jessica Rinaldi and Patrick Garvin, who contributed the author photo and map, respectively.

Peter Canellos, a fellow alumnus of *The Daily Pennsylvanian* (DP), has been a sage mentor and friend for twenty-five years. At every stage of this book, Peter offered the right mix of critique and encouragement to keep me on track.

I appreciate the many educators who helped shape me, including Steve Fortin, whose fourth-grade journaling assignments made writing joyful and rewarding, and Bonnie Weiss and Martha Remsen at Needham High. Mrs. Weiss's red pen taught me the real work of writing comes with revising; Mrs. Remsen brought winking humor to the classroom and predicted that I'd write a book. I was saddened to learn both had passed away before I could thank them again. At Penn, I took two formative seminars with Paul Hendrickson, and I can still picture him pacing the room, emphasizing spare prose—keep it moving like "the prow of a ship."

Those lessons, coupled with smart editing at my longest professional homes (the *Globe*, New Hampshire's *Concord Monitor*, and *The Standard-Times* of New Bedford, Massachusetts), prepared me to embrace feedback and try again whenever a first (or third) draft missed the mark—all leading to a successful collaboration with Charles. He's encouraging, attuned to structure, respectful of a writer's voice, and candid if something isn't working.

I also appreciate unflappable assistant editor Hannah Pierdolla for her attention to detail throughout. Thank you to everyone at St. Martin's, including cover artist Rob Grom, interior designer Omar Chapa, and the marketing and publicity team of Michelle Cashman and Kathryn Hough. Copyediting was a joy, working with Susannah Noel, Allan Fallow, and Amelie Littell.

My research budget was extended by family, friends, and friends of friends who hosted me in New York, Detroit, and Seattle. Special thanks to Ted and Michelle Clark, who lent me their Volkswagen Tiguan to explore Snoqualmie Pass and Lake Keechelus; I repaid the favor by driving it over appalling roads.

I've benefited from talking through the process or blowing off steam with friends from every phase of life, especially my student-newspaper days at the DP, including Ben Geldon, Nick Plagge, Rick Haggerty, and Sebastian Stockman (a native of Alma, Missouri, along the race's route). I'm grateful to all the friends who've buoyed me in so many ways, watching Celtics games, coaching soccer, playing trivia, or lifting me with a call or text. Special mention to Will Durbin for being one of the world's great listeners.

I'm especially indebted to family. My brother Scott has been a trusted sounding board throughout. His sharp edits coupled with encouragement helped me strengthen the Goodland chapter while cutting it in half. My parents, David and Ellen, filled our childhood with books and museums, raising us to appreciate road trips and Americana. As a kid drawn to history, I peppered them with questions about the past while asking still more questions of the grandparent I knew best, Libbie Moskowitz, whose ninety-five years stretched from a Hoboken childhood where her father briefly ran a horse-drawn moving company to the car-centric suburbs of the 1950s to the twenty-first century. She understood that books are vital. Near the end, as her health faltered, she sustained herself with the fresh bag of library titles we brought weekly. I can imagine what joy this book would have brought her.

When I stumbled upon this story, I was twenty-nine and single. I cross the finish at forty-six, married a decade, a father of two. This book is dedicated to my wife, Hannah Swartz, and our sons Arlo and Isaac (Izzy to us), whose love and encouragement made this all possible. Years ago, Hannah asked me to tell her about the main characters, intuiting that these were "the people we're going to be living with." Arlo provided my favorite moment along the way, surprising me on my Seattle trip with folded notes hidden in my luggage. Izzy, who makes everyone laugh, is the only one who could ask, nightly, "Did you finish your book today?" without any pressure, only curiosity. As I neared the end, I loved sitting on the kitchen floor with Hannah amid scores of photographs as she helped select the winners to include. Thank you all for believing in me.

Finally, in memoriam: I lost three people dear to me while writing this book. My DP friend Rod Kurtz, a skilled journalist and entrepreneur, charismatic and sincere, deserved to turn forty-six and deserves to be remembered. My spirited mother-in-law, Sarah Silberstein Swartz, a talented professional editor, provided considerable help when I was flailing with an unfinished proposal. Within the family we had a special connection around writing. She was rooting to see this through to publication. Sadly, she passed away as I was writing the final chapters.

Andrew Goldman was my first friend, my best friend. He was agile, magnetic, generous, and unable to resist directing his considerable wit at groaner puns. I couldn't believe my luck that we remained close for four decades, whether a bike ride away or continent apart. In October 2022, Drew was driving home to San Francisco after an extended work trip in Boise. Stopping in Reno, he visited the National Automobile Museum for me, home to the Thomas Flyer pathfinder car, among other historic autos. That afternoon, we exchanged a flurry of texts, and Drew sent twenty-three photos capturing compelling cars from all angles. The very next night, I got the shattering news that he was gone. I keep a photo of us as kids near my desk and have thought about him daily while working on this book.

NOTES

For all the gaps that remain, I could not have written this book with anywhere near this depth of material twenty years ago or even ten. Widespread digitization of old newspapers, magazines, genealogical records, city and state directories, fire-insurance maps, railroad timetables, travelogues, chamber of commerce brochures, regional histories, corporate records, postcards, archival photographs, atlases, and other materials made it possible for me to immerse myself in the rolling landscape of 1909 from my laptop, augmented by research trips to archives in Detroit (multiple visits to The Henry Ford's Benson Ford Research Center, hereafter BFRC) and Seattle (the University of Washington Libraries and the Museum of History & Industry, MOHAI) as well as New York City (the Municipal Archives and the New York Public Library) and Philadelphia (Simeone Foundation museum library), and by many hours peering at conventional microfilm. Even then, I sometimes discovered that reels I had ordered via interlibrary loan just a few months earlier—and painstakingly scrutinized, page by page—had been digitized subsequently and were now easily searchable.

I reconstructed the action in the race primarily from newspapers, drawing chiefly on firsthand coverage from nearly two hundred different local newspapers along the route from New York City to Seattle; these papers typically covered the race as the cars passed through, often extensively, sometimes with just a sentence or two. The leading wire services of the day also produced regular updates, reprinted widely, while a few large newspapers with far-flung correspondents carried their own distinct dispatches at key junctures. Beyond those papers, I found useful coverage in the cities where the cars originated (i.e., Boston, Detroit) and in other large metro areas. Several 1909 magazines devoted to "automobiling" also covered the race, some in great detail: *The Club Journal*, the biweekly publication of the Automobile Club of America; *Ford Times* (hereafter *FT*), the biweekly organ of the Ford Motor Company and its dealer network; and the weekly publications *The Automobile*, *Automobile Topics Illustrated* (hereafter *AT*), *The Horseless Age* (hereafter *THA*), and *The Motor World*, as well as the monthly *MoToR*.

Digitization meant I was also able to review several thousand newspaper stories from the early 1900s, for details of the race and to gain context about the characters, places, and businesses that populated these pages. I also gleaned biographical material for major and minor characters by reviewing myriad genealogical records on Ancestry.com and FamilySearch. Likewise, I built family trees for a few dozen of the most intriguing figures in the book, while attempting to reach out to descendants of nearly all of them. In some cases, that yielded a studio portrait or an intriguing passed-down anecdote; in the case of Earle Chapin and Elbert Bellows, the stars aligned, and I connected with descendants holding troves of letters and other original materials from the race, and who generously shared them with me—bringing those characters, and their journeys, to life with the richness of their own words and perspectives.

While I amassed a small library of automotive-history books, and borrowed more through my local library, Archive.org made it possible to search and access a wealth of titles that helped illuminate one corner of this book or another, particularly rarities from the 1920s to 1950s, noted in the following pages.

In lieu of presenting an exhaustive list of over a thousand endnotes for newspaper sources alone, I've condensed the most relevant highlights into chapter-by-chapter sketches that follow. For additional information on any sourcing, please contact me.

In geographic order (east to west both by state and within each state), these are the papers where I found local coverage of the race to construct the narrative:

New York: In Brooklyn, *The Brooklyn Citizen* and *The Brooklyn Daily Eagle;* in Manhattan, *The Evening Sun, The Evening Telegram, The Evening World,* the *New York American, The New York Herald, The New York Press, The New York Times, New-York Tribune, The Sun,* and *The World;* and beyond New York City, *The Yonkers Statesman, Poughkeepsie Daily Eagle, The Pokeepsie Evening Enterprise, Albany Evening Journal, The* [Albany] *Argus, The Schenectady Daily Union, The* [Schenectady] *Evening Star, Amsterdam Evening Recorder and Daily Democrat, The* [Herkimer] *Evening Telegram, Utica Herald-Dispatch and Daily Gazette, The Utica Daily Press, The Utica Observer, The Syracuse Herald, The Syracuse Journal, The* [Syracuse] *Post-Standard, The Auburn Citizen, The* [Rochester] *Democrat and Chronicle, The* [Rochester] *Post Express, The* [Rochester] *Union and Advertiser, The Rochester Herald, The Buffalo Commercial, Buffalo Courier, Buffalo Evening News, Buffalo Evening Times, Buffalo Morning Express,* and *The* [Dunkirk] *Evening Observer.*

Pennsylvania: *Erie Daily Times, The Erie Dispatch, The Erie Evening Herald, Girard Cosmopolite,* and *The* [Meadville] *Evening Republican.*

Ohio: *Conneaut News-Herald, Geneva Free Press-Times, The* [Elyria] *Evening Telegram, The* [Norwalk] *Daily Reflector, The* [Norwalk] *Evening Herald, The Bellevue Gazette, Fremont Daily News, Toledo Blade,* and *Toledo News-Bee.*

Indiana: *Goshen Daily Democrat, Goshen Daily News-Times, The Elkhart Truth, The South Bend Tribune,* and *The Lake County Times.*

Illinois: *The Chicago Daily Journal, Chicago Daily News, The Chicago Evening Post, Chicago Examiner, The Chicago Record-Herald, Chicago Daily Tribune, The* [Chicago] *Inter Ocean, The Joliet Daily News, Joliet Evening Herald, Morris Daily Herald, Dwight Star and Herald, The Pontiac Daily Leader, The* [Bloomington] *Daily Pantagraph, The Atlanta Argus, Lincoln Daily Courier, The* [Lincoln] *Daily News-Herald, Illinois State Journal, Illinois State Register,*

The Springfield News, The Springfield Record, and *The Edwardsville Intelligencer.*

Missouri: *St. Louis Globe-Democrat, St. Louis Post-Dispatch, The St. Louis Republic, The St. Louis Star, The St. Louis Times, St. Charles Banner-News, St. Charles Cosmos and Monitor, Warrenton Banner, The Jonesburg Journal, The* [Mexico] *Daily Intelligencer, Mexico Evening Ledger, Centralia Fireside Guard, Columbia Daily Tribune, The Columbia Statesman, Omar D. Gray's Sturgeon Missouri Leader, Clark Chronicle, Moberly Daily Monitor, Higbee Weekly News, Armstrong Herald, The Glasgow Missourian, The Slater Rustler, The Marshall Republican, The Weekly Saline Citizen, Saline County Weekly Progress, Weekly* [Marshall] *Democrat-News, Miami Weekly News, The Corder Journal, The Higginsville Advance, Kansas City Journal, The Kansas City Post, The Kansas City Star,* and *The Kansas City Times.*

Kansas: *The* [Lawrence] *Daily Gazette, Lawrence Daily Journal, Lawrence Daily World, The* [Lawrence] *Jeffersonian Gazette, The Topeka Daily Capital, The Topeka State Journal, The* [Manhattan] *Daily Mercury, The* [Manhattan] *Daily Nationalist, The Manhattan Republic, The* [Junction City] *Daily Sentinel, The* [Junction City] *Daily Union, Abilene Daily Chronicle, Abilene Daily Reflector, The Salina Daily Union, The Salina Evening Journal, The Ellsworth Messenger, Ellsworth Reporter, Kanopolis Journal, The Russell Record, Ellis County News, The* [Hays City] *Republican, The Hays Free Press, The Ellis Review-Headlight, Gove County Advocate, The Oakley Graphic, The Colby Tribune, The Goodland Republic and Goodland News,* and *The Sherman County Record.*

Colorado: *The Burlington Republican, Rocky Mountain News, The Denver Express, The Denver Post, The Denver Republican, The Denver Times, The Brighton Blade, The Brighton Register,* and *The Greeley Tribune.*

Wyoming: *The Cheyenne Daily Leader, Cheyenne State Leader, The Wyoming Tribune, Laramie Boomerang, The Laramie Republican, Carbon County Journal, Rawlins Republican, Rock Springs Miner, Rock Springs Rocket, Green River Star,* and *The Kemmerer Camera.*

Idaho: *Montpelier Examiner, The Soda Springs Chieftain, The Pocatello Tribune, American Falls Press, Rupert Pioneer-Record, Twin Falls News, The*

Glenns Ferry Gazette, Mountain Home Maverick, Evening Capital News, Idaho Daily Statesman, Payette Independent, and *The Weiser Semi-Weekly Signal.*

Oregon: *The Baker City Herald,* the [Baker City] *Morning Democrat,* and *La Grande Evening Observer.*

Washington: *The* [Walla Walla] *Evening Bulletin, The* [Walla Walla] *Evening Statesman,* the [Walla Walla] *Morning Union, Wallula Gateway, The Pasco Express,* the [Kennewick] *Twin City Reporter, The Prosser Record,* the [Prosser] *Republican-Bulletin, The Sunnyside Sun, The Yakima Daily Republic, The Yakima Democrat, The Yakima Herald, The Ellensburg Capital, Cle Elum Echo, The Issaquah Independent, The A.-Y.-P. Daily News, The Seattle Daily Times, The Seattle Post-Intelligencer, The Seattle Republican,* and *The Seattle Star.*

Where two or more stories listed different times for a car's arrival, I typically averaged the times if they were within the ballpark of each other; if there were multiple stories with similar times and one outlier, I used my judgment or avoided specifying the time.

Epigraph

The Kipling quote comes from a 1904 letter to Filson Young, reflecting as an early adopter on how far automobiles had come since 1897. It begins: "I like motoring because I have suffered for its sake. I began seven years ago in the days of tube ignition, when 6 h.p. was reckoned fair allowance for a touring car, and fifteen miles an hour was something to talk about. My agonies, shames, delays, rages, chills, parboilings, road-walkings, water-drawings, burns, and starvations, at which you laughed . . . all went to make your car to-day safe and comfortable." From *The Kipling Journal* (Vol. 58, No. 229, March 1984), 30.

1. The Starting Gun

The Model T idling rate comes from a 2024 interview and ride-along with Steve Lang of Lang's Old Car Parts, a supplier of mail-order parts to Model T owners since 1981. Steve's father, Don, gave me my first ride in a Model T in 2009, when I wrote a *Boston Globe* story about the centennial of the race—as well as a 1959 collectible-reprint copy of Ford's 1909 advertising brochure recounting the tale of victory, as penned by H. B. Harper (*The Story of the Race: How the Ford Car Won the Transcontinental Contest for the Guggenheim Trophy Told by One of the Crew on Ford Car No. 1*), an invaluable resource.

The phrase "saturnalia of reckless speeding" comes from *Automobile Topics* (hereafter *AT*), May 8, 1909, not from an article about the race itself but from the wider debate over whether lawmakers should legislate one-size-fits-all numerical speed limits or allow a driver to use "reasonable and proper" discretion.

At the end of 1908, an industry survey counted 253 American automakers, in an exhibit submitted to Congress as domestic automakers lobbied to maintain the protective tariff on European imports, *Tariff Hearings Before the Committee of Ways and Means . . . , Sixtieth Congress 1908–1909. Schedule C* (Washington: Government Printing Office, 1909). Given the frequency with which firms folded and started, "250 or so" seems safe.

The pathfinding Thomas Flyer's travails were thoroughly chronicled, including in a series of exclusive (and agonizing) *St. Louis Post-Dispatch* (hereafter *SLPD*) accounts filed by the expedition's leader, L. W. Redington. The detail about the sheepherder who struck the car with a bullet while ostensibly aiming for a coyote comes from "Welcomed to Seattle by Mayor," *Seattle Star* (hereafter *SS*), May 20, 1909.

The phrase "ocular demonstration" may have originated with T. Francis "Tom" Moore's initial partner, John Kane Mills. Guggenheim hired the duo's pioneering promotional firm ("Acceleration of Sentiment a Specialty," their letterhead crowed) for $10,000, plus a $4,000 bonus if they procured twenty entries, but the partnership cracked up amid the pressure campaign against the race—and frequent mockery from publications sympathetic to AAA in the ACA-AAA rivalry—leading Mills to fall on his sword in May. Moore remained as sole promoter.

Beyond press coverage, several memos from Moore related to the planning of the race are preserved in the New York City Municipal Archives, as part of the McClellan mayoral papers, in Box 15 alphabetized under incoming correspondence for January–March 1909 and April–June 1909. A letter from Russell Field on behalf of the Manufacturers' Contest Association emphasizing their opposition to the race can be found in Box 8. Considerably more evidence of the pressure campaign can be found in the Library of Congress's William Howard Taft Papers, including a copy of Moore's "Wall Street Special" advertising pamphlet, submitted to Taft in a letter from the editor of *The Motor World* as damning evidence of "the true character of the race," in Series 5, Case File 2521. Thank you to the LOC's Lewis Wyman for helping me navigate those papers, digitized but not searchable.

The ACA-AAA feud and the role of the MCA have been mischaracterized at times. My understanding comes from accounts in the automotive press and from phone and email interviews with automotive historian H. Donald Capps; in this truncated retelling, I have tried not to introduce any new errors.

The *New York Times* (hereafter *NYT*) editorial on Stolp's behalf ran April 23, 1909 ("Shouldn't Be a Race of Dollars"). The detail about Stolp finding his car in pieces comes from *The Brooklyn Citizen*, June 5, 1909.

On price and specs: The Ford Model T numbers are well established. The Acme was reported to be a six-cylinder with 48 horsepower or 45–50 horsepower. A 1909 Acme brochure (at the Simeone) shows two models with those specifications and a body design matching photos of the No. 4 Acme racer, the Type XX Special and Type XXI Special. Both sold for $4,500, but with different wheelbases and weights (126 inches and thirty-four hundred pounds for the XX, 118 inches and thirty-three hundred pounds for the XXI). It appears to me to be the XXI Special. Fire prevented Shawmut from advancing into serious production, but a 1907 brochure owned by Bruce Chapin, Earle's grandson, listed the Model A Roadster for $4,750 and the Model B Touring Car for $5,000. The two were identical under the hood, but the stock roadster had a 108-inch wheelbase and seating for three (a rumble seat in back), weighing 2,675 pounds; the touring car had a 112-inch wheelbase and seating for five, with a rear tonneau and weight of three thousand pounds. Some accounts assumed the No. 5 Shawmut was a touring car, but it was instead a roadster modified with a rear tonneau. News stories at the time put the Shawmut weight at four thousand to forty-five hundred pounds, but that seems excessive, unless it also counts crew and gear. The Itala price and specs are harder to pin down; the car was widely reported as a four-cylinder, typically 45–50 horsepower, sometimes 40 or even 60. This was the very same car entered by the Itala Import Company and partner coachmaker A. T. Demarest in the sweepstakes race that christened Willie Vanderbilt's Long Island Motor Parkway in October 1908, also with Lechleitner at the wheel. *MoToR*'s 1908 guide to autos and chassis lists an unfinished 40-horsepower Itala chassis (124-inch wheelbase) at $7,000, including tariff. Demarest bodies typically started at $1,000-plus and could exceed $3,000, according to clips and ads from the era. Later accounts indicated that Guggenheim may have paid $8,000 for this car.

The "Western cowboy" line appeared in multiple stories. August Lechleitner (born September 8, 1881) lived on First Avenue in Yorkville in the 1900 census; his father's birthplace was listed alternately as Germany and Austria. His bio (and many Itala and Demarest details) comes partly from transcribed testimony in a lawsuit filed by an Itala customer that reached the New York Supreme Court, Elizabeth B. Colt v. A. T. Demarest & Co. Lechleitner had previously worked as a machinist for J. Walter Christie, the pioneering race-car designer and driver who would later create the modern military tank.

Acme's corporate depiction comes from Beverly Rae Kimes and Henry Clark's extraordinarily valuable *Standard Catalog of American Cars, 1805–1942* (Iola, Wisconsin: Krause Publications, 1989), hereafter Kimes; from *Historical and Biographical Annals of Berks County, Pennsylvania* (Chicago: J. H. Beers, 1909); and from an assortment of news clippings. Jeremiah "Jerry" Price's pinkie accident was reported in *Reading Times*, November 28, 1903. His daughter, Congresswoman Florence Price Dwyer, was born July 4, 1902.

The generalized production numbers come from multiple sources. I found three books to be especially valuable for early industry history and statistics: Ralph C. Epstein, *The Automobile Industry: Its Economic and Commercial Development* (Chicago: A. W. Shaw, 1928); E. D. Kennedy, *The Automobile Industry: The Coming of Age of Capitalism's Favorite Child* (New York: Reynal & Hitchcock, 1941); and Lawrence H. Seltzer, *A Financial History of the American Automobile Industry* (Boston: Houghton Mifflin, 1928).

I could fill a volume with the trail I followed on the real George Salzman and the con artist who plagued him. More details follow in the epilogue, with related notes there.

The Travel Magazine estimate comes from the October 1908 issue.

Depictions of Ford and the development of the Model T come from many sources, especially Allan Nevins, *Ford: The Times, the Man, the Company* (New York: Charles Scribner's Sons, 1954); Steven Watts, *The People's Tycoon: Henry Ford and the American Century* (New York: Knopf, 2005); Robert Lacey, *Ford: The Men and the Machine* (Boston: Little Brown, 1986); Bruce W. McCalley, *Model T Ford: The Cat That Changed the World* (Iola, Wisconsin: Krause Publications, 1994); and Philip Van Doren Stern, *Tin Lizzie: The Story of the Fabulous Model T Ford* (New York: Simon & Schuster, 1955).

The portrait of Guggenheim (born May 17, 1885) comes from numerous articles in New York, New Jersey, and Seattle papers and from John H. Davis's *The Guggenheims: An American Epic* (New York: William Morrow, 1978), as well as Irwin Unger and Debi Unger, *The Guggenheims: A Family History* (New York: Harper Perennial, 2006); Edwin P. Hoyt, *The Guggenheims and the American Dream* (New York: Funk & Wagnalls, 1967); and my own phone interviews with Robert Guggenheim's grandson, Dan. He listed his height at five foot eight in a 1920 passport application as well as his World War II draft registration card, though in the starting-line photo he appears to be multiple inches shorter than Ford, who stood about five foot nine. The "Robert the Young" profile ran December 20, 1908.

The first coverage I found of the proposed race in the Seattle press is

"Plan New York to Fair Auto Race," December 3, 1908, *The Seattle Post-Intelligencer* (hereafter *SPI*), which credited Sheffield with the idea.

Ford's "first real auto contest" quote ran widely, including *NYT*, April 12, 1909.

The definitive history of the Selden suit is William Greenleaf's *Monopoly on Wheels: Henry Ford and the Selden Automobile Patent* (Detroit: Wayne State University Press, 1961); the definitive history of Ford's relationship with the press and public is David L. Lewis's *The Public Image of Henry Ford: An American Folk Hero and His Company* (Detroit: Wayne State University Press, 1976).

The BFRC prepared an online guide ("Henry Ford's Residences") identifying every home the Fords lived in. The negotiations with Durant have been characterized in multiple books, including *Men, Money, and Motors: The Drama of the Automobile* (New York: Harper & Brothers, 1929), by Theodore F. MacManus and Norman Beasley; Lawrence Goldstone's *Drive! Henry Ford, George Selden, and the Race to Invent the Auto Age* (New York: Ballantine Books, 2016); and Arthur Pound's *The Turning Wheel: The Story of General Motors Through Twenty-Five Years* (Garden City, NY: Doubleday, Doran & Company, 1934).

The "Tennessee mules" quote comes from *AT*, February 6, 1909, "President Elect is to Get That $12,000 Appropriation." Both *SPI* and *The Seattle Daily Times* (hereafter *SDT*) carried the "Go, with best success" quotes.

The 4,106-mile figure was tallied by the pathfinder.

2. Up Automobile Row

The depiction of Earle Chapin (born September 6, 1882) comes primarily from genealogical records and newspaper clippings as well as family scrapbooks and letters retained by grandson Bruce Chapin. Firsthand memories came from phone interviews with Bruce's older cousins, siblings Craig and Bob Chapin, who were already in their twenties when "Paps" died in 1964 and knew him well.

The Duryea history is told in detail in Richard P. Scharchburg, *Carriages Without Horses: J. Frank Duryea and the Birth of the American Automobile Industry* (Warrendale, PA: Society of Automotive Engineers, 1993).

The depiction of Lucius J. Phelps (born October 8, 1850) comes from numerous sources, including genealogical materials, newspaper and automotive-magazine clips, corporate records from Massachusetts and Maine, and materials saved by his family and shared by a granddaughter, Susan Phelps Reynolds Howard, along with Susan's daughter and son-in-law, Betsy and James Mark. Lucius Phelps's son, Earle B. Phelps, became a pioneering public-health scientist in the fields of water and wastewater treatment. Tragically, seventy-four-year-old Lucius disappeared from Earle's New Jersey home on July 6, 1925, bound for New York by train with a handbag carrying his latest in a lifetime of inventions, a set of cylindrical locks, hoping to interest manufacturers. Possibly suffering from mental illness, he never reached his destination; the story, and related search, made national news, but Lucius was never seen again.

The name Elliot Cabot Lee (born April 16, 1854) and his image, with motoring cap and Garibaldi beard, appeared frequently in the automotive press of the era. The Phelps materials from the Howard-Mark family included correspondence between Lee and Phelps as well as Phelps's diary and a stock certificate signed by Phelps and Lee.

I reconstructed Shawmut's corporate history from Boston and Stoneham newspaper articles; from annual financial summaries included in yearly *Abstract of the Certificates of Corporations Organized Under the General Laws of Massachusetts* volumes digitized by the Massachusetts Office of the Secretary of State; and from microfilm records reviewed in person at the Secretary of State's office. Bruce Chapin shared Shawmut promotional literature from 1907 ("an exquisitely refined and sensitive mechanism . . .") and 1908; the BFRC has a 1906 brochure.

Quincy Adams Shaw Jr. was born July 30, 1869, a first cousin of the late Robert Gould Shaw, the Civil War officer killed while commanding the 54th Massachusetts Infantry, the Black regiment depicted in the film *Glory*. His age here (thirty-eight) corresponds with Shaw's heavy involvement with Shawmut in 1907–1908. The "best known clubmen" line comes from *The Boston Herald* (hereafter *BH*), March 10, 1908, "Auto Show Now off on Real Run."

The "hardest test ever given" line, about the 1908 Bay State endurance run, comes from the *Boston Evening Transcript*, October 3, 1908, "Auto Efficiency Proven." Waite's "we had the goods" quote is from *BH*, October 4, 1908, "Shawmut's Fine Work No Surprise."

I pieced together the story of the fire from the November 13, 1908, editions of the *Boston Evening American* (hereafter *BEA*), *Boston Daily Globe* (morning and evening editions), *BH*, *Boston Evening Transcript*, *Boston Post*, *Boston Traveler*, *Fall River Daily Globe*, *Wakefield Daily Item*, and *Woburn Daily Times*; the November 14 *Stoneham Independent*; the November 16 *Wakefield Daily Item*; and the 1908–1909 annual reports of the towns of Stoneham and Wakefield.

The related business in Watertown was called Power and Speed Controller.

Depiction of True Arthur Pettengill (born December 17, 1877) comes from genealogical and newspaper records, from the Stoneham Historical Society collection, and from materials shared by great-granddaughter Susan Lustig.

The nickname "Hod" for Horace Waite appears in the Vicennial Record for Yale's Class of 1891.

The "down to the last bolt" *Boston Post* quote comes from "Ready for Ocean to Ocean Contest," May 23, 1909.

The Shawmut crew's experience in New York comes primarily from Chapin's letters.

Ford's American branches in 1909 were located in Boston, New York, Buffalo, Philadelphia, Chicago, Cleveland, Detroit, St. Louis, Kansas City, Denver, and Seattle. The definitive history of Ford's early branch-and-dealer network is Henry L. Dominguez's *The Ford Agency: A Pictorial History* (Osceola, WI: Motorbooks International, 1981). I drew on that book as well as on multiple phone interviews I conducted with Dominguez, plus Lewis's *Public Image*, original records at BFRC, and *Ford Times* accounts.

Ford's challenge, including the "does not believe in" quote, ran in *FT*, May 15, 1909, "That Ocean to Ocean Contest," and elsewhere.

On Broadway's Automobile Row: The "liveliest 2 miles" comes from *Motor Age*, December 23, 1909, "Big Year Ahead for New York." Acme dealer Cordner occupied 1540 Broadway, at Times Square. Ford (1721–23 Broadway) sat between Fifty-Fourth and Fifty-Fifth Streets. Hol-Tan had recently moved to 1741 Broadway, near Fifty-Sixth. The Demarest Building occupied the southeast corner at Fifty-Seventh.

F. B. Whittemore Jr. was born July 26, 1888, making him nearly twenty-one. Sheffield, which blended practical science education with the liberal arts, had a shorter course of study than Yale College. The previous year, Whittemore's famous grandfather had suffered a stroke in the heat at his Yale graduation, then died of ptomaine poisoning contracted at a graduation clambake, with his death front-page news in the *New-York Tribune*.

The description of Elbert E. Bellows (known to family as Bert and E. E.) comes from genealogical records and news clippings as well as letters and mementos saved by family, including a twenty-one-hundred-word tribute ("My Dad") published by his daughter—Elisabeth Bellows Cantwell, born a week before the race—in 1972 in the *Franklin Historical Review*, Vol. 9.

Broadway was first paved with asphalt from Columbus Circle south to Fourteenth Street in 1900, but paving of the longer (and wider) expanse north of Columbus Circle to the northern tip of Manhattan was not completed until the end of 1906, making it "now indeed a smooth, clean and broad way," in the words of *Good Roads Magazine*, January 1907.

3. A "Frenzied, Foolhardy Speed Terror"

In the John Gerrie section, "heap of debris" comes from "The Deadly Railway Crossing," *AT*, November 2, 1901. His "midget competitors" quote appeared in "Ford Cars Score Great Victory in Seattle Race," *New York American*, June 27, 1909.

With Bernard W. "Bert" Scott and Charles James "Jimmie" Smith, I

faced a nickname-spelling conundrum. Most accounts during their Ford tenure spelled Scott's nickname as Bert and Smith's as Jimmie, occasionally Burt and Jimmy. In Smith's case, the obituary that his family placed in the *Detroit Free Press* (hereafter *DFP*), May 15, 1955, called him "Jimmie," cementing it for me. Most records in Scott's lifetime referred to him formally as B. W. or Bernard, though his wedding announcement in the May 7, 1907, *Port Huron Daily Times* called him "Bert," as did a feature obituary in the January 15, 1940, *Port Huron Times Herald.* However, when Scott's own son, Jack, wrote a book about his father and the race in the 1980s (*The Big Race*), he spelled his dad's name "Burt." But Jack Scott had named one of his own sons Burt with a *u*, and that son told me his father may have conflated the spellings in the book, with Bert more likely accurate for his grandfather's phonetic nickname during his lifetime.

Depictions of Scott (born February 25, 1883) and Smith (born December 28, 1884) come from a mix of genealogical records and news clippings. The depiction of Frank Kulick (born August 1, 1882) comes largely from Rob Heyen's excellent two-part feature ("Frank Kulick: They Should Make a Movie") in the March/April and May/June 2022 issues of *Model T Times*, supplemented by newspaper and genealogical records and my own interview with a Kulick relative. The biographical sketch of Henry B. Harper (born June 23, 1880, known as H.B. and Harry) comes from newspaper and genealogical records.

Toledo dealer Stanley Roberts (born December 27, 1883) was featured in *FT,* January 1, 1909, as he left the corporate office to become a dealer. The Pelletier depiction comes primarily from Lewis's *Public Image* and news clips. The Hawkins bio comes from multiple books and articles, including *People's Tycoon* as well as "Norval Hawkins: The Greatest Salesman in the World," *Ypsilanti Gleanings*, Summer 2014. The "daddy of super-salesmen" line comes from his *DFP* obituary, August 19, 1936.

Pettengill's compass resides at the Stoneham Historical Society and Museum.

The depiction of Fremont comes from various sources, including

Sanborn fire insurance maps; a series of 2016–2019 local-history columns in the *Fremont News Messenger* by Roy Wilhelm; *Twentieth Century History of Sandusky County, Ohio*, edited by Basil Meek, and published by Richmond-Arnold Publishing (Chicago, 1909); and phone interviews with Wilhelm and John Ransom, head librarian at the Rutherford B. Hayes Presidential Library & Museums.

The *Blade*'s Jerry Winters (born Cyrus Bertrand Winters) was known as both Jerry and Bert. I found the story about the bullet in the *Sandusky Evening Star*, June 9, 1903, "Bullet."

Harper's telegram was reprinted in *The Brooklyn Daily Eagle* (June 5, 1909) as well as Minnesota's *Bemidji Daily Pioneer* (June 17, 1909), among others.

4. Muscling Through the Middle West

The "first class condition" line comes from a set of transcribed telegrams sent by the crew to Waite and retained by Chapin's family; my hunch is that the company stenographer transcribed the originals to distribute to the family of the crew.

The Ohio and Indiana speed laws (and other state-by-state motoring laws in this book) come from "Motor Car Laws," *MoToR*, June 1909.

The "Blue Book" for the race (*Route: New York to Seattle Automobile Contest*) can be found at BFRC among the Fair Lane Papers, Box 169, in the Racing 1906–1921 folder. Originally, the race organizers intended to package the instructions with extensive photos taken by J. S. M. Eley, a member of the pathfinder expedition, and sell it to the public as a lavish book. Either they ran out of time or the cost was prohibitive. Instead, they issued a slim booklet to the racers before the start with no photos, then repackaged these same directions shortly after the race with a smattering of photos—portraits of officials and scenes from the starting line, not Eley's pathfinder documentary work—and dozens of advertisements for auto-friendly businesses along the route, for sale to intrepid motorists who wanted to attempt to drive some or all of the route. A photostat of that booklet (*Transcontinental Automobile Guide, Ocean to Ocean Automobile Contest, M. Robert Guggenheim Trophy*) published by J. G. Dresen of Seattle can be found in Accession 717 at BFRC, in the folder "Ocean to Ocean Race—Planning—History of 1909 Race."

In researching road guides of the era, I scoured searchable newspaper ads and notices in trade publications to determine release dates. For wider history I drew on the work of John T. Bauer, University of Nebraska at Kearney, in "Navigating Without Road Maps: The Early Business of Automobile Route Guide Publishing in the United States" from Proceedings of the International Cartographic Association, 1, 2017, and Bauer's "The Official Automobile Blue Book, 1901–1929: Precursor to the American Road Map" in *Cartographic Perspectives*, Number 62, Winter 2009, as well as phone and email correspondence with Bauer.

Amid the Stolp coverage, the *Chicago Daily News* quip comes from June 7, 1909.

The Tom Hay depiction comes from genealogical materials and several dozen newspaper and magazine stories. "Tom Hay, the 95% Manager," *FT*, March 15, 1909, was especially vivid; a *Motor World* account from July 18, 1917 ("Trade's Biggest Men Form New Association") had a helpful capsule biography. Hay's role in Indianapolis's significant bicycle history comes from *Hyman's Handbook of Indianapolis* (Indianapolis: M. R. Hyman Co., 1897) and Stephen J. Taylor's "Keep Your Sauerkraut Away from My Bicycles," posted to the Historic Indianapolis website October 26, 2015.

My broader understanding of the 1890s bicycle boom and bust comes from multiple sources, including Bruce J. Schulman, "Pedaling Toward Modernity," *Reviews in American History*, September 2016, Vol. 44, No. 3, and Thomas Burr, "Market Cycles: Bicycles, Riders, Industries, and Environments in France and the United, States, 1865–1914," *The American Journal of Economics and Sociology*, April 2013, Vol. 72, No. 2, as well as Michael Kranish's *The World's Fastest Man: The Extraordinary Life of Cyclist Major Taylor, America's First Black Sports Hero* (New York: Scribner, 2019), which documents the Hay-Taylor connection.

The Chris Sinsabaugh anecdote comes from *Public Image* and Sinsabaugh's own memoir, *Who, Me? Forty Years of Automobile History* (Detroit: Arnold-Powers, Inc., 1940), which also covers the Cubs coinage; some baseball histories have misspelled his name as "Charles Sensabaugh."

The Harper telegram appeared multiple places, including in a *Syracuse Herald* ad, June 20, 1909, placed by a local dealer, the Syracuse Motor Car Co. Magneto's column ran June 6, 1909, with the headline "2 Autos in Ocean to Ocean Race Have Reached Chicago."

The mood in the Shawmut comes from Chapin's letters. The Chicago Automobile Club's grand clubhouse was described in *The Architectural Record* (September 1907), *The Automobile* (July 4, 1907), and *Motor Age* (July 11, 1907).

Railroad fares and amenities from Karl Baedeker's *The United States, With Excursions to Mexico, Cuba, Porto Rico, and Alaska: Handbook for Travellers* (Leipzig: Karl Baedeker; New York: Charles Scribner's Sons, 1909).

On tires: Henry Copley Greene's entertaining *Atlantic* essay, "The Romance of Motoring," ran in the August 1908 issue. *The American Cyclopedia of the Automobile, or, Motor Cars and Motoring Self-Taught* (New York: Thompson & Thomas, 1909) is a six-volume reference that proved especially valuable as I tried to gain a technical understanding of automobiles and automobiling in 1909. And Dorothy Levitt is fascinating; her *The Woman and the Car* (London and New York: John Lane, 1909) is a lively read.

5. Guile at Glasgow

The Whitman quote comes from the National Park Service page for the Eads Bridge, within the Gateway Arch National Park website. Eads tolls come from "Three Cents is Cost of a Walk Over New Bridge," *SLPD*, November 23, 1910, which compared the established Eads rates with those for the new McKinley Bridge; the "high toll" complaints come from "A Few Words about St. Louis Traffic," *The Sister Republics*, June 1906.

The "nerve-destroying rush" is from "Itala Breaks Down," *St. Louis Star*, June 8, 1909.

Genealogy librarian Preston Petermeier of the St. Louis Public Library tracked down a rare copy of *Missouri State Automobile Blue Book* and tallied the numbers (St. Louis: The Auto Review Publishing Co., 1908).

Degener and Sorensen portraits from Nevins and other sources, including the reprint of Sorensen's 1956 autobiography, *My Forty Years with Ford* (Detroit: Wayne State University Press, 2006). His *NYT* obit (August 14, 1968) credited him as the executive who "held Ford together between the time the company slipped away from the aging Henry Ford and his grandson, Henry Ford 2d, could take over." A feature photo of the eight senior-most employees posing with the fifteen millionth Model T engine on the assembly line can be found in The Henry Ford's digital collection, Object ID 84.1.1660.P.O.2571.

The description of Fuzzy Anderson comes from numerous sources, with *FT* especially fruitful, including an August 1, 1908, profile ("Who is St. Louis?").

The escape of circus lions "Denver" and "Caesar" was front-page news in the June 3, 1909, *SLPD* ("Lions Escape at St. Charles, Crowd in Panic").

The "betcher-life" quip comes from *The Jonesburg Journal*, June 10, 1909.

The Gutelius portrait comes from a variety of sources, including genealogical records and newspapers from several states. His father, Calvin, published the *Public Press* of Northumberland, Pennsylvania.

The "flicker of a motion picture machine" line is from "Auto Racers Here Tuesday," *Centralia Fireside Guard*, June 11, 1909.

The Glasgow scene has been constructed from several months of *The Glasgow Missourian*; from State Historical Society of Missouri archival photographs; from the National Register of Historic Places Registration Form for the Glasgow Commercial Historic District; and from correspondence with Glasgow historian J. Y. Miller. William Barton Stevens appears to have taken over the ferry in early 1908 and relinquished it in October 1909, though he fished and hauled freight on the river for many years. His name appeared frequently in the local paper in advertorial content for a patent medicine, Doan's Kidney Pills, attesting to the supposed relief they had provided the "sharp pain" in his back and kidneys.

Meade portrait from various genealogical and newspaper sources, as well as "Kansas City and C.C. Meade," *Ford Times*, June 1, 1908. "Lightner the Wizard" from Henry Ridgely Evans, *History of Conjuring and Magic* (Kenton, OH: International Brotherhood of Magicians, 1928) and other sources; his height and weight come from his World War II draft registration card and "Sporting Comment," *Kansas City Star*, June 1, 1932.

I winced when I first spotted the line in the June 10, 1909, *Glasgow Missourian* about little Henry Rose stepping on a nail, and was relieved to learn from genealogical and newspaper records that he lived a full, healthy life, with an obituary in the January 4, 1987, *Columbia Daily Tribune*.

Weston's harrowing experience on the Glasgow bridge comes from one of his daily *NYT* dispatches (May 5, 1909) and from Wayne Curtis's book on Weston's journey, *The Last Great Walk* (New York: Rodale, 2014).

The conclusion in nearby Mexico that the ferryman was bribed appeared on page one of *The Daily Intelligencer*, July 10, 1909 ("Motorists Foiled Ferryman's Plans").

The "swayed exhaustedly" observation came from an *SLPD* correspondent in Kansas City (June 9, 1909, "Autos in Coast to Coast Race Make Kansas City a Twenty-Hour Run"). Harper was quoted at length in that day's *Kansas City Journal*.

Bryan's speech was covered in the June 8, 1909, *Kansas City Times*. Information about the Baltimore Hotel, also known as the Hotel Baltimore, is from *The Baltimore Illustrated* (Kansas City: Hotel Folder Publishing Co., 1909), an extensive folder detailing the hotel's renovations; Keith Eggener, "The Uses of Daylight," *Places Journal*, May 2012; and multiple 1909 Kansas City newspaper ads and articles.

The Gustin letter was included in the transcribed telegrams retained by the Chapin family.

6. "Mud, Water, and Glue"

The Kulick quote appeared in *The Parsons Daily Sun*, June 9, 1909. Henry Ford contrasted with the inventor of "far-away expression" comes from the June 9, 1909, *Kansas City Star* ("Runabout the Coming Car").

Though his name was frequently misspelled, W. H. Gillmore showed up regularly in motoring clips in Nebraska and then Kansas City. His record-setting trip was covered in the August 4, 1907, *Kansas City Journal* ("Waiting for Good Roads"), August 3 *Denver Post* ("Auto Smashes Kansas City to Denver Record"), and with a full-page spread in the August 24 *Kansas City Post* ("Following Joe Wittman on His Record Run to Denver"). The July 9, 1908, *Kansas City Times* ("Answers") established that the record still held, and I found no faster trip by June 1909.

Meade's scouting was covered in the May 27, 1909, *Abilene Daily Reflector* ("Making a Road Map"), which spelled it "Mead." The young Kansas friends originated in St. John, where their travel dispatches were carried in *The St. John Weekly News* and *The County Capital.*

My understanding of acetylene headlamps comes from my ride-along with Lang, interviews with Dominguez, and other sources, including YouTube demonstration videos.

On gumbo mud: The "long-lost brother" description comes from the October 18, 1919, *American Lumberman*, 79. Alice Ramsey called it "mucilage" in *The Travel Magazine*, May 1910. Lillian Hoyt's quote comes from June 12, 1909, *Salina Evening Journal* ("Gave it up at Hays"). Hoyt is an intriguing figure, running her own business (a high-grade millinery), owning her own car (a Maxwell, like Ramsey), and living with another woman (identified as a "partner" in the 1910 census) as well as their own housekeeper.

"Canadian steel" mishearing comes from the June 9, 1909, *Lawrence Daily World.*

Guild's teaser ("Cars Coming Today") ran in *The Topeka Daily Capital*, June 8, 1909. The superlatives about Paul Mulvane's Motor Car Supply Co. come from the June 21 *Daily Capital.* Soon after the race, he would sell to a man named Terry Stafford and get into ranching.

The press sometimes spelled the Hotel Gillett as "Gillet" or "Gillette," but photos indicate the sign said "Gillett," matching the name of proprietor, Rube Gillett. The description of the men as "road drags" comes from Manhattan's *The Daily Nationalist* (June 9, 1909); the "mud wallow" passage is from *The Manhattan Republic* (June 11).

The Eisenhowers figured regularly in Abilene newspapers—Dwight had cut his face a few weeks earlier running into a fence while chasing a fly ball—but young Bessie Coulson (born June 12, 1902) attracted coverage across the state and beyond, including in the March 12, 1909, *Kansas City Times*.

George Weisgerber's dealership and garage, built in 1908, was known as the Central Kansas Automobile Co. He formed it with two partners, Dave Maynard and Ed Donmyer, who served as Ford pilots here out of Salina.

The Ellsworth description ("smiling ornaments") comes from *Sights and Scenes from the Car Windows of "The Overland Route,"* ninth edition (Omaha: Union Pacific Railroad Co., 1901), which proved helpful for context about many of the points in Kansas.

The Paul Warner (born September 14, 1889) portrait comes from various clips and genealogical records, including "Baker's Own Story," *Motorcycle Illustrated*, May 28, 1914, and the July 3, 1914, *Norton Daily Telegram*.

The bank president with the flag was J. H. Ward. *The* [Hays City] *Republican* reported June 12, 1909, that the Shawmut "was in the city limits first but ran out of gasoline and stopped at Cox's garage for nearly an hour," leaving it ambiguous whether they ran out of gas before or after reaching Cox's. The garage advertised as an "Auto Hospital" in the July 31, 1909, *Hays Free Press*.

A widely printed wire story had Whittemore driving and Bellows unable to handle the car, but that correspondent appears to have reversed the names; Bellows's own letter indicates that he needed to do the driving, commensurate with their respective levels of motoring experience.

The New York paper declaring the contest "a thrilling one" was *The Standard Union* of Brooklyn, June 11, 1909. "Turn It Off," begged *The Oakley Graphic*, June 11, 1909.

Chain-drive care is from *The American Cyclopedia of the Automobile*, Vol. 1, 179–81.

The Harper telegram ran June 12, 1909, in *The Brooklyn Daily Eagle.*

Ellsworth Reporter timetables had the eastbound 102 arriving at 2:20 AM. Walter Brown (born February 13, 1892) was the son of mill operator Casper Brown. His bio and brother John's business interests come from newspaper and genealogical records.

The Colby Tribune coverage ran June 17, 1909.

7. Captured in Goodland

I found the Bateman photos at the BFRC in Accession 1854, Binder 15, on my first visit, and wondered immediately about the backstory. I searched for possible T. E. Batemans but thought it was unlikely the photographer lived all the way off in Concordia. Then I encountered a copy of the 1942 letter from Bateman's son to Ford in a vertical file ("Racing-Transcontinental—1909," no. 2 of 3) on my second visit, confirming the identity; I gained biographical details from newspaper and genealogical records, including about Bateman's trip to explore a mining investment opportunity in Idaho Springs, Colorado, and from connecting with a great-grandson, Mark Bateman, as well.

To visualize Goodland, 1909, the city's two newspapers (*The Sherman County Record* and *The Goodland Republic and Goodland News*) provided a robust starting point, augmented by photos and insights from Samantha Windle of Goodland's High Plains Museum.

The harrowing Patterson story ran in detail on page one of the June 18, 1909, *Republic* ("Mrs. Patterson a Heroine"), though it referred to her only as "Mrs. A.T. Patterson." I learned her given name, age, and other details from genealogical records.

8. Ford's Man in the Mile-High City

The depiction of Charlie Hendy (born September 30, 1875) comes from numerous sources, including genealogical records and newspaper articles from Nebraska, Colorado, and beyond; a *Ford Times* full-length profile ("Our Denver Branch," May 1, 1908) as well as a caricature (September 15, 1908); and multiple books, including a biographical entry on Hendy in *History of Colorado, Illustrated, Volume IV* (Chicago: The S. J. Clarke Publishing Co., 1919), and an entry for his father in *An Illustrated History of Lincoln County, Nebraska, and Her People, Volume II* (Chicago and New York: The American Historical Society, 1920).

The "score of Spaniards" send-off for the student volunteers appeared on page one of *The Nebraskan*, May 6, 1898 ("Bid Farewell to the Boys"). The same paper referred to Hendy "trying to get the Spanish out of his system" on September 23, 1898 ("Among the Greeks in Absentia").

For the portrait of Denver in 1909 as a modern, "healthful," motor-mad city, an official weekly publication from that era called *Denver Municipal Facts* was especially useful, replete with statistics. For atmospherics I drew on railroad and tourism guides, including *Denver, the Beautiful*, published in 1902 by the Colorado Press Bureau of Information; *Denver: The Queen City of the Plains*, published 1906 by L. H. Nelson Co., Portland, Maine; and *Over the Range to the Golden Gate*, a guide issued by R. R. Donnelley & Sons Co., Chicago, 1908. The column observing the hunger for homes with "a lawn to mow" appeared in the August 4, 1908, *Denver Post* ("Prospering Denver").

The photo of Hendy with the three women in a Ford, along with the quote here, comes from the November 23, 1908, *Denver Post* ("Passes 29 Autos in Night Race to Denver After Game"); the Denver-Carlisle football carpool was highlighted in the December 6, 1908, *Post* ("Leads Auto Race to City After Big Game").

Though his name was not always spelled correctly (sometimes "Henry"), I pieced together Hendy's prerace movements from multiple digitized newspapers, including the May 26, 1909, *Laramie Republican* and May 30, 1909, *Sunday News-Times* of Denver.

From here, most of the quotes are noted in the text alongside the newspapers where they appeared.

The record-setting Denver-Cheyenne run was covered in the August

22, 1908, *Denver Post*, which recorded it as 3 hours 34 minutes; that day's *Rocky Mountain News* had it at 3 hours 35 minutes in a story ("Brinker with Chalmers Car Breaks Record"), though a Chalmers ad in the same paper called it 3 hours *24* minutes. The *Wyoming Tribune* identified the Shawmut's Denver-Cheyenne guide as "Mart Fetcher," meaning Martin B. Fetcher, who taught Denver's fire chief to drive and appeared regularly in Denver's auto pages in those days.

By Warren's own recollection, Cheyenne was a town where every "man slept with from one to a half-dozen revolvers under his pillow, for depradations [*sic*] of every character could be expected at any hour, day or night," per his biography in the Wyoming Historical Society's online encyclopedia.

9. Beware the Unexpected

Pettengill's letter ran in *BEA*, June 21, 1909, "Close Battle in Ocean to Ocean Race."

When the Inter-Ocean Hotel (sometimes Inter Ocean) burned in 1916, *The Wyoming Tribune* said the register included the names of Ulysses S. Grant, Rutherford B. Hayes, William McKinley, William Howard Taft, Theodore Roosevelt, and Woodrow Wilson.

That the Shawmut crew informed Guggenheim immediately about Kulick comes from a Shawmut telegram to Waite, June 14. The crew would not mention any suspicion about the No. 2's axle until Seattle, per coverage of the post-race controversy.

The numbers of cars in Cheyenne and other Wyoming communities come primarily from a special auto-themed issue of *The Wyoming Tribune*, June 10, 1909 ("This Is the First and Only Automobile Edition Ever Issued by a Wyoming Newspaper—Isn't It a Dinger," the front page declared).

Cheyenne garage details come from a variety of newspaper and auto-magazine briefs, as well as city directories and Sanborn fire-insurance maps. Lial D. Branson (born June 18, 1888) was about to turn twenty-one; his name was sometimes misspelled in print as Lyle.

A photo of the Borgeman sign can be seen in *Retracing the Pioneers:*

From West to East in an Automobile, a chronicle by San Francisco liquor wholesaler Hugo A. Taussig of a cross-country drive he took with friends going eastward in June and July 1909, printed privately in 1910 but digitized by the Library of Congress. A flurry of stories about Borgeman and his privately imposed toll appeared in the Laramie and Cheyenne papers in June 1909, with a panoply of spellings and assumed ages. His brother-in-law visited the *Laramie Boomerang* to defend him (June 10, 1909, "Two Sides to the Question"). Genealogical records indicate he was born January 22, 1876.

The case for an automobile in Laramie was made in "The Automobile on the Plains of Wyoming," September 2, 1908, *THA*, by J. Tidball, meaning Volney Jean Tidball, a future judge. The "electricity and ozone" quote comes from a brochure ("Albany County, Wyoming: The City of Laramie") that appears to have been printed in early 1909 by The Laramie Republican Company.

Elmer Lovejoy (born February 2, 1872) was extensively covered by Wyoming newspapers in his lifetime. A collection of his personal papers, largely digitized, is archived through the University of Wyoming's American Heritage Center. His Diamond connection to Shawmut is an inference; a March 1911 *Motor Field* article identified Lovejoy as a Diamond tire man then, but I could not find any reference to the type of tires he favored or sold in 1909.

Hendy initially telephoned his Laramie agent from Rawlins to say he would go east to Medicine Bow to meet the lead Ford, but he appears to have stopped at Fort Steele.

The Itala's harrowing experience at Glasgow comes primarily from a Bellows letter, as well as the June 15, 1909, *Kansas City Star* ("Six Days Late, But Racing") and June 17, 1909, *Glasgow Missourian*.

The depiction of the pathfinder crew fending off aggressive hoboes with wrenches comes from the April 21, 1909, *Cheyenne Daily Leader* ("'Bos Attack Pathfinder"). Weston's relevant *NYT* dispatches include June 8 ("Wind Bowls Weston Over Embankment"), June 14 ("Weston Badly Handicapped"), and June 15, 1909 ("Sheriffs Protect Weston").

My description of the terrain owes much to Kelia McCuddy of the Carbon County Museum. Wyoming's Board of Sheep Commissioners counted 5,131,182 sheep to start 1909, according to the guide *Wyoming: Resources, Population, Industries, Opportunities, and Climate* (Omaha: Union Pacific Railroad Company, 1909).

The depiction of Hendy waiting with the armed guard comes from Chapin's sworn testimony in Seattle, "Axles of Cars Stamped Alike," *SS*, June 29, 1909.

10. "A Damned Crooked Deal"

The "energetic young ladies" line is from the July 15, 1909, *Wyoming Tribune*; "brown as berries" comes from that day's *Cheyenne State Leader.*

The Fort Steele description is from numerous sources, including the site's 1969 National Register of Historic Places Inventory—Nomination Form; Barbara Fifer's *Wyoming's Historic Forts* (Helena, MT: Farcountry Press, 2003); a 1977 Historic American Buildings Survey; a "Fort Fred Steele" history pamphlet prepared by the Wyoming Department of State Parks and Cultural Resources; census records; multiple statewide gazetteers and directories from the period (*R.L. Polk & Co.'s Wyoming and Idaho Gazetteer and Business Directory*, 1908–1909; the rival *Wyoming State Business Directory* for the same period, from Denver's The Gazetteer Publishing Co.; and the next Gazetteer Publishing entry in that biennial series, 1910–1911, all provided by the Wyoming State Archives); materials from the Carbon County Museum in Rawlins; and phone and email correspondence with Lonnie Porter, superintendent of the state park that includes the Fort Steele remnants.

On Earl King: Wyoming railroad historian and former Union Pacific dispatcher James Ehrenberger told me by email that many station agents in this era lived in their depots and worked all hours, on call. Newspapers and railroad journals often reported the comings and goings of station agents. The April 1909 issue of *The Railroad Telegrapher* and the April 8, 1909, *Cheyenne Leader* each mentioned King stationed at Fort Steele, where his wife had recently given birth to a boy. In the 1910 census, he was still stationed there, with wife Beatrice and sons Richard (four) and Jack (one). On May 1, 1912, he advertised a registered Llewellin setter ("finest prize winning stock") in Fort Steele in the *Cheyenne State Leader*, but resigned his position soon after, per the June 21, 1912, *Shoshone Journal*. The later bio is from military records and an obituary in the February 13, 1951, *Tacoma News Tribune*. Neither Chapin's letters nor contemporaneous coverage of the race mentions the station agent by name, but context indicates King.

The date of the Saratoga bridge is from the April 13, 1905, *Saratoga Sun* ("Built Saratoga's Iron Bridge").

The Cosgriff Bridge was named for brothers who dominated sheep-rearing and shearing in the area and ran a network of mercantile stores. It washed out in late-May flooding, amid extreme rains coupled with the melting of exceptionally substantial snowpack, according to *The Wyoming Tribune* ("Ft. Steele Bridges Goes Out," May 31, 1909) and others.

Chapin's letter and multiple news accounts indicate the Shawmut reached Fort Steele first, though a wire story that ran in *The Denver Republican* and some other papers reported that the No. 2 Ford had instead caught the Shawmut in Hanna, just before Fort Steele. All corroborate that the two lead cars were running close here, that the Shawmut was held up overnight, and that the trailing No. 1 Ford also passed it the next morning while the Boston crew still waited.

The Chapins married June 17, 1908, in Springfield, Massachusetts.

The rebuke of Hendy ran in *The Laramie Republican*, June 16, 1909 ("Ford Loses Wheel After Leaving City").

Hendy's description of crossing the ties appeared July 25, 1909, in an extensive account of the race he authored for Denver's *Sunday News-Times* ("Story of Ocean-To-Ocean Race of Autos, Won by Ford Machine"). Ramsey's description comes partly from her book *Veil, Duster, and Tire Iron* (Covina, CA: Alice Huyler Ramsey, 1961) and partly from her May 1910 account in *The Travel Magazine*.

On the total delay: Chapin would attest in Seattle that they were delayed "more than 16 hours"; a lawyer for Shawmut would put it at sixteen hours.

The "man for breakfast" phrase was widely used to describe the wildest parts of the West. The venerable John McPhee applied it to Rawlins in *Rising from the Plains* (New York: Farrar, Straus and Giroux, 1986).

Jack Booth was a nickname for Elijah Minor Booth, whose birthdate varied but was often listed as August 23, 1867. Biographical details are from genealogical and newspaper records. The livery and stable man who died from a tangled-pistol accident was C. R. Bell. Booth rode broncos in exhibitions at Rawlins and elsewhere. His tax protest occurred in late 1907. The gunplay between the Booths and their future brother-in-law was covered in multiple papers in summer 1905. A great-granddaughter of Booth's sister told me, regretfully, that the family rift endured across multiple generations. Booth's travails with a "dishonest patent attorney" were covered in the October 13, 1910, *Rawlins Republican*, which indicated he'd invented the post two years earlier.

Stevenson quote from his *Across the Plains: With Other Memories and Essays* (London: Chatto & Windus, 1892).

D. V. Bell information comes primarily from "Old Timer David V. Bell Passes," in *The Union Pacific Coal Company Employes' Magazine*, July 1943, which favored the old spelling of "employes." Early petroleum production figures are from *Report of the Federal Trade Commission on the Petroleum Industry of Wyoming* (Washington: Government Printing Office, 1921). More recent figures are from the Petroleum Association of Wyoming.

The episode in which Guggenheim helped dig the pathfinder out of the muck was covered in many papers, including "Pathfinder Car has Tough Trip Across Wyoming," *SLPD*, April 25, 1909.

Rock Springs depiction from multiple sources, including newspapers, maps, statewide directories and gazetteers, and considerable materials and insight provided by Jennifer Messer, coordinator of the Rock Springs Historical Museum, including the photo of the No. 2 outside the Rock Springs Lumber Company garage.

Multiple early motorists wrote dramatically about Marston Wash, including businessman J. M. Murdock in "A Family Tour from Ocean to Ocean," a detailed promotional booklet published by the Packard Motor Car Co. about the Murdock family's 1908 trek.

Hendy praised Thomas in his *Sunday News-Times* recap. The shooting was covered over multiple stories in the *Carbon County Journal*, July 1904, concurrent with a legal notice about the divorce in the July 22, 1904, *Wyoming Star*; the April 15, 1905, *Rock Springs Miner* carried a notice that Mary Thomas sought the ranch as alimony. Thomas's unusual legal defense appeared in the August 14, 1905, *Wyoming Tribune* ("Is a Dead Shot").

11. Broken Down by Bancroft

The Kemmerer depiction is from Sanborn maps and newspapers, including the *Kemmerer Camera*, where Ming earned frequent notice.

Harper's depiction is from *The Story of the Race*.

The Pocatello Tribune, an evening paper, reported June 17, 1909, that the No. 2 Ford was broken down at Cokeville, without specifying a reason. The Shawmut telegram sent that night from Soda Springs, Idaho—after passing the No. 2 at Cokeville—referred to Ford's trouble as a "broken piston." Harper, writing about the "victory" for Ford before the illicit engine swap had been exposed, glossed over Cokeville entirely except to say that the two cars decided to split up there, moving at different paces. Hendy also skipped over the breakdown in his written account that July. Twenty-six years later, Scott gave an interview to the *DFP* ("Michigan Gasped as Speed Demons Hit 35 Miles an Hour," July 14, 1935) in which he remembered that they "cracked a piston"; he placed the incident at Granger, eighty-five miles east of Cokeville (though the reporter interpreted it as Granger, Washington, not Granger, Wyoming). In 1959, a thirty-page typewritten history prepared by Ford Motor Company researchers as an internal memo while preparing for the fiftieth-anniversary campaign identified the problem as a broken connecting rod ("Chronological Story of the New York–to–Seattle Transcontinental Endurance Race," at BFRC,

Accession 717, "Ocean to Ocean Race—Planning—Planning Notebook," folder 2 of 10).

That Cokeville had no garage in 1909 comes from a master's thesis (Errol Jack Lloyd, *The History of Cokeville, Wyoming*, Utah State University, 1970) and biennial directories. Each Model T expert I consulted (including on the MTFCA forum) gave a slightly different estimate of the time it would take to remove and replace a connecting rod in a 1909 T, compared with swapping out the engine, mainly within a ballpark range.

In Salt Lake City, Consolidated Wagon had been advertising the Model T locally since January, but the Montpelier branch didn't receive its first T until mid-June. The same *Montpelier Examiner* issue that covered the race (June 18, 1909) reported the sale of that car to Cruikshank. When Ford researchers reached out to newspapers and libraries across the country in 1959 seeking clips about the race, they discovered from Montpelier's successor *News-Examiner* that Cruikshank was still alive; their resulting correspondence can be found at BFRC, Accession 717, "Ocean to Ocean Race—Clippings—Requests/Replies," folder 10 of 14. Other Montpelier information comes from the Polk directory, Sanborn maps, news clippings, and a master's thesis from 1957 (A. McKay Rich, "The History of Montpelier from 1864 to 1925," Utah State University).

Details about John J. Jones and his father, crack investigator Joseph Jones, are from assorted newspapers and genealogical records as well as materials shared by Roger Jones, a grandson of John. The "terror to box-car thieves" comes from *Men of Affairs in the State of Utah*, issued by the Press Club of Salt Lake, 1914.

Auto pioneer Percy Megargel, who recorded three of the first eight successful cross-country drives, was nearly overcome by the altitude trying to pump his tires at Soda Springs. "The slightest exertion causes a person to pant violently, while harder work causes one not accustomed to the mountains to bleed at the nose, mouth and ears," he wrote in *From Hell Gate to Portland* (Detroit: Oldsmobile Motor Co., 1905).

Guggenheim's speeding episode made national news, but the quote here is local, from the June 18, 1909, *SS*.

Railroad times are from *The Soda Springs Chieftain*, *Pocatello Tribune*, and other sources.

The memory of the armed fireman comes from the August 24, 1945, *Reading Chronicle*, "Team Reunion Recalls Great Transcontinental Auto Race."

The Pocatello shops description is from *The Railway Age*, March 28, 1902, "Oregon Short Line Shops at Pocatello, Idaho," and *Engineering News*, October 15, 1903, "Recent Improvements on the Oregon Short Line R.R."

Messer remembered the "hurry up" ribbing when he spoke to reporters in Seattle for "Shawmut Car Wins Second in Big Race," *SS*, June 24, 1909.

The Trist and Turner depictions are from a variety of genealogical and newspaper records. The August 12, 1909, *Pocatello Tribune* referred to Trist as Pocatello's "automobile doctor."

12. No. 2 to the Fore

Though the *Montpelier Examiner* didn't know the reason for the long delay at Cokeville, the June 18, 1908, issue pinpointed the No. 2's departure to 4:45 AM. In his own post-race account, Hendy called it 5 AM, noting that departure matter-of-factly without mentioning why the car had been stalled there for so long.

The dealer registers (BFRC Accession 387) were an invaluable resource—and a joy to examine.

The portrait of Rice (born October 15, 1873) is from a variety of genealogical sources and news clips, including the June 1896 issue of *The Land of Sunshine*, which carried a headshot of Rice among four dozen prominent national cyclists; "Suicide from Grief," in *The Newton* [Illinois] *Press*, August 1, 1899; and "New Records for Rice and the Model T," in the November 1911 *Ford Times*.

The April 26, 1909, *Pocatello Tribune* captured a taste of the debate over the best route westward. Idaho historian, author, and postcard collector Ron Yates provided considerable insight on the Snake River corridor and Idaho's overall geography and topography. I also drew on a report ("Historic Survey of Roads in Idaho's State Highway System, Volume 1: Historic Context") prepared for the Idaho Transportation Department in 2019 by consultants Mead & Hunt.

The Twin Falls depictions and context are from photos, from Yates, and from media coverage, including "The Transformation of a Desert," *Pacific Monthly*, August 1907. Sadly, the *Twin Falls News* and *The Twin Falls Times* microfilm have gaps for the period during which the race came through.

Information on Lorenzo Lloyd Evans is from newspaper and genealogical records as well as the 1908 edition of *The Gast-Paul Directory of Bankers and Attorneys Throughout the United States and Canada*. The story of his mother, Winnifred (Gwen) Lloyd Roberts Evans, is documented online at BYU's Welsh Saints Project. His brother, David Lloyd Evans, was a founder of the enduring D.L. Evans Bank and grandfather of Idaho governor John Evans.

Harper detailed the fiasco from American Falls in *Ford Times*, July 15, 1909.

The Idanha depiction comes partly from *The Idanha: Guests and Ghosts of an Historic Idaho Inn* (Caldwell, ID: The Caxton Printers, 1983), by Idaho historian Dick d'Easum.

The 505-mile figure for Hendy's journey is the combined track mileage on the Oregon Short Line and Oregon Railroad & Navigation Company (both Union Pacific subsidiaries) from Cokeville to Baker City, inferring that Hendy orchestrated the Cokeville engine swap in person; if he set it in motion while remaining in Montpelier, the mileage figure becomes 473.

13. The Shawmut Charges Back

The arrest in Buhl on June 18, 1909, of an outlaw ultimately identified as William Matthews made national news and is the subject of an article by Tommy R. Thompson, in *Nebraska History* 63 (1982), "The Great Omaha Train Robbery."

Fairchild was a subject of derision in the local press in the 1910s and

1920s, but later accounts treated him with nuance, including "Congress May Protect Land Of Deserving Idaho Widow," *Idaho Daily Statesman*, February 15, 1932, and "Buhl Oldtimer Believes in Magnetic Healing," *The Times-News*, Twin Falls, June 29, 1978.

Syster's Winton was featured in the June 12, 1908, *Twin Falls News*, "Forsakes Broncho for Auto."

Sherman Johnson (born June 15, 1889), son of Ford dealer J. C. Johnson, had just turned twenty; he was also a crack marksman. Shawmut guide Allen G. Randall (born August 11, 1872), according to news clips and genealogical materials, started small ("Auto Livery," *Idaho Daily Statesman*, November 8, 1906) but by the time of the race ran a large Boise garage and dealership, the Randall-Dodd Auto Company, that had expanded to Salt Lake City as well.

14. A Case of "Auto Intoxication"

The Baker City depiction is from the 1909–1910 *Polk's Oregon and Washington Gazetteer and Business Directory* and news clips. The "real highway" quote comes from Baker City's *Morning Democrat*, May 14, 1909, "The Pathfinder."

The name of the Geiser Grand day clerk came from the racing passport prepared by the pathfinder and issued to each crew, with a page for each checkpoint. Because the Itala did not finish the race, Bellows retained a rare copy of that passport, which his family shared.

While researching Dr. Carl Patterson, it took my breath away to discover a bevy of detailed Patterson materials, including photos of his office and waiting room, via the Baker County Library Digital Archive. I'm grateful to my keen-eyed wife, Hannah Swartz, and physician friends Brian Schulman, Henry Cheng, and Maireade McSweeney for helping interpret Patterson's handwriting on a medical note preserved by the Chapin family.

15. Henry, Edsel, and the Crack Train of the Northwest

The Chicago papers first identified Frank Dunnell (born July 18, 1883, and identified in the 1905 New York census as a "demonstrator") as driver of the late-breaking Ford entry at Crown Point on June 9, 1909; his original role with Duerr was affirmed in the February 1, 1909, *Ford Times*. The *Chicago Examiner* reported June 18 that Ford dropped out of that race because the car "did not reach the track in time for the driver to familiarize himself with the course or tune up the car," while the July 1, 1909, *Ford Times* said the special body needed for the chassis was not finished in time. A year later, Ford would move to reenter road racing at the first Elgin National Road Races in Illinois, again persuaded by Hay, with two stock cars entered in a class for cars with 161 to 230 cubic inches of piston displacement. When his two Ts—including one with Kulick at the wheel—failed to meet the fourteen-hundred-pound weight minimum, "Henry Ford positively refused" to meet the requirement with weighted seats or other ballast, *The Automobile*, September 1, 1910.

Newspaper coverage in Washington established that the Fords took the North Coast Limited. The description of enticements comes from "Roads Hot After A.-Y.-P. Travelers," *SPI*, June 24, 1909. The mail speed made national news, including "Seattle in 4 Days for New York Mail," *NYT*, May 22, 1909.

The Disher departure made the *Idaho Daily Statesman* ("Expected on Wednesday," June 20, 1909) and a few other papers, his name misspelled as Disches. His given name was Hiley Peter Disher (born October 4, 1885, per multiple records, with some discrepancies), and he featured periodically in local auto coverage as a Ford mechanic and burgeoning racer, including "Disher May Race on Big Speedway," July 24, 1910, *The Seattle Sunday Times*. In 1919, a Texas society heiress would appeal to police to help locate him after he vanished with money and jewels ("Widow Seeks Flyer from Indianapolis," *The* [Evansville] *Journal-News*, November 26, 1919). He surfaced in Boston, married to a different heiress, where he had multiple scrapes with the law before killing his wife, the former Elsie Cheney, and himself ("Disher Kills Wife Takes Own Life," *The Boston Daily Globe*, September 11, 1923, and others).

16. "The Greatest Thrill of My Life"

Bellows's path through the Blues is reconstructed from a letter and newspapers.

The portrait of Smith from genealogical records and news clippings comes primarily from *La Grande Evening Observer* (*LGEO*), including ads and notices for his repair shop. The "live hustler" classified can be found July 30, 1908, in the summarized *La Grande Weekly Observer.* The detail about checking the spelling of the word "garage" before painting it comes from "L.C. Smith Auto Veteran," *LGEO*, November 11, 1916.

Description of the Grande Ronde Valley and surrounding region comes from multiple sources, including *An Illustrated History of Union and Wallowa Counties, with a Brief Outline of the Early History of the State of Oregon* (Western Historical Publishing Company, 1902), the 1909–1910 Polk directory, and insights from Stephen Wadner of the Union County Museum.

I first came across the death of Summerville's "Walter Wetherall" in Baker City's *Morning Democrat* ("Cigarettes Cause of a Fatal Disease," June 27, 1909). Probing, I found items in other papers, with varying phonetic spellings for Walt or Walter "Weatherall" or "Witherell." His death certificate confirms the spelling "Walter L. Witherell," with the attending physician listing this cause of death: "Bronchial asthma due to the excessive use of cigarettes and whisky."

The depiction of the Toll Gate comes from numerous sources, including Irene Barklow, *From Trails to Rails: The Post Offices, Stage Stops & Wagon Roads of Union County, Oregon* (Enterprise, OR: Enchantments Publishing of Oregon, 1987); the October 1908 issue of Walla Walla's *Up-to-the-Times Magazine* ("Toll Gate on the Summit of the Blue Mountains was a Famous Place"); an extensive 1961 history by Mary Arlie Rouanzoin ("The Toll Gate Story & The Woodward Family") provided by the Frazier Farmstead Museum in Milton-Freewater, Oregon; the Eastern Oregon University Library Digital Archives; and contemporaneous and retrospective news stories.

Scott's son, Jack, corresponded with Hubbs and included the anecdote in *The Big Race.* Additional details are from genealogical records and a biography of Oland "Olie" Hubbs on the Walla Walla University website, for the Oland F. Hubbs Memorial Theology Scholarship.

17. Going on Nerve Alone

A photograph of Inland Auto can be found in *THA*, April 21, 1909, page 573.

Portrait of Walla Walla from multiple sources, including a circa-1909 "Walla Walla: The Garden City" promotional booklet and R. L. Polk & Co.'s 1909–1910 *Directory of Walla Walla City and County*, from Whitman College's extensive digitized Arminda Collections.

The "merry sport of 'chuffing'" comes from the June 18, 1907, *Evening Statesman*. The wheat assessment, and what it would mean for local auto sales, comes from the July 1909 *Up-to-the-Times*. The *Bulletin*'s "one long macadam road" line is from June 6, 1909, while the "anxiety and ado" quote comes from Walla Walla's *Morning Union*, May 15, 1909. The "buzz-cart" assessment appeared in the *Evening Statesman*, June 21, 1909.

The portrait of Archie Gilbert Henderson (born October 21, 1880, son of prominent contractor Smith F. Henderson) and his tenure selling Fords comes from genealogical records, news clippings, and the BFRC dealer registers.

The rancher James Angus McKenzie consistently spelled his surname without an *a*, but his father, Roderick MacKenzie, an even more prominent rancher, favored the *a*.

Depiction of the Hotel Dacres comes from photographs and other sources, including *The Coast*, March 1908, "Hotel Dacres, Walla Walla"; "Dacres Grill to Have Orchestra," *The Evening Statesman*, January 19, 1909; and the National Register of Historic Places Inventory—Nomination Form for the Dacres.

Kerrison's warning about "mulcting" appeared in his automotive column May 11, 1909.

The number and location of the bundled telegraph wires comes from a special *NYT* "Building Supplement" all about the skyscraper now known as One Times Square, published January 1, 1905. The thirty-five-words-a-minute transcription rate for telegraphers in newspaper telegraph rooms in the early 1900s comes from Joe Alex Morris, *Deadline Every Minute: The Story of the United Press* (New York: Greenwood Press, 1968).

The Inland Auto interior depiction comes from *THA*, April 21, 1909.

The portrait of Dick Tyson (born Charles Richard Tyson, October 24, 1883) comes from newspaper and genealogical records. Late in life he was featured in the May 18, 1952, *Walla Walla Union-Bulletin.*

S. O. Jayne of the Department of Agriculture noted the seepage in the Kennewick Canal in *Irrigation in the Yakima Valley, Washington* (Washington, D.C.: Government Printing Office, 1907). The depiction of Horse Heaven is from *Polk's Oregon and Washington Gazetteer* and other sources.

The fire in Prosser, a dramatic episode told with slight differences in each account, is reconstructed from coverage in *The Prosser Record*, Prosser *Republican-Bulletin, La Grande Evening Observer, The Evening Statesman, Daily Oregon Statesman, Daily* [Oregon] *Capital Journal, Morning Oregonian, The Seattle Star, Wallula Gateway*, and *The Evening Bulletin*, as well as *The Story of the Race.*

18. Clawing Through Central Washington

The portrait of Wallula is from numerous sources, including contemporaneous news clippings; local and statewide Polk directories; a 1909 Sanborn map; the Washington Trust for Historic Preservation's online Revisiting Washington project, which reinterprets the 1941 Federal Writers Project book *Washington, A Guide to the Evergreen State*; D. W. Meinig's *The Great Columbia Plain: A Historical Geography, 1805–1910* (Seattle: University of Washington Press, 1983); and the Wallula entry (Essay 10524) at HistoryLink.org, an extensive encyclopedia of Washington State history. The Meriwether Lewis quote comes from his May 1, 1806, journal entry, available through the University of Nebraska Press's Journals of the Lewis & Clark Expedition online.

The portrait of Ivan "Ive" Doak (born December 13, 1881) is from genealogical and newspaper records. The *Elsie May* and Captain Pitman appeared in numerous clips, including the shaggy-dog story from 1905 about the federal agent and the fine, covered in the *Port Townsend Daily Leader* ("Deputy Collector Has Hard Time," November 14, 1905) and elsewhere.

The Hovers received regular coverage in the automotive press in 1908–1909; the later *NYT* feature ran July 20, 1949 ("Pair, 81 and 72, Who Have Toured Million Miles, Plan 50,000 More").

The June 23, 1909, *Twin City Reporter* mention of German airships reflects news that dominated headlines at the time, about the recent nine-hundred-mile flight by Count Ferdinand von Zeppelin, so incomprehensible that people debated whether it might end warfare entirely or usher in a new age of aerial terror.

Alva R. McLane (born October 16, 1874), a jeweler, optician, bank vice president, and Prosser city councilor, mounted a failed bid the previous year to drive from Prosser to Philadelphia as a promotional venture for *The Pacific Monthly*.

Roscoe Sheller's account comes from "The First Automobile to Cross from Ocean to Ocean," part of a previously unpublished collection gathered by his daughter and preserved online at the "Sheller Stories" WordPress site.

The railroad dinner-dance was recorded in the July 3, 1908, *Ellensburg Dawn* and July 4, 1908, *Seattle Sunday Times*.

The "Who'd a thought it? Apples bought it" rhyme comes from "The Modern Eshcol," *Pacific Builder and Engineer*, October 24, 1908.

I reconstructed the comings and goings of North Yakima's garages from 1906 through 1909 from over two dozen articles in local newspapers and national trade magazines, cross-checked with entries in annual directories.

Mottinger (the man and his ranch) was featured in *The Pacific Monthly*, March 1905. More information came from a variety of sources, including Edmond S. Meany's "Origin of Washington Geographic Names [Continued . . .]" from *The Washington Historical Quarterly*, Vol. 11, No. 3, July 1920.

19. Bearing Up Under the News

The description of the routes between North Yakima and Ellensburg are from various sources, including W. D. Lyman, *History of the Yakima Valley, Washington*, Vol. 1 (The S. J. Clarke Publishing Co., 1919); Edward Lange's "Birdseye View Map of Yakima Valley and Central Washington" (1907); A. P. Neyhart's 1926 Automobile Club of Washington map, "Winter Routes from Wenatchee South"; and Jennifer Ott's "Walla Walla to Seattle Historic Corridor Wagon Roads," HistoryLink.org Essay 10757.

Cle Elum was featured in the April 1905 issue of *The Coast*, also called *Wilhelm's Magazine*. General anxiety about tramps was captured in the July 3, 1909, *Cle Elum Echo* ("Tramps are Terrors"), while the violent episode with the bandits was covered June 26 ("Broke into Hades").

The Cle Elum State Bank description comes from multiple sources, including photos from the digitized collections of the Northern Kittitas County Historical Society and Central Washington University Libraries.

Depictions of Harry Tucker (born May 2, 1886) and his father come from newspaper and genealogical records, in addition to *An Illustrated History of Klickitat, Yakima and Kittitas Counties* (Interstate Publishing Company, 1904) and correspondence with Harry's grandson, Don DeFrancq, and great-granddaughter, Leslie DeFrancq, who shared photos and other materials.

Ford's rail-station exchange with former employees in North Yakima was captured in *The Yakima Herald*, June 23, 1909, "Ford Still Leads Race."

20. Snoqualmie Pass

The description of Snoqualmie Pass in 1909, as well as of Lake Keechelus, comes from a multitude of sources, including dozens of newspaper and magazine stories from the era; Yvonne Prater's book, *Snoqualmie Pass: From Indian Trail to Interstate* (Seattle: The Mountaineers, 1981); material from the Snoqualmie Valley Museum; United States Geological Survey maps; the biennial reports of Washington's highway commissioner, starting with the first in 1906; and interviews and emails with Milwaukee Road "High Line" historians Allen Miller and Andrew Craig Magnuson.

The "hardest test" comes from the October 22, 1911, *Oregon Sunday Journal* ("Strenuous Trip of Auto Party is Record Breaker"). The "Blitzens!" letter appeared in *MoToR*, May 1909.

Seattle statistics are from the 1909–1910 Polk statewide directory. Snow's "energy of Hercules" quote appeared in the February 28, 1909, *SPI*. The road-funding history comes from the highway reports and from the published *Session Laws of the State of Washington* for each biennial session.

Guggenheim's visit with Taft was widely covered, including in the April 13, 1909, *NYT* ("Taft to Start off Autos"), with that paper elaborating on the road appropriations the following Sunday ("Automobilists Want Transcontinental Highway," April 18). He also touted the Idaho and Washington investments when he met with McClellan ("Test for Auto Parts," *New-York Tribune*, April 16, 1909). The $1,000 King County appropriation was noted in the April 8, 1909, *SS* ("Hanford Party Leaves to Meet Pathfinder") and elsewhere.

The offer by capitalist H. C. Henry (Horace Chapin Henry) to former mayor J. T. Ronald (James T. Ronald) was reported in the March 28, 1909, *SDT* ("Autos to Cross Water by Ferry").

Easton church-saloon ratio is from the 1909–1910 Polk directory.

For the re-creation of the Keechelus environment, I'm indebted to the considerable help and materials provided by BranDee Bruce, historian and national history program lead for the federal Bureau of Reclamation (known as the Reclamation Service in 1909), and Kate Hovanes, a bureau historian based in Yakima, including numerous photos, Yakima Project annual histories from 1902–1913, maps, diagrams, and two modern reports (Christine Pfaff's *Harvests of Plenty: A History of the Yakima Irrigation Project*, from 2002, and what's known as an HAER, or Historic American Engineering Record, for Keechelus Dam, HAER No. WA-80).

The nature and extent of the timber comes from a 1915 Reclamation Service advertisement soliciting contractors to clear the site, after Flanagan's exit. The Patrick Flanagan portrait comes from genealogical records and newspaper accounts, principally from Washington and Ohio, though the $10 toll made news in Chicago ("Ferry Makes Money on Auto Tourists," October 17, 1909, *The Inter Ocean*).

Smith's recollections come from "The Reminiscences of Mr. C. J. Smith," conducted in 1951 as part of the Owen W. Bombard interviews series, Accession 65, BFRC. The contention that someone from the Ford side delayed the ferry was reported in the post-race Shawmut allegations.

21. Breaking the Tape

"Autos Expected in Seattle Today," *Morning Oregonian*, June 23, 1909.

Cle Elum road description is from multiple period maps, with additional insight from Charlene Kauzlarich of the Northern Kittitas County Historical Society.

Depictions of Les Reinovsky (sometimes misspelled "Reinosky") and Christian Hansen (name spelled a variety of ways) come from genealogical records, news clippings, and federal reports. The detail about the cash under the pillow comes from "Lake Keechelus Man Robbed of $85," *SDT*, July 26, 1907, which noted that "C. Hansen, a bachelor who has lived at the foot of Lake Keechelus for a number of years," was robbed of $85, equal to nearly $3,000 in 2025. Police suspected two women from Easton who'd been seen in the vicinity—"one of them the notorious Nell Pickerell, who is wearing man's apparel and going by the name Harry Allen." Today, Allen would be recognized as trans. He led a life at once vibrant, tortured, and misunderstood, continually running afoul of the law and making appearances in the press across the Northwest for two decades, prior to his premature death in 1922, acknowledged by Peter Boag in "Past as Prologue: Harry Allen in the Northwest and the Slow History of Trans Acceptance," Northwest Public Broadcasting, February 5, 2021. Newell's testimony about Hansen comes from a House Committee on Irrigation hearing, February 3, 1909.

North Coast Limited arrival time is from the daily "King Street Passenger Station" timetable, *SDT*, and other sources.

Harper acknowledged that the No. 1 drove over the railroad bed in *The Story of the Race.* In the fall of 1909, the newspaper *The Philadelphia*

Press organized a coast-to-coast automotive relay, involving numerous vehicles and drivers, to carry a message from President Taft to the Alaska-Yukon-Pacific Exposition shortly before it closed. A *Seattle Sunday Times* account from the motorist who handled the journey over Snoqualmie Pass ("Dotzer Describes Rough Trip," October 10, 1909) said a surveying party at the summit advised them to take the Milwaukee railroad bed for part of the descent, suggesting "the cars in the New York–to–Seattle race" did the same.

The road-sprinkling issue was raised in a June 23, 1909, *SDT* editorial, and elsewhere. Information on the Seattle fire chief's Autocar and chauffeur Bradford Dean Kuhn are from newspaper and genealogical records and photographs.

Second Avenue was paved with vitrified brick, a popular choice for urban streets, per the October 9, 1909, issue of *Southwest Contractor and Manufacturer* ("Vitrified Brick Street Paving in the Northwest").

The tourist who described the "mass of surging humanity" was Frank L. Dodge, writing home to California's *Hanford Kings County Sentinel.* He thought the bedraggled Scott and Smith "looked like a pink night shirt drawn through a sheep dip."

For depictions of the fairgrounds and surrounding neighborhood, in this chapter and the next, I'm indebted to the 2009 book *Alaska-Yukon-Pacific Exposition, Washington's First World's Fair: A Timeline History,* by Alan J. Stein, Paula Becker, and the HistoryLink.org staff, published by History Ink/HistoryLink in association with the University of Washington Press, and to a wealth of materials preserved by the University of Washington Libraries Special Collections and MOHAI, Seattle, in addition to 1909 newspaper coverage.

Fairgrounds finish line, stadium, and Mines Building scenes were re-created from numerous photographs in the UW Libraries Special Collections and from news accounts. Towering guard Fred Bloom appears prominently in multiple photos (including Nowell x2204 and x2195); in the finish-line photo reproduced in this book, with the car entering the fairgrounds, Bloom is the uniformed figure standing in the otherwise-parted path with his back to the camera. He was featured multiple times in the Seattle press, including "Giant Finn to Teach Gentle Grappling Art," *SPI*, September 29, 1910, and "Bloom, Former Marshal, Dies," *SDT*, December 19, 1935.

22. A Scrap in Seattle

The prominent logger who assisted the Shawmut was Albert Schafer of the noted Schafer Brothers; his trip in his "handsome new" $4,000 Stoddard-Dayton was reported in the June 28, 1909, *Aberdeen Herald*. Schafer's nephew, Dionis "Dio" George Reinig, who helped out on that occasion and who later became a successful Snoqualmie Valley businessman, remembered that exciting night assisting the "Shawmot" car in "Grandpa, Tell Me a Story," a series of reminiscences set down in 1966 for his family and preserved by the Snoqualmie Valley Museum.

Pettengill's postcard is from the Stoneham Historical Society.

James Blake Howe details are from news clippings and books as well as correspondence with descendant Joan Branch, who produces a "Howe's the Family" newsletter.

Ford's seemingly high-road quotes are from "Protest Heard in Automobile Race," *SPI*, June 26, 1909. The phrase "generalship" appeared in all three Seattle papers between June 24 and 26. I found Edsel's original postcard to his mother at BFRC in folder "EBF—Correspondence; 1902–1914," number 18–13, in Accession 1 (Fair Lane Papers).

The depiction of the suffering Itala crew in Cheyenne comes from a Bellows letter.

The estimated Guggenheim sum includes $10,000 to promoter Moore and the cost of the Itala, among other expenses he footed. The Seattle Automobile Club raised an additional $5,000 in local subscriptions toward the cost of the race.

The Salzman account comes from "Ford Cars Are Under a Cloud," *The Baker City Herald*, June 26, 1909.

The premier Kansas City investigator who visited Glasgow for Shawmut was Clarence W. Tobie, per the July 1, 1909, *Glasgow Missourian*. Two years later, Tobie would help crack the so-called "crime of the century"—the new century, so far—a deadly bombing of the *Los Angeles Times* building.

Antero's inspection of the markings on the car was described in Walla Walla's *Evening Statesman*, July 6, 1909, "Igorrote Called to Decide Race." The MOHAI collection includes an image of Antero (Image Number 1990.73.110) inspecting the Shawmut inside the roped-off display in the Mines Building, with the Acme and No. 1 Ford also visible, as well as the trophy. Notably, the space where the No. 2 resided is empty in that photo. Given reports that the damaged frame was straightened out for the July 8 victory-tour departure, the car had presumably been removed for this work at the time of Antero's visit; this begs the question of whether Antero was able to inspect the No. 2 with the other cars, either at the Mines Building or elsewhere, and whether the original engine had already been swapped back in at this point or was put in when the car was removed from display to prepare it for departure.

Photos of the No. 2 poised for departure ran in *Ford Times* ("On the Back Trail," August 1, 1909) and Denver's *Sunday-News Times* ("Ford Car That Won Race to Seattle Will Be Exhibited at Frontier Days," August 15, 1909). The banner language is not fully visible in either photo, but I pieced it together from additional views of the car on the return trip in BFRC, Accession 1854, Binder 15.

The Ford ads sampled here come from *The Cairo Bulletin*, June 30, 1909; *The Daily Express*, Kirksville, Missouri, June 28, 1909; and *Lindsborgs-Posten*, Lindsborg, Kansas, July 30, 1909.

The "pluck and energy" ad ran in both the Sunday *Detroit News Tribune* and *DFP*, September 19, 1909. The Pontchartrain scene comes primarily from the September 21 *Detroit News* and *DFP* and *Ford Times*, October 1, 1909.

Searching newspaper databases, I found coverage of the fabled No. 2 visiting dealers in Philadelphia that October, followed by Washington, D.C., and Richmond, Virginia, in November. *The Dayton Herald* reported that the car had reached that Ohio locale January 31, 1909 ("Ford Racer is Here"), "driven by the youngest expert mechanic and driver in the city,

Earl DeVoe, age 12 years." He was really sixteen, according to genealogical records for Earl C. DeVoe (born December 10, 1893), younger brother of auto dealer Ralph DeVoe. At that point, the No. 2 had "been driven about 32,000 miles in all sorts of road and weather and over all kinds of roads," per the *Herald*. The brothers still had the car in March 1910, when it anchored their display at Dayton's automobile show, captured in a feature photo in the March 5, 1910, *Dayton Herald* ("The Ford"). Its whereabouts afterward are elusive, but even celebrated cars were often scrapped in that era at the end of their useful life.

The ACA hearings are reconstructed from reports in *The Club Journal* and various newspapers, though the evidence, affidavits, and minutes from the hearings themselves do not survive. The portrait of Robert Lee Morrell (born July 13, 1866) comes from a variety of newspaper, magazine, and genealogical sources, as well as photos in the Detroit Public Library's National Automotive History Collection. Assorted clips about his college rowing success put his height between five foot two and five foot five and a half, and his weight at 101 to 110. The *SDT* reported that "duplicate express receipts" served as a smoking gun in the ACA ruling, in "Ford Disqualified; Won by Fraud," October 29, 1909. John Jones's central role in gathering the evidence comes primarily from the December 31, 1909, *Montpelier Examiner*, "Prizes Awarded to Shawmut Car," which also established definitively that the original Ford engine was removed and replaced with the sly substitute at Cokeville. And while it's clear that the engine was removed and replaced at Cokeville, it's less clear where the repaired engine got swapped back in. Several reports (including the *SDT*) indicated it may have happened at Weiser, though I find it unusual that *The Weiser Semi-Weekly Signal* of June 23, 1909, gave the race just a brief paragraph as the cars passed through, and did not note an unusually long stop on the part of the Ford or any other car.

The yarn about Chandler and the farmer ran in several papers, including the April 3, 1910, editions of *The Washington Post* ("Automobile Notes"), *DFP* ("Dug Up the Gold"), and Chicago *Inter Ocean* ("Buried Gold Buys Ford"). The Fred Sweeney anecdote comes from *The Oakes Times*, May 19, 1910 ("City Local").

Model T production and shipping figures come from McCalley, *Model T Ford*.

23. Carrying On

Shawmut financial figures are from the Massachusetts Secretary of State sources cited in chapter 1. The South Boston relocation saga played out in Boston dailies and South Boston weeklies, with particularly full coverage in *The Boston Herald*, *The South Boston Gazette*, and the *South Boston Inquirer*. Harvard Business School's Baker Library has a Boston Chamber of Commerce archive, formed from the chamber's surviving holdings when it moved offices in 1949. With Baker staff assistance, I spent two days searching archival boxes and files in hopes of finding the elusive Shawmut report from 1909, without success.

The "slightly used" classified ad is from the April 22, 1911, *Boston Evening Transcript*; the "excellent bargains" ad appeared in Boston's *Sunday Post*, March 24 and 31, 1912.

The "honest car" poem comes from the Stoneham Historical Society. The Pettengill post-race portrait comes from a variety of sources, including materials from the Stoneham Historical Society and Susan Lustig, articles and ads throughout his life in Stoneham papers, and 1955 obituaries in *The Stoneham Independent*, *Wakefield Daily Item*, and *Manchester* (New Hampshire) *Union Leader*. The details of the Messer-Chapin arrangement and Chapin garage services come from articles and notices in the Stoneham and Wakefield papers and ads in annual directories.

The fates of the Thomas and Acme come primarily from Kimes. Flink's *The Car Culture* was published in 1975 (Cambridge, MA: The MIT Press).

The ten millionth Model T was covered in *Ford News*, June 8, 1924. According to McCalley's *Model T Ford*, Ford reduced the base price of the Model T with touring car body from $295 to $290 effective December 2, 1923. That price held until February 11, 1926, when Ford raised it to $310. The "saturation point" quote comes from "Automobile Psychology," *NYT*, May 31, 1925. The Middletown quote comes from Robert S. Lynd and

Helen Merrell Lynd's *Middletown: A Study in American Culture* (New York: Harcourt, Brace & World, 1929), 256.

The Will Rogers witticism has appeared in numerous books, sometimes with third-person wording ("whether he helped us"), sometimes addressed to Ford directly ("whether you have helped us"). It originated in an *NYT* letter to the editor from Rogers printed July 31, 1929, acknowledging Ford's sixty-sixth birthday. It starts in the third person ("He has had more influence on the lives and habits of this nation . . .") but ends in the second person: "So good luck, Mr. Ford. It will take a hundred years to tell whether you have helped us or hurt us . . ."

The related 1959 Ford Motor Company research and promotional materials fill the ten boxes of Accession 717 (Ocean to Ocean Race Reenactment Subseries), BFRC.

Smith's concession that the engine might have been changed after all appears on page 74 of Stern, *Tin Lizzie.*

The wider portrait of Chapin here is from interviews with his grandsons. The *Globe* story (Arthur Kelley, "Reading Man Recalls 1909 Auto Race," June 7, 1959) focused on Chapin's recollections about the race.

Epilogue

The post-race portrait of Kulick comes primarily from Heyen's "Frank Kulick" stories. A photo of movie stars Pickford and Fairbanks in the ten millionth Model T, with Kulick advising from the rear seat, can be seen in the The Henry Ford's Digital Collections online, Object ID 64.167.833.P.38626.

The H. B. Harper portrait: From multiple stories, including a June 1, 1910, *Ford Times* article about his promotion; a story about his Studebaker promotion in the November 26, 1921, *Chippewa Herald-Telegram*; and his August 28, 1948, *Atlanta Constitution* obituary.

Bert Scott: From *The Big Race* and from numerous newspaper stories from Australia as well as the United States, with his obituaries in the *Port Huron Times Herald* obituary (January 15, 1940) and *DFP* (January 16, 1940) especially valuable. Jack Scott's article that preceded *The Big Race* ran in the June 1968 issue of *Driver: The Traffic Safety Magazine of the United States Air Force*. I'm grateful to Jack's surviving children, Barbara Parrent, Bev Faitz, and Jack B. "Burt" Scott II, for sharing their memories and artifacts to augment the written record.

Jimmie Smith: From his 1951 interview and multiple newspaper stories, including July 31, 1938, *DFP* coverage of seventy-fifth birthday festivities for Henry Ford.

Fuzzy Anderson: From a variety of news stories and books, including Neil Baldwin, *Henry Ford and the Jews: The Mass Production of Hate* (New York: PublicAffairs, 2001); Peter Golenbock, *The Spirit of St. Louis: A History of the St. Louis Cardinals and Browns* (New York: Avon Books, Inc., 2000); and Anderson's December 20, 1945, *SLPD* obituary. A column in the June 24, 1924, *Rockford Register-Gazette* ("Sports Done by Brown") mentions Anderson as Ringling's "warm personal friend."

R. P. Rice: From numerous articles, including "R. P. Rice, Seattle Ford Manager, Is Promoted," *Seattle Sunday Times*, July 2, 1916; "Ford Men Honor R. P. Rice," June 24, 1926, *The Kansas City Times*; and "A Link to Car History," January 15, 1948, *Kansas City Times*.

Charlie Hendy: From a variety of newspaper and genealogical sources, including February 14, 1912, *The Kemmerer Camera*; the October 17, 1913, *The Denver Post* ("Big Livestock Receipts, New Factories Add to Prosperity"); and "Charles Hendy Jr. Promoted to Head Ford's Chicago Branch," *The Denver Post*. His involvement with the antitheft business was covered in multiple publications, including *Automotive Industries*, July 14, 1921. The considerable correspondence between Hendy and E. G. Liebold, Ford's secretary, appears in BFRC Accession 285, Box 135, Folder 16, which also provides insight into Hendy's short-lived experience with the Wills Sainte Claire and his feeling that Wills left him high and dry. The rare Model K Six-Forty at the junkyard was highlighted in *The Denver Post*, April 3, 1921 ("Here's Ancient 6-Cylinder Flivver, and It's Still Going"), which may be how Hendy learned of it. That article, which called it "the only one in captivity in the west," named the owner as "J. A. Hayutin of the Auto Wrecking and Metal company"; genealogical records indicate he was Jacob Abraham Hayutin (born December 25, 1895). Obituaries for Hendy appeared in Omaha's *Evening World-Herald*, November 2, 1954, and *Automotive News*, November 15, 1954; *The Denver Post* reported November 16, 1954, that a $700,000 bond had been posted for his estate as the will went to probate, reflecting the value of personal property, not including real estate.

James Hemstreet: From multiple sources, including *NYT* obit ("J.A. Hemstreet Dies; Auto Travel Expert," June 16, 1935) and information from corresponding with extended relatives via Ancestry. Various records indicate that James Albert Hemstreet (born October 3, 1875) was initially a teacher; he simultaneously advertised himself as a "penman and designer" in the *Asbury Park Daily Press*. His mother, writing as Mrs. Mary A. G. Hemstreet, published poetry in *The Brooklyn Daily Eagle* and elsewhere.

Jerry Price: From multiple newspaper and genealogical sources, including considerable materials provided by a great-grandson, Dr. Richard Gregg Dwyer. A feature obituary appeared January 16, 1947, in *The Salem News* in Ohio, where Price managed the Mullins plant.

George Salzman: As mentioned in the notes for chapter 1, I could fill a volume with what I learned about Salzman—and still be left with as many questions as answers. I reconstructed his life by combing genealogical and newspaper records. Coverage of the purported Patent Holding and Manufacturing Company of Spokane appeared in numerous places, including Spokane's *Spokesman-Review*, January 5, 1910 (which referred to "George A. *Selzman*"), and *THA*, January 12, 1910 (which called him "George *E.* Salzman"), both of which named him as a graduate of Princeton and what was then called Boston Tech while identifying him as the famed Salzman associated with the Thomas car. (The real George Salzman wrote to correct the record in *THA*, January 26, 1910, as he and others from Thomas had previously done in 1909; nonetheless, *Motor Age* carried the same erroneous report February 17, 1910, prompting another letter from the E. R. Thomas Motor Company.) The fraudster genuinely raced aviator Lincoln Beachey in July 1911, an event covered in the *Elmira Star-Gazette* (hereafter *ESG*), which also reported the following year (May 10, 1912) that the same George Salzman—definitively identified as the local car salesman who had raced the aviator in 1911 and "won second prize" in the Ocean-to-Ocean Race in 1909—was considering entering a three-hundred-mile race in Savannah. That same individual married June 21, 1912, in Steuben, New York, giving his name as George S. Salzman, his age an unlikely twenty-two. The check-fraud arrest made news in multiple Detroit newspapers on December 31, 1914, and in Ohio's *Allen County Republican-Gazette*, January 5, 1915. The *ESG* reported November 16, 1917, about his alleged misrepresentation of character when his wife sought to annul their marriage. The clips about his supposed Great War heroism are as numerous as they are preposterous, including the August 18, 1918, *Buffalo Express* and August 30, 1918, *ESG*. Multiple papers reported on his contemplated transcontinental flight, including the April 23, 1919, *ESG*, and July 28, 1919, *Buffalo Enquirer*, which included a photo of "Capt. George Salzman." He genuinely served in the war, his more modest Royal Naval Volunteer Reserve records associated with the name George Anthony Salzman, born July 6, 1888. A passport application filed by the same George A. Salzman in 1920 listed his birthdate as July 6, 1887. The coverage of his subsequent criminal activity in the 1920s is considerable in the Elmira, Rochester, and Buffalo papers, with some still using the term "War Hero" in headlines. The clippings trail goes quiet after his garage burned in 1926, followed by a false statement on a driver's license application in 1927. In 1930, he was living in Pittsfield, Massachusetts, working for an auto accessory shop; by World War II he was living in Warwick, Rhode Island, working for an automotive electrical firm. He returned to Canisteo, New York, half a year before his death, November 19, 1962, with no known survivors and with personal property valued at $1,000.

Robert Messer: From newspaper and genealogical sources, including obituaries for his father, Charles W. Messer, in the November 9, 1945, *Stoneham Independent*, and for Messer himself in the October 9, 1952, issue. Given that Messer was close with his parents—they traveled to New York for the start of the race; he succeeded his father at the funeral home—I wondered if he might have sent them letters. However, he was an only child who had no children of his own, with no direct descendants today who might have inherited and preserved such materials. His obituary noted many friends but just one cousin; I tracked down her daughter in Maine, but she was unfamiliar with Messer's story. I also tried the successor to the Charles W. Messer & Son funeral home at 4 Common Street in Stoneham, renamed Anderson-Bryant, wondering if there might be materials in the attic. I had a wonderful conversation in 2022 with Jack Anderson, a Stoneham native who died in 2023 at eighty, and who appreciated local history. He knew the Pettengills and "knew of" the Messers in boyhood, but by the time he bought the funeral home from the succeeding Bryants in 1984, there was no trace of the Messers, scrapbook or otherwise.

Earle Chapin: From previously cited sources and interviews and material provided by his family, including a March 1964 tribute pamphlet with eulogy, produced by Chapin-Nichols, Inc., "Reading's Oldest Automatic Heating Company."

Arthur Pettengill: From previously cited sources, including news clippings and other artifacts made available by the Stoneham Historical Society and great-granddaughter Susan Lustig. The quote from the 1945 Rotary Club reunion appeared with slightly different wording in the August 24, 1945, *Reading Chronicle* ("by mutual agreement") and August 17, 1945, *Stoneham Independent* ("by natural agreement").

Gus Lechleitner: From various newspaper, automotive-magazine, and genealogical records from the United States and Australia.

F. B. Whittemore Jr.: From clippings and genealogical records, and from information provided by granddaughter Linda O'Connor.

Elbert E. "Bert" Bellows: From newspaper and genealogical records, and from photos and materials made available by granddaughter Janice Bellows Feaman (a daughter of Bert's son James W. Bellows, an Okinawa combat veteran who became a dentist) and great-granddaughter Sarah Bellows Upbin (a granddaughter of Bert's son Elbert George Bellows, a Navy veteran who became a lawyer). The feature on the Gray-Bellows Motor

Company appeared in the February 10, 1915, *Motor World.* I'm indebted to the previously cited "My Dad" biography written by Bert Bellows's daughter, Elisabeth (a teacher who became a stay-at-home mother, then earned a master's and became a college librarian), known to family and friends as Sally.

M. Robert Guggenheim: From numerous accounts in books (cited in chapter 1) and newspapers as well as phone and email correspondence with grandson Dan Guggenheim. The "disaster and discredit" quote comes from the February 1, 1910, *Seattle Daily Times*, where the jump-page headline was especially damning ("Malignant Fate Stalks in Wake of Guggenheim"). The "dump it into the East River" line was the kicker of a wire story that ran in many papers, including "One Automobile Has Made a Millionaire Peck of Trouble," *Cleveland Plain Dealer*, November 17, 1910.

INDEX

ABOUT THE AUTHOR

Jessica Rinaldi

Eric Moskowitz spent twelve years at *The Boston Globe*, where he covered transportation and was part of the team that received the Pulitzer Prize for coverage of the Boston Marathon bombing. He has written for *The Atlantic* and *The New York Times*, and his work has appeared in *The Best American Sports Writing* and *The Best American Newspaper Narratives* anthologies. He studied American history at the University of Pennsylvania and lives near Boston with his wife and children.